Charlie Chaplin, Director

DONNA KORNHABER

CHARLIE CHAPLIN, DIRECTOR

NORTHWESTERN UNIVERSITY PRESS
EVANSTON, ILLINOIS

Northwestern University Press
www.nupress.northwestern.edu

Printed in the United States of America

10 9 8 7 6 5 4 3 2 1

Library of Congress Cataloging-in-Publication Data
Kornhaber, Donna, 1979– author.
    Charlie Chaplin, director / Donna Kornhaber.
       pages cm
    Includes bibliographical references and index.
    ISBN 978-0-8101-2952-8 (pbk. : alk. paper)
    1. Chaplin, Charlie, 1889–1977—Criticism and interpretation. 2. Motion picture
producers and directors—United States. 3. Motion pictures—Production and
direction—United States. I. Title.
PN2287.C5K67 2014
791.430233092—dc23

                                                                    2013035621

∞ The paper used in this publication meets the minimum requirements of the American
National Standard for Information Sciences—Permanence of Paper for Printed Library
Materials, ANSI Z39.48-1992.

For Cyrus and Sophia

I am always saying that we must let the films themselves teach us how to look at them and how to think about them.

—STANLEY CAVELL, *Pursuits of Happiness*

CONTENTS

Gallery follows page 206.

ACKNOWLEDGMENTS

There are many people who have made this book possible. My first order of thanks goes to those who listened so attentively and commented so perceptively on my musings on film behind the gates of Columbia University. I am indebted especially to Martin Puchner for his sharp readings and shrewd advice over more than a decade now, to Julie Stone Peters for her elegant commentary, and to Maura Spiegel for her willingness to be a patient and wise sounding board. I also want to offer my thanks to Matthew Wilson Smith for always being willing to listen or to read and to Amanda Claybaugh for offering such helpful guidance. The seeds of this work began to germinate even before Columbia, during my many years at New York University. Special thanks go to David K. Irving, who chaired the film program during my time there, and to Leonard Jenkin in the Department of Dramatic Writing, for their example and inspiration.

Ultimately this work truly came into being during my time at the University of Texas at Austin, and I am deeply grateful for all the support I have received here. I owe a special debt of gratitude to Elizabeth Cullingford, chair of the Department of English, for her remarkable support and general administrative genius, which were instrumental in making the completion of this work possible. I am also thankful to Roger Louis, director of the Program in British Studies, for his support in all regards. And I will be forever grateful to Douglas Bruster, whose thoughtful, meticulous, and incisive commentary on this manuscript helped make it what it is in ways both large and small. A robust round of thanks belongs to my colleagues in the Department of English at the University of Texas at Austin, where I have had the good fortune of discovering a community of scholars that gives full meaning to both of those terms. Special thanks go to Alan Friedman, for his ongoing guidance and encouragement; Martin Kevorkian and Wayne Lesser, who have taken pains to make teaching here such a pleasure; and Elizabeth Scala for being both friend and mentor. A full accounting of all the individuals who have so richly defined my experience at the University of Texas would be too long to include here. Instead, I must offer my thanks to a few in particular: Samuel Baker, Janine Barchas, J. K. Barret, Daniel Birkholz, Mia Carter, Matt Cohen, James Cox, Brian Doherty, Patricia García, John González, Lars Hinrichs, Heather Houser, Coleman Hutchison, Julia Lee, James Loehlin, Allen MacDuffie, Carol MacKay, Lisa Moore, Gretchen Murphy, Domino Perez, Lindsay Reckson, Elizabeth Richmond-Garza, Snehal Shingavi, Jennifer Wilks, Michael Winship, Hannah Wojciehowski, and Marjorie Woods. It has been a great privilege to find myself among such scholars, colleagues, and friends these past years. I must also acknowledge the generous support of Randy Diehl and Richard Flores in the College of Liberal Arts, who have made available research and subvention funding to support this work. Finally, I owe thanks to my students, far too many to name here, who were among the first to hear many of these ideas in detail and who were invaluable in helping them take their current shape.

Is it possible to thank a city? This work began in New York, but I cannot help but feel that it might not be quite the same had I not had the opportunity to complete it in Austin. While writing this book, I had the chance to see many of the films discussed here and others of the period the way they were meant to be seen—in packed theaters with enthusiastic audiences. Even in today's world, there is simply no better way to see a film, and I have to think that aspects of this project were shaped in part by my experiences at the Paramount Theatre, the Alamo Drafthouse, and other venues around town. While on the subject of film viewing, I also want to thank the folks at Vulcan Video North, a veritable archive of obscure and out-of-circulation films and perhaps the greatest video rental joint left standing in the world.

Portions of chapter 8 can be found in *Quarterly Review of Film and Video* 31, no. 5, and portions of chapter 9 in *Movie: A Journal of Film Criticism* 4, no. 1. I am grateful to the editors of these journals for permission to use this material here. For the images reproduced in this book, I am deeply thankful for the cooperation of a number of parties, most centrally the Charlie Chaplin Estate / Roy Export S.A.S. as well as Universal Studios Licensing LLC, the Harold Lloyd Trust, and the Kobal Collection.

Most especially, and with much appreciation, I wish to thank my editor at Northwestern University Press, Mike Levine, whose dedication to this project over the course of multiple years and through many stages of development has been extraordinary. This project would not be what it is without him. Likewise, I owe a special thanks to the entire team at Northwestern University Press, whose thoughtfulness and care have made every step of this process a pleasure.

In particular, I want to thank Anne Gendler, Rudy Faust, Marianne Jankowski, Alma MacDougall, and Steven Moore.

Turning to my inner circle, I would like to thank my mother, Donna, for always believing in my abilities as a writer and a scholar and for nurturing my love of reading, writing, and the cinema. To Diane Dickinson, who has been there from the beginning, thank you for helping me get here. Thomas Dickinson; Christopher, Jenifer, and Amelia Popolizio; Michael and Jennifer Popolizio; and Pamela, Lester, and Stephanie Trotto—thank you for your love and encouragement through it all. Jon K. Williams, thanks for your camaraderie from the very start of this journey. To my uncle John, thank you for your reassurance and support. And to my grandparents Grace and John and my great-aunt Nina, gone too soon, my thanks and love.

There are no words to thank David Kornhaber, my partner in life and in love, for his generosity and all-around brilliance. It is impossible to imagine this book without him. I am indeed lucky to be able to share my world and my work with him every day.

Finally, I would like to thank my children, Cyrus and Sophia. In his concluding speech in *The Great Dictator*, Chaplin warns, "We think too much and feel too little." I am never in danger of this with them in my life, and I treasure the happiness they have brought with them. I dedicate this book to them with love and admiration.

Charlie Chaplin, Director

Introduction

I think I'm a better director than an actor," Charlie Chaplin told an interviewer for *Life* in 1967. There is perhaps no statement with which Chaplin's critics have disagreed more. He received no shortage of praise, of course, during and after his career. George Bernard Shaw famously called him "the only genius developed in motion pictures." For Andrew Sarris, he is "the single most important artist produced by the cinema." Edmund Wilson declared him to be "among his age's first artists." And yet, from early in his career through some of the most recent assessments of his work, Chaplin has been criticized as a director even as he has been extolled in almost all other respects. Orson Welles summed up the majority opinion: "Chaplin's a great artist—there can't be any argument about that," he declared. But, Welles said, Chaplin was simply not "a man of the cinema." In a contemporary review of *Modern Times* (United Artists, 1936), Otis Ferguson took this idea as one of the central points of his analysis. Chaplin was not, he said, "a first-class picture-maker" because "he keeps on refusing to learn any more than he learned when the movies themselves were just learning." Thirty-six years later, Richard Schickel repeated this thought in a retrospective of Chaplin's work on the occasion of his much-anticipated return to the United States, aptly titled "Hail Chaplin—The Early Chaplin." As a director, he writes, Chaplin is "inadequate"; despite the genius of his early shorts he has refused to accept or incorporate almost "every stylistic and technical change which has come to the movies since the end of World War I." Reviewing the last film of Chaplin's career, *A Countess from Hong Kong* (Universal, 1967)—one of only two films that Chaplin directed in which he did not star—an unsigned article in the London *Times* returned at length to this question of directorial ability:

> It is always difficult to separate in one's mind the various functions of a great composite: how much of the effect of a classic Chaplin film is due to his direction, how much to his writing, and how much to his own central performance? The suspicion has always persisted . . . that he might be at best a director of very modest competence who just happened to have a rare knack of showing off his own work as a performer to maximum advantage. . . . Now that Mr. Chaplin has again ventured on a film denied the special support of his own performance in a central role, we can take stock. And sadly, it must be said that *A Countess from Hong Kong* confirms our most pessimistic imaginings.[1]

The reviewer's reflections were anonymous but not anomalous. To most critics, Chaplin's career ended with a final confirmation of his failures as a director, reinscribing in the critical consciousness the idea that his talent and expertise consisted chiefly of his masterful comic performances and that his greatest cinematographic achievements could only properly be considered as efforts to show off "his own work as a performer to maximum advantage."

The bias against Chaplin's work as a director is not limited to the opinions of his fellow filmmakers and popular critics. If anything, it is expounded at greater length and at times with even more fervor by the scholarship that has grown up around his body of work. Dan Kamin offers an effective summary of the common complaints against Chaplin's visual style: "Chaplin's camera is often immobile, or moves just slightly, and he frequently frames shots widely. Individual shots often go on for much longer than shots in other movies." He also has a "cavalier disregard for some basic elements of movie craft, such as continuity in his editing." He is, in Kamin's reading, a kind of "stubborn curmudgeon of cinema."[2] Kamin's analysis is similar to one offered by Michael Roemer, though Roemer acknowledges extra-filmic influences on Chaplin's technique. "The staging and camera work are derived from the theatre," Roemer contends. "Space is treated two-dimensionally: sets and action are photographed from a single vantage point—most often from the center of the missing fourth wall; there are few reverse shots and we never see one character from the point of view of another. The camera seldom moves."[3] If Roemer attributes Chaplin's visual prejudices to the theater, Kamin contends that such an opinion is a misreading. "Despite their vaunted staginess," he writes, "Chaplin's films could *not* effectively be reproduced on stage. The full figure onscreen might be fifteen feet high, making possible a subtlety in performance that would be lost on the stage."[4] More common is Eric Flom's analysis, echoing Ferguson and Schickel, which finds a kind of abrupt abridgment in Chaplin's development some time during the early silent era, rendering him an antique specimen preserved even into the latter half of the twentieth century:

The silent film technique which Chaplin learned at Keystone Studios utilized a fairly immobile camera, allowing the actors to simply play and improvise in front of the lens. Chaplin naturally began his directing by imitating this style. . . . But while technical and creative techniques advanced by leaps and bounds during the last 15 years of silent cinema, Chaplin did not always move rapidly to adopt or experiment with these new methods. . . . While other directors had learned to heighten dramatic effects by varying shots or scene composition, Chaplin rarely strayed from his proven mode.[5]

In most readings of Chaplin's visual handicaps, what has allowed him to survive in our consciousness and to thrive as a filmic artist and sometime critical darling is the unmistakable and undisputed power of his performances. In David Cook's words, Chaplin's "genius was as an actor and a mime. So long as the little tramp character stood at the center of his films, they were masterworks of comedy and pathos. When the tramp disappeared, the limitations of Chaplin's directorial ability became increasingly apparent. With few exceptions, it was Chaplin's *presence* in his films, rather than anything in their formal structure, that made them interesting, important, and distinguished."[6]

What is perhaps most remarkable in the discussion of Chaplin's abilities as a director—that is, as the organizing intelligence behind the narrative development and visual apparatus of his films and the interplay between them—is that so few commentators have come to his defense. Chaplin has no shortage of admirers, defenders, and promoters as regards his filmmaking more broadly. But regarding his directorial abilities or even his basic visual technique, few have contested his critics on their own terms. Many sidestep the issue, while others offer some compensatory accomplishment that might even the artistic balance sheet. John Kimber declares Chaplin "a great poet of the cinema," yet no sooner does he offer this judgment than he redefines the term to exclude technical matters. "I want to enlist for Chaplin the serious attention deserved by one who is both original and who also draws strength from theatrical and social traditions older than the cinema," he writes. "I dearly hope that in my use of the term 'poet' I can avoid the extravagance of film criticism by which workmanlike, craftsmen film makers have been transformed into cinematic Prousts and Tolstoys."[7] In Kimber's reading, Chaplin's standing as an artist relies on his transpositions of non-cinematic aesthetic traditions to the screen rather than his abilities as a filmic "craftsman"; on the matter of visual style alone he is perhaps more than workmanlike, but less than a genius.

Others, like Charles Silver, offer the totality of emotion in Chaplin's films as a kind of recompense for these films' supposedly lackluster visuals: "Chaplin's style was profound in its simplicity, and he was always too preoccupied with depth of feeling to worry about depth of focus."[8] Silver's conclusion is a common one. For instance, Chaplin has had the benefit of few commentators more perceptive or effusive than the inimitable André Bazin, yet even Bazin sees Chaplin as a maker of mythologies more than a maker of movies: his Tramp character "is a mythical figure who rises above every adventure in which he becomes involved. . . . For hundreds of millions of people on this planet he is a hero like Ulysses or Roland in other civilizations."[9] It is a profound compensation for what he sees in the end as Chaplin's relatively limited formal gifts. "The reality of the work resides in the symbolism of the situation and the characters," he declares of Chaplin's filmmaking, not in "the meaning of the formal aesthetic problems of the narrative and the direction."[10] There is not much to say, Bazin concludes, about Chaplin's technique: "Even in the best-made of his films the so-called structural qualities are the most extrinsic to them, the last by which we would determine their excellence."[11]

More remarkable still is that in his monumental *The American Cinema* even Sarris, like Bazin one of Chaplin's most ardent and intelligent defenders (though much less mythologically inclined), essentially cedes the issue of technical and visual capability while admitting Chaplin into the "pantheon" level of directors. There he calls Chaplin's body of work an example of "cinematic biography on the highest level of artistic expression" and exempts his muted cinematic style on the grounds that it is secondary to his persona, that Chaplin's "other self on the screen has always been the supreme object of contemplation."[12] For Sarris, Chaplin's stature as a filmmaker ultimately rests on his status as the cinema's "most extraordinary performer" and his ability to combine this remarkable acumen with a commitment to exploring his own identity on screen. He was, in Sarris's words, "the supreme exemplification of the axiom that lives and not lenses stand at the center of cinematic creation."[13]

Sarris's argument runs parallel to many of the attempts to gerrymander Chaplin into great director status. He was, the logic goes, at least a great director for himself. Kamin offers a version of this approach, though he admits (unlike Sarris) that it is a kind of aesthetic second-place prize:

> The purpose of Chaplin the director . . . is to properly showcase the remarkable performances of Chaplin the actor. In this respect, his directing is not merely adequate—it's brilliant. . . . Audiences leave the theatre knowing that they've witnessed a performance of extraordinary physical skill, even if they're largely unaware of the level of filmic sophistication necessary to create that impression. Further, the display

of skill is fully integrated with the film, not a tangential stunt or non sequitur; it illuminates Chaplin's character.[14]

Gilberto Perez makes an argument along a similar premise. According to Perez, it was only "when he [Chaplin] became his own director that he was able to perfect his craft as an actor and to develop an unerring sense of where to put the camera with a minimum of elaboration, bringing his pantomime comedy to a peak of refinement."[15] In these readings, Chaplin the director is a kind of profound craftsman but only insofar as that craft serves the greater craft of his performances. This position is similar to that taken by Jeffrey Vance, who reads Chaplin's directorship as designed to facilitate not just his own acting but the performances of his entire company. "His rudimentary approach to camera placement and lighting was a conscious decision to remain focused on the actors and to leave the performance area accessible for improvisation at all times," he writes.[16] It was, in his reading, as much a pragmatic concern as an aesthetic one: "Complicated camera set-ups required time. When the mercurial Chaplin was ready to act, he did not want to be waiting on technicians."[17] Unlike most of Chaplin's commentators, Vance allows for some innovation in his visual style, but it is limited almost entirely to his treatment of the mise-en-scène—his penchant for "imbuing the décor with symbolism" and "using objects for their metaphoric and metonymic value."[18]

The idea of a Chaplinesque visual style that goes beyond the level of the actor (and perhaps the immediately surrounding objects and scenery) seems for the most part an impossibility. Indeed, Chaplin himself did little to help his cause and much to aid such analyses in several of his own statements about his filmmaking, his protestations to *Life* about his abilities as a director notwithstanding. "I am the unusual and I do not need camera angles," he once told an assistant director.[19] Similarly, he declared that his camera angles "don't have to be interesting—I am interesting."[20] It is on the basis of such exclamations that Peter Bogdanovich explicitly (and with no small degree of judgment) places Chaplin among Hollywood's greatest actors in his series of oral histories of the film industry—"If ever there was an actor's remark, that's it," he says of Chaplin's comments on camera angles. Tellingly, he does not include Chaplin in his volume of conversations with the great directors, his own version of Sarris's "pantheon."[21]

Perhaps the only sustained attempt to elucidate Chaplin's merit as a director on something approaching the terms by which other film directors are evaluated comes from Gerald Mast. Mast starts with the basic criteria on which we might judge any film for its visual stylistics and narrative organization regardless of the strength of the particular performances—its cinematography, its editing, and its mise-en-scène. Yet for all the energy behind Mast's claims, his defense itself is remarkably feeble. On Chaplin's cinematographic skill, he praises only the particular camera angles that Chaplin selects for pivotal scenes, noting how in certain sequences "the camera has found precisely the right angle to communicate the pictorial, intellectual, and emotional values of the shot." Mast even claims that "although Chaplin prefers the fixed composition of a passive camera, he does know how to use a moving camera on the rare occasion when he wants that sort of effect." On editing, Mast mostly defends Chaplin's choices on the grounds that they do not detract from the interest of a given scene. "It is true that Chaplin edits very sparingly," he writes. "But this is extremely effective editing for Chaplin because the scenes remain hypnotic regardless of their length." Chaplin does not allow his cutting to "become intrusive and destroy the magic." The relatively simple mise-en-scène in his films is likewise praised mostly for being unobtrusive. "Chaplin seems to perceive that elaborate and careful décor—usually a cinematic virtue—can be a great fault if it diverts the viewer's attention from the film's central human and comic matters." In Mast's reading Chaplin's technique is entirely functional, designed with no greater purpose than to be serviceable and invisible to the action on screen. In the process of mounting his defense, Mast in fact discredits visual composition as anything other than a neutral point of transmission, as though language could never carry inflection. "There has never been a better film technician than Chaplin because Chaplin's technique was perfectly suited to communicate what he wanted. And that's as good as technique can ever be," he declares.[22]

For Graham Petrie, the absence of anything approaching a sustained formal analysis of Chaplin's work is itself one of the great issues in Chaplin scholarship. "Such unanimity is remarkable in film criticism and it raises several, potentially disturbing, questions about the nature of Chaplin's art," he writes. "Nowhere . . . can one find a detailed analysis of the structure or technique of any major film or even of an important sequence within such a film. There is no serious dissection of Chaplin's camera style, editing, use of sound or music, or of the narrative or image patterns to be found within his work." Petrie's article has been widely cited and anthologized since it first appeared in 1977, but it has as yet brokered no substantial change in critical readings of Chaplin. According to Petrie's coverage of the literature, most studies of Chaplin's work situate themselves squarely at the level of character and acting, concentrating on "the Chaplin persona and its significance rather than on the structure or style of the films themselves." They deem the filmic output of Chaplin's labors essentially illegible. For critics favorable to Chaplin, his work "has reached a level of such universal simplicity and transparency, that he speaks so directly and clearly to his audience, that there is nothing left for the critic to do"—essentially a recapitulation of Mast's defense of Chaplin's supposedly unadorned technique.[23]

On the other hand, Petrie points out that "a more sophisticated and also more prosaic generation of critics seems . . . to have drawn the obverse conclusion to this: if criticism of Chaplin's films lacks subtlety, ambiguity, depth, rigor, it is simply because the films themselves lack these and provide no opportunity for the kinds of criticism in fashion." Even among Chaplin's admirers, Petrie observes, what this perspective has produced is in many cases a scholarship of Chaplin-as-springboard, his films used frequently as a launching point for speculations that not only outstrip formal readings but have no formal origin point at their base at all. He laments the "flights of ecstatic prose that seldom descend to the level of accurate examination of the images and their arrangement" so common in Chaplin scholarship and writes that "it is almost as if, having accepted as a working premise the belief that Chaplin had no specifically cinematic talent, they feel obliged (or free) to write about his work from a purely mythic, psychological, philosophical, or sociological viewpoint, using the bare narrative of the films as a point of reference."[24]

It is true that, more than most other filmmakers, Chaplin has entered prominently into discussions beyond the scope of film studies and that sometimes have little to do with the discipline at all. In the wider public consciousness, he is, as Bazin declares him to be, as much artist and mythologizer as filmmaker. But as Petrie points out, this transcendence leaves behind a puzzling lacuna in film studies, one which resonates well beyond the immediate domain of Chaplin scholarship and reaches to questions of cinema scholarship at its most general level. "And yet. And yet," Petrie writes, "how could someone so woefully ignorant of the very basics of his medium produce some of the greatest films (not novels or plays or music hall turns but *films*) ever made?"[25] Or, to unpack the question that lies just beneath Petrie's: Do we even know what films are if Charlie Chaplin cannot be said to have made them well?

Such questions turn ultimately on what we mean by "film." Mast comes close to framing the central issue in his opening salvo against those who would criticize Chaplin's visual technique. Criticism of Chaplin's directorial work, he writes, "assumes that 'good' cinematic technique is fixed rather than a function of the particular work."[26] The second half of Mast's sentence flattens the depth of insight offered by the first, again evacuating style from technique and neutering the idea that formal and stylistic analysis across any body of works is a profitable critical pursuit. But Chaplin does not need to be protected by such scorched-earth techniques for exactly the reason that Mast initially identifies.

There is in nearly all the criticisms leveled at Chaplin's directing an implicit telos, one that culminates consistently and unproblematically in the Hollywood classical paradigm, what David Bordwell, Janet Staiger, and Kristin Thompson together define as "a distinct mode of film practice with its own cinematic style and industrial conditions of existence" that constitutes "a determinate set of assumptions about how a movie should behave, about what stories it properly tells and how it should tell them, about the range and functions of film technique, and about the activities of the spectator."[27] Such is the depth to which most formal criticisms of Chaplin's work are embedded in assumptions central to the classical paradigm that perfectly descriptive, declarative observations of his technique are understood, immediately and without further elaboration, to impugn against his directorial ability. Chaplin uses an immobile camera. He uses a consistently wide frame. He does not vary his camera angles. He cuts infrequently. Criticisms of Chaplin's technique are essentially written in a critical code so widely understood that it does not need to be fully spelled out at any point. These are not neutral statements but normative condemnations. Chaplin uses an immobile camera *when he should obviously avail himself of the mobile frame.* He uses a consistent middle-distance perspective *when he should clearly vary his framing according to the action on screen.* He does not vary his camera angles *when everyone knows that cinematographic variety is a necessary tool of visual inflection.* He does not cut often *even though editing is integral to filmic language.* Chaplin should be moving his camera, varying his shot distances, experimenting with new angles, or editing frequently within a scene because these are the sanctioned uses of technique within the specific mode of filmic composition that came to dominate the cinema in general, and Hollywood in particular, just after Chaplin's film career began.

Hence the recurring historical component to criticisms of Chaplin's technique—Schickel's complaint that he resisted "every stylistic and technical change which has come to the movies since the end of World War I" or Flom's statement that Chaplin did not "adopt or experiment with these new methods" even as "technical and creative techniques advanced by leaps and bounds during the last 15 years of silent cinema." Chaplin's manner of framing, filming, and editing space, time, and movement are taken to have essentially ossified at a point before the cinema came to properly know itself, rendering him irredeemably antediluvian. Chaplin is ultimately suspended in a kind of unpermitted opposition to what is taken as a general industry consensus on what constitutes acceptable film practice, a consensus that consolidated sometime before or around 1917 and that thereafter, in Thompson's words, achieved "stability" by consistently rewarding "conformance to its established filmmaking approaches."[28] Chaplin's technical and formal choices do not read as choices but as mistakes because they are not constituted as choices within the horizon of permissible decisions in the classical model. His visual style is seen as illegible because it is written in a language that does not seem translatable to classical norms.

Yet this sense of incompatibility and even opposition is arguably one of the animating features of Chaplin's visual approach. The individual techniques that Chaplin privileged in his filmmaking tend to be those that predate classical consolidation, yet they are not in themselves inimitable to the sanctioned uses of style in classical filmmaking. The long take, staging in depth, an austere cinematography, a relatively immobile camera, to name just a few of Chaplin's favored techniques: each of these elements may be found, alone or in combination, in films that are easily compatible with classical dictates. They are not the forms of composition that were most emphasized in studio-era filmmaking, but neither did they constitute a body of forbidden or forgotten forms. They might properly be considered "residual" to the classical style in the sense developed by Raymond Williams, constituting that which "has been effectively formed in the past, but . . . is still active in the cultural process, not only and often not at all as an element of the past."[29]

What would relegate Chaplin to the margins of classical-era filmmaking, then, is not the nature of his technique so much as the degree to which his application of it was organized in purposeful opposition to some of the basic philosophical grounding points of the classical paradigm. Or, to put it another way, reading Chaplin's directorship on the level of technique alone within a classical paradigm is perhaps the very genesis of the view that he was only a passable director. The animus of Chaplin's directorship only comes alive if one recognizes the degree to which he was deploying these techniques in an active critique of classical assumptions about the organization of image and narrative. For classical style, far more than simply offering a battery of approved formal tactics, ultimately operated around a common set of assumptions regarding the proper functioning of the filmic image, typically privileging ideas of clarity and comprehensibility in film construction. At its core, it offered what Robert Ray calls a "tacit guarantee of a constantly optimum vantage point," though the understructure of classical style goes even further than this—for any guarantee of comprehensibility to even be operable, there must already be in place an assumption that such a thing as an optimum vantage point is an extant or estimable visual element and that the object of attention in any given filmic moment is stable enough to allow for, at a minimum, the fiction of an ideal view.[30]

Classical style, then, is a form that demands at least a working sense of conceptual stability, presupposing, in Bazin's analysis, in "its very nature the unity of meaning of the dramatic event."[31] This stability was not something Chaplin was usually willing to grant within his films. If other filmmakers attached to Hollywood on occasion questioned or challenged basic classical assumptions within their standard working methods, few did so with Chaplin's consistency or fervor. His perspective on the world could not easily be accommodated to a visual system that assumed, of necessity, a stable center of meaning in any given shot. In Raoul Sobel and David Francis's analysis of the nature of Chaplin's comedy—which works equally well as a description of the origin point for his manner of filmic construction in general—he is "a man who confronts us with a looking-glass world," a filmmaker obsessed with showing us "the overthrow of order, the sudden inversion of all we take for granted."[32] Chaplin's style is built not on an assumption of the stability of meaning but rather on a fascination with visual and conceptual malleability and instability, conceived in philosophical counterpoint to the classical model.

It is not in the broader history of film an entirely unique position: it bears traces of the cacophony of competing film techniques and aesthetic philosophies of cinema's earliest years while at the same time anticipating and pointing forward to the paradigmatic disruptions that classical style would undergo in the wake of the Neorealist and New Wave movements. Yet for a filmic approach developed in the shadow of the Hollywood studio system, it seems remarkably out of time, written in a language that is not supposed to exist either anymore or yet again. Debates about when classical style became consolidated to the point of a normative industry standard in the United States vary, but so long as Chaplin's work is construed as existing sometime before that final consolidation he is largely forgiven his idiosyncrasies and oppositions; he is simply participating in a moment of stylistic indeterminacy in the development of narrative film when, in Charlie Keil's description, "filmmakers are still experimenting with [classical] techniques, viewing them as innovations to be tested."[33] Hence Schickel's willingness to grant Chaplin his artistry during only his earliest periods. "Chaplin never again achieved the perfection of those first years," he writes.[34] Chaplin worked best before "the movies . . . underwent radical change, became more and more resistant to his particular gifts."[35] Schickel's is a particularly pronounced distension, across all of Chaplin's artistry, of a prejudice that relegates any visual achievement solely to the period of Chaplin's early shorts but still allows for compensatory artistic developments beyond the visual realm in Chaplin's later work.

Yet if in this reading Chaplin is too late in his continued adherence to preclassical modes of filmmaking, he is also in another way too early. The hegemony of classical technique would not be unbroken or unchallenged across the twentieth century; yet Chaplin is not generally regarded as part of the narrative of its disruption and dissolution. Early challengers to classical constrictions are typically considered to have come from within the paradigm itself, just as its final assailants have generally been identified as arriving from other national traditions. The early challengers were masters of the classical style's basic strictures as much as they were innovators against them: Welles most prominently, but also figures like Josef von Sternberg or King Vidor. According to Bordwell, this is evidence of Leonard Meyer's observation that "for any specific style there is a finite number of rules, but there is an indefinite number of possible strategies for realizing or instantiating such rules."[36] Those who prominently and openly opposed themselves to the classical aesthetic both philosophically and compositionally did so, at first, only outside the American studio system and only after the supreme paradigmatic disruptions of history itself—after the tumult of the Second World War, when, as Gilles Deleuze writes, political and social dislocation "has greatly increased the situations which we no longer know how to react to, in spaces which we no longer know how to describe."[37] From those spaces would be born new concepts of filmic representation, new visual styles that would unconsciously rehabilitate methodologies supposedly long abandoned like the long take or disruptive, unhidden editing.

Chaplin stands apart from and before all this, and there is simply no model for a prominent Hollywood filmmaker who would, in the span of a single career, outlast the rise and fall of the classical approach, marking himself at one and the same moment old-fashioned and ahead of his time—for decades. To compose films as Chaplin did during the specific time frame that he did and within the specific locus of production that he did—in the very heart of the American film industry—must only be to compose them poorly, either actively to fail at or indolently to abstain from achieving fluency in a manner of composition so omnipresent that it must surely have been his guiding framework as well. There is no other language within a typical classical framework or a typical film history to describe his directorial work other than the language of failure.

For Chaplin's filmic artistry to be properly conceived, it must be conceived in the negative space of the classical style. The absence of one technique must be seen instead as a marker for the presence of another: his failure at one approach must be recast as evidence of his success at a different one. Where the classical style favored techniques of the camera, Chaplin focused on composition in the mise-en-scène. Where it advocated sequence, he emphasized simultaneity. Where it drove toward unity, he opened toward multiplicity. Where it demanded clarity, consistency, or concision, he delighted in obfuscation, decentering, and diffusion. Seen in such a light, Chaplin did not fail at classical film construction but instead created within his body of work a model for an alternate, counterclassical system of composition, one grounded on different visual—and ultimately philosophical—values.

From very early in Chaplin commentary and scholarship, traces of such approaches to his artistry can be found, usually phrased in the language of escape or transcendence. T. S. Eliot described Chaplin's artistry in this way in 1923: "The egregious merit of Chaplin is that he has escaped in his own way from the realism of the cinema and invented a *rhythm*. Of course the unexplored opportunities of the cinema for eluding realism must be very great."[38] Chaplin's escape from realism in the strictest sense is certainly no greater—and arguably much less so—than that of either of his major slapstick peers, Harold Lloyd or Buster Keaton. Eliot seems instead to be speaking not of reality per se but of the paradigmatic structuring of its representation—what passes as reality within the classical mode—to which Lloyd and Keaton were much more firm adherents. To Eliot, Chaplin has not failed at this representation; he has skipped it altogether, substituting for it another premised on a different set of aesthetic values but with as many possibilities, perhaps more. Hence the language of Louis Delluc in describing Chaplin's work as essentially supra-filmic. Chaplin's films, he writes, place us "in a country which is splendidly illimitable"; a Chaplin film at once "justifies all that one can expect from the cinema" and at the same time "is something above the art of the cinema."[39] Chaplin is not in violation of paradigmatic codes so much as he is unconstrained by them, operating in another system of possibilities.

Some aspects of that system have been described by theorists trying to grapple with the cinematic medium not in any single historical moment but rather in all its manifold potentialities, looking for what Jean Mitry calls "the essential components of film expression . . . [that] define the rules of its existence."[40] Outside the imaginative constraints imposed by historically and paradigmatically situated readings, Chaplin at last begins to emerge. Mitry recognizes in Chaplin a kind of special scripting of cinematic space and movement. "Whereas so many other films are no more than the pictorialization of a story already written, the expression of an idea existing in itself independently of the medium which translates it . . . Chaplin's films create their own signification and emotion for and from themselves. They are self-defining . . . [and] they are irreducible to all forms of expression other than the cinema."[41] Deleuze, one of Chaplin's most perceptive contemporary interpreters, finds in him too something that stands outside other modes of classical construction. Deleuze's theory of cinematic movement and time, as espoused in *Cinema 1* and *Cinema 2*, is at least in part an apparatus designed to reinforce our existing sense of filmic periodization, a conceptual division of visual practices that largely aligns to classical and postclassical modes of composition.[42] What he calls the "movement-image" is roughly analogous to the running together of separately composed shots that is the basis of analytical editing as favored in classical filmmaking, in his words "a single movement whose very halts are an integral part of it and are only a vibration on to itself."[43] Yet in his analysis of Chaplin, Deleuze recognizes a unique departure from some of the visual norms of the classical era, an insistence on what he calls an "irreducible simultaneity"—a refusal to visually or intellectually isolate items or actions within his scenes in contrast to the classical prescription. In his view, Chaplin is always taking disconnected or even opposing actions, emotions, situations, or even characters and "doing both together . . . without the one obliterating or diminishing the other."[44]

Looking back on Chaplin from the vantage of the new paradigmatic space of the French New Wave, Éric Rohmer finds a similar phenomenon: a concentration on space as an organizing principle of composition above and beyond cinematography proper, focusing not on a movement between images but on the arrangement of the single image centered within an unbroken radius of space. Rohmer attributes to Chaplin "a perfect understanding of the demands of cinematic perspective, of the difference between the screen and scenic space" and praises his creation of a unique cinematic approach that allows his characters to "evolve inside a universe where their smallest intentions were immediately translated into spatial language."[45] And Bazin himself, though he found little to say about Chaplin's formal merits, laid a groundwork for Rohmer and others to re-understand Chaplin in his own critical challenges to classical orthodoxy. In his landmark essay "The Virtues and Limitations of Montage," Bazin propounded a new "law of aesthetics" to run counter to traditional classical assumptions about the treatment of cinematic space in a way that mirrored much of Chaplin's own oppositions. For Bazin, "when the essence of a scene demands the simultaneous presence of two or more factors in the action, montage is ruled out" and can only again "reclaim its right to be used . . . whenever the import of the action no longer depends on physical contiguity."[46] Chaplin is mentioned only briefly (almost teasingly) at the end of the watershed essay, the further implications of his participation in this new "aesthetic law" left for others to explore. Chaplin's comedy, Bazin writes, "succeeded before the days of Griffith and montage . . . because most of its gags derived from a comedy of space, from the relation of man to things and to the surrounding world."[47] But Bazin's brief statements opened the door to new perspectives on Chaplin's directorial priorities—as in Dudley Andrew's brief extrapolation on Bazin's remarks. "Imagine a Chaplin film shot with conventional editing," he writes. "The comedy would no longer exist because the space would be destroyed.

Bazin here has debunked one aspect of the commonplace notion that Chaplin was an unimaginative director because he failed to change his shots or come in for close-ups."[48] Mitry, Deleuze, Rohmer, and Bazin speak only briefly to Chaplin's form and technique, often in works whose main concerns lie elsewhere. (When Mitry and Bazin write at length on Chaplin, they are concerned largely with his mythos.) Yet they offer a view on his visual artistry and manner of filmmaking that is uniquely unencumbered, open to a positive conception of his agenda as reaching toward new goals rather than falling away from established ones. They suggest a critical perspective open to the idea of a Chaplinesque directorial style.

This book seeks to record and interpret that style, to find in Chaplin the unique tenets and principles of a manner of filmmaking whose visual approach was purposeful, intelligible, and rich. It is, on one level, an attempt to bring Chaplin's style into view, to recover the specific techniques of cinematography and framing, editing, and mise-en-scène that recur throughout Chaplin's work and that constitute the foundational visual properties of his filmmaking. On another level, it is an effort to render that style meaningful, to draw from it a philosophy of organization and arrangement that speaks to Chaplin's conception of the world as he was able to represent it and to the process of that representation itself.

It is an excavation of style that operates at the level of the director, though it is not ultimately auteurist. Chaplin, like all directors, functioned within a series of larger industrial and cultural networks and processes that shaped, enabled, redirected, and constrained his artistic output; even the very idea of what it meant to "direct" a film changed substantially between his early days on the Keystone lot and the conclusion of his career in the 1950s and 1960s. He cannot be considered apart from those contexts. Yet the degree of his embeddedness need not preclude an investigation into a manner of filmmaking that we might rightfully call his own, one that he would develop and refine over the full course of his career even as the industry transformed around him. The identification and analysis of Chaplin's cinematic style is a function of looking across his films for elements that recur or iterate under a variety of conditional factors, forming identifiable patterns of technique and of approach—and within those patterns, even identifiable periods—that seem attachable to him. The composer Carl Davis, who has worked intimately on several Chaplin score reconstructions, has offered in this spirit a defense of the idea of distinctive Chaplin musical style across the sound films, a point that can be extrapolated across much of Chaplin's visual and storytelling work as well: "It is amazing—from *City Lights,* the first thing recorded, right to the end—how consistent it is.

And of course if it was being written by other people, how is it that the 'Chaplin style' maintains itself through widely differentiating and widely changing arrangers? There is a line that goes through, no matter who is working with him."[49] The search for consistent patterns across disparate films can be said to allow for the uncovering of a degree of personal style or individual perspective in any filmmaker—a case that is not limited to the figure of the director but that can be made from a cross-film analysis of any number of major production figures, whether actor, editor, producer, cinematographer, or production designer, to name only a few.

It is, in the end, a particularly powerful methodology in the specific case of Chaplin, for there is arguably no other single figure in the history of film who has had so great a degree of independent control over his productions for so long a time. For the better part of his career, during the nearly thirty years he spent with United Artists, he was not only his own star and his own director and his own writer but also his own producer and his own studio head, even his own distributor. (That is to say nothing of his work, credited or de facto, as composer, editor, and casting director on his films.) He owned his own back lot, hired his own technical personnel (and even his own office staff), and cultivated his own rotating company of actors. Only the bookends of his career saw him working under the aegis of a production company that he did not control, at Keystone and Essanay in 1914 and 1915 and then at Universal Pictures in 1967. Even his early contracts with Mutual and First National for distribution of his shorts stipulated that he had complete artistic and financial power over his own work. (While he was working under contract with First National Chaplin even built the studio in Hollywood that he owned for most of the rest of his life.) Chaplin, in other words, was largely inoculated against outside artistic or financial interference in his filmmaking, a direct product of the outsized revenue his work produced even from very early in his career. Reinvesting much of that money into his own filmmaking, he evinced an unusual degree of control over his own processes and artistic products, and he limited his collaborators to a relatively small circle: a few scenarists in the days of his early shorts, his longtime cameraman and de facto director of photography Rollie Totheroh, a stable of actors largely drawn from alumni of Fred Karno's music hall company and competing slapstick film outfits, and, most important, his half brother Sydney, both financial adviser and artistic confidant. Story line details and gags were almost all improvised on set, shot and reshot sometimes for days or weeks on end until Chaplin felt satisfied with the outcome. He acted out all the parts himself and asked his ensemble to precisely mimic him, often to the chagrin of the more experienced players. He gave explicit orders to Totheroh about framing and shot composition, even instructing his camera operator to follow his timing during fade-outs.[50] (Vance describes Totheroh, a camera operator from Essanay who worked almost exclusively with Chaplin for his entire career, as ultimately "an elemental film technician who provided the director exactly what he wanted.")[51] If there was ever an artistic figure in Hollywood who approached the status of an independent auteur, constructing an entire industrial apparatus tailored to his control, it was Chaplin. More so than can be said of most directors, he enabled his own fingerprint to be seen in nearly every aspect of his work, artistic and industrial alike, constructing an entire production system aimed at the development and expression of his individual vision.

Ultimately, the Chaplin that emerges from a recognition of this vision and from an engagement with the assumptions and motives that lie behind it is not a figure radically unknown to his other interpreters or to his wider viewership. But he is a figure who has been only partially and often imperfectly seen. He is, for one, a technical craftsman far more in touch with the history of his medium and the techniques of his peers than is generally acknowledged: carefully and selectively preserving tactics from the era before classical consolidation even while repurposing and reconceiving techniques from his classical contemporaries and his slapstick cohorts. He is also a more self-conscious critic than most readings of his work will allow, subtly and sometimes explicitly attacking on artistic or philosophical grounds the narrative or visual prescriptions of classical style both during the silent era and in the age of sound. He is an artist as well with a powerful conception of his own visual style as something to be preserved and developed across his films, as much a marker of his artistic legacy as the Tramp himself. And he is a compositionalist with a deep commitment to space as a foundational concern of the filmic medium, an approach that grounds his visuality and places him in opposition to classical arrangements and organizations of the filmic frame on the basis of principle and method more than willfulness or ineptitude. Most important, though, he emerges as a filmmaker motivated by a profound philosophical skepticism, an aspect of his art only partially glimpsed by those who examine his performance or his mythmaking alone. Chaplin's visual world approaches the anarchic in the degree to which it refuses to commit to the solidity or ultimate validity of any attempt to order, capture, or render sensible the world. Chaplin's film, viewed on its own terms and against its own goals, is a kind of anti-film that both anticipates and in some ways exceeds many of the most drastic challenges to classical technique of the later twentieth century.

The story of Chaplin's visual style is a historical one, beginning with his entry into the film industry in 1914 and extending to his final film in 1967, where, even at the end of his career, he still sought to adjust and reconfigure his style to keep pace with developments in his own filmmaking and in the world around him. The first section of this book concerns the origins of that style in the film industry as Chaplin first knew it—in the broad context of a dynamic period of visual and narrative transformation and within that context in the unique domain of silent slapstick comedy, first as practiced at Keystone Studios and then as developed by Chaplin's most immediate comic peers. Chapter 1 begins with an examination of Chaplin's earliest Keystone shorts set against the backdrop of the artistic environment in which they were created, one where the classical style is not yet the inevitable and inherent mode of storytelling supposedly destined to arise from cinema's prehistory but still a developing historical product itself. That style would mark the consolidation of a series of narrative and technical experiments for which D. W. Griffith in particular came to be known, experiments which were designed to transform the cinema away from an earlier ideology of uninflected space that was seen to hamper the medium's new narrative aims. Yet even from the outset, Chaplin's comic work showed a deep antipathy to many of the technical developments that were becoming prevalent at the time, aligning itself both philosophically and visually with modes of composition still present in the industry but quickly becoming outmoded. Chapter 2 considers Chaplin's early work in the context of its creation as part of the mass-produced slapstick work of the Keystone Studios. Contra the system of visual organization beginning to dominate Hollywood stood the early slapstick comedies, sequestered from the experiments of Griffith and others by their wholly unique set of narrative demands. Composed in sequences of micronarrative gags that depended for their effect on an unimpeded view of the comedian's interaction with an uncooperative environment, the slapstick tradition stood at a clear remove from the dictates of classical visual discourse. Chaplin's visual style evolves from and in many ways purifies these techniques. Chapter 3 explores slapstick's moment of transformation early in Chaplin's career, the point at which it can no longer fully evade an increasing encroachment of classical narrative demands and still sustain its own popularity. Harold Lloyd and Buster Keaton, Chaplin's greatest competitors during the apogee of slapstick comedy in the 1920s, each negotiate a compromise between slapstick tradition and classical technique unique to their own comic talents and artistic prerogatives. These realignments help to frame the visual and narrative choices that Chaplin himself would make in confronting the dual demands of slapstick and story as his career flourished.

The second section of this book concerns the development of Chaplin's visual style during the silent era, beginning with his Essanay, Mutual, and First National shorts and concluding with his refusal to unconditionally enter the sound era in *City Lights* (United Artists, 1931). Chapter 4 seeks to identify the foundational elements of Chaplin's filmmaking technique across the silent era. Uncommitted to the narratorial camera and editing work that would become the classical norm, Chaplin developed alternate methods for ensuring a necessary clarity of story even while preserving a principled commitment to the representation of unbroken space. Chaplin essentially turned space itself to narrative ends, organizing his frame into discrete units that would allow for the development of narrative action over space instead of time and choreographing movement both of himself and others in the frame to direct and control the spectators' attention in lieu of cinematographic cues. Chaplin's alternate system of composition-through-space was, in part, an adaptation from his background in the British music hall and in part the product of a dedication to some of the cinema's earliest principles of filmic composition (principles that Griffith and others had tried to supersede or erase). Chapter 5 examines the philosophy and worldview that lay behind Chaplin's unique approach to composition and technique. It is a philosophy grounded at its core in a pervasive skepticism, a disposition that reaches extremes in Chaplin's work and undergirds his refusal to organize his films according to typical classical techniques of concision and abridgment. Chaplin refuses to accept the unitary and self-assured perspective that such an approach requires and insists instead on pointing always toward multiplicity and simultaneity, toward a universe that resists division and representation and that can be rendered on film only imperfectly. For Chaplin, to make a film is always to question the very purpose or potential of film itself. Chapter 6 takes *City Lights* as an apotheosis of Chaplin's work in the silent era, an achievement all the more pointed for its highly strategic incorporation of sound into what is still essentially Chaplin's stylistics of silent film construction. Thrust toward a consideration of representation itself in the moment of film's greatest transition and armed with the new technical element of sound, Chaplin creates the film widely considered his masterpiece as a direct meditation on his own style of filmmaking in its moment of greatest crisis.

The third and final section of this book considers the transformation and redemption of Chaplin's approach to filmic composition and construction in the sound era. Chapter 7 presents a reading of *Modern Times* and *The Great Dictator* (United Artists, 1940) as self-conscious grapplings with the inevitable breakdown of Chaplin's directorial technique in the face of the talkies. More than a technical change for Chaplin, the coming of sound was a philosophical challenge: a redoubling of classical certainty and mimetic illusionism that posed an existential threat to his filmmaking philosophy. *Modern Times* dramatizes that threat, warning of the epistemic dangers of sound and dialogue even while the film demonstrates its own deterioration. *The Great Dictator* performs a postmortem on that deterioration as the inevitable product of speech, painting a dark picture of aesthetic subjection as powerful and central as the film's political concerns. Chapter 8 considers Chaplin's attempts to adjust and reconfigure his compositional approach in his sound films of the 1940s and 1950s, *Monsieur Verdoux* (United Artists, 1947), *Limelight* (United Artists, 1952), and *A King in New York* (Attica-Archway, 1957). The films are markedly less assured than his silent and early sound transitional works, and much of this decline can be attached to a kind of aesthetic free fall in Chaplin's direction. Accepting sound as a transformative element in film yet unwilling to abandon a visual style set in philosophical opposition to the certainty implied by sound, Chaplin's sense of filmic construction begins for the first time to falter. The shortcomings of these later works actually illuminate what had once made Chaplin's style so inimitable, and the films demonstrate through their decline the near impossibility of reconciling his standard working method to the exigencies of sound. Chapter 9 offers a radical rereading of Chaplin's final film, *A Countess from Hong Kong,* as a deliberate departure from his previous sound films and a belated restitution of his unique manner of filmic composition. Typically dismissed by critics and scholars as substandard to the rest of Chaplin's work (in large part for the absence of any identifiable traces of his famous Tramp), the film, taken on its own aesthetic terms, in fact presents a profound point of resolution to the problems of sound first introduced in *Modern Times* and *The Great Dictator.* Chaplin here refigures speech to a point of ontological equivalency with action, stripping it of meaning in its content and leaving it only functional importance. Late into the sound era and near the end of his life, he thus finds a means of returning to the filmic priority once given to space and movement and to the position of aesthetic instability that had first defined his style and his approach to making films.

This book concludes with a brief consideration of Chaplin's legacy as a director in the mid- to late-twentieth century. Despite the reluctance of film critics and Chaplin scholars alike to afford him credence as a director, generations of filmmakers who sought alternatives to the hegemony of the largely American classical system took him as their champion. Filmmakers of Italian Neorealism and the French New Wave, from Vittorio De Sica to Federico Fellini, from François Truffaut to Jean-Luc Godard, saw Chaplin not just as a performer and even as something more than a director; they saw him as a fellow oppositionalist and trailblazer, a figure who stood in conflict with paradigmatic modes of filmmaking long before they did and whose way of making films—Truffaut saw in those films an "explosiveness" that can only be known to those who have experienced "total misery"—called into question even the assumptions that underlay their own rebellions.[52]

The filmmaker these later innovators saw when they looked at Chaplin was not, in the end, the superlative comic performer or the expert craftsman of sentimental stories or even the powerful mythmaker of most critical accounts. He was a figure deeply committed to exploring film as a consummate medium of expression, to challenging accepted cinematic orthodoxies, and to questioning what it means to make a film. This book aims to recover what that figure looked like.

PART I

CHAPLIN IN CONTEXT

Chaplin at Keystone, Griffith at Biograph

harlie Chaplin's directorial debut marks a seemingly inauspicious start to a monumental career. *Twenty Minutes of Love* (Keystone, 1914) is a "park" film like any number of others produced by Keystone during the early teens, when Los Angeles's Echo Park and Westlake Park (now MacArthur Park) provided easy alternatives to studio-based shoots.[1] Chaplin plays an early version of his Tramp character, first introduced two months prior in Henry Lehrman's *Kid Auto Races at Venice* (Keystone, 1914): the bowler hat, the mustache, the cane, even a nascent form of the famous walk are all present, though the character himself is mostly still embryonic.[2] The story is simple: the Tramp encounters a series of lovers on an afternoon stroll through the park, relieves a pickpocket of a watch stolen from one of the lovers, tries to use that same watch to woo one of the lovers himself, and initiates general mayhem and confusion. It is quick work—the story line and comic bits more or less improvised on site, the characterization and timing clearly rough hewn and imprecise. It is awkward cinematographically as well, governed by a visual logic that seems more suited to the theater than the screen. Almost the entire short is played in the foreground, the actors grouped into the spatial plane closest to the camera, with the middle ground and background of most shots obscured. In fact, the deeper planes of screen space seem almost consciously masked: bushes, trees, and almost anything else that was at hand within the park are placed directly behind the line of actors most of the time. It is as though the actors, all Keystone regulars, were positioned on a thin strip of stage, limited in their movements to a single plane of focused space on the left-right axis, prohibited from moving toward the camera or away from it. Even the entrances and exits seem marked by this logic. Though the setting is ostensibly a park, surrounding each character in 360 degrees, characters tend to enter or exit the frame from a single point on either side, as though the park, like a stage space, had wings.

It is tempting to think that Chaplin simply carried with him a theater artist's mindset from his recent days in the British music hall, where action must always conform to the limitations of an unchanging proscenium, viewed and viewable along only a fixed axis. Chaplin's compositional decisions in creating *Twenty Minutes of Love* seem especially to suffer from a theatrical handicap. The film largely adheres to the tradition of shot-scene correspondence that marked many of the earliest narrative films. Chaplin essentially refuses to cut within a scene. The camera remains unmoved during each of the comic bits—the encounter with each pair of lovers, the stealing of the watch—waiting for the action to transpire before cutting to the next comic moment, again filmed in whole. It is typical to say of these early shorts that Chaplin is "just filming the action," but what is perhaps more accurate is that he is just filming the space.[3] Chaplin does in fact prove willing to interrupt the action of a given scene. In the film's opening bit, the Tramp encounters a pair of overeager lovers on a bench and mimics their passion by swooning over a tree. The action of the scene is all of a piece, but Chaplin readily cuts between the lovers on the bench and the Tramp next to the tree because the spaces can be held distinct. Though they are presumably near each other, the lovers are not aware of the Tramp's mockery; he can be construed to be standing at a remove, in a separate space. Yet as soon as the Tramp invades the lovers' space and attempts to take a seat on their park bench, the camera remains unmoving for the duration of their extended fight. Chaplin's film is organized around its spaces.

Or, put another way, the film is organized to privilege spatial unity over the narrative. In one of the key plot points of the film, Chaplin's Tramp surreptitiously steals a watch from a pickpocket who is gloating to himself at his new acquisition. The logic of the sequence demands that the pickpocket remain unaware of Chaplin's presence, like the earlier lovers on the bench, but also that the two figures stand next to each other and occupy the same screen space. Chaplin proved perfectly willing to cut between the Tramp and the lovers on the bench so long as their spaces could be held distinct, but he will not cut between the pickpocket and the Tramp. If ever there was a moment in the short to cut between two figures in the same space it is here, providing a much-needed emphasis on the pickpocket's obliviousness to the Tramp's presence, as Chaplin did in the film's opening sequence between the bench and the tree. But Chaplin films the bit in one continuous take, the pickpocket and Chaplin on opposite sides of a tree. The logic of spatial coherence insists that the scene be unbroken and the space of the action not be segmented, regardless of what the narrative demands. A similar approach is employed in the short's climactic chase, when the Tramp must try to evade just about every character he has met during the short. Chaplin breaks up the action but he will not break up the space. Each shot is tied to a particular location in the park—next to the lake, away from the lake, on a path; he cuts back and forth between them but never breaks up the action within them. As in many of the earliest "chase films" that dominated the cinema some years before, Chaplin privileges the coherence of the spaces that make up the chase above the generalized action of the chase itself.

Throughout the film, then, an uncompromising logic of spatial coherence predominates: once a radius of space is defined by the frame, it cannot be further subdivided. Action is broken, segmented, and divided into parts, as witnessed in the chase or in the cutting between the lovers and Chaplin's mockery of them. Time is even broken in the film. Although it is titled *Twenty Minutes of Love,* the short lasts only about ten minutes, and there are several instances of intercutting that complicate our sense of elapsed time, as when one of the lovers searches for his lost watch while Chaplin tries to use it to woo his paramour in what may be construed as an instance of simultaneity. But space remains the indivisible unit of the short, unable to be compressed or rearranged once it is established. The limitations that Chaplin places on the actors' movements can be seen as a reaction to this basic fact. Unwilling to subdivide space for narrative emphasis, Chaplin pushes all the action to the front, where it cannot be lost. He would rather mask the actual dimensions of his space and play each bit in only one plane than allow our perspective on that space to be altered or redirected by a cut. Chaplin conforms his diegesis to a perfect uniformity and coherence of space within a scene, even to the point of robbing that space of its natural depth.

Twenty Minutes of Love is journeyman work, filmed in a single afternoon hardly two months after Chaplin had made the switch from acting onstage to acting in film. But it was also a proving ground. According to later accounts, Chaplin had quickly grown tired of acting under other filmmakers' direction; only months after starting his job at Keystone he is said to have put his entire life's savings—fifteen hundred dollars—on the table to guarantee Mack Sennett, Keystone's founder and studio head, that he could direct a film that would be worthy of release if Sennett would only give him the chance.[4] If it is far from a major work in the Chaplin canon, *Twenty Minutes of Love* was certainly pivotal in Chaplin's career. So it is perhaps all the more remarkable that the film is so out of step with many of the filmmaking trends of the time. The problem of how to deal with the often competing demands of space and narrative was, in effect, already "solved" by 1914, worked and reworked by a number of filmmakers during the rapid transformation of cinematic form between approximately 1907 and 1913, when techniques of analytical editing like crosscutting, cut-ins, eye-line matches, and shot/reverse-shot sequencing, as well as techniques of deep staging and depth of field, began to enter common practice. Compare *Twenty Minutes* to almost any D. W. Griffith short of the same period and Chaplin's work seems like a throwback to an era of filmmaking that had already passed, if only recently. Even among other Keystone films of its moment it was unsophisticated. There were other Keystone shorts that shared its theatrically styled entrances and exits, its overframing and boxing-in of space—the first Keystone short in which Chaplin appeared, Lehrman's *Making a Living* (1914), is notable for this. And most of the Keystones maintained a basic unity of shot and scene, as much for reasons of economics and expediency as art. But the extremely shallow field in which Chaplin plays his action and the other contortions he must bring to bear in maintaining an obsessive unity of space are conspicuous. Chaplin was still learning his craft. He would in fact learn it remarkably quickly, such that before the end of 1914 his mastery of the camera arguably matched or exceeded any of the other directors at Keystone—more than just being releasable, his shorts became among the studio's most profitable. But what is perhaps most remarkable about this sudden ascension is that even as Chaplin's technique improved, his filmmaking still participated in the same kind of visual system that is seen at work in *Twenty Minutes of Love.*

Chaplin, in other words, remained committed to an unbroken integrity of space, even as he learned to master that commitment more adroitly. This held true even as he began to erase ties to the visual mindset of the theater, where the proscenium itself is a given. And it held true as he eventually moved his films from the universe of absolute slapstick into a place of undulating pathos and tragicomedy. As much as Chaplin's earliest directorial effort marks a series of quick decisions by an inexperienced filmmaker, it also marks an early manifestation of what would eventually develop into a cinematic style and philosophy, one grounded in considerations of space before it is grounded in the arrangement of narrative. It was, for its time, both a reactionary and a radical move: reactionary in its approval of and adherence to some of the earliest techniques of photographing space used by filmmakers in the cinema's prenarrative days; radical in the proposition that these techniques and their associated aesthetic values might still be reconciled with the need to tell stories on film.

By the time Chaplin began his work at Keystone in 1914, the American cinema had already emerged from one of the most rapid and profound periods of stylistic transition it would ever know—an emergence that pointed toward a consolidation of technique around a filmmaking style very different from the one that Chaplin employed. As a performer and director, Chaplin began working in film at almost the exact moment of Griffith's commercial and aesthetic ascendance, when the manner of storytelling that Griffith and other like-minded directors championed seemed capable of reaching the level of an industry standard. To make films like *Twenty Minutes of Love* and the more successful shorts that came after it, Chaplin would need to ignore or rewrite important parts of the recent history of filmmaking, a period indelibly marked by efforts to alter or expand prevalent conceptions of filmic space and narrative. To understand Chaplin's early shorts in context and to appreciate the notable departures in the treatment of space they represent, it is necessary to understand the vital changes in the conception and handling of cinematic space that came before them.

CHARACTERISTICS OF SPACE IN EARLY NARRATIVE FILM

The treatment of space can be considered one of the foundational problems in the development of narrative cinema. In the years before the widespread growth of narrative film, the ability to record an unbroken unity of space and to unobtrusively chronicle the objects and bodies within it was regularly considered a basic property of the camera and due cause for the initial mass appeal of film. Film's very ontology was premised, in David Cook's words, not in the ability to create but to "simply *record* some real or staged event which occurred before its lens."[5] To watch early examples of events recorded and publicly presented simply for the wonder of the recording itself, what André Gaudreault and Tom Gunning have pivotally termed the "cinema of attractions," is to watch a filmed world defined by unbroken space and its necessary corollary, uninterrupted time.[6] Early attractions like the Lumière brothers' *Workers Leaving the Lumière Factory* (Lumière, 1895) or *Railway Station Scene* (International, 1897) displayed a world rendered in its spatiotemporal components like the one we know from experience: tethered to a specific spatial locus that can be framed but not subdivided, bounded in time that is equally unalterable. Even many of the earliest fictional films mimicked the basic spatiotemporal structure of the *actualités* and *documentaires,* providing a total perspective into a notable historical event as in the Edison Company's "trick" film *The Execution of Mary, Queen of Scots* (1895). The apotheosis of this approach might be seen in the early filmed panoramas like *Mt. Tamalpais RR No. 2* (Edison, 1898) or *Panorama of the Flatiron Building* (Biograph, 1903), extrapolations from the Victorian tradition of painted panoramas. Each of these took the depiction of terrestrial space in motion as an end in itself, whether the thrilling motion of a train ride as in the Edison example or the more pedestrian motion of simply looking up and regarding a building from its base to its pinnacle as in the Biograph example. Here, the attraction lies not only in the recording ability of the camera and its magical capacity for mystifying the commonplace by rerendering and thereby enchanting otherwise ordinary activities; the attraction of the panorama lies equally or more so in the ability of the camera to stand in for the human eye and provide a perspective on the world otherwise unseeable to the average viewer—not just to re-create an already known image but to transmit an otherwise inaccessible image, maintaining the coherence of a fascinating or exotic space as part of its main purpose.

Narrative was a part of film from very early in its history, of course. The Lumière brothers' first bill at the Grand Café in 1895 included a one-shot comic narrative titled *The Gardener* (*The Sprinkler Sprinkled*), and some film historians like Marshall Deutelbaum and Gaudreault argue for a basic narrative awareness even in such *actualités* as the early Lumière films.[7] More significantly, the idea of cutting between spaces and bringing together multiple unbroken spatial units to create a narrative sequence, a method which first arose with the development of the newspaper cartoon strip in the 1890s, took hold quickly.[8] You can see it in the narrative and spatial sequencing of Georges Méliès's thirty-shot *A Trip to the Moon* (1902) or the Edison Company's move from a protonarrative one-shot like *The Execution of Mary, Queen of Scots* in 1895 to their fourteen-scene adaptation of *Uncle Tom's Cabin* in 1903 or their fourteen-scene Western, *The Great Train Robbery*, directed by Edwin Porter that same year. Though only a minor part of cinema's earliest years, narrative film expanded rapidly: according to Charles Musser, a "new phase of rapid expansion" in the film industry from 1903 onward can be attributed largely to the "popularity of story films."[9] Exactly when narrative film achieved dominance against its documentarian predecessors has been a point of considerable debate, but Kristin Thompson reasonably divides the earliest years of cinema into two broad phases, with 1895–1902 being dominated by one-shot actuality films and 1902–8 being dominated by multi-shot story films.[10]

But the question of narrative ascendance is a different one than the evolution of cinematic space, for by and large the earliest narrative development took place entirely within the bounded and unmoving spatial units of the shot-as-scene multi-shot film, a kind of fictional counterpart to the unchangeable spaces of cinema's earliest documentarian days. In Gaudreault's apt description:

> Early filmmakers were more or less consciously considering each shot as an autonomous, self-reliant unit; the shot's objective is to present not a small temporal segment of the action but rather the totality of an action unfolding in an homogenous space. . . . Before releasing the camera to a subsequent space, everything occurring in the first location is necessarily shown. Spatial anchorage prevails over temporal logic.[11]

Indeed, single-shot filmmaking—the epitome of a narrative that is bounded by a space that lies above and beyond its dictates—continued to dominate the industry until around 1903 and remained in regular practice until at least 1906. It wasn't until around 1907 or 1908 that the treatment of space in narrative film became thrown into question, as the entire film industry reorganized around the rise of the film exchange and the nickelodeon. Film exchanges, which purchased films from production companies and then leased them to exhibitors, dramatically lowered the costs of film exhibition, leading to the "nickelodeon boom" of 1905–8 that essentially turned film from a specialized attraction, largely presented at existing vaudeville theaters, to a mass-market entertainment in its own right. With the rapid growth in exhibitors came a rise in demand that nearly overwhelmed the leading studios, such that by 1907 the general manager of Biograph would declare that the company was "pushed to the limit of its capacity by the demand for new subjects."[12] At the same time, individual filmmakers found themselves in increased artistic competition with one another as studios responded to the crisis of demand by attempting to establish new levels of consistency and quality within their output, vying for name recognition in an increasingly crowded marketplace.[13] In Musser's words, "The year 1907 was pivotal for the institution of American cinema," exacting changes in everything from production systems to forms of narrative and representation.[14]

Exactly how these changes affected the development of cinematic narrative is a question that has no single answer, but what the intensity of the debate around narrative transition in this era points to, almost in perfect correspondence, is the force of the rapid evolution at work in the film industry at that moment.[15] In her breakdown of early film periods, Thompson marks the years 1908–9 as the beginning of a "transitionary phase," a movement beyond the age of one-shot *actualités* and shot-as-scene multi-shot narratives alike.[16] If single-shot shorts could still be found with some frequency in 1906 (and would continue even as late as 1908), they would be all but gone within only a few years. By 1913, a year before Chaplin entered the film industry, one begins to see a cinema that looks markedly more like what we recognize as such—an early ancestor, to be sure, but quite obviously of the same genetic material. Though cinematic style was obviously still evolving, beginning in 1913 one can, as Charlie Keil has argued, "find most of the techniques that collectively constitute the classical style already in use"; the year would mark the beginnings of a consolidation of "changes in filmic representation that would mark a departure from previously established modes."[17] That is not to say it was a uniform transition. Gunning goes so far as to argue that the cinema of attractions of film's early years and the "cinema of narrative integration" that would take its place during this time "represent less two different diachronic periods than different synchronic approaches, often present within the same film."[18] And Keil cautions that in the transitionary phase "filmmakers are still experimenting with such techniques, viewing them as innovations to be tested" before moving on, ultimately, to "engage in a process of refining and honing elements of style they will enlist systematically during the classical period."[19] But the sum total of efforts from around 1907 to the very early teens marks a decisive stylistic shift in the early film industry, one that would both anticipate and define much of cinema's development for the century to come.

Spatial Unity in the Transitionary Phase

Although the period between 1907 and 1913 was rich with cinematic innovation, the techniques that would interrupt the integrity of space within a scene and enable the move within early cinema from a necessary world of shot-as-scene construction to one of shot-as-scene component were actually developed, in their most nascent forms, even before Thompson's transitionary phase and were at least a small part of the visual lexicon of early cinema years before they were adopted by directors like Griffith or Thomas Ince, figures who would become the public faces of a newly narrative-driven cinematic style. Barry Salt, among many others, has declared it a mistake to attribute "to D. W. Griffith the complete invention of 'film language.' Griffith may have been the best director working in the years from 1908 to 1915, but that does not prove he invented everything."[20] Early antecedents of the disruption of cinematic space date back as early as 1899, with Méliès's framing of a courtroom scene in *The Dreyfus Affair* from an unnaturally high angle, placing the principal actors in the deep background of the frame and a crowd of onlookers in the frame's middle and foreground. For Salt, it can be "considered to be the first occurrence of a purely 'cinematographic' angle in fictional film"—though as a technique it was actually not uncommon in *actualités* of the era.[21] It was an acknowledgment, perhaps the first, that fictional cinematic space might be perspectivized at a level beyond the straight-on, middle-distance shot as a point of narrative emphasis; it may be the first instance of harnessing the depiction of space itself to a narrative end, a subtle but important downgrading of space's consummate status in early film. Two years later, James Williamson's *Stop Thief!* (Williamson, 1901) presaged the development of the "chase film" by passing a continuous action across multiple shots, allowing for the unity of space within a shot but disregarding the idea of that unity as an unbreakable barrier for the individual actions of the film. But perhaps the greatest innovations in this direction came in two developments in 1903. In Wallace McCutcheon's *A Search for Evidence*

(American Mutoscope and Biograph, 1903), a series of long shots of a woman searching for her cheating husband in a hotel are intermixed with point-of-view shots as seen through the perspective of the keyholes through which she peers. At the film's climax, the wife breaks into the room where her husband is cavorting with another woman, at which point McCutcheon shifts the axis of the frame by ninety degrees and cuts to a shot of the wife coming through the door from inside the bedroom, with action-matching to link the two perspectives. Space in McCutcheon's short, though not actually broken, is capable of being used subjectively: the objectivity of the long shots married to the point-of-view shots into the bedrooms (shot through keyhole-shaped mattes), the angle on space calibrated and shifted according to the needs of the scene at the narrative's peak moment. Porter's *Gay Shoe Clerk* (Edison, 1903) would take the impulse behind such developments one step further, marking what seems to be the first instance of a close-up cut into the narrative action of a scene: a close-up of a shoe being fitted cuts to a long shot of a shoe store scene, with effective angle and action matching. The principle it establishes is powerful—the space of a given scene can be represented in more than one way (and in more than one shot) across the duration of the action in that space. The space in which a narrative takes place has been broken, if only quickly; tentatively, space has become a feature of the story and not a constraint upon its telling.

Such early innovations are the forerunners of the profound experimentation of the transitionary period. The central techniques of analytical editing and associated forms of emphasis that would begin to enter common usage—cut-ins, irises, crosscutting, eye-line matches, and the shot/reverse-shot—are further developments of the basic principles of editing seen in these earliest examples, ways of emphasizing features within a given space by naturalizing spatial and perspectival breakages within a single line of action and subsuming the ordering of spatial sequences to narrative need. But if the precursors from which these techniques were drawn were already in existence before the transitionary period, the sure conviction that they represented an improvement on filmic form—a proper and profitable response to the ballooning demand for narrative films—was lacking. Even as directors like Griffith turned with greater frequency to such techniques and helped develop them into their classical forms, the critics of the film industry trade press showed no assurance that such flourishes might not in fact pay a disservice to the basic structure of the cinematic image and interfere with audience comprehension.[22] According to the journal *Nickelodeon,* from an article at the outset of the transitionary phase in 1909, moving picture photography (here called "motography") is founded upon a requirement of "the art of the picture being developed fully in the scenes themselves before the motion picture camera is called upon to receive them."[23] It is a statement against the techniques of photographic storytelling—

the whole battery of devices that comprise analytical editing—in favor of a filmic style that essentially privileges the unelaborated depiction of photographed space such that the narrative may play out inside of what is captured and not through the means of its capturing. It is, moreover, a testament to a kind of static cinematography that stood against the techniques of emphasis like cut-ins, close-ups, and irises. In 1911, *Moving Picture World* and *Nickelodeon* would both agree on the impropriety of such techniques, stating that "the fundamental rule to be observed in this matter is that no figure should appear larger than life-size to the eye" and that "distance is an absolute requisite to any kind of idealistic illusion."[24] Even the advisability of cutting between too many scenes within a single film was occasionally called into question, with *Moving Picture World* criticizing that "three times the proper number of scenes are used to cover up the thinness of Director Griffith's on-the-flap-of-an-envelope stories" and decrying the spread of his technique: "A twenty scene drama is run up to fifty or sixty scenes, with an average time length of from fifteen to eighteen seconds each. Acting is not possible. Clarity of story is not possible. Unfolding of plot is not possible. There is a succession of eye-pleasing scenes, but no stories."[25]

But if the tastemakers of the early cinematic universe held on to conservative notions of spatial unity, premised both on cinematic tradition and on the supposedly inherent properties of motion photography, the mass-market appeal of many of the new experimental shorts often pushed filmmakers into new territory. Gunning has productively argued that the varieties of early film experiments might be divided into "genres" not based on their content but on their varying approaches to "filmic space and time" and specifically their stance toward editing.[26] And perhaps no "genre" did more to advocate for a loosening of mores around the interruption of filmic space and to set the general direction of the transitionary period than the burgeoning "chase" genre. The chase film, which predates the transitionary period by a number of years but continued in force until at least 1908, was far and away one of the blockbuster genres of film's early transitionary years.[27] Filmmakers turned frequently to the format to fulfill the overwhelming demand for shorts emanating from the new nickelodeons around 1907 and 1908, especially because such films proved easily replicable—an essential factor with studios overburdened by demand. With only minimal narrative pretext, filmmakers could hold audiences' interest time and again by filming a pursuit over a sequence of locales. The basics of the chase film beyond the particular narrative contrivance at hand were simple and stable, as evidenced in Gunning's effective summary of the form:

> The pattern is consistent: a character is chased by a group of characters from one location to the next. Each shot presents the chased character

running at some distance from the pursuing mob. The shot is held until first the pursued, and then the pursuers, exit from the frame. The next shot begins with the entrance of the pursued, and the movement through the frame begins all over again. The action continues through a series of shots until the fleeing character is captured.[28]

The success of the chase film demonstrated beyond any doubt that audiences would accept and take as natural a cinematic story that unfolded over multiple sequential spaces. For Gunning, the breakdown of spatial barriers inherent in the chase film is even a key part of its strange and long-lasting appeal: "Every chase film," he writes, "exploited the permeable barriers of the frame and created, through editing, a synthetic space in which exits from one shot or location were immediately sutured to an entrance in another shot or location.... It would seem the form's fascination lay in the spatial continuity it rehearsed, the possibility of stitching together a larger spatial whole from separate shots."[29] But the breakage of space that the chase film represents is still ultimately limited, for in each of these works narrative is, in the end, subsumed to the demands of spatial coherence. This is most true in the earlier chase films, which treat the unity of space as the ultimate determinant of narrative development. In works like McCutcheon's *Personal* (Biograph, 1904) and *The Escaped Lunatic* (Biograph, 1904) and Porter's *Maniac Chase* (Edison, 1904), the protagonists and antagonists must each pass through a locale, one after the other, before the filmmaker moves on to the next location, where the escape and pursuit is repeated once again—in Keil's words, they ensure that each "space is completely 'used up.'"[30] Later films ease up on these restrictions, allowing the movements or implied movements of single characters across supposedly linked locations to constitute a kind of spatial unity even if no literal chase occurs: a kind of subgenre of the chase film that Gunning calls the "trajectory film."[31] But in neither version of the chase film is space entirely subjugated to action; the films do not cut from the exasperation of the pursued to the determination of the pursuers, nor do they cut from one member of the pursued party to another, moving back and forth between subsections of the same greater space. Regardless of how they are organized in the trajectory film, the spatial nodes of the chase still form the core structure on which the narrative is overlaid.

GRIFFITH'S INNOVATIONS AT BIOGRAPH: PRIVILEGING THE DEMANDS OF NARRATIVE

Griffith's directorial debut and first entry into the chase genre, *The Adventures of Dollie* (Biograph, 1908), provides an exemplary case of both the promises and limitations of the chase genre. It is, in Gunning's description, a "trajectory film" that "immediately reveals Griffith's debt to, and quick mastery of, the visual and narrative forms of films before his debut."[32] The short depicts a well-to-do family whose daughter is kidnapped by a traveling gypsy and hidden in a barrel. The father catches up to the gypsy but abandons the search when he cannot find his daughter in the gypsy's wagon. As the gypsy crosses a river to escape with his prize intact, the barrel floats away down the river and eventually returns, with the daughter still inside, to the family. It is an ingenious rewriting of the basic dynamics of the chase genre: a linear narrative structure is transformed into a circular one; a narrative of failure and separation is paralleled, reversed, and ultimately completed by a narrative of success and reunion; and a narrative form seemingly dependent on agency is successfully resolved only in agency's abandonment.[33] Griffith's treatment of space within the film is likewise relatively more advanced than others of the genre. The recursive structure of the film renders the repetition of opening and closing spaces—the park where the daughter is kidnapped and then reunited—narratively significant, providing an alignment of the film's spatial units, its narrative structure, and its thematic concerns. Even Griffith's willingness to repeat the use of spaces already seen was an innovation for the genre. And yet, for all of the film's forward-looking features, like other films of its time it is still inescapably organized around a sequence of spatial nodes. The park, the gypsy's camp, the various spaces of the chase in between—all of them once established remain cinematically unbroken, governing the points through which the narrative must pass and the pace at which it may do so. The case is especially evident in the daughter's return to her family via the river. Griffith segments the total space of the river into a series of discrete locales, but within each locale the only event that can transpire is the event that the location most immediately dictates: the barrel must pass down the river, over the rapids, past the rocks, or by whatever other feature the environment affords. Any intercutting of the daughter's worry, of onlookers' concern, or of any other narrative features beyond the most basic progression of the action is forestalled.

For a filmmaker trying to tell a story, such an approach to narrative has substantial and obvious limitations. Foremost among these is simply the difficulty of conveying the locus of narrative attention when there is only limited possibility for visual emphasis. It was not an uncommon problem, and it was one that the trade publications frequently lamented and sought to find ways to resolve. Taking the preservation of filmic space as a given, most proposed solutions revolved around the careful composition and arrangement of action in the frame. Thus for *Moving Picture World*, the issue had to be addressed through a thoughtful use of the foreground plane of the screen: "Keep your active characters down front as much as possible. By active characters is understood those who are advancing the story at the moment."[34] But the range of possible solutions developed in early film was significantly more varied and sophisticated than just this. As David Bordwell has shown, nuanced strategies for the arrangement of information in the frame, what he calls "the long-take, 'scenic' method" of film construction, were commonplace in the era before classical consolidation.[35] "The primary solution," he explains, "moved characters around the frame so as to highlight salient action, using glances and composition to funnel attention."[36] In this manner, early directors "smoothly choreographed the brief glances and shifts of position, the outstretched arms and slightly swiveled bodies, the occluding of a background detail until the drama necessitated that it be apparent to all" so as to manage and direct viewers' attention in the frame, leveraging "the resources of set design, aperture framing, and figure movement" to create "highly functional staging patterns."[37] Yet the more complicated a scene, the more cumbersome and potentially ineffective such solutions could become. The problem, according to a *Nickelodeon* article from 1911, is that numerous actors on screen means numerous centers of attention, "any one of whom may do something, and consequently must be watched. It is a three-ring circus effect, where in trying to watch all rings at once, one really sees none of them."[38] Attempting to resolve issues of clarity within the frame was often an imperfect solution, especially when a degree of overlapping activity and visual cacophony was supposed to become an active part of the scene at hand.

One of Griffith's very early one-shots, *Those Awful Hats* (Biograph, 1909), fully displays these limitations. At only three minutes long, the piece needs to convey its narrative information quickly and efficiently. Such economy of message was in fact part of the purpose of the piece: it was designed as a humorous way for theater owners to remind female patrons to remove their hats before the film (an amusing predecessor to our contemporary reminders to silence our cellular phones in the theater). But for a work whose purpose is founded upon sending a prompt and uncomplicated message, the short is remarkably unclear. Griffith sets his camera in long shot and captures the busy auditorium of a nickelodeon as spectators watch a film-within-the-film. The general location and the film-on-film conceit of the piece are clear enough from the outset, but the actual details of its very simple narrative are difficult to discern. A series of patrons come and go from the auditorium as characters likewise move back and forth on the screen-within-the-screen. More than one woman with a significant hat enters the theater to the consternation of those around her, but were it not for the title of the short these interactions might be entirely lost. The hat incidents seem of no greater or lesser importance than any of the other interactions happening simultaneously among the patrons captured in the film—for that matter, they seem no more or less important than any of the business in the film-within-the-film that is also captured. What finally draws our attention to these particular instances of incivility is the appearance at the end of the short of a completely unexpected deus ex machina: the metal claw of a mechanical crane that swoops down from the ceiling and bodily removes the hat-wearing patrons to cheers from the rest of the crowd. (It is one of the few instances of trick photography in Griffith's entire body of work.) The short is ultimately effective in its ends, but only barely so. Without the ability to cut within the preestablished space of the nickelodeon to frame and highlight the most important action for the audience, Griffith's power to succinctly and effectively convey his narrative is limited. There are, of course, ways to circumvent such problems without subdividing the space within the initial frame. Griffith faced almost the same issue in another short from the same year, *A Drunkard's Reformation* (Biograph, 1909), wherein he would need to demonstrate an alcoholic's conversion while watching a temperance play. He resolved the matter by framing his view of the interior of the theater to show the two central characters prominently in the bottom-left quadrant of the frame, sacrificing the broader mise-en-scène of the theater hall for a closer alignment of screen space and narrative interest. But in *Those Awful Hats* Griffith is intent on showing the busy atmosphere of the modern movie hall, even if it means some sacrifice of narrative focus. As Griffith quickly learned, though, in complicated, multi-character scenes—the shot of the crowded nickelodeon can be read as a small-scale precursor to the kind of epic crowd shots for which Griffith would become famous—the demands of spatial coherence and the priorities of narrative communication might often find themselves at cross-purposes.

This central tension between spatial integrity and narrative clarity was well understood by other filmmakers of the transitionary period, and most early attempts to resolve this tension sought to foster a more perfect alignment of space and narrative such that the two might be developed in tandem within a film. One approach that achieved particular popularity between 1907 and 1908 and continued to be used through 1911 focused on developing stories that could unfold on opposite sides of some kind of diegetic spatial divider, as in *The Last Cartridge* (Vitagraph, 1908), which depicts an attack on a British colonial building during the Sepoy Rebellion in India with the action of the film taking place on either side of the building's gates.[39] Solutions such as this, what Keil calls an emphasis on "contiguous" spaces, proved an intermediary step toward balancing the demands of space and narrative—this approach allows for editing within a space broadly construed, but it forestalls that editing from subdividing the space by already predividing the space within the diegesis of the film.[40] As Keil recounts, "any act of cutting from an established space can risk producing spectatorial confusion," and thus contiguity shooting was a means of trying to mitigate that confusion absent the driving narrative linkages of something like the chase genre.[41] A related approach employs what Keil calls "proximate" space, a more general form of contiguous space which involves pinning the story to a series of otherwise adjoining physical spaces as a means of fully interlacing the visual and narrative sequencing of a film.[42] Sidney Olcott and Frank Oakes Rose's adaptation of *Ben Hur* (Kalem, 1907) provides an example wherein Ben Hur's home is situated vertically atop an arch under which many of the public events of the film transpire, allowing for easy movement between the public and the domestic spheres without the need for cutting—much as one might attempt with the set of a play. Such approaches, of course, had their obvious shortcomings. If the former severely limited the kinds of stories one might tell, the latter resulted in any manner of strange spatial contortions. ("Why would Ben Hur's home be located on top of an archway?" Keil asks.)[43] Yet many early filmmakers felt that such alignments between space and story might be a necessary aspect of filmic form, much as they would be in a stage play—at least as a means of reducing confusion in cuts between locations. (As Sergei Eisenstein recounts in "Dickens, Griffith, and the Film Today," the response that Griffith received from the Biograph studio heads upon suggesting a cut between disparate geographic locations in his early short *After Many Years* [Biograph, 1908] was, "How can you tell a story jumping about like that? The people won't know what it's about.")[44] While such an approach might significantly distort one or the other poles of narrative and space, either foreshortening narrative or distending and contorting spatial logic, it did effectively preserve an inviolable coherence of space while still making accommodations to film's narrative drive.

Within its purposes, such joinings of narrative to space could work effectively to mediate between their competing demands, and Griffith would use the device early in his career. *The Sealed Room* (Biograph, 1909) is one of his more sophisticated examples. Combining elements of both the contiguous and proximate approaches (in fact, the film switches between the two tropes midway through the action), *The Sealed Room* tells a macabre tale of infidelity and revenge: a king constructs a windowless room as an amorous retreat for himself and his queen, discovers that his queen is using it for an affair, and orders that she and her lover be secretly sealed into the room by a wall that he constructs over the opening as they are distracted by their tryst. As the film ends, the king gloats on one side of the wall while the queen and her paramour plead for their lives from the other side. It is an ingenious pairing of story and space, and the spatial organization does in fact help to organize the narrative of the film. The earliest scenes of the short are able to convey only the broadest outlines of the story: the king's pride at the room he has constructed, his public displays of affection for his wife. With a line of characters crowding the forward space of the frame, most of the interpersonal dynamics are easy to miss. We naturally focus our attention on the king, as that is where the characters in the short focus theirs as well; the more subtle exchanges between the queen and the musician who turns out to be her lover are hardly noticeable. Griffith has only limited means to convey the idea of a private affair in a public setting; only with some prior knowledge of the story might one think to focus on the behaviors of the musician and the queen, separated by other courtiers, amid the many actions and poses unfolding on the screen.

It is through the spatial dynamics of the film that Griffith is able to create emphasis. As soon as the queen and her lover retreat to the king's sanctuary, our understanding of their relationship is recast. We can track the movement from public space to private across the adjoining rooms and know for sure of the affair and its broader implications; the very location of the affair helps to communicate the depth of betrayal that it represents—a violation of private trust and public trust alike. And it is this act that precipitates the transformation of what was originally a place of transition between adjoining, proximate spaces into a wall of division between spaces that have become contiguous but separated, as in *The Last Cartridge*. There is a thematic overlay to the closing of the open space between private and public that results in the isolation of the queen and her lover. But, on a more technical level, it also allows Griffith the chance to focus separately on the actions of the king and of the queen and her lover without sacrificing spatial coherence. Griffith can move *as if* in close-up between the two parties, intercutting their pleas and exclamations. The wall gives him permission to jump between the two, to focus the narrative first on one character's experience and then on the other's, while still maintaining the unity of the core spatial components. The cuts that Griffith might otherwise want to make between characters in the film's climax are literally built into the architecture of the filmic space.

Of course, Griffith would soon discard such diegetically motivated spatial arrangements and would cast forward with a significantly new conception of cinematic space. If compromise is the goal, then a short like *The Sealed Room* can represent an effective halfway position between the needs of space and narrative. But it is also a limiting and cumbersome form of storytelling and one that Griffith would quickly abandon. Narrative, in Griffith's hands, would ultimately be subordinated to nothing. If we follow Salt in questioning Griffith's innovative role in the introduction of new filmic techniques, we are still left with the impact of the total system of filmic storytelling—what Gunning calls Griffith's "cinema of narrative integration"—that he helped to develop:

What is missing in these earlier filmmakers, although it appears at points in their work, is an unambiguous subordination of filmic discourse to narrative purposes. Under Griffith, the devices of cinema that were generally displayed for their own sake as attractions in the work of earlier filmmakers became channeled toward the expression of characterization and story. The often free-floating filmic attractions of early film became part of a narrative system as film unambiguously defined its primary role as a teller of tales, a constructor of narratives.[45]

Griffith may have been only one of many filmmakers to approach the cinema as a narrative form, in other words, but he was arguably the first to so consistently and uncompromisingly bend the possibilities and techniques of the medium to meet narrative demands. It was an imperative that would rely in fundamental ways on the rewriting of the role of space within filmic form, for it was the ideology of spatial coherence inherited from cinema's prenarrative beginnings that proved one of the greatest handicaps to the visual systems that Griffith meant to explore, the cause of so much contortion and compromise in films like *The Sealed Room* or *Ben Hur.* In Eisenstein's famous anecdote, it is not actually Griffith's privileging of narrative that is the cause for such consternation but his surprising disregard for the privileged place that space was supposed to have, his insistence that jumps that literally cross the world might be countenanced and understood simply by virtue of their narrative necessity, as though the spaces captured on film and the connections between those spaces might be made subordinate to the events happening inside them and the connections between those events. "When Mr. Griffith suggested a scene showing Annie Lee waiting for her husband's return to be followed by a scene of Enoch cast away on a desert island, it was altogether too distracting," Eisenstein writes.[46] Too distracting, that is, because of the spaces covered and the lack of contiguity between them. But Griffith's ambitions and his rethinking of cinematic space would be only just beginning.

The foundations of these new ambitions can be seen in so early a short as *Corner in Wheat* (Biograph, 1909), one of Griffith's earliest works, made in the same year as *The Sealed Room* and *Those Awful Hats,* and yet one of his most sophisticated. The basic spatial dynamics are in keeping with his other works: Griffith cuts between locations but he does not interrupt or subdivide a given space once it is introduced. But even if the integrity of space remains respected within the film, it is clearly not the organizing principle of the piece. The short tells a broad-ranging story of economic plight and excess. We begin with a series of one-shot scenes of farmers and their families, their lives revolving around the planting, harvesting, and selling of wheat. Then we make the jump to a series of scenes involving a wealthy investment tycoon, who schemes to "corner the market" in wheat. His success leads to the plight of the working families and this is indicated through a series of intercut scenes of these families struggling to survive as the tycoon holds an elaborate dinner party. The story resolves when the tycoon accidentally falls into one of his own grain elevators and is buried alive, restoring the farming families to their previous way of life. With such an elaborate narrative to cover, Griffith's adherence to the unity of space within each scene is little more than a politeness. Gone is any regard for spatial continuity across the various parts of the story. The contiguous spaces of a work like *The Sealed Room* are long forgotten, but even the spatial sequencing of a chase film like *The Adventures of Dollie* are abandoned. In the chase film, narrative logic works to make the sequence of spaces within the film seem contiguous or at least proximate, the totality of space covered by the film capable of being described more or less by the totality of scenes. The narrative, in other words, works not just to protect the integrity of each individual space but to give a sense of a bounded total space. (The same dynamic is at work in *Twenty Minutes of Love,* where the total sum of the scenes seems to describe a discrete area of the park environment.) *Corner in Wheat* explodes this notion. There is no means of knowing the spatial relationships between the scenes of working-class life and the scenes of the financiers. The total space they cover may be as great as the United States. Even within each segment, the various locales—a farm field, a bakery, a business office, a trading floor, a storage silo, a private estate—have no clear and obvious geographic relationship to one another. You cannot mentally map the spatial relationships between them, as you can in many shorts of the era. Space is respected but it is also harnessed to something else: the thematic prerogative. The jumps between the spaces of the suffering farm families and the celebrating millionaires are not jumps in physical distance so much as economic distance. The geography being mapped is moral more than it is spatial, though it is still conveyed through space. We do not see close-ups of the suffering farmers or the gloating businessmen; we see only their broad locations and the actions within them—a man planning seeds, families waiting in line for bread, socialites in a festive room. As in *The Adventures of Dollie,* what the space most immediately allows for is what Griffith is able to show. But the point of such showing is divorced from concerns about the integrity of space and tied to an abstract idea of injustice and inequality.

The treatment of space in *Corner in Wheat* represents a pivotal point in the development of Griffith's filmmaking, initiating a mode wherein ultimately the dynamics of space are wholly subsumed to concerns that emanate from, if not directly represent, the narrative thrust of a film. The opening of Griffith's short *The Mothering Heart* (Biograph, 1913) helps exemplify an early consolidation of this approach. The short begins with an iris on Lillian Gish regarding a flowering tree and slowly widens to reveal the garden in which she stands. A housekeeper enters the frame and gives her some information to which she responds by beginning to move, but her gaze is caught by something on the ground ahead of her. Griffith cuts to two puppies, one of whom has got its head caught in an open can. An intertitle reads "The Mothering Spirit" as we cut to Gish's bemused reaction and back again to the dogs. Gish kneels among the rose bushes to free the puppy, then in another shot takes them to sit with her on a bench. We cut to her beau entering the garden and stopping as he sees her with the puppies, then back to Gish (now holding the puppies). We return to the beau, and then cut back to Gish with her beau now entering the frame. Gish places the puppies on the ground, but when Griffith cuts to them we see that they are unwilling to leave her and scurry on only reluctantly. And at last we are back to Gish and her beau, readied for the actual narrative of the short to begin.

The information presented in this short opening is remarkable for the time: twelve cuts, an iris, and an intertitle in just over a minute's worth of film, all before the plot of the piece even begins.[47] Any sense of an integrity of filmed space has been abandoned. We are given a general sense of spatial parameters: Gish seems to move no more than a few feet throughout the shots, and we are led to believe she is describing a very small section of the garden and that most of that section is captured in one shot or another. We can in some sense mentally map the space traversed through the sum of the shots. But that is all we can do. At no point are we given an establishing shot of the garden or any kind of perspective that might allow us to see the total space at once. Griffith in fact opens the short with the opposite of such an approach: a tight iris around Gish and the greenery, only slowly pulling back to reveal a thin sliver of the garden space. Far from an organizing principle, space has become utterly sub-divided and deployed, harnessed to demonstrate Gish's "mothering spirit." We are given only pieces of a total space—those pieces that most serve the narrative drive of the moment, in this case a drive toward characterization. The spot near the tree, the spot near the dogs, the spot with the bench: these are not discrete locations as in *Twenty Minutes of Love*, indivisible and coherent spaces in which action entirely unfolds. They are segments of a garden space that we are made to understand is larger than what we are being shown, pieces that can be retreaded, recombined, and broken into other pieces still larger or smaller than what we have seen. What organizes the space is unseen: it is a general sense of Gish's character. Space has become not a feature but a function.

SPACE AND SUBJECTIVITY:
GRIFFITH'S FEATURE FILMS

The subjugation of space to story helps to explain the success, both narrative and thematic, of Griffith's breakthrough full-length works, those films that would most define and transform the nascent film industry. To view Griffith's early feature-lengths in light of the experiments of his Biograph shorts is to observe a continuity and consolidation of his earlier stylistics. These show where the film industry would move, the almost complete resolution of what Gunning calls the "period of ambivalence and contestation" that marked the transitionary phase.[48] In other words, Griffith's full-length achievements would not be possible without the rethinking of filmed space that first appears in his shorts. Nowhere is this more true than in *The Birth of a Nation* (D. W. Griffith, 1915), the film that Roger Ebert aptly calls "Griffith's sin"—the work that both fulfilled the revolutionary technique he had developed up to that point at Biograph and the one "for which he tried to atone all the rest of his life."[49] The impact of the film has perhaps been overstated, as Salt and others have argued.[50] But it marked a turning point in the industry nonetheless, both technically as a foray into the full-length features that would become Hollywood's mainstay and commercially as what may still be, accounting for inflation, the highest-grossing film of all time. And it was a turning point within Griffith's own career, not least for confirming suspicions he raised as early as 1909 about the obsolescence of spatial coherence and its utter irrelevance to the future of motion pictures.

The famous Ford's Theatre scene, which re-creates the assassination of Abraham Lincoln and provides the turning point of the film from Civil War to Reconstruction, is perhaps the most salient example. The scene can be read as a return to the issues Griffith encountered in *Those Awful Hats* and *A Drunkard's Reformation*, where the crowded space of the theater proved particularly resistant to easy narrative arrangement. Unlike his approach in the shorts, however, Griffith neither shies from the broad establishing shot nor hesitates to divide it once presented. His establishing shot of the theater, which raises exponentially the confusion and commotion of the nickelodeon in *Those Awful Hats,* is one of the great set pieces of Griffith's career: it is "an historical facsimile of Ford's theatre as on that night, exact in size and detail, with the recorded incidents," in the words of the film's intertitle. But it is revealed only in relation to the characters of narrative interest. Griffith begins the sequence with an iris on Elsie Stoneman (Lillian Gish), which widens slowly, first to reveal Phil Stoneman (Elmer Clifton), and then—in a kind of counterpoint to the move used in *The Mothering Heart,* where the widening iris provides only a portion of the spatial environment—to broadly encompass the totality of the theater as seen from behind the Stonemans' balcony seats. It is a powerful reveal, reminiscent of a curtain being drawn on the historical re-creation and paralleled by the opening of the actual curtain in the scene only moments later. For Griffith, the totality of space represented in the establishing shot and the commotion of the characters within it is a feature of the sequence—perhaps its central, most spectacular feature—but it is not the organizing principle. Griffith proves entirely unhesitant to divide, recombine, isolate, and reframe any and all components of the space to move his story forward. He moves among the establishing long shot (which he returns to throughout the sequence), middle-distance shots of the action on the stage, and a middle distance reverse-shot which puts the Stonemans in the center of the frame so that we can watch their reactions to the play. The establishing shot provides a set of coordinates that tie together the other shots of the theater: most of the shots in the sequence are mappable back to that long shot, such that we can easily follow the constant breakdown and reconstruction of the space. But these principles are not inviolable. Griffith proves perfectly willing to disorient the spectator and throw his viewers into spatial limbo when he cuts to the entrance of Lincoln's party arriving through a back hallway. After a title card announcing Lincoln's entrance, the viewer is wrenched from the established framework of the theater space into an unknown and heavily shadowed realm, defined in contrast to the broad curvatures of the theater space by its tight, rectangular angles. Griffith plays a kind of game with the audience: as the characters exit the unplaceable hallway space, they enter slowly into the coordinate system of which we are already aware: first, a medium shot of the presidential box which we may remember from the long shot, then a reaction shot of the Stonemans, and finally a return to the long shot placing the Lincoln party firmly in the established space and making the spatial system whole again. A similar game marks the appearance of John Wilkes Booth. Our attention is drawn to him first by the Stonemans, who notice the celebrity actor's presence during one of their middle-distance shots. Booth then appears in a tight iris shot, leaving us to wonder where he exists within the space of the theater. Griffith only gradually switches to a wider iris that still segments the theater space but places Booth clearly to the side of Lincoln's box. The revelation of characters in space becomes not a precondition of Griffith's narrative but a part of the suspense of that narrative's development. Understanding the space that a shot represents and the locations of the figures within it can become a kind of proxy for following the narrative itself: a reversal of earlier traditions where the narrative had to follow the development of the space.

There is still some trepidation in Griffith's handling of the unruly theater space he has unleashed. He refuses, for instance, to show Booth outside of an iris shot. The presentation of Booth is a halfway compromise between the techniques in *Those Awful Hats* and *A Drunkard's Reformation*. The iris widens at times to encompass more of the mise-en-scène lost in the tight shots of *A Drunkard's Reformation*. Yet the shots with Booth are always bounded and delimited by the iris, escaping the generalized confusion of *Those Awful Hats*. Griffith doesn't trust his epic spatial creation not to fully subsume his narrative if given the chance, even in a case where the basic dynamics of that narrative could not be more well known to his viewers. Yet he is also willing to play with the idea of the space enveloping the story, so long as it is at the right point in the story's development. Immediately after the assassination has occurred, Griffith cuts back to the medium shot of the Stonemans for their reactions and then cuts to the long shot of the theater. It is in the long shot, in the bottom of the frame, that we see Elsie Stoneman faint—an incident that is quite easily missed in the commotion shown throughout the rest of the frame. Griffith could have easily shown Elsie's collapse in the medium shot before jumping again to the total space; however, the difficulty of noticing her faint has become part of the point. Griffith is willing to strategically lose the locus of narrative interest if it serves the greater thematics of the scene, in this case a representation of the grand commotion that the assassination has caused. The Stonemans' story has been subsumed for the moment by the national story, a portrait in miniature of the film's overall movement between the localized personal stories of the Stoneman and Cameron families and the national drama of the Civil War and Reconstruction. In a far more sophisticated sense than in *The Sealed Room,* the jump between spaces, here the personal space of the Stonemans' seats and the public space of the theater writ large, aligns with the overall thematic interest of the work.

The Ford's Theatre scene in *The Birth of a Nation* demonstrates Griffith's willingness to subdivide and play with the space of a scene, but it still evinces an almost conservative respect for spatial coordination. We are mostly able to locate ourselves within the overall space of the sequence throughout—that is, there is still a kind of moderate privileging of filmed space, even if Griffith proves more than willing to subdivide and recombine its elements to narrative or thematic effect. Space still helps to organize a scene, even if it does not prove its *causa finalis*. Griffith's further development of these techniques in *Intolerance* (Wark, 1916) demonstrates a new and in many ways more radical commitment to making the spatial features of a scene only one component among many, to stripping them entirely of any organizing function. Spatial connections as such are almost wholly abandoned in the logic of *Intolerance*. The film is an apotheosis of the governing logic of a short like *Corner in Wheat,* where the intercutting of spaces might encompass a geography as vast as the country.

Indeed, geography is a quaint concern here, with intercutting that spans nearly the full breadth of human civilized history, from ancient Babylon to twentieth-century America, all purposed to the thematic exposition of "love's struggle through the ages."[51] And though Griffith is more than willing to turn space into spectacular attraction—as in his famous long shots of Babylon's great walls and lavish festivities, inspired by *Cabiria* (Itala, 1914)—he is also willing to leave it strategically untouched, as in the film's third-act trial scene. Here, a young husband is put on trial for a murder that he did not commit as his loving wife looks on. Griffith opens with an establishing shot of the courtroom as grand as anything in *The Birth of a Nation*: it would seem to be the trial of the century from the packed gallery it has drawn and the grand courtroom it has been assigned. Yet there is something suspect in this shot. It is preceded by an intertitle that reads "Nearing the end of the Boy's trial for murder"; and, in fact, as grand as the shot is, it is framed at the edges by an iris. We are told, in effect, to ignore any sense of precision in the timing of the sequence we are about to see: it is not even "near" the end of the trial, simply "nearing." And we are similarly denied a comprehensive picture of the scene before us. The iris emphasizes this denial, insisting that we recognize that we are being given only a taste of the grandeur of the occasion and entreating us not to take the establishing shot as a comprehensive picture or plan of orientation.

And indeed, such orientation would do us no good, as nearly the entirety of the remaining scene plays out in a series of tight iris shots of the individuals in the courtroom: the testimony of a policeman, the arguments of the prosecutor, the sober expression of the judge, the appearance of the boy on the witness stand, the desperate worry of his wife, the shifting of the jury members, the guilty squirming of the murderess in the gallery. Only the boy's inexperienced lawyer is shown in an iris that encompasses another figure as well, revealing the reactions of the experienced prosecutor to the defense attorney's blundering. Even when the boy and the prosecutor interact during questioning, Griffith insists on showing them one after the other in isolated irises. We are never given a chance to understand how any of the figures may be oriented to one another spatially, and we return to the establishing shot only once during the proceedings of the trial—when the boy takes the stand, a means of reemphasizing the enormous pressure he must feel. All the other shots hold tight around the figures of the narrative, and the scene is an almost impressionistic sequence of faces and bodies, worry and agony. It is a scene about the subjective experience of the trial, not about its actual mechanics. We are prevented in every way from seeking any grounding in the space—or, for that matter, any sense of the time that may elapse. We cannot tell if any of the expressions that we see are meant to be simultaneous or overlapping in time, whether they truly represent a sequence, whether they occur in real time, or whether there might be gaps in time between each shot. The scene gives to us a sense of the experience of the trial at the expense of a full understanding of its action. And the space of the trial, insofar as it is presented at all, serves only to emphasize particular aspects of its experience: that is, it does not truly function as space at all. Or, in other words, Griffith has at last fully abstracted his narrative from any kind of spatial grounding.[52]

Not all of Griffith's work would be so austere in its abandonment of space; *Intolerance* may be considered a high point in this regard. But even as his narrative focus became again more grounded, the intense subjectivity developed to a frenzy in the *Intolerance* trial scene would continue as a dominant trope of his filmic style. Even the most action-oriented scenes, those dependent entirely on a sense of space for their full execution, would be presented through a lens of subjective experience. This is the approach embodied in one of the climactic moments from *Hearts of the World* (Famous Players–Lasky, 1918). Funded by the British government to drum up American support for entering World War I, *Hearts of the World* depended for its effect on an implacable insistence on German menace.[53] In a climactic scene, an American boy and his French sweetheart find themselves trapped in a room with German soldiers pounding on the locked door, determined to enter. It is an inversion of the climactic moments of *The Sealed Room:* here, the villain and his henchmen demand entry into an inescapable bedroom holding a boy and his lover, where before it was the boy and his lover who demanded exit from an inescapable room from the king and his servants. As in *The Sealed Room,* Griffith cuts frequently from one room to the next, the spatial divisions of the scene serving as a proxy for the narrative and thematic distinctions of good and evil, pursuer and pursued. But the evolution between the two works is notable. In *Hearts of the World,* each space is treated not just as a distinct location but as a set of distinct experiences. Griffith cuts between the objects and locations that preoccupy the worried lovers: a close-up of the door beginning to give way to the pounding of the German soldier, the boy and girl in each other's embrace, the worried panic of the girl, the desperate reassurances of the boy. On the opposite side of the threshold, Griffith cuts between the menacing face of the German commander and the eagerness of the soldiers ready to kill the boy and girl. The basic dynamics of the scene are in line with those of *The Sealed Room*—contrasts of panic and excitement, violence and despair—but the execution is of another order. The impressionism of *Intolerance*'s trial scene is coupled here with a tactical use of spatial coordinates. We are made to focus on the experiences of the main characters and to focus on the objects that hold their attention—the lock, the door—but we are aware at all times of the physical relationships that they have to one another, the intense proximity of pursuer and pursued creating the suspense of the scene.[54] There is only a door that separates them, and a not-too-solid one at that. The space here serves the urgency of the narrative and in fact serves nothing else. There is no sense of spatial coherence as an end in itself: the space is divided and redivided by Griffith's editing, broken into a parcel so small as a door lock and so wide as a hallway. There are no spatial games or careful revelations of location. There is only spatial separation as an instigation to greater suspense and as a tool for demonstrating the growing panic or determination of the characters. The space here is made to serve not only the development of the narrative but the characters' subjective experience of the narrative as well.

The Promise of Classical Style

What Griffith managed to develop over the course of his shorts and early features was nothing less than a model of cinematic technique that would help define what modern film would become. Griffith's approach would not be a perfect forerunner to the consolidation of classical Hollywood style. "With Griffith," Gunning writes, "the emphasis on the tasks of storytelling is brought to a particular intensity," prohibiting Griffith from the kind of stylistic transparency that would become part of the classical paradigm.[55] Or, as Gunning later puts it, "In Griffith, what is rendered 'invisible' in later cinema still remains visible."[56] But Griffith's approach would nonetheless create the blueprint from which the classical style would be built: a style defined, in Robert Ray's terms, as "the systematic subordination of every cinematic element to the interests of a movie's narrative. Thus, lighting remained unobtrusive, camera angles predominantly at eye-level, framing centered on the principal business of a scene. Similarly, cuts occurred at logical points in the action and dialogue."[57] More than a toolbox of techniques, however, the classical style is also a kind of promise to the viewer. As Ray writes:

> Each shot results from dozens of choices about such elements as camera placement, lighting, focus, casting, and framing (the components of mise-en-scène); editing adds the further possibilities inherent in every shot-to-shot articulation. Not only do things on the screen appear at the expense of others not shown, the manner in which they appear depends on a selection of one perspective that eliminates (at least temporarily) all others. . . .

> The American Cinema's habitual subordination of style to story en-
> couraged the audience to assume the existence of an implied contract:
> at any moment in a movie, the audience was to be given the optimum
> vantage point on what was occurring on screen. Anything important
> would not only be shown, but shown from the best angle. . . .
>
>   This tacit guarantee of a constantly optimum vantage point con-
> stituted so fundamental a part of Hollywood's stylistic that the best
> filmmakers, even when working in the detective genre, violated it only
> surreptitiously.[58]

It is a promise, in other words, premised on a compensation for the abridgment and distortion of space. There is nothing in itself natural about the way
that Griffith's technique cuts, reedits, and reorders the spaces and figures it
represents: that is, nothing that actually parallels our experience of the world,
even if it aims in its final form to mirror our subjective encounters with our
environment. It is, in Joyce Jesionowski's words, a " 'spontaneous way of seeing'
that makes the cinema world seem more *present* than everyday reality," but it
is also a deliberate and careful construction.[59] Griffith's approach, Jesionowski
writes, was to create a mode of filmic presentation wherein "disarmingly 'realistic' effects are based on alarmingly abstract construction. . . . Griffith's brand
of screen reality is characterized by spatial and temporal elisions, bridged by
formal suggestions, that convince viewers that a continuity of screen action
and screen narrative they perceive has, in fact, occurred on the screen before them."[60] In this way, Griffith's technique mimics a subjective shifting of
focus and emphasis—a "spontaneous way of seeing"—but it is a preordained
spontaneity, not one of our choosing. To encounter the world exempt from
such filmic styles—or, correspondingly, the world re-rendered on film in an
unbroken image of space—is to encounter a series of perceptual choices: we
ourselves can deem where best to place our focus or hone our attention, when
to shift, how long to linger. Classical technique anticipates this process and
forecloses our choices. It is based on what Stanley Cavell calls "the image of
perfect attention," wherein the cinema discovered in "the altering frame . . . the
possibility of *calling* attention to persons and parts of persons and objects."[61]
The reason that one can miss points of narrative emphasis in so simple a short
as *Those Awful Hats* is that one can choose where to focus and might choose
wrongly. But one cannot choose at all in a sequence like the trial scene from *Intolerance* and one can hardly choose, or choose only in brief, isolated instances,
in something like the climax of *Hearts of the World* or even the assassination
scene in *The Birth of a Nation*. With the removal of space comes the removal of

options—perceptual choice is made for you. Classical technique promises that the choices will be the right ones.

It is a promise that in its full execution approaches a kind of metaphysics of the image. The classically organized film is not given from the single vantage point of a single observer but from a concomitance of vantage points tied to no particular observer. It offers ultimately a subjectivity without a subject, a perspective on the world without a person holding that perspective. This is what Cavell terms the "automatism" of film, a divorcing of perspective from the point of perspective and the fulfillment of a wish for a continually perfect viewpoint, even "for the condition of viewing as such."[62] The classical film offers a perspective that transcends the limits of space and time as we know and experience them. Narrative is offered as its only organizing framework. It is a guarantee that in a world where you cannot possibly make your own perceptual choices, those being made for you will be significant and connected; they will tell a story. What Griffith promises is that the images he shows us and the rapid movements between them will add up to something: seeing them in this order, in this way, will lead to a total understanding of the events unfolding, a total understanding of the broken and reordered world before us. At the end of that stream of images the sequence, and the world, will be made whole again. In this sense, narrative is not simply that element which is privileged in the Griffithian mode of filmmaking or in the classical tradition. Narrative is given as compensation for the breaking of the world.

Chaplin's First Response: *Dough and Dynamite*

Griffith offers a promise that lies at the beginning of what cinema would become. Even if he was not, on his own, the entirety of that beginning, he would give a name—his name—to it in the popular imagination. As James Agee wrote of Griffith, "To watch his work is like being witness to the beginning of melody, or the first conscious use of the lever or the wheel; the emergence, coordination and first eloquence of language; the birth of an art: and to realize that this is all the work of one man."[63] Jean-Luc Godard would take Agee's praise one step further. "I think one should mention Griffith in every discussion about the cinema," he declared.[64] Even Chaplin would seem to agree. Asked in a magazine interview from 1925 to name the "best pictures ever made," Chaplin listed, in order, *The Birth of a Nation, Intolerance,* and *Hearts of the World.*[65] These films were to Chaplin, as to so many others, what film might best become. But they were not, nevertheless, what he made when he made films.

For even as Chaplin honed his craft, he would never truly come to participate in the discourse that Griffith was developing. Even as Chaplin joined forces with Griffith as a producer, creating United Artists in 1919 along with Mary Pickford and Douglas Fairbanks to jointly distribute the films that each made independently, Chaplin still did not make films that *looked* like Griffith films. He did not make films that shared in their visual assumptions or techniques. By 1914, when Chaplin began directing shorts, all the techniques that Griffith would deploy in his feature-length works were already in widespread use, in large part from the success of Griffith's own shorts. They were already coalescing into an acceptable mode of filmic style, long before Griffith's debut feature. They were, in other words, already established.

Yet they entered into Chaplin's early directorial technique hardly at all. Even in what is arguably Chaplin's most accomplished work from his pivotal first year at Keystone, he is obviously pushing in directions other than those explored by Griffith, directions that speak to a separate set of concerns and that would only grow stronger as his career and craftsmanship developed. A late 1914 short like *Dough and Dynamite* (Keystone) is not an exploration of the ways in which spatial coherence might be subverted, circumvented, or reprioritized. It is instead a study in how spatial concerns might be artistically rethought without being abandoned, how they might be made even more artistically potent. Widely considered among the best of Chaplin's work at Keystone—and among the best work that Keystone would produce from any artist—*Dough and Dynamite* centers on a revelry of comic space caught on film. Chaplin, once again an early version of the Tramp character, is a waiter at a restaurant where the bakers have suddenly gone on strike; he and another waiter must take their place baking in the basement to fill the customers' orders. Though it is a film that covers multiple locations in the exposition of its first half, its narrative coalesces toward the single, grand location of the basement bakery in the short's second half. It is a film, in other words, whose narrative drives toward spatial coherence with a unified and unbroken location as the site of its most important developments and final resolution. And what a location it is: the fiery basement room, as much culinary dungeon as food preparation site, is an ingenious comic set, a space that might overwhelm even the most experienced baker let alone the novice waiters who are its newest inhabitants. Chaplin's handling of the space shows the extent of his rapid maturation as a filmmaker, *Dough and Dynamite* coming only six months after *Twenty Minutes of Love*. Chaplin essentially splits the basement area in two while maintaining a commitment to unbroken space. The room is always presented in one of two possible framings: the half with the entrance, or the other half with the ovens. Chaplin essentially treats the single space of the basement like the contiguous spaces of shorts like *The Sealed Room,* spaces with their own identity that are joined at a common meeting place. Only here, the "rooms" that are adjoined are merely segments of a larger, total room: an inventive adaptation of established technique to comically exaggerate the size of the space. It is a space that exceeds the desire to maintain its coherence, a space beyond filmability—if the space is *that* big, our hero cannot stand a chance.

It is, of course, a great comic setup, and in its sophistication it is of a piece with Chaplin's other directorial choices throughout the film. Gone is the clumsy masking, the foreshortened playing space, the awkward framing, and the forced entrances and exits—all of the most notably unpolished aspects of his directorial debut only a few months earlier. Chaplin confidently distributes his actors across all three planes of framed space, and even seems to overprivilege the front-back axis of the frame. Nearly all of the major spaces of the film are oriented in this way: a long counter pushes away from the camera into the deep space of the frame, a row of tables stretches away from the lens in the same direction. The basement even shares this orientation, its leftmost section defined by an entry ladder in the background of the frame, its rightmost section defined by a series of ovens that reach toward the backmost plane. Chaplin ingeniously invents a world where the primary axis of movement is forward and backward, only to throw the rules of that world into comic jeopardy when the waiters must navigate the left-right spatial orientation of the basement itself. The contrast leads to any number of calamities: the Tramp accidentally knocking the other waiter in the head with a long wooden peel that runs across the screen, the need to evade flying dough bags and return fire across the left-right axis of the room as a food fight erupts with the bakery's owner. The geography of the basement literally upends the spatial orientation of the rest of the film, just as it narratively upends the working experiences of the Tramp and his fellow waiter.

Chaplin's decision to film the outsized space in two adjoining frames further amplifies the comedy that the basement itself creates. By essentially masking one half of what is otherwise an uninterrupted and contiguous space, Chaplin adds a layer of micro-distance between the way events unfold in that space and the way in which they transpire for the audience. In this way he can prevent us from anticipating a joke, sometimes even prompting us to forget that the joke might be coming. When the Tramp removes his long peel from one of the ovens, for example, we cannot see the butt of the paddle headed for the other waiter's head. Chaplin must cut to the other half of the space, where we are suddenly reminded of the waiter's presence just in time to see it make contact. When the Tramp finds himself in a food fight with the bakery's owner, we do not see an unbroken volley of dough bags flying back and forth. We watch each bag's launch and then, only after we have suffered through the delay of the cut between spaces, can we be surprised and delighted by where it lands or how it is avoided. Likewise, when the Tramp drops an enormous bag of flour into the basement and traps his coworker underneath, we forget all about the incident as the Tramp unthinkingly moves on to the frame with the ovens. When he returns at long last to the other side of the basement and finds his coworker still trapped in the background of the frame, just where he left him before, the effect is far more surprising than had we been watching the poor fellow the whole time.

Chaplin's technique here is brilliant, but it is also highly retrograde. The contiguous space approach of shorts like *The Sealed Room* was passé by the time Chaplin created this film, but he finds means of resurrecting this basic approach and making it viable once again. What *Dough and Dynamite* evinces is not just a filmmaker quickly mastering his craft but a filmmaker interested in issues and approaches that would seem to have been already left behind in film's rapid growth as an industry and an art form. Here is a filmmaker concerned with one of the issues most central to narrative film's development before he ever arrived in the industry: the question of how to maintain a coherence of space as an artistic practice. Chaplin does use more advanced techniques in *Dough and Dynamite.* He offers two facial close-ups, for instance: something Griffith would not even yet incorporate in any meaningful way into *The Birth of a Nation,* released the following year. But these are flourishes placed at transition points in the film. The preponderance of Chaplin's effort is constructed inside a world of spatial continuity, one where the coherence and explicability of space is still central to the filmic form. It is a world that needn't yet offer any promises, as it hasn't yet broken anything. And it is a style of filmmaking that stands apart from Griffith and his inheritors. It did not belong entirely to Chaplin, as it developed in significant ways from the slapstick tradition, but it was a style, and beyond that a philosophy, that he would ultimately come to make his own.

The Slapstick Exemption

In 1908, the year that D. W. Griffith began directing films at Biograph and six years before Charlie Chaplin joined Keystone, the French film studio Pathé Frères had one of their greatest successes on the American market with the comic short *The Runaway Horse* (1907). It was of course only one of many comic films to be released that year, though for Richard Abel it helps identify the moment when "Pathé's prominence on the American market probably reached its peak."[1] (It was also something of a minor cultural touchstone in itself. In Barry Salt's telling, it was "so successful a film" that it would have been hard for anyone with an interest in the new art form of moving pictures "to avoid seeing it.")[2] The short remains of interest to historians of early film because it is remarkably advanced in its technical composition for works of the era. The film presents an early instance of narrative crosscutting and showcases an ability to navigate what Don Fairservice calls "telling stories as single progressing continuities," which was still far from an established industry norm.[3] More than that, it includes a number of advanced techniques of continuity editing, including a difficult—and for the time unusual—cut on movement. It was, in other words, a remarkably well-executed early example of the kind of narrative-driven and continuity-focused editing that would soon become constituent of the classical style of filmmaking. But it was also a work divided into "two equal parts," as Abel puts it, of which only the first has any engagement with a "sustained sequence of alternation," crosscutting between a delivery man who is delayed while making his drop-off in a walk-up apartment building and his horse, who gets into an open bag of feed on the street outside.[4] For all the critical attention focused on this opening sequence and on the end of the film, the places where the crosscutting and continuity editing occur, the least technically noteworthy section of the film was arguably the greatest (and possibly the only) cause for the film's popularity. What Abel identifies as the second half of the film, in which the delivery man's horse escapes from his master and, newly energized by the bag of oats, wreaks havoc on the streets of Paris, is composed almost entirely in standard shot-as-scene format with straight cuts, not unlike any number of other preclassical films. But what it depicts within those static frames—sheer mayhem, an exuberant cacophony of bodily peril and material destruction—is something remarkable. It is by genre a chase film, wherein each scene compels a new aggrieved party to chase after the main subject until at last a virtual mob is in pursuit of the overfed and overexcited horse of the film's title. But it is not so much the chase as the causes for the chase that are the main attraction here, which is to say the extent of the havoc the horse manages to wreak: knocking over carriages, a baby stroller, a kiosk, market stalls, two sets of scaffolding, and the display pieces at a pottery shop—all culminating in the actions of a stable boy who steps in to defend the horse by turning loose a watering hose on his pursuers, pushing them down the Parisian street like so many pieces of curbside litter.

Despite the sophistication of the film's editing and narrative composition, it was arguably these anarchic scenes that comprised its greatest appeal. *The Runaway Horse* inspired a number of derivative films and overt copies (including one directed by Griffith himself), yet, tellingly, not one of them sought to emulate the film's technical mastery—not even Griffith's version. As Fairservice observes, the success of the film would make one think that "this kind of continuity editing was now well established; that the innovative reverse angle cutting . . . had become commonplace. But that was not the case at all. These continuity linkages between shots would not become widely adopted for several years."[5] What other filmmakers sought to copy was instead the masterful execution of the scenes of distress and destruction, moments of comic bedlam that were far from original for the time but that were particularly inventive and well articulated, presented with as much formal simplicity as possible and as much diegetic pandemonium as could be achieved. The film's elaborate falls, crashes, fights, and collapses—indignities of the body and destructions of the material world—were the subjects of emulation. *The Runaway Horse* did not actually need such a sophisticated compositional structure of crosscutting and continuity editing; it did not have a complicated story to tell or a sense of subjective experience to evoke. It needed far simpler things: an escaped horse, a frantic delivery man, a cityscape full of collisions waiting to occur. It was a work of slapstick. And for audiences at the time, all of its editing tricks and achievements were just so many superfluities. What they wanted was not sophisticated storytelling. What they wanted was comic action and a good laugh.

As the particular case of *The Runaway Horse* illustrates, slapstick as such stands apart from other forms of fictional filmmaking. This has become a point so oft repeated in the study of the genre that some critics have worried about a kind of critical ghettoization. Writing in 1988, Peter Krämer cautioned that "the history of North American cinema has often been written in relationship to the dramatic genres," with slapstick regarded simply as a "site of heterogeneity" with "neither its form nor content fitting existing models of classical American cinema in the teens."[6] Reflecting on the scholarship since Krämer, Tom Paulus and Rob King reiterated his concerns some twenty-two years later: "Insofar as the study of dramatic filmmaking practice set the terms of scholarly debate, slapstick quickly came to be framed as 'other.' . . . While these path-breaking studies made exemplarily clear the structural gap separating early comedy from dramatic filmmaking, they nonetheless risked omitting much by defining their object principally from an assumption of difference. The recognition and categorization of difference, we would suggest, can only ever be one step in an understanding of slapstick as a cultural practice."[7] To be sure, though, the assumption of slapstick's difference from other forms of fictional cinema has not been a universal given in the scholarship. David Bordwell, for one, acknowledges a degree of difference but finds it a critical dead end: slapstick is for him an example of "transtextual ends such as genre" and is more or less reducible to other generic tropes, its notable features remaining separate from an otherwise general convergence between the substance of its comedies and the basic "narrative economy" that defines the classical form.[8] Similarly, Kristin Thompson acknowledges that "every film contains a struggle of unifying and disunifying structures" and uses the term "excess" to define features that are "counter-narrative" and "counter-unity," but she generally excludes slapstick tropes from this category, arguing alongside Bordwell in a case study of Buster Keaton's *Our Hospitality* (Buster Keaton, 1923) that "virtually every bit functions to support and advance the cause-event chain of the narrative."[9] In Henry Jenkins's words, by the 1920s a filmmaker like Keaton, among many others, could be seen to operate "fully within classical norms and showed few signs of his previous allegiance to the vaudeville aesthetic."[10]

Looking at slapstick from its inception in the earliest days of film to its culmination at the end of the silent era, both sides of the debate hold some truth. Slapstick can and in many cases did remain distinct from the move toward classical technique that marked other forms of film in the teens, yet it also engaged throughout the later silent era in an ongoing series of negotiations with classical style and narrative, adjusting and renegotiating the degree to which it might allow itself to conform to prevalent filmmaking modes. It is into this ongoing dialogue that Chaplin entered when he joined Keystone in 1914, and as he learned and relearned how to direct for the screen he was forced to make his own choices about the classical system. To decipher Chaplin's approach to this interchange, one must understand the world of comedic film at the moment of his arrival: its possibilities and limitations, the problems that Chaplin and other silent film comedians would need to overcome to make slapstick something of a continuing commercial power even as the basic assumptions of what it meant to make a film changed beneath their feet. Slapstick first emerged in America at a time when its distinction from what would ultimately become classical style was no great matter; it was an instance of heterogeneity without being a source of heterodoxy. But over the course of Chaplin's early career all of this changed and slapstick became something unique: a genre that might succeed with audiences and yet still evade classical technique in ways both obvious and subtle, imagining a different way to organize and present the world.

THE SLAPSTICK EXEMPTION

More so than narrative drama, slapstick can lay claim to have stood at the very beginnings of film. The only one of the Lumière shorts to tell a story at their Grand Café presentation in 1895 was, not incidentally, a kind of slapstick comedy. *The Gardener* (*The Sprinkler Sprinkled*) is not much for story: it depicts, in one shot, a boy who steps on a gardener's watering hose and then releases the water into the gardener's face. It is, in effect, a glorified gag. But slapstick's origins run deeper, even to what may be the first film ever made (depending on whether it is dated to 1889 or 1892) and what is in either case the earliest surviving copyrighted motion picture—Edison's *The Sneeze* (copyright 1894), which, in three seconds, depicts the face of Edison employee Fred Ott, who was known at the company for creating comically exaggerated sneezes to entertain the other workers. *The Sneeze* fits easily into the concept of the cinema of attractions: its appeal, such as it is, lies almost entirely in the act of its recording itself. It is a picture of life, rendered on film and played back to us, and its interest is mostly bound up in its own ontology—it is interesting as a film simply because it is a film. But the interest of *The Sneeze* also exceeds this. To recognize the sneeze in *The Sneeze* as a comically exaggerated one is to recognize a matrix of expectations and norms beyond the act itself to which the act immediately connects: expectations about the proper expression and proportions of the face, norms of social decorum and comportment, all of which are thrown, momentarily, asunder. Comic sneezes would have a proud history in slapstick: *That Fatal Sneeze* (Hepworth, 1907) consisted almost entirely of a progression of comic sneezes and became one of the most influential slapstick films of its age.[11] Considered as a recording of a slapstick gag, *The Sneeze* embodies much of what slapstick would try to depict: the human body in exaggerated distress, beyond help and beyond the reach of social norms, and yet (usually) relieved of any real danger or consequence. Physical humor like that in *The Sneeze* can be placed in a narrative context, and indeed it frequently was, even from cinema's earliest days. But it does not need to be. It can be interesting—and funny—on its own.

There may be no greater proof of the degree to which slapstick comedy can escape from narrative demands than D. W. Griffith's own work in the genre. Such was his aversion to comedy in general and his general avoidance of it in his later feature films that it can be easy to forget that Griffith directed several comic shorts while under contract at Biograph. But there is something telling in Griffith's Biograph comedies in comparison to his other work at the studio. *The Curtain Pole* (Biograph, 1909) is among the best examples. Starring none other than Mack Sennett, who would soon leave Biograph to found Keystone, its story is exceedingly simple: a man sets out to buy a long curtain pole and creates all manner of chaos as he tries to bring it home—hitting people on the street, destroying furniture, and damaging buildings, even at one point getting his carriage stuck in a perpetual circle around a street pole. Cinematographically, the film conforms entirely to shot-scene correspondence and uses none of the editing or camera techniques with which Griffith was experimenting elsewhere. It is, by genre, a chase film: an accumulated chase where the space is "used up," to use Charlie Keil's term, as both Sennett and then an increasing number of consternated parties pass through it before the next space is introduced.[12] And it is utterly standard for the genre, showing none of the nascent narrative or filmic ingenuity of Griffith's more sophisticated "trajectory" chase from 1908, *The Adventures of Dollie*.[13] That *The Curtain Pole* was filmed in 1909 is remarkable; that same year Griffith would create one of the most complex forerunners of his hallmark visual style and storytelling approach in *Corner in Wheat*. Even more remarkable is the fact that Griffith would continue making shot-as-scene comedies as late as 1911, when the cinematic experiments that would come to define his identity as a filmmaker were in full development.

What could explain this? The typical justification is simply that Griffith put little effort into his comedies and cared little for the outcome. The seeming lack of sophistication in these works is taken as evidence of the filmmaker's distraction.[14] And yet, to use a phrase not inappropriate to early slapstick, this seems like putting the cart before the horse. What would a short like *The Curtain Pole* look like if Griffith had treated it as if it were, say, *Death's Marathon* (Biograph, 1913) or *The Musketeers of Pig Alley* (Biograph, 1912)? The basic situation might be enhanced to create a sense of urgency about Sennett's return with the curtain pole, allowing for some typically Griffithian crosscutting and suspense as in *Marathon*. And Griffith might have easily given us close-ups of Sennett's reactions to the various mishaps that befall his character, creating a deeper sense of personality and subjectivity as in *Musketeers*. But such refinements would have irredeemably changed the texture of the piece, transforming it into a story about *this* man's journey with *this* curtain pole—placing it into a unique context of narrative and character—rather than what it is: an exegesis on all the mishap that can be caused by a curtain pole and a study in bodily contortion and physical destruction. In fact, there is much originality and innovation in *The Curtain Pole;* it just occurs within the static frame. The short was Griffith's answer to *The Runaway Horse,* and he copies almost verbatim some of the more iconic images of carriages in turmoil. But he also invents his own devices. The scene in which the curtain pole catches on a street pole and sends the carriage in circles, though roughly executed, is in its conception as elegant and outlandish as anything that might appear in a Keaton film. *The Curtain Pole* is not a study of characters on a mission so much as it is a study of bodies and objects in space, and Griffith seems, for once, content to hold his camera still as he focuses his innovation on that aspect. All of Griffith's Biograph comedies would end up looking more or less the same. The very fact that they are so consistent when so much else of Griffith's work at the time was marked by diverse experimentation should in itself speak to the kind of stylistic exemption that Griffith gave to his comedies. While Griffith struggled in so much of his filmmaking to make his visual fingerprint unique and immediately distinguishable, he would allow his comedies to comfortably resemble nearly every other comedy being made at the time, from the shot-as-scene works at Pathé to the similarly structured pictures being produced by their fellow Parisian competitor in mayhem at Gaumont. Even beyond Griffith's own hand, slapstick seemed largely exempt from cinematographic innovation well into an era when nearly every other extant genre—from romances to gangster films to Westerns—was undergoing a series of trials and experiments in style and technique.

This quality of exemption can be seen as foundational to the origins of large-scale, dedicated slapstick production in America with Sennett's creation of the Keystone Film Company in 1912. Sennett inherited a visual style—or lack thereof—directly from his work with Griffith. Griffith's influence on early American slapstick has been sporadically noted, though generally it has been overshadowed by commentary on the poverty of his comedic efforts. Walter Kerr is dismissive of what he calls Griffith's "undeveloped" sense of humor, but he nonetheless makes a case that Griffith gave slapstick "its quintessential American shape. . . . Understanding film as he did, Griffith plainly foresaw what its comic patterns might be or ought to be."[15] Barry Salt has more recently also remarked on the influence—and the general lack of attention given to it by film historians—arguing that "D. W. Griffith had a strong, and unrecognized, influence on the form of American film slapstick. . . . The only thing surprising about this is that no-one has remarked on it."[16] But Sennett himself was not shy to attribute his debt to the era's master filmmaker. In an incident recounted in his memoirs, he speaks of learning to direct films from a series of long walks he supposedly took with Griffith while he was still just an actor under the master's sway:

> When Griffith walked, I walked. I fell in, matched his strides, and asked questions. Griffith told me what he was doing and what he hoped to do with the screen, and some of what he said stuck. I thought things over. I began to learn how to make a motion picture.[17]

What Sennett learned from Griffith is unclear, for very little that he would direct or produce at Keystone or afterward would look anything like the works for which Griffith is best known. They would look, instead, like the Griffith comedies that are largely forgotten: typically based on a simple shot-as-scene construction, set persistently in medium or long shot, and heavily reliant, as Salt observes, on Griffith's studio staging technique of "room-to-room movement in side-by-side spaces filmed from the front."[18] They are not at all like the works for which Griffith is best remembered as he practiced an early version of classical style but rather like the preclassical works that he is remembered for replacing. Or rather, they are like the comedies Griffith himself made that looked so unlike his other films.

One of Sennett's early directorial efforts, *An Interrupted Elopement* (Biograph, 1912), made while he was still at Biograph and under Griffith's supervision, is a case in point. Sennett places the action in the foreground, the players arranged in lines along a right-left axis. There is some use of background space, particularly with entrances and exits often happening along the front-back axis perpendicular to the frame, but by and large Sennett seems intent to thrust the action to the front to make sure none of it is missed. Griffith moved beyond such simple compositional structures in his non-comic efforts as early as 1908, but it has a purpose in Sennett, as it arguably did for Griffith in his comedies. Sennett is not telling a story so much as he is presenting a series of actions—or rather, a series of comic bits. The story of the film is nothing special: a father refuses to allow his daughter to marry her betrothed, his friends promise to kidnap the minister to force the wedding, they kidnap the father instead by accident, and the young man, in a flash of insight, pretends to fight off the friends and save the father. There are moments where Sennett's composition seems to actively work against what little narrative there is. In the climactic confrontation, the friends don't leave the frame—in fact, they don't even leave the foreground—when the young man fights them off, but simply move to the side and snicker at the ruse, a few feet away from the father. But narrative logic isn't Sennett's goal and his shots are not arranged to that end. He wants to show us moments that are meant, in and of themselves, to be funny: the father with a sack over his head, the comic punching that constitutes the fight between the young man and his friends. And to do so he needs to show not a succession of independent images but stretches of continuous space and time; he needs to let the gags unfold in the context of the environment around them. One result is that the actual narrative of the film is not clear at every moment. Remarking on Sennett's earliest directorial work at Keystone, Salt observes that "the most obvious feature . . . is the way they are relentlessly crammed with action and continual movement, so that the detail of the narrative is difficult to follow. It is a matter of 'Why the hell is he doing that?' most of the time, to a degree that I have never seen anywhere else in a film."[19] But a perfect conveyance of narrative was never Sennett's main aim. What he wanted to show us—by literally pushing it to the front of the frame in his earliest efforts—were the indignities of the human body as it moved through the world.

The Gag as Organizing Principle

The relative consistency of visual style that can be seen across the earliest slapstick comedies, from Pathé and Gaumont to Griffith and Sennett, is perhaps the clearest indication that cinematographic innovation was not a major area of concern for slapstick's performers and directors. Their focus lay elsewhere. The stylistic uniformity is a mask for the real arena where differentiation occurs and where slapstick's artistic focus lies: in the gag, which occurs at a level that we might consider separate from (though not always independent of) narrative, what Donald Crafton calls the "vertical domain of slapstick" as opposed to the "horizontal domain of the chase."[20] Of course, "gag" is hardly a clinical term. Even in detailed discussions of slapstick the word is used to cover everything from moments of social or bodily transgression to deliberate pranks to the visual punning of sight gags. According to Tom Gunning, "defining it can be as difficult (and self-defeating) as defining what makes us laugh," and he settles in the end only on the definition of the gag as "a comic action."[21] Given the manifold varieties of gags, Gunning's definition is not a bad one, but it could be taken further still: the gag, we might say, is an action or series of actions that in itself produces laughter, from a comic pose to a comic fall, and that typically is linked to a set of expectations of correctness or congruity, questions of whether it is "right" for a body, a person, or an object to behave in such a way. In Noël Carroll's schematic, summarizing what is known as the incongruity theory of humor, "amusement is provoked by the juxtaposition of incongruous elements. . . . The perception of incongruity in an event or situation amuses us, which in turn causes the risible situations—laughter, for example—that we feel in response to humor."[22] The incongruity at the heart of a gag may be a matter of event or situation as Carroll lays out, but it may also be a matter of bodily distortion, of social transgression, or even of simple confusion. As slapstick developed, it would come to encompass all such possibilities, though as Carroll notes it began at Keystone mostly at the level of transgression: "Whereas the trick film transgressed the laws of physics, films by people such as Mack Sennett tended to transgress the laws of society, especially in terms of the norms of respect appropriate to the handling of persons. In both cases, the comedy in question proceeded simply by displaying transgressive material."[23]

It is important to distinguish, however, that the gag is not in itself synonymous with all silent comedy, only with slapstick. While a case could be made for slapstick being the most popular and widespread genre of early comedy, it competed in its earliest years with the more narrative-driven strain known as "genteel comedy." Genteel comedy might best be considered as the narrative cinema's natural comic style, the comic analog to genres like melodrama. If slapstick depends for its appeal in large part on the humor of its individual gags, genteel comedy is based unquestionably on its story; it is more derivative of the legitimate theater's tradition of farce and the comedy of manners than the variety acts of vaudeville and the British music hall, and it tends more closely to follow the visual trends of narrative film and move in the direction of classical style. An early genteel comedy like *A Cure for Pokeritis* (Vitagraph, 1912), starring John Bunny, one of the genre's most popular early figures, has the same shot-as-scene structure as many slapstick films, but its humor is grounded entirely in its story—even to the point that it eschews or avoids moments of potential slapstick. Bunny plays a gambling-addicted husband whose wife cooks up a plan to save him: her cousin will make his Bible study group dress up like policemen and raid the poker game, at which point she and the other wives will break in and save the husbands from the police, thereby curing them of their gambling habit. Aside from its moralistic concerns, a common trope of the genre, the setup is not unsuitable for a traditional slapstick romp. Yet at the pivotal moment of the plot, when the fake police have broken into the card game, the film cuts almost immediately to the wives preparing to enter. The entire breakup of the poker game—surely a battle royal just waiting to happen if Sennett were directing the film—consists mostly of a series of entrances and exits, the police followed by the wives. The most and worst that we are allowed to actually see in the sequence is an overturned table and some threatening looks shot from policemen to poker players. Even the scene of the Bible study group dressing up as policemen—which might present its own comedic possibilities, no violence required—is handled quite matter of factly. Insofar as there is comedy in a film like this, it is entirely the comedy of situation and narrative development.

Slapstick begins to look and function differently than narrative cinema, of which genteel comedy is a straight derivative, when it is actively concerned with, rather than avoiding, the gag—when, as in *The Curtain Pole,* the point is to see the destruction wrought by the pole in all its varieties more than it is to learn the story of that pole's acquisition. That the gag is one of the few filmic elements on which narrative may founder is a point that was perhaps made most powerfully and directly by Crafton. Writing against those who see in slapstick's focus on the gag a kind of narrative inadequacy, he declares that "the distinction between slapstick and narrative has been properly perceived, but incorrectly interpreted. I contend that it was never the aim of comic filmmakers to 'integrate' the gag elements of their movies. I also doubt that viewers subordinated gags to narrative. . . . If gags were so scorned, then why did the gag film linger on for so long, an important mode of cinematic discourse for at least forty years? And is there not something perverse about arguing that what is 'wrong' with a film form is that which defines it to begin with?"[24] Crafton offers a case for the gag as narrative "excess"—"what lack of economy!" he declares to those who would argue for the gag as just an elaborate means toward narrative ends—and he provides a pocket history of how this development might have occurred, drawing on Gunning's concept of the cinema of attractions.[25] "The disruptive gags of slapstick can be regarded as an anachronistic manifestation of the cinema of attraction," he argues. "While other genres work to contain their excesses, this opposition is fundamental to slapstick. Furthermore it is carefully constructed to remain an unbridgeable gap."[26] But the question of narrative's relationship to the gag is also at its heart a formal one even before it is historical and chronological; the unanswered question of Crafton's essay, in other words, is *why* the gag so often and for so long proved largely inhospitable to the narrative and stylistic techniques that developed in other genres of early cinema—and whether this turn is only a historical product or speaks to some more fundamental separation of formal interests.

History can help to provide an answer to this formal question. If we look backward across slapstick's development—from the golden age of its grand compromises with narrative in the 1920s to its earlier manifestations as little more than a collection of gags with only minimal narrative connection (what Gerald Mast describes as a "series of jests, unified solely by the figure performing them"[27]) in the aughts and teens and even further backward to slapstick's origins in the almost entirely narrative-free, self-contained pranks of the earliest gag films from *That Fatal Sneeze* or *The Gardener* and before that to the frequently a-narrative (and sometimes antinarrative) compartments of vaudeville and music hall variety acts—the dynamics of the gag as a mode of performance become more clear. The history of the gag in silent comedy is largely one of increasing accommodation to narrative over time, but its deeper origins point to something else: even entirely absent narrative structuring or narrative stakes, the gag can be said to have a significance that is immediate and independent. That is, in its ability to produce laughter even in the total absence of larger context, it can immediately answer the question of "Why should I devote my attention to this?" Or, to borrow a slightly different phrase that Paul Woodruff uses in a theatrical context, what makes this "worth watching"?[28] The gag is often used within a narrative context and deployed to narrative ends, to be sure, but in a fundamental sense it does not *need* narrative. It is one of only a few filmic elements that can be presented with no narrative framework and still command our rapt attention. (Other such elements include the dance and the fight—like slapstick, both spectacles of the body.) In other words, it can be made "worth watching" entirely on its own. Indeed, audiences spent decades doing just that in the heyday of vaudeville and the music hall, where the only narrative present (if any at all) was usually just the micronarrative that was internal to the gag routine itself.

This potential for independent significance has powerful implications for visual style and particularly for the treatment of cinematic space in the slapstick film, justifying and sometimes even demanding an engagement with unbroken space in a manner more reminiscent of the cinema of attractions than of classical construction. In dividing the world into a rapid sequence of individuated shots, classical technique delays significance. Typically, any single isolated part of a classical narrative sequence cannot justify its own existence; it cannot make itself worth watching. Only through the accumulation of those parts can classical narrative develop significance.[29] The promise of the total picture and the significance that will come with it allows for and justifies the endless division and redivision of space and time. This stands in contrast to the cinema of attractions, wherein the undivided image and the continuous event can be made worth watching simply by virtue of being displayed on film. Yet in this sense it is not quite enough to say that slapstick is a remnant of the cinema of attractions in the manner that Crafton implies. Rather than a synonym of the cinema of attractions, slapstick might more accurately be said to be its homonym: significance in slapstick comes not from the act of displaying but from the action displayed. The power of slapstick, in other words, lies not so much in capturing the event as such, a mode wherein the appeal of the unbroken image is bound up in its capacity to present before us an instance of unbroken space and time stolen from the world; rather, its focus lies in cap-turing a specific performance of action, where the unbroken image that it pre-sents is primarily a byproduct of the necessary time in which that action must unfold. In terms of what is captured, the result is similar or the same, but the prerogative behind it differs. The cinema of attractions revolves around ques-tions of the instant, of the moment or moments that it captures on film and the time and space contained therein.[30] Slapstick is instead organized around the actual actions that occur within those instants, a focus which ultimately can be accommodated, if uneasily, to classical narrative.

Bodies, Machines, and the Image System of the Gag

Ultimately, then, the gag is not antithetical to narrative—or, by extension, to classical construction. But it is that rare filmic specimen that can actually stand apart from narrative with its own independent discourse structure. The most iconic sequences of the slapstick era—Harold Lloyd hanging from the sky-scraper clock in *Safety Last* (Hal Roach, 1923), Keaton standing erect as the side of a house falls on him and he passes through a window opening in *Steamboat Bill Jr.* (Buster Keaton, 1928)—are eminently watchable even when entirely di-vorced from their narrative context. More than that, they can be scrutinized apart from questions of narrative; they contain a significance unto themselves tied to their investigation of the human body in space. Indeed, most theorists of slapstick premise the genre's power—its ability to inspire enjoyment and critical commentary alike, long after the genteel comedy is quite forgotten—on a core concern with interrogating and depicting the frailties and indignities of the human body against an implacable environment. Thoughts on the specific categories of frailty and indignity to be explored vary, though there is more consistency across the breadth of the century than one might expect. None other than Sennett himself focuses on the psychosocial and the ontological as the categories of slapstick's main concern. "There are only a handful of possible jokes," he claims. "The chief members of this joke band may be said to be: The fall of dignity. Mistaken identity. Almost every joke on the screen belongs, roughly, to the one or the other of these clans."[31] Carroll would more or less agree nearly a century later, linking the significance of early slapstick (and Sennett's work in particular) to "the transgression of social inhibitions about the proper way in which to treat the human body," a formulation that can roughly encom-pass both of Sennett's pet indignities and a handful of others as well.[32] And Alan Dale all but recapitulates Sennett's concepts in more sophisticated lan-guage. "The essence of a slapstick gag is a physical assault on, or collapse of, the hero's dignity," he writes.[33] This may take many forms—"a superexaggeration of the hero's obliviousness and ineffectuality" or even "an unawareness of a standing circumstance," but to Dale they are a "difference of degree, not kind."[34]

What stays consistent across much of the theory on slapstick, both in its own era and in ours, is the idea that the human body in a state of social or physical peril, impediment, or inefficiency is inherently interesting as a topic of examination. Slapstick is, according to Alex Clayton, essentially a study of a basic condition of human existence itself: an investigation of our own materiality and the inherent indignities therein. As Clayton writes, "The ever-present possibility of slipping on an olive is a condition of being embodied, something we all have to learn to live with. Embodiment, in this sense, suggests nothing more, or less, than the fact of having, or being, a body. . . . The condition of embodiment constitutes one of the genre's major subjects."[35] Slapstick then is a virtual laboratory of experience, a look at our state in the world that is presented, typically, in a kind of suspended animation where consequences are only ever free, mollified, or (in the case of a villain) justified. (For we typically know by virtue of the genre that the frailties will not be fatal, the indignities will not be crushing—though we cannot always be assured.) But if slapstick is an exploration of these ideas, then it is also, even more than that, an exploration of them in its isolated images and sequences alone; that is, an exploration of them through the vehicle of the gag almost regardless of the narrative context into which it is placed. In James Agee's pivotal 1949 *Life* magazine essay on slapstick, "Comedy's Greatest Era," which is widely credited for rekindling both critical and popular interest in slapstick comedy two decades after its demise, no particular story or theme draws out the author's nostalgia. It is the isolated spectacle of the human body in motion that he remembers: "All these people zipped and caromed about the pristine world of the screen as jazzily as a convention of water bugs. Words can hardly suggest how energetically they collided and bounced apart, meeting in full gallop around the corner of a house; how hard and how often they fell on their backsides; or with what fantastically adroit clumsiness they got themselves fouled up in folding ladders, garden hoses, tethered animals and each other's head-long cross-purposes."[36] The body in motion, so often in itself a kind of peril, becomes an independent point of exploration in slapstick, whether it is the kinesis of bodies and objects together in space as in Keaton or the internal kinesis of the human body itself that distinguishes Chaplin's performances. Slapstick marks its significance and its interest immediately in the very substance of what it depicts, and it doesn't need narrative to lead us toward what that significance might ultimately be.[37]

More than that, slapstick marks its significance in images that are inimitably, and fascinatingly, tied to a particular moment in time—the time of the rise of the machine age. The body alone is what lies at slapstick's heart and what sustained it through decades of development in the vaudeville theaters and music halls of the nineteenth century. But if slapstick as a filmic genre represents an inheritance from and further development of the kind of isolated and minimally narrative physical comedy that developed on the vaudeville and music hall stage (and which, in turn, has its own ancestry lines in commedia dell'arte, stage farce, and Aristophanic comedy, to name only a few sources), it is a development based in no small part on the moment at which it came about. For slapstick as it was practiced by Sennett and the great silent film clowns emerged—could only emerge—at a moment of rapid technological development. It is itself a product of the mechanism of the camera. Thus, much of the bodily peril that slapstick film explores is specifically the peril of the machine and, more generally, the mechanical itself. It is not just the giant machines of *Modern Times,* the ocean liners and locomotives of Keaton's work, or the endless car races and car crashes that Sennett put out; it is also the way in which Lloyd must reduce himself to a mechanical repetition of actions to successfully climb the skyscraper in *Safety Last,* the kind of "comic rapport" (to use George Wead's phrase)[38] that Keaton achieves with machines of all shape and size, the trope of breakdown—bodily and mechanical alike—that recurs so frequently in the genre. It is in this context that we might best understand Henri Bergson's famous remarks, issued just before slapstick's true emergence in the early 1900s, on the nature of laughter as a response "in exact proportion" to the degree to which the "body reminds us of a mere machine."[39] Though frequently repeated and scrutinized in studies of slapstick, it is in many ways a perplexing analysis—it seems to mistake a subset of the humorous for its substance. Surely there is laughter that emerges from that which we might consider organic, not only from an intrusion of the mechanical. But Bergson was writing at a moment when the body in peril and the body in mechanical peril were almost one and the same. When he speaks of the body as a machine, he is thinking not of the efficient or even the repetitive; he is thinking quite explicitly of the weighty and lugubrious, that which is as prone to total breakdown as to iterative functioning. Bergson contrasts the mechanical not with organic roughness but with organic perfection, with the "gracefulness and suppleness in the living body," a vitality that stands in contrast to the heavy materiality of the actual body—a body that "is no more in our eyes than a heavy and cumbersome venture, a kind of irksome ballast which holds down to earth a soul eager to rise aloft."[40] It is in this sense that the body is rendered mechanical—in its weight, in its breakdowns: that is, in its indignities. "Matter," Bergson writes, "is obstinate and resists," and it tries forever to "convert" gracefulness to "its own inertia and cause it to revert to mere automatism."[41] The mechanical is for

Bergson the opposite of the graceful, and by extension the humor of slapstick becomes the humor of a world fighting against its own regression and the disappearance of grace.

Walter Benjamin gives what is perhaps the best explanation of the degree to which the fact of slapstick's coemergence with the heights of industrialization permeated its whole depiction of the world, an extrapolation on Bergson's thesis. Writing specifically on Chaplin, he observes, "Whether it is his walk, the way he handles his cane, or the way he raises his hat—always the same jerky sequence of tiny movements applies the law of the cinematic image sequence to human motorial function."[42] In Benjamin's reading, Chaplin has become an embodiment of the cinematic machine that creates his image; he has left, in Michael North's words, "traces of mechanical reproduction written into [his] performance style."[43] Thus the mechanical is more than a particular subject matter of some individual slapstick films; it is, in Bergson's and Benjamin's formulations, one of slapstick's earliest and most pervasive aesthetic conditions. North wonders whether slapstick is not actually, for everything else it is, also a manifestation of the inherent comedy of the mechanical age itself. Slapstick, he writes, poses the question "whether there might be something potentially comic in mechanical reproduction itself. . . . If there is something inherently funny in mechanical reproduction, then it is also possible that modernity itself is governed by a comic rhythm, even when it is not particularly amusing."[44] This is not to dislodge the central place of the organic body in slapstick's humor, an inheritance—its most direct and important—from its vaudeville and music hall origins. But it is a means of further defining slapstick's ability to produce images and moments of self-contained significance and to offer even in the absence of any story an exploration that holds in itself power and interest for the new modern world. To see a car collide or a bomb explode, as occurs so frequently in the later Sennett comedies, is to see both a body in peril—for where there is a machine in slapstick there is always somewhere near it a human body, visible or implied—and to see, and sometimes react against, a new world made of peril.

Such is King's analysis in his reading of the Keystone oeuvre: "No other aspect of the studio's output ever received such unanimous praise, as, week after week, reviewers wrote in amazement of the films' 'mechanical contrivances,' 'trick, mechanical effects,' and 'uproarious inventions.' . . . They thus participated in the emergence of a distinctly modern comic form—one that may have played a role in mediating the experience of mechanization for audiences whose own encounters with technology . . . often betrayed startling ambivalences."[45] Eileen Bowser takes King's reading of Sennett's place in the formation of a new mass culture for the mechanical age one full step further. For Bowser, a figure like Sennett might even be construed as the ideological counterweight to an icon of the machine like Henry Ford. If Ford created mass production, Sennett created a kind of fantasized mass destruction—setting up a factory for the creation of images of the modern world's demolition that seemed to try to demechanize the world, one car crash at a time, almost as quickly as Ford meant to mechanize it. In Bowser's words, "Henry Ford brought us affordable cars for the common man and Mack Sennett gave us slapstick comedies that did their best to take apart, deform, and destroy the wonderful new machines."[46] If it was not a clear ideological stance, it was at least a statement on (and revolt against) the condition of the mechanized modern world and the human body within it. More than that, it was a statement that could be broadly understood even in the absence of any narrative context. As a mode, slapstick consistently produced a kind of image that didn't need narrative to make its meaning known. It was an image system that had its own means of organization and composition based on whole actions unfolding in space and time—a demand to show the whole car crash, the whole pratfall—and was resistant to the cinematographic division of space and time that classical narrative demanded. Where the cinema of attractions stood against classical technique, so too did slapstick for its own set of reasons.

MACK SENNETT'S PURIFIED SLAPSTICK

In this sense, we might regard the work that Sennett created as a kind of slapstick in its purest distilled form. Sennett's obsession, from Keystone's founding in 1912 to his output under Mack Sennett Comedies in the later silent period, was consistent: movement for its own sake, peril for its own sake, destruction for its own sake. In short, Sennett created kinesis practically for its own sake in his films, and he prided himself on doing so. He became famous for having his cameramen significantly undercrank the film, artificially speeding up the action on the screen to levels beyond what the material world itself could ever allow, creating an alternate filmic universe defined by its accelerated motion. More than that, he would proudly have his editors remove frames from the film stock to accelerate the action further still, sometimes taking out as much as every third or fourth frame. Even as he grew more removed from the creation of individual films in his studio and left most of the directing to the stable of artists he had under contract, Sennett would still insist on watching dailies, editing and recutting them to give them what he thought to be the proper dynamics of frenetic motion. (Indeed, he would boast in an essay from 1918 that "when one of our comedies is finished, it is usually about five times as long as it is when the public finally sees it.")[47] Chaplin in fact grew so frustrated with Sennett's habit of cutting up his films—and so incensed that Sennett was debilitating anything but the most basic broad comic strokes with his editing choices—that he learned to do his best comic business while he was entering or leaving the scene, so that Sennett couldn't take it out.

Of course, it wasn't simply speed itself that fascinated Sennett; it was the prospect of what might be shown with that speed, even if those depictions didn't have anything near the subtlety that figures like Chaplin desired. Sennett seemed to never meet a pie-in-the-face that he didn't like, a car he didn't want to destroy, or a chase he didn't want to include, especially if it ended with everyone falling into a body of water. (Idiosyncratically, he insisted on calling the chase, which typically brought about the culmination of each Keystone short, the film's "rally"—an appropriately athletic term that also gives to the chase a kind of structural pride of place, as though the motion of the chase itself was enough to top off any story, regardless of content.) It is curious and fascinating that nearly all of the slapstick elements that Sennett introduced or promoted—he would give to the world the first pie-in-the-face in *A Noise from the Deep* (Keystone, 1913) and he raised the chase to new heights through sheer ubiquity—were perfected by artists who either had left Sennett's studios or who had never actually worked with him. Chaplin would offer the first (and still perhaps the best) full-fledged pie fight, beating Sennett at his own game two years after leaving Keystone in his Mutual short *Behind the Screen* (1916). And the chase scenes created by Keaton, who never worked for Sennett, are beyond compare, particularly the daredevil motorcycle chase in *Sherlock Jr.* (Buster Keaton, 1924) and the over-the-top police chase in *Cops* (Comique, 1922), involving hundreds of extras meant to represent the entire Los Angeles police force. Similarly, nearly all of the artists that Sennett discovered would go on to do their best work after leaving his studios, from Chaplin to Roscoe "Fatty" Arbuckle to a young Frank Capra. (Mabel Normand, who many commentators say was simply in love with Sennett and refused to leave, is one of the few exceptions.) Many observers have taken these facts as a testament to Sennett's fecklessness, his lack of vision, his authoritarian style, or maybe his tightfisted salaries. In Kerr's words, "Sennett hurt himself most, and most surprisingly, by his insensitivity to quality in the performers he had discovered. Beyond question, he had an instinct for talent. . . . But Sennett invariably lost his people as they began to find themselves."[48] But it can also be seen as evidence of a kind of generic purity. Sennett seemed persistently unconcerned with perfecting or building on slapstick's core fundamentals and was happy to part with those who wanted to develop the genre beyond anything but its most basic construction. He sought mainly to replicate and mass-produce slapstick's basic elements, which he found in themselves endlessly entertaining. Fights, falls, chases, collisions—these are the substrata of all slapstick and the surface structures of almost everything Sennett produced.

Sennett's films, then, are more than disconnected gags, but not much more. His shorts are consistently marked by only the thinnest narrative glaze and seem to possess almost no visual flourish. Sennett, who had his performers and directors largely improvise their work (a common working method throughout the slapstick era), was particularly averse to almost any narrative beyond the most basic scenario construction: a day at the park, a car race. This trait went back to the beginning of his career. Sennett actually came up with the scenario for one of Griffith's most famous rescue films while the two were working at Biograph—*The Lonely Villa* (1909), wherein a young mother tries to evade burglars as she waits for her husband to return home and save her. It is a significant work for Griffith's move toward what Gunning calls "narrative integration," one of the first shorts in which parallel editing "becomes a narrative structure, a way of shaping the relations of space and time."[49] Yet even as Sennett helped to introduce one of the earliest instances of narrative-driven crosscutting, a key component for the development of filmic suspense, he would go on to parody and lambaste his own work in another Biograph short that he directed, *Help! Help!* (1912). Here, the wife's call for help is based on a mistake—it is merely a poodle that has moved the curtains—and the husband's journey home is marked by one mishap after another: his car breaks down (twice) before finally exploding, at which point he must commandeer a farmer's cart, but he can't get the horse to move and ends up being chased by the farmer. There are delays in the husband's journey in *The Lonely Villa*, but, as Simon Joyce recounts, Sennett "extends this into the logic of a comedic nightmare."[50] Sennett seems to be parodying here not only *The Lonely Villa* but also the very idea of narrative itself: in his view, narrative is just a construction, a careful arrangement of contrived events (an actual burglar, a troubled-but-successful journey home) designed to produce maximum emotional effect; don't believe it, the film seems to say. The film itself is, of course, closely tied to narrative by nature of being a parody of narrative (a rare case in Sennett where the car breakdown is funnier in its narrative context as part of a string of mishaps on the husband's journey than it is purely on its own terms), and Sennett would return to this kind of parody many times throughout his career. (In Agee's phrase, "Sennett made two kinds of comedy: parody laced with slapstick, and plain slapstick.")[51] But the film contains a very specific kind of relationship to narrative: the comedy in a work like *Help! Help!* is rendered in a standard narrative format only to subvert and ultimately question narrative itself.

What Sennett seems to have wanted to do more than tell stories was to show us things—things that would make us laugh. Hence the kind of bifurcation that ultimately appears in Sennett's later output, premised on a direct presentation, narratively and visually, of the mechanical and the bodily elements at the core of slapstick. On one hand, there are the mechanical excesses of shorts like those made by one of Sennett's top stars of the 1920s, Billy Bevan. These are films premised, in Mast's words, on "motion, frenzy, and the multiplication of absurdity," typically involving a multiplicity of automobiles (colloquially called Lizzies at the time): car racing and car crashes in *Lizzies of the Field* (Mack Sennett Comedies, 1924); full-sized remote-control cars in *Super-Hopper-Dyne Lizzies* (Mack Sennett Comedies, 1925); a collision between cars and streetcars in *Wandering Willies* (Mack Sennett Comedies, 1926).[52] They are symphonies of mechanical mishap and destruction, and the visual goal of the films seems to be to simply present such mayhem as completely as possible. The culmination of *Lizzies of the Field* is a case in point. Premised on a car chase between rival auto garages, the film reaches a fever pitch of car collisions in the climactic final moments. With almost every car that is added to the pileup, we gain a new angle on the destruction—a long shot, a medium shot, even a point-of-view shot of a car about to crash. This is not, however, the montage of classical technique, the framing and reframing of space toward a promise of ultimate narrative clarity. The sequence of images of the crashing cars adds up to nothing more than what we knew at the very beginning: there is a huge collision occurring. We don't even cut to any of the participants in that collision, so that the different angles might add up to some expression of a collective experience. Sennett (who produced the film, the director is unknown) merely wants to show us the action in as interesting a way as possible—in fact, in as many interesting ways as possible. The film stands, visually, at the halfway point between classical style and the spatial configurations of the cinema of attractions. Sennett does not break the space in the way true classical technique most probably would—cutting, for instance, from an exterior shot of the crash to the expressions of those inside the cars and back again to create a sense of the story of the car crash. Yet neither does he prove unwilling to interrupt and reframe the space as in the cinema of attractions and its earliest narrative descendants. Sennett means to show us the full action of mechanical destruction, and the visual stylistics of the film insofar as they exist are based around this goal.

There stands in contrast to this exuberance of the mechanical the case of Harry Langdon, one of Sennett's last great comedic discoveries and perhaps the purest representation of Sennett's fascination with the comic body. In his heyday in the mid to late 1920s, Langdon rivaled Chaplin, Keaton, and Lloyd in popularity. But he has proved a curious subject for later critics. He was the closest Sennett would ever come to matching the kind of narratively sophisticated, character-driven 1920s work of Chaplin, Keaton, or Lloyd, and he was in many ways very much the creation of Sennett himself, even though he only stayed with the producer for three years before forming his own production company. Sennett saw something in Langdon, who was nearing middle age as a vaudeville performer when Sennett came to know of him, and put him on contract largely on an instinct that he might be successful. In Kerr's account, "When he first hired Langdon, Sennett hadn't the faintest notion of what to do with him. He had a hunch, he was stubborn about it, and he then washed his hands of it, assigning to his staff the task of turning an already aging, essentially slow-moving, thoroughly un-Sennettish wool-gatherer into some sort of film comedian."[53] Unlike Chaplin and the other major silent clowns, Langdon proved unable to create on his own a character sustainable for film, and he would not conceive and direct his work to nearly the same degree as would his peers. It was largely Capra, at Sennett's behest, who would invent and direct Langdon's screen persona: a distant, sad, and almost otherworldly clown, as much an overgrown, innocent infant as a full-grown man. It is the extremity of Langdon's persona that has proved so disconcerting. He is, in Mast's description, "a vague, internalized mixture of shyness, immaturity, an almost subhuman intelligence, with few clear outer characteristics at all" or, in Richard Dyer MacCann's telling, a "sad incompetent clown, a lost soul perhaps from some European circus, slow-moving and slow-thinking, embarrassed, rejected, fumbling."[54] Indeed, in Capra's description, he is almost entirely without agency: "the helpless elf whose only ally is God."[55]

In this regard, Langdon is perhaps best understood as a kind of apotheosis of Sennett's slapstick vision. He is almost pure body, stripped of agency, intelligence, and almost entirely of personality. To see a great Langdon moment, like his perilous brush with a cliff edge in *Tramp, Tramp, Tramp* (Harry Langdon, 1926), is to see a body in space and almost nothing else, or perhaps as close as one can come to such an abstraction and still have any degree of characterization from one film to the next. Langdon's characterization is a kind of anti-characterization. Trying to escape a flock of sheep (which he mistakenly, and gratuitously, thinks are cows—as if to dehumanize him further), Langdon climbs over a fence, not realizing that it sits at the edge of a cliff. As he begins to absentmindedly slide down the fence to his doom, his shirt and belt become caught on a protruding nail—Capra's hand of God at work. To see Lloyd or Keaton or Chaplin in such a moment would be to see a furious intelligence conniving how to escape the situation; it would be to see a body in space but also to see human ingenuity along with it. Langdon gives us only the body. He hangs limply, and his one effort to save himself by removing another nail from the fence and hammering his shirt to the post is actually only an effort to preserve his situation, and one that further worsens it by weakening the fence. We do go to close-up, but the move is almost a subversive one, a near parody of classical assumptions: we don't see in Langdon's expression any inner intelligence or agency at work but rather an almost complete vacancy, the lack of a person. The long shot of Langdon's body hanging from the fence is a truer expression of the situation than any close-up of his reaction. In these moments, Langdon himself can represent a kind of uninflected slapstick that is interested only in bodies, only in objects.

THE NARRATIVE IMPERATIVE AND
THE TRANSFORMATION OF SLAPSTICK

Sennett's total vision represents a pure construction of slapstick, one that stands in contrast to the narrative negotiations that Chaplin, Lloyd, and Keaton would all pursue within the form. But it was a vision, while long-lasting, that did not always succeed. Sennett's career was lucrative, to be sure, and he would declare himself in the title of his 1954 memoir to be the "King of Comedy," but he was also in his day considered something of a hack. In an age when Chaplin was being feted as a genius, Sennett was having a hard time achieving anything more than the esteem (not insubstantial of course) that monetary success alone can bring. He made money, but he didn't always make friends among the critics. One *New York Times* review of a new Sennett comedy from 1921 begins: "Mack Sennett's alleged comedies have seemed so often utterly dull to the writer, and he [i.e., the writer] has so often said as much or wearily ignored them entirely."[56] The idea of Sennett's "alleged comedies" being "utterly dull" is important, for Sennett's work was nothing if not repetitious. There was occasional innovation, to be sure, but once Sennett found a comic trope that worked he was happy to repeat it (the pie fights, the car crashes, the "rallies"). King thus describes Sennett's aesthetic as one of "accretion, multiplication, and repetition."[57] Sennett's output is remarkably consistent—consider, for instance, the significant artistic development that Chaplin displays between *Twenty Minutes of Love* in 1914 and *The Kid* (First National, 1921) made only seven years later, as compared to almost any two Sennett shorts from any period. That consistency, especially in the face of the significant artistic development that other slapstick figures outside of Sennett's orbit displayed, seems to indicate that Sennett missed a moment of transition that affected nearly all the major slapstick filmmakers. As King records of Sennett's work in the 1920s, "In a decade that witnessed the successes of Buster Keaton and Harold Lloyd, the launching of the Hal Roach 'All-Star' comedies, the continued ascendancy of Charlie Chaplin, and the institutionalization of the slapstick feature, Sennett's approach to comedy changed little."[58] It would not be entirely for lack of try-ing. Sennett was obsessed with increasing the prestige of his work and ex-perimented throughout his career with different means of achieving greater acclaim. At Keystone he produced the first six-reel comedy, *Tillie's Punctured Romance*, in 1914, a year before Griffith's *Birth of a Nation* would help to estab-lish long-format narrative film as Hollywood's dominant mode. And in 1915 he formed a consortium, the ill-fated Triangle Film Corporation, with Griffith and Thomas Ince, arguably the two most prestigious directors of the age, to jointly distribute their films—and perhaps have some of their esteem rub off on him. Indeed, Sennett was never shy about placing himself in a lineage even more esteemed than Griffith and Ince: "The comedies of Aristophanes were pretty lusty too when they set out to put stuffed togas in their place. At any rate you will find that the downfall of pretension runs through most great comic works, emphatically including Shakespeare."[59]

But the changes that Sennett was willing to make to achieve the status he so desired were mostly structural changes, matters of production and distribu-tion. The change that slapstick comedy seemed to undergo in the mid to late teens was more a matter of story and of style than of simply changing the na-ture of its billing. Several film stars and commentators talked about their sense of a transition around the middle of the decade. In an interview from 1915, Mabel Normand declared that "the comedy of four or five years ago was a very different affair from those made today."[60] A series of articles from *Photoplay* in that same year came to a similar conclusion, claiming that "it is the situa-tion that makes for real comedy and not foolish, childish acting, such as has been indulged in so freely in the past and of which the public has now become tired and disgusted."[61] Slapstick moved toward a greater engagement with nar-rative, prompted by what Thompson identifies as an industry-wide embrace of new artistic models, "a change in influences from the other arts, from an initial close imitation of vaudeville, to a greater dependence on short fiction, novels and legitimate drama."[62] Such forms provided both a model of success-ful narrative construction to match the public's ever-growing demand for fic-tional film and, not incidentally, an association with greater cultural prestige. In Jenkins's extrapolation from Thompson's thesis, vaudeville becomes only a niche influence in the cinema, "restricted either to certain marginalized classes of films (B-movies, serials, comic shorts, cartoons) or to short sequences of slapstick or spectacle safely sequestered within larger story structures."[63] Thus by 1926, a film like Keaton's *The General* (Buster Keaton) would be constructed in such a way that several textbooks later considered it a case study in classical technique; take almost any silent short from the early or middle 1910s—and almost any Sennett short even from the 1920s—and it would be anything but a classical exemplar.[64] By the end of the 1910s, most film comedians realized that slapstick would have to find a way to come to terms with the increasing dominance of classical filmmaking and the narrative and visual assumptions that went with it.

This was perhaps inevitable, not so much for external pressures as for factors internal to the mechanics of filmed slapstick and the nature of its transition from vaudeville stage to national screen, factors that Sennett ignored at his own peril. The critique often made of Sennett's work can be directed at nearly all slapstick—it is repetitious; King's descriptor for Sennett's Keystone aesthetic, "accretion, multiplication, and repetition," may on some level be taken as a motto for the genre. The elevation of a relatively small number of slapstick films to canonical status tends to obscure the astounding degree of repetition that marked the work of even its most accomplished artists. To view the gamut of any slapstick comedian's output is to note a pervasive recycling of gags, running from the most mundane to the most elaborate. Even within the major works of the great silent clowns borrowing and repetition is rampant. In *A Dog's Life* (First National, 1918), Chaplin hides behind a curtain and uses his arms as if attached to another person's body, a common vaudeville bit; Lloyd offers a similar moment in *The Freshman* (Harold Lloyd, 1925). Chaplin carries a giant pole over his back and knocks all those around him on the head in *Behind the Screen;* Keaton does the same when he is tied to a stake in *The Paleface* (Comique, 1922). Both are variations on gags that go back at least to *The Curtain Pole*. Even the famous moment in *Steamboat Bill Jr.* where the side of a house falls on Keaton but misses him because of an open window restages a gag from Arbuckle's *Backstage* (Comique, 1919). As Bryony Dixon records, cataloging gag repetition in slapstick is almost too easy: "The 'outing' of joke thieves is today a popular pastime for internet contributors, and a great way for people to show off or to reinforce their allegiance to a particular performer."[65] But Dixon questions whether repetition was a form of thievery, as some commentators from the silent era to our own day have claimed. "Comedy relies on a common pot of gags and business," she asserts. "Is it possible to have an original prat-fall?"[66]

Repetition in slapstick was not a tactic of convenience or evidence of a dwindling comic imagination; it was an inherent structuring principle. For all its reliance on improvisation, slapstick was as much an art of recombining and repositioning an established retinue of gags and bits as it was an art of originality—and in this respect was much more akin to ballet choreography, which draws from a finite set of moves and positions, than it was to what we may think of as improvisation today. This process of recombination from a set of finite possibilities is a direct inheritance from slapstick's origins in American vaudeville and the British music hall. For while vaudeville and music hall performance (Robert Knopf helpfully links the two together under the umbrella term "variety stage"[67]) developed a reputation for the anarchic and carnivalesque in the kind of humor they often promoted, they were also highly practiced arts that required intensive training, not unlike what we might expect a circus performer to go through today. Lupino Lane, one of the less remembered silent clowns of the 1920s but one of the few to make extensive notes of his experiences, recounts the training he underwent as part of a family of British music hall performers in a manual that he published in 1946 titled *How to Become a Comedian*. Describing the training through which "each member of my family, male or female, has been put . . . by the elders of the family," he catalogs the following: "ballet, tap, juggling, acrobatics, fencing, boxing, costume design, music composition, mime, singing, producing plays, Shakespearean acting, lighting, elocution, building scenery, as well as all sorts of falls and slapstick play."[68] Lupino's list is effusive but conveys the difficulty of the arts that the variety performer had to achieve and master. Indeed, the regimentation of variety theater training and technique was refined to such a degree that it depended in part, if one can believe the often exaggerated and mythmaking accounts of slapstick artists themselves, on a system of formal numbering. The "108"—what David Madden describes as "a comic fall involving a split and sudden backward somersault that lands the actor flat on his back, a feat involving great risk and skill"—was apparently the sine qua non of the true slapstick performer.[69] Keystone actor Ben Turpin was known for being quite accomplished in his version of it, and, apocryphally at least, Chaplin performed one during an audition for Sennett that helped land him the Keystone job.

On stage, the repetition inherent to the variety theater never posed the structural problems it would in film. It was an effective means of standardizing training and passing down technique, and whatever monotony might threaten such a system was almost entirely dampened by the production arrangements of the variety stage. Vaudeville and music hall performances were based mostly on a touring tradition, with acts operating as independent economic units that competed to find a place on the evening bill of a national network of independent local theaters. Novelty was prized, to be sure, but it was typically construed as something other than simply coming up with a series of new gags; novelty was comprised of the ways in which gags might be combined and the costuming and persona that went with them, what Dixon calls the variety entertainer's "brand."[70] Thus, whatever threat there was of audiences growing tired of the same kinds of routines was mollified by a compensatory delight in comparing the technique and acumen of different performers, of trying out one brand after another. Even beyond the idiosyncrasies and levels of talent that separated individual actors, there were broader differences between the types of comedians who operated on the variety stage, each drawing from Dixon's "common pot of gags and business" but bringing to it a different kind of comic focus and inflection. As Knopf recounts, "The variety stage . . . encompassed diverse types of performers within every category of performance. Not only was variety comprised of musicians, comedians, magicians, dancers, and specialty acts, but each category contained subcategories. Just as the larger category of dancing acts include everything from tap dancing to chorus lines, so did 'comedians' include double-talk teams, stand-up comedians, and mimes."[71] Even among the mimes there were sub-subcategories, broadly divided between "comic acrobats" like Keaton and "pantomime clowns" like Chaplin.[72] In other words, the structures of the variety theater's production arrangements—the venues, the performers, the brands, the subcategories and sub-subcategories, the traditions from which they drew—helped mitigate gag repetition within the acts themselves. Attending a variety show was in part an act of comparison. Repetition was part of the fun.

Transferred to film, however, such repetition could become deadening: the number of performers was vastly smaller, the scope of the total audience vastly larger. While the assemblage of silent film comedians extended well beyond canonical figures like Chaplin, Keaton, Lloyd, and Langdon, the total number of leading comic figures employed by Hollywood was nowhere near the number of individual comic performers on the American vaudeville circuit or in the British music halls. Coupled with this telescoping of the talent pool was a concept utterly new to the traveling variety actor: an essentially instantaneous national audience. By the early 1910s, film distribution systems looked broadly like they look today, with films being distributed to exhibitors nationwide in a more or less single release. Coming from a world in which they might tour a single act across the country for a year or more as they moved from venue to venue, variety performers now had to adjust to an industrial system that in its heyday was producing one or more new slapstick films per studio per week. The kind of repetition that had been one of the variety theater's most appealing features was exploded by the new production and distribution systems of the film industry. The shrewder film comedians understood that something would need to change, lest they end up, as many of the lesser silent clowns did (including many of the stars who never broke out of Sennett's orbit), making only slight variations to the same kinds of films over and over again. To do so risked limiting the scope of their appeal and their success. If the need to meet a popular demand for film spurred the development of classical narrative beginning around 1907, so too would oversaturation push slapstick closer to classical technique a decade later. Slapstick could hold an audience's attention and carry their interest forward from scene to scene in a way that few other preclassical modes of filmmaking could. But could it hold that audience's attention at the level of production that audiences were beginning to demand, across hundreds of films per year? Narrative—actual storytelling, not just a simple scenario—offered a means of forever changing and re-inflecting the constant repetition of gags that was slapstick's curse. And it was here that the great slapstick artists would make their most important mark on the form: Chaplin, Lloyd, and Keaton, each in his own way, would evince within their greatest works a careful negotiation between the slapstick gag and the narrative tale, crafting from a common point of comic origin works that were remarkably varied in tone and story and style. Just as classical ballet would take a finite set of moves and set them to music, choreographing its way into uniqueness, in the hands of its most successful practitioners slapstick would take its own moves and learn, essentially, to set them to narrative.

Harold Lloyd, Buster Keaton, and the Classical Style

In 1915, only one year after Charlie Chaplin entered the film industry, the magazine *Photoplay* ran a four-part series on his career, already proclaiming him "the most popular comedian that the motion picture industry has yet produced."[1] Chaplin, the magazine contends, never fit in with his cohorts at Keystone, which he left at the end of 1914. "Chaplin introduced a new note into moving pictures," the second article reads. "Theretofore most of the comedy effects had been riotous boisterousness. Chaplin, like many foreign pantomimists got his effects in a more subtle way and with less action. . . . Chaplin enlarged the field of all motion picture comedies."[2] The fourth article laid bare the nature of this "new note" and the way in which the field of motion pictures had been expanded: "It is plain to the careful observer that Chaplin is working toward something entirely new in pictures. In a general way, his idea is that comedy should be more subtle and have more real story."[3] The period that we think of as the golden age of slapstick comedy—what James Agee called "comedy's greatest era" in the essay that revitalized the study of the period—was in fact a time of transformation, when slapstick comedy moved from the depiction of physical mayhem in its purest form (as expressed in Mack Sennett's films) to a compromise with classical technique, exemplified in distinct ways by the canonical slapstick features of the twenties.[4] Film comedy would not yet reach the level of classical standardization of the late 1930s, what Frank Krutnik calls "formalized comedian comedies" wherein "the twin demands of representation and presentation are articulated and contained within a stable and predictable formal mode."[5] The films of the slapstick era are still part of a moment in which "aspects of the classical representational paradigm coexist with a presentational mode of attraction that has its roots in such variety forms as vaudeville and burlesque."[6] As Krutnik observes, comedy "has always been slower than other genres to fall in line with industrial practices of standardization."[7] Yet by the 1920s it was clear that the minimally narrative, a-narrative, or even antinarrative slapstick of the first decades of the century would need to enter into dialogue with the tenets of classical technique, even if the endpoint of standardization was not yet clear.

Perhaps no one recognized the nature and necessity of the transition more than Chaplin, whose characterization was among the most nuanced and distinctive and whose narratives were among the most varied and complex of any of the silent clowns in their artistic maturity. But Chaplin's own negotiations with classical form occurred in the context of a series of parallel negotiations as each of his rivals sought his own way forward from gag-reel to film, efforts that defined a horizon of approaches against which Chaplin's evolution as a filmmaker might be judged. The terms of the negotiation between slapstick's traditional modes and classical style's normative demands would not look the same from comedian to comedian; they would vary across the last two decades of the silent era but most especially across the individuals who would come to define the form—based on each figure's filmmaking style and philosophy, to be sure, but also on the history and training that he brought with him, and even, pivotally, on the contours of his body and the ways in which he knew how to perform in and around a given radius of space. The development of Chaplin's hallmark visual style was the product of a series of stylistic and narrative choices, but Chaplin did not make these choices in isolation. He stood always in the presence of other performers and filmmakers, former vaudevillians and screen-born actors alike, who had to navigate their own way through this new terrain. To know Chaplin's filmmaking and the cinematic style that he would develop to support it, we must first turn to two of his peers in particular: Harold Lloyd and Buster Keaton. The arc of their choices would help define the matrix of options from which and through which Chaplin's own brand of cinema emerged.

Harold Lloyd, Student of Slapstick

By financial standards, the most successful figure in negotiating the transition to a new era of slapstick in the 1920s was the one most opposite to Chaplin: the youthful, all-American Lloyd. He personified gumption, optimism, and upward mobility, in contrast to Chaplin's perpetually downtrodden outsider. Though Chaplin's business acumen (or, more precisely, that of his half brother Sydney Chaplin) made him among the most powerful figures within the Hollywood film industry, Lloyd was objectively the more successful during slapstick's silent heyday. His films drew the largest audiences and made the most money of any of the silent comedy stars; his forty-room, twenty-two-acre estate in Beverly Hills was the stuff of Hollywood legend, "the most impressive and expensive of all the movie star estates ever built in Beverly Hills."[8] That Lloyd integrated slapstick into classical style is perhaps not surprising: he was the only major slapstick star with a background not on the variety stage but on the legitimate stage. Lloyd's love of performance began not in the virtuosity of vaudeville but in the theater proper, and he was among the most open in wedding slapstick to a new style and manner of filmmaking.

Lloyd was less a natural performer of slapstick than a student of it. His success was not, as for Chaplin and Keaton, the result of years of stage training but of years of study—of observing, copying, and when necessary changing what was successful in the work of his peers. Lloyd's background in the theater was quite modest, more a matter of aspiration than achievement—minor roles and amateur theatricals mostly.[9] He came to Hollywood determined to learn the craft of comic filmmaking; and though he was determined, he wasn't exactly a quick study. The story of Lloyd's rise in the film industry is almost like something out of one of his films, with the hero rising to stardom through sheer pluck. Lloyd started as a bottom-tier extra on the Keystone set; in fact, he was never even approved by Sennett or anyone else at Keystone as an extra—he simply figured out a way to sneak past the studio guard by mixing with the other extras as they returned from lunch, hoping he might get called into a short.[10] While at Keystone, Lloyd made friends with another extra higher up in the pecking order—Hal Roach, who went on to become one of the great slapstick producers. When Roach suddenly came into money in 1915, he set out to start his own slapstick studio and decided to make his friend Lloyd his first star, improbably launching one of the great slapstick careers of the era.

Even with such strokes of luck, it took Lloyd a long time to develop his comic persona and style. Chaplin made only one short at Keystone before inventing the Tramp character that became his mainstay. Keaton made some fifteen shorts as a second-string funnyman at Roscoe Arbuckle's Comique Film Company, but his first starring work, *One Week* (Comique, 1920), was a full-fledged classic with Keaton's stone-faced screen persona fully intact. Lloyd, by contrast, made more than seventy films with Roach before discovering the character—what he called simply the "glasses character" or sometimes "the boy with the glasses"—that became his trademark.[11] And even then, the nearly one hundred short one-, two-, and three-reel "glasses comedies," as Lloyd called them, never rose to the level of Chaplin's or Keaton's shorts; it was in features that Lloyd excelled.

Lloyd's short films were more a training ground than an artistic body of work: a way for him to learn and practice some version of what Chaplin and Keaton had grown up with on the variety stage. What he lacked in training,

Lloyd tried to make up for in deliberation and persistence. In Roach's recounting: "Of course he wasn't funny in himself; he needed his writers and a constant stream of gags. I remember in our early days together he was always so concerned about being a comedian all the time. A transition shot might just call for him to walk out of a door and across a room. Midway he'd stop in his tracks, turn to me and say, 'What do I do to be funny?' "[12] Lloyd even began in direct imitation of Chaplin, as though trying to master his technique, creating in his Lonesome Luke character (and for a short time before that, a similar character called Willie Work) a kind of cut-rate version of Chaplin's Tramp, his great distinction being simply a kind of physical inversion of clothing—"too small instead of too big," in Lloyd's description.[13] But Lloyd never matched Chaplin in the art of pantomime. (Any of the Lonesome Luke shorts gives ample testament to this fact.) Nor did Lloyd match a figure like Keaton in the precision of his acrobatics. For someone with no formal training or prior experience, Lloyd's moments of pure slapstick are exceptional. There is an excellent moment of mechanical acrobatics in *Bumping into Broadway* (Rollin, 1919) where Lloyd tries to get to a theater by secretly riding on the back bumper of a car. It is no small feat, but it pales in comparison to a similar moment in *Cops*, where Keaton grabs onto the back of a passing car and is dragged into the air, fluttering behind the moving vehicle like a human flag. Where Lloyd achieved impressive physical feats, Keaton achieved a kind of artistry.

Lloyd's epiphany came when, after indirectly apprenticing himself to Chaplin, he determined that he could never compete with the other silent clowns on their own terms. He would have to discover those characteristics that might make him unique. He all but risked his career on this move, abruptly ending a lucrative but inglorious distribution deal with Pathé for the Lonesome Luke shorts as a kind of second-tier Chaplin substitute in favor of trying to sell the distributor on his untried glasses character. In Lloyd's recollection, the turning point came when he was at a screening of one of his films and overheard a young boy say, " 'Oh, here's that fellow who tries to do like Chaplin.' . . . If I knew where that boy was, I'd send him a medal, because that settled it for me. I went back and told Roach I was going to quit. I wasn't going on forever being a third-rate imitator of anybody, even a genius like Chaplin."[14] Lloyd had two notable characteristics in his favor. For one, he had simple, boyish good looks hidden under his Tramp-like outfits—an uncommon trait among silent comedians, even for Chaplin and Keaton, who typically made their living on the basis of some degree of bodily distortion. He was a figure capable of playing the romantic lead: a potential matinee icon as well as a comedian. Lloyd's famous glasses, which were a prop only and not prescription, were designed to emphasize this aspect of his persona, calling attention to both his handsome features and his youth. As he writes in his autobiography, "When I came to choose a pair . . . the vogue of horn rims was new and it was youth, principally, that was adopting them. The novelty was a picture asset and the suggestion of youth fitted perfectly with the character I had in mind."[15] The glasses became an essential component of the new leading figure he constructed—in the fashion context of the era, they mark him as a boy just on the cusp of manhood, poised on the precipice of an adult sexuality that was not typically so direct a part of the slapstick universe.

Beyond his physical appearance, Lloyd also had what Alan Dale calls a kind of "effort and athleticism" that might help to compensate for his lack of acrobatic training and acumen and that was being largely wasted in his pantomime-based work as Lonesome Luke. It was not virtuosity, to be sure, but it was at least a highly advanced form of "the kind of physical skill the average boy is much more likely to have developed," in Dale's words.[16] Lloyd might never be able to achieve the extreme flourish of Keaton's car-grab moment, but from the right position he could attach himself to the outside of a moving automobile without injury, which was no small feat in itself. Whereas Keaton might turn the world into his gymnasium, Lloyd offered something else: not a spectacle of elegant motion but a demonstration of frenzied endurance, a man of seemingly average physical abilities caught in a world that demands from him extraordinary feats that he, in the end, can barely muster. Lloyd would become the handsome boy who finds himself caught in an ignominious world and must fight his way to success. His own description of the character is apt:

> The glasses would serve as my trade-mark and at the same time suggest the character—quiet, normal, boyish, clean, sympathetic, not impossible to romance. I would need no eccentric make-up, "mo" or funny clothes. I would be an average recognizable American youth and let the situations take care of the comedy. The comedy should be better for not depending upon a putty nose or its equivalent and the situations should be better for not being tied to low-comedy coat tails; funnier things happen in life to an ordinary boy than to a Lonesome Luke. Exaggeration is the breath of picture comedies, and obviously they cannot be true to life, but they can be recognizably related to life.[17]

In essence, Lloyd found his filmic hallmarks in the nature of his performing body—in his physical features and abilities. These were hallmarks that led him closer to classical technique, both visually and narratively, than the performing styles of his immediate peers would allow. For there is little of immediate, independent significance in a boyish face; it needs a boyish mission and ideally a boyish romance to make itself of interest. And athleticism in and of itself cannot hold the same attention as acrobatics. Athleticism is a matter of sustained physical activity over time, not encapsulated moments of virtuosity; it asks for actions to unfold in a meaningful sequence. It asks, like Lloyd's good looks, for a story. Thus Lloyd was better poised than any of his peers to draw up a compromise between slapstick tradition and classical technique, for his version of the former depended on the latter. To be sure, it was a compromise that he came to in collaboration with a number of artistic associates. To speak of Lloyd as a filmmaker, rather than as a performer, is to use his name in a corporate sense—unlike Chaplin and Keaton, he did not direct his own features and he worked with a wide circle of collaborators in developing his scenarios and his gags. Yet he was understood by all involved as the driving artistic force behind his trademark films: Lloyd was not only his own star but also, like Chaplin and Keaton, eventually his own producer and his own studio head. (Walter Kerr puts his controlling influence in particularly sharp terms, writing that Lloyd simply "did not take a directorial credit on his films.")[18] Lloyd's pictures were built ultimately on his prerogatives and, in turn, on the particular dynamics of the character he created, one who was uniquely suited to a narrative of ascendancy and maturation.

Indeed, it is this thread of narrative necessity that stitches together an otherwise highly divided career. Though he was known as the "King of Daredevil Comedy"—the strain of his work for which he is remembered today—Lloyd was also one of the few slapstick clowns who could effectively and convincingly play a romantic lead, and the bulk of his major films, from *Grandma's Boy* (Hal Roach, 1922) and *Girl Shy* (Harold Lloyd, 1924) to *The Freshman* (Harold Lloyd, 1925) and *The Kid Brother* (Harold Lloyd, 1927), are coming-of-age stories with no real daredevilry to speak of. Lloyd's body of work essentially bifurcated slapstick into what seem like the extremities of the genre, focusing on acts of daredevil danger on the one hand and narrative-driven work on the other. As a performer, he seems to manage to exist on those two extremes, shuffling easily between them, but the difference is perhaps not so great. In the end, all of Lloyd's films reduce to an essentially similar construction of the boy becoming a man, whether through romantic trials or extreme physical feats. His "boy with the glasses" must surmount any number of encumbrances to this process. As Dale recounts, "In his features, Lloyd has to overcome cowardice, hypochondria, an untenable situation caused by his having written letters home to his country girlfriend about his success in the city, pathological shyness that causes him to stutter in the presence of girls, overeagerness, scrawniness, impracticality, and, of course, bad luck."[19] But whatever the obstacle, Lloyd's stories always come back to the same injunction, to "make a man of yourself," as Kerr puts it, quoting the very first reel of Lloyd's first feature-length film.[20] Lloyd's financial success arguably rested on his particular ability to marry slapstick comedy and such an archetypal mode of storytelling, his comedy always leaning heavily on his narrative for justification and resonance.

LLOYD'S DAREDEVIL COMEDY AS CLASSICAL COMPROMISE

Lloyd's reliance on narrative holds true even for his most egregious acts of daredevilry. On one hand, his daredevil features like *Safety Last* (Hal Roach, 1923) and associated shorts like *High and Dizzy* (Hal Roach, 1920) and *Never Weaken* (Hal Roach, 1921) seem to boil slapstick down to its essence as pure attraction, evincing a more austere focus on the human body in peril than even the work of Sennett. In *Safety Last,* Lloyd famously climbs to the top of a department store skyscraper with only his bare hands. In *Never Weaken,* he must try to extricate himself from skyscraper scaffolding. In *High and Dizzy,* he must traverse the high-floor ledge of a skyscraper while drunk. Such moments are intrinsically interesting in themselves: one can easily extract the pivotal sequences from any of Lloyd's daredevil works and marvel at the almost sublime level of peril that they present, a series of urban high-rise nightmares made manifest. They seem a kind of holdover of the cinema of attractions, à la Donald Crafton's formulation of the history of the gag.[21] If Biograph in 1903 could produce a panorama film that merely showed a perspective on the Flatiron Building, with the camera panning from the street level up toward the top of the building, imagine the appeal had there been a man climbing that building. It is not too hard to imagine an *actualité* or *documentaire* on a professional building climber, or "human fly," that looked not too distant from what Lloyd shows in his fictional works.[22] As much as Lloyd is giving us a comedy, he also seems to be giving us the pure attraction of his body in extreme states of danger.

But what makes these moments funny—as opposed to terrifying—begins to point at the subtle influence of narrative on Lloyd's most seemingly straightforward slapstick moments. As Gerald Mast has observed, very little in the sequences themselves makes them funny over and above any other reactions that we might have. "Where Harold's near-fatal, near-miss stunts produce whoops of laughter in an audience," he writes, "the climax of Hitchcock's *Saboteur* [Frank Lloyd/Universal, 1942]—which uses the Statue of Liberty for its 'high-rise' tension—keeps an audience tense and anxious."[23] The high-stakes sequences in *Safety Last, Never Weaken,* and *High and Dizzy* are not self-consciously marked as moments of virtuosity or artistry that render them aestheticized and safe. They are not aerial ballets as Keaton might have produced; Lloyd does not display a masterful elegance and precision of movement as he navigates his vertical climbs or horizontal balancing acts. He awkwardly juts out his rear as he climbs up the building face in *Safety Last,* balances one foot in front of the other desperately and unevenly in *Never Weaken.* He looks like a man who is unpracticed at what he is doing and who may fall at any moment. Mast's reference to *Saboteur* is an effective counterpoint: a moment where a very similar kind of peril as that presented by Lloyd is meant to evince suspense and fear rather than chuckles. So how does Lloyd mark his comic moments as such? Mast, speaking of comedy more broadly, lays the answer squarely with genre: all comedy finds ways of marking itself as such, announcing in advance its suspension of normal rules of consequence. Mast uses the term "comic climate" to explain how "an artist builds signs into a work to let us know that he considers it a comedy and wishes us to take it as such. . . . If comedy does indeed depict matters of life and death, then the reason such depiction remains comic is because it *has not been handled as if it were* a matter of life and death."[24] This perspective holds true for a film like *Safety Last* in a highly literal way. Lloyd opens the film with what seems like the imagery and language of death: the boy seemingly behind bars, what seems like a noose dangling behind him, his fiancée and her mother separated from him and looking at him longingly, and a prison guard and a minister appearing behind the bars, all explicated by a title card speaking of the boy's "long, long journey."[25] Within moments, though, Lloyd dislodges all of our expectations as the camera pulls back to reveal the false constructions to which we have been subject (a favorite comic visual technique of his): the bars are just a separator in a train station, the noose in the background is actually a device for giving messages to the train conductors, the supposed prison guard is just a train conductor, and the fiancée, the mother, and the minister have simply come to see the boy off to the city. Lloyd's opening foreshadows the peril that the boy will find himself in later in the film and announces to us in advance that it will not be fatal.

But the laughter that accompanies the pivotal sequences in Lloyd's daredevil works is ultimately more than a matter of generic self-identification, for the removal of consequences might just as soon render the main scenes safe and interesting without necessarily also rendering them funny. What makes it humorous to see a man desperately climbing up the side of a building even after we have been made aware that he will not suffer dire consequences is the fact that it is not just any man climbing the building but *this* man, this frenzied novice—that is, Lloyd's fresh-faced "glasses character." It is all too easy to reduce Lloyd's daredevil films to their daredevil moments alone. But Lloyd goes through extraordinary pains to provide for us a narrative context for his film's signature moments. Compared to Keaton's work, where a short like *One Week* takes only a few minutes to arrive at the home construction site that provides the film's comic landscape or where a feature film like *The Navigator* (Buster Keaton, 1924) uses only a few short scenes to introduce the characters on land before setting them adrift in the great luxury liner set piece, Lloyd's central slapstick features are introduced only after extensive preparations. In *Never Weaken,* the first half or so of the short is concerned with establishing the boy's love for a secretary in a nearby office and the extreme physical feats he will go to in order to win her favor. His placement atop the skyscraper scaffolding is the improbable result of a suicide attempt undertaken when he thinks that the secretary has betrayed him, rendering his ventures up there the actions of a young man who has a proven level of physical dexterity but who is already in extreme distress. It is this interplay of characteristics that we watch as much as the actual actions undertaken to get down from the scaffold. In *High and Dizzy,* Lloyd again dedicates the first half of the short to introducing his new iteration of the boy, this time a struggling doctor who falls instantly in love with one of his patients. He is thus not just any man who winds up on a skyscraper ledge through a series of narrative contortions; he is a bright young man who is heartsick for his patient, torn between saving himself on the ledge and maintaining a modicum of dignity and decorum by not improperly entering an apartment where she might be sleeping.

Lloyd is not committed in these shorts to any kind of originality or sophistication of narrative per se—the stories are simple and flagrantly contrived; rather, he is committed to the kind of characterization that can be achieved through narrative action, an approach that reaches its height in *Safety Last.* There, the building climb marks only the last third of the film; the bulk of the feature concerns the boy's relationship with his fiancée, his struggles at work, and his friendship with a roommate whom he discovers, in a scene that foreshadows the climactic climb, is actually an adroit building climber. The narrative of the film as such is quite simple: the boy has trouble making it in the city, contrives a building climbing stunt as a way to draw a large publicity bonus at work, and finds himself to be the one climbing the building when his friend cannot do it. But the actions that go into this story—which set up the building climb but are in no real way requisite to it—help to establish the humor of that climb. In the pre-climb sections of the film, we see the boy as both a bumbling naïf in the department store scenes, overwhelmed and nearly torn to shreds by female shoppers, and as a dedicated and persistent striver (although one with a tendency for fibbing and exaggeration), arriving extremely early for work and writing his betrothed a letter as he waits for the doors to open. It is this combination of characteristics that informs our viewing of the daring building climb.

We know from the film's generic announcement at the outset that its actions will have no dire consequences, but more than that we know that the boy's efforts to climb the building will be both incompetent and dogged—that he will climb the building poorly but will be persistent in his efforts nonetheless. If the film's generic announcement gives us permission to laugh from the beginning, it is this incongruous combination of ineptitude and determination, carefully built over the course of the film, that gives us an actual reason to laugh. The person climbing the building, the way that he climbs it, is funny; the act of climbing itself is not assumed to be so—the scene in which Bill Strother as "The Pal" climbs a smaller building to escape a policeman is meant to be impressive, not comical. Thus, Lloyd's film actively points to the fact that it is not just any man but *this* man who is climbing the building in the film's climax. In Keaton's work, a feature like the building climb might tend to be more isolated and detached from narrative setup, an action rendered interesting in itself. His characters, particularly in the shorts, have little background or personality beyond his general screen persona. It is the act of struggle with the physical environment that is made humorous, with the humor couched in (and enhanced by) an almost archetypal vagueness. For Lloyd, the humor lies in specificity: in knowing the man who ends up climbing the building—and knowing all the ways that he is unlike the man who was supposed to climb it.

More than a narrative move, this specificity would have significant implications for Lloyd's visual style. The cinematics of Lloyd's daredevil works mark a kind of compromise between the unbroken time and space of slapstick's origins and the cut-up world of classical film. The medium and medium long shot are Lloyd's distances of choice. In part, this is a matter of necessity. Whereas Keaton would make the long shot his preferred distance, in large part to give evidence of the lack of contrivance in his stunts, Lloyd in fact relied on contrivance to achieve his effects and needed the camera to hide his work. The skyscraper in *Safety Last,* for instance, was not as it seemed. Lloyd selected a building situated on a hill to make it seem higher relative to the street behind it, and on that building's roof his crew built an additional two stories. Filmed from the right angle, Lloyd would look like he was suspended high above the city when he was in fact never more than a few stories off the actual roof of the building, with mattresses laid out to break his fall. (The real danger, in fact, was not from falling off the building but from falling off the constructed set, bouncing off the mattresses, and then falling off the building—as happened when Lloyd tested his safety mechanisms with a dummy.) Thus, the nature of Lloyd's slapstick necessitated both a closer shot distance than a figure like Keaton and a greater degree of cutting and angling than nearly any other comic.

But Lloyd's approach to slapstick also represented a visual compromise in another sense, as a balance between space and character. In the climb sequence in *Safety Last,* we can see a fair amount of the environment around Lloyd's character at any time—at least what seems like a fair amount of the environment—but we can also always see him as a person, a young man whose reactions to and anticipations of his perilous situation are real to us at every moment. Lloyd doesn't go into close-up often, but he does when he wants to highlight his character's reaction to a particular mishap—when he lies dangling by a rope from a high window, when he bangs his head against a ledge as the rope is raised back up. These are accent moments, meant to convey in detail the specificity of the boy's experience when it reaches its most extreme points (his most extreme peril, his most extreme pain). For reasons as much technical as aesthetic, Lloyd never goes into close-up in the film's most iconic sequence where the boy is hanging from the clock, but neither are such close-ups necessary. The medium shot holds within it both Lloyd's person and his environment, the two components necessary for his slapstick shots to work: to go into close-up at this point would emphasize the one over the other.

More typical of the sequence than the close-up is Lloyd's use of the iris. Framing out the boy's experience while still capturing his most immediate background, the iris highlights the specificity of the boy's climb without fully sacrificing the clarity of the world around him, the cause of all his dangers. At the very end of the climb, Lloyd even provides an extremely wide iris that merely blacks out the four corners of the frame. It is little more than a stylistic flourish, as the iris is masking hardly anything at all; rather, it emphasizes the degree to which even the broadest perspective on the situation conveys the boy's particular experience. Lloyd has turned to some of the most basic techniques of narrative emphasis to draw attention not to the narrative per se but to the character within that narrative. He has created a world where it is not just the body of the performer but the temperament of the character that imbues the slapstick with humor and where his filmmaking must walk a line between that character and the world around him. And it is, by necessity, a cut-up world. Lloyd's medium and medium long shots would be distinct from Chaplin's, for they cannot capture the whole of the world that they depict. Chaplin would never attempt such large-scale daredevilry as Lloyd or Keaton; his comedy exists on a human scale and thus his medium or medium long shot captures an unbroken sphere of human action. Lloyd's shots are a subdivision of the larger vertical space of the skyscraper, divided both narratively and visually into a sequence of floors, each with a different challenge for Lloyd's character to master. His comic world is highly personalized, but it is not visually continuous. To find a compromise between the specificity of his character and the epic scale of his actions, Lloyd must create a world divided, a world that in the end looks not unlike that depicted in classical film technique.

SLAPSTICK SUBSUMED: LLOYD'S ROMANTIC COMEDIES

Lloyd's kinship with classical technique becomes even more explicit in his romantic pictures, films less remembered now but as popular or more so than his daredevil stunts in his own day. The degree to which these films were committed to detailed narrative arrangement is remarkable for works that can still fall under the slapstick banner; they seem as much descendants of John Bunny's genteel comedies (and before that, the long stage tradition of narrative-driven comedy) as they are of Sennett's early mayhem. *The Freshman,* perhaps the most successful of Lloyd's romantic pictures, is a case in point. The basic arc of the story adheres to what Kerr lays out as the shape of all Lloyd's feature films: the injunction to "make a man of yourself." Here, a boy goes off to college hoping to become the most popular student on campus and must learn that throwing lavish parties will not win him true success; acclaim finally comes to him only through gumption and determination during a pivotal football game. It is a simple story, but the intricacies of the narrative development very nearly match anything from much later versions of adolescent comedy. There is Lloyd at home dreaming of his college days, a classic "meet cute" with his future love interest, a run-in with the president of the college, an embarrassing mishap at orientation, a lavish party sequence, scenes of football practice, and of course the climactic home game. Unlike so many slapstick works, the film is not organized around a single physical set-piece: the football game, which holds the same narrative space and takes about the same amount of time as the climactic climb in *Safety Last,* is a culmination of the film but not its raison d'être. It is actually an outgrowth of earlier events, the physical comedy subsumed by rather than led up to by the narrative development of the story.[26] In fact, *The Freshman* is remarkably verbal for a silent comedy, with many of its funniest moments organized around words rather than actions: an early sequence in which the boy's father uses a shortwave radio to accidentally listen in to his son practicing phrases he will use in college; a moment where the boy and his future love interest try to solve a crossword puzzle together with clues like "sweetheart" and "darling" so that they look to all the world like cooing lovers; a moment of humiliation where the boy winds up onstage and must give an impromptu speech (in a silent film!) to the assembled student body. It was not uncommon for slapstick comedies to embed jokes or satiric comments in their intertitles, but Lloyd's work is something else entirely: it is actively wanting for dialogue, not just for additional moments of humor but for its own narrative development. Before it is a slapstick comedy, *The Freshman* is a story.

That is not to say *The Freshman* does not have its share of physical humor, but it is offered in excess on top of a story that could work just as well without it. It is a flourish to the story rather than the reason that the story was concocted. Hence the film's central party sequence, where the boy throws a lavish ball to help make friends but arrives with his tuxedo only half stitched together; his tailor follows him around to repair it as it breaks apart. Crafton's description of slapstick's relationship to narrative as being one of "excess" and "lack of economy" particularly suits this sequence.[27] The party scene is clearly organized around a series of physical stunts that fit into the narrative but are excessively indulgent to their own spectacle: Lloyd pretending to sit at a table as he in fact lies nearly prone, his legs stretched out behind a curtain as the tailor repairs his pants, or Lloyd hiding a sleeveless arm behind the same curtain as the tailor lends his own arm to cover up the ruse and shake hands with fellow partygoers. And yet, while such moments of physical contortion provide the substance of the party sequence, they are not the only reason it exists. The party caps the unknowing indignities that the boy has suffered as his fellow students exploit him for money and good times even as they make fun of him behind his back. Lloyd's perpetual loss of clothing—culminating, inevitably, in losing his pants before the entire assembly of guests—parallels the dignity that is being shed as he comes to realize his true position. He is caught with his pants down emotionally as well as physically, and the climax of the scene comes not in physical action—the lost pants are in fact quickly replaced—but in narrative revelation: the boy is finally told to his face what a fool everyone thinks he is.

In fact, Lloyd occasionally makes the choice in *The Freshman* to elide those moments most suited to physical comedy altogether, offering us only the implication of slapstick, as in the boy's audition for the football team. Rather than let the boy on the team, the coach decides to dupe him into being used for tackling practice. We see a few moments of clobbering as Lloyd happily takes his punishment for the good of the team, followed by a shot of a line of football players stretching into the distance. But instead of a long succession of tackles made humorous by a series of continuous bodily contortions each more elaborate than the next, Lloyd opts to skip the sequence altogether, cutting only to the last few tackles as night falls and the boy appears on the verge of collapse. We can get the necessary idea—the boy's endurance and dedication to the team—as effectively by elision as by seeing it directly. It is in a way the ultimate triumph of classical technique over slapstick's visual independence. Whereas traditional slapstick would insist on seeing the body pummeled—such would be the attraction, and the significance, of the whole sequence—classical narrative can do without. The pummeling is consigned to the implied excisions of montage: we see the beginning of the tackling line, we see the end of the tackling line, and we can connect the two ourselves. This unseen surfeit of injury may be substantive within the visual system of slapstick, but it is extraneous to the classical system of narrative.

From this perspective, *The Freshman*'s climactic football game is both an apotheosis to and a kind of dismantling of the classical-slapstick compromise of *Safety Last*'s climactic climb. If characterization helps to drive the comedy in the skyscraper ascent, it becomes the organizing principle in the football game. We are not watching a comic football game as such; we are watching Lloyd's character react to and overcome the indignities he has faced throughout the film. Where other characters insist on keeping him out, he insists on being let in. Where other characters know the rules, he is practically oblivious to how the game is played. But his newfound doggedness coupled with his outsider status help to create his success. The boy bends the rules and finds new ways to thwart the other team in part because he doesn't know any better: he pretends to leave the football lying on the field to divert the other team and then grabs it at the last minute by the cord of the unwound football lace; he walks casually down the field with the ball hidden behind his back so the other team won't know he has it; he continues to progress toward the end zone even when tackled because he simply doesn't know any better. We are given ample images of the body in pain—all of the comic tackles, with Lloyd lying crushed on the field or landing upside down on his head, that were denied to us in the earlier training sequence. But we are given them here because they serve a narrative purpose and are not a function of pure comic repetition: each painful tackle serves to both heighten our awareness of the boy's incompetence and demonstrate his growing resolution to win the game, showing us in action the same combination of ineptitude and dedication that was Lloyd's hallmark in *Safety Last*.

Yet unlike the building climb in *Safety Last,* the big game in *The Freshman* does not seek any compromise between narrative and slapstick: there is only slapstick harnessed to the needs of narrative, and the visual style of the sequence reflects this breakdown. The football game is a kind of checklist of classical technique. Gone is the progressive sequence of medium and medium long shots that marked Lloyd's ascent to the top of the skyscraper. Instead, we have a steady mix of long shots, medium shots, and close-ups as well as point-of-view shots, shot/reverse-shot sequences, cuts-in-action, and a tracking shot that follows Lloyd down the football field. There is even a textbook moment of montage where we see Lloyd running down the field, cut to a whistle blowing (though not the referee's whistle), and cut back to Lloyd prematurely stopping his progression down the field, Eisensteinian construction here rendered comic through the misapprehension of the hero. We are not given the game as uninterrupted spectacle; we are given it as narrative accumulation. It is composed of slapstick units, but those units are not ends in themselves. It is not actually a slapstick world but a world broken into small slapstick parts, meaningful not in themselves but in their combination toward a narrative end. They are funny, but they are not allowed to be the only reason that we watch. This is not slapstick informed by classical technique but slapstick utterly subsumed to it and to the divided, reconfigured world it builds.

BUSTER KEATON'S SEARCH FOR A NEW CINEMATIC LANGUAGE

Lloyd's technique stands in contrast to that developed by Keaton, who among the major silent clowns might be said to have developed a visual style that most sought to present slapstick on its own terms. Like Lloyd, Keaton was an inveterate collaborator: he worked with a codirector for a number of his pictures, and he typically developed his stories and gags with a team of trusted scenarists. Yet he was understood, like Lloyd, to be the driving creative force on his films—his own star, his own cowriter, his own codirector, and, for most of the 1920s, his own producer and studio head. In fact, Keaton has traditionally been considered the most cinematic—and often the most classically cinematic—of the great silent comedians. David Bordwell, Kristin Thompson, Donald McCaffrey, and Daniel Moews have all made cases for Keaton as an exemplar of classical style in the Hollywood comedy.[28] Mast likens him almost to a camera himself: "Keaton's physical comedy is essentially a synthesis of malleable human flesh and Bergsonian encrusted machine. . . . Keaton is both machine and man at once. Keaton's interest in machines and mechanical processes also influences the way he handles the camera, that cinema machine."[29] Or in Kerr's phrase, "Uncovering the camera's workings, he made it master in its own house, established its identity."[30]

There is no doubt that Keaton's films are more interested in their own workings qua films than those of any of his peers. Keaton was fascinated with the possibilities of cinema from almost the first moment he stepped onto a film set. In his memoirs, Keaton recounts how on his first day on set with Arbuckle at the Colony Studios, his new mentor and boss "took the camera apart for me so I would understand how it worked and what it could do."[31] For all his mechanical inclination, though, Keaton's real thrill seems to have been much more expansive than a matter of film stock and lenses:

The greatest thing to me about picturemaking was the way it automatically did away with the physical limitations of the theatre. On the
stage, even one as immense as the New York Hippodrome stage, one
could show only so much. The camera had no such limitations. The
whole world was its stage. If you wanted cities, deserts, the Atlantic
Ocean, Persia, or the Rocky Mountains for your scenery and background, you merely took your camera to them. . . . The camera allowed
you to show your audience the real thing: real trains, horses, and wagons, snowstorms, floods. Nothing you could stand on, feel, or see was
beyond the range of the camera.[32]

Keaton was undoubtedly enamored of the camera, but Kerr reminds us that
he also, every bit as much as Chaplin and far more than Lloyd, had a lineage
in clowning and that his films were ultimately shaped to a vaudevillian's end:
"Keaton is a comedian like other comedians, a clown making use of the standard vocabulary of clowns. He tells us stories that are meant to be both stories
and funny; he uses gags because they are gags."[33] Keaton was in constant dialogue with classical technique to be sure, but his cinematic achievements were
as much a matter of what Robert Knopf calls the "formidable artistry in his gag
and stunt sequences and the complex ways in which these sequences interact
with the narrative" as they were about anything more typical of the classical
style.[34]

    In fact, we might say Keaton's own struggle was not so much to find a com-
promise point between slapstick and classical style as it was to find a new filmic
vocabulary entirely, one that might be able to capture the grand scope of his
particular comic vision. There is indeed no silent film comedian—and hardly
any film director of any genre, in his time or since—more absolutely elemental
in his cinematic imagination than Keaton. Keaton composed at the level of
the monumental. Houses, trains, steamboats, ocean liners—these are not set
pieces for Keaton; they are actual objects to be manipulated by the filmmaker's
vision and sometimes by the characters themselves within the diegesis of the
film. The forces against which Keaton's character would contend are almost
biblical in their magnitude (indeed, natural disasters from hurricanes to torna-
does would play a greater role in his comedy than in that of any of his peers). If
Lloyd's struggle was to personalize slapstick, to bring it down to the level of the
individual character even in a scenario so mammoth as climbing a skyscraper,
Keaton's project was something of the opposite: finding ways to increase the
scale of cinematic storytelling, to hold the human figure constant but explode
the magnitude of the environment around him, all without losing the intimacy
or detail necessary for successful comic work. In this search, Keaton would not

infrequently borrow from the retinue of classical technique, but his choices can never really be said to be in service of classical aims. Keaton is in search not of the clearest means of telling a story but, most frequently, of the clearest means of conveying man and his surroundings in opposition, regardless of the narrative need of the moment. In Kerr's evocative description, "The elements with which he is at odds and in which he is so much at home—wind, water, the natural geometry of a universe God made and washed His hands of—already swirl, pivot, fold and unfold about him, defying his efforts to nail them together with a hammer."[35] He is, in fact, searching for a new cinematic vocabulary on the opposite artistic territory from that which most interested Chaplin, whose own search would focus not on the level of individual character and achievement like Lloyd or on the level of the epic and elemental like Keaton but ultimately on the social and the interpersonal, with his visual style built to match. Yet Keaton's achievements put into perspective the alternate choices and approaches that would surround Chaplin's decisions as he sought to achieve his own particular marriage of slapstick and film.

KEATON'S DUAL INFLUENCES: ROSCOE "FATTY" ARBUCKLE AND THE VARIETY STAGE

A substantial degree of Keaton's cinematic innovations might be traced to the particular mode of his entry into the world of film. Tellingly, Keaton was the only one of the major silent clowns never to have worked with Sennett and thus never to have been a part of the most rudimentary forms of cinematic comedy that he produced. Keaton never personally knew the world of limited visual assumptions, shot-as-scene constructions, and kinesis for its own sake that marked Sennett's work and that served as the entry point for so many of the variety comedians who tried to make the transition to film. He was, in fact, only one step removed from Sennett—but it was a significant step. Keaton began his film career as a supporting funnyman under Arbuckle, who was one of Sennett's earliest stars at Keystone (and a frequent collaborator with Chaplin during his tenure at the studio) and who set out at the turn of 1916–17 to form his own comedy studio, the Comique Film Corporation. But to begin one's career at Comique was a far cry from beginning at Keystone. Arbuckle's innovations as a comic star and comic director have been generally underrated by film historians, in part because he arguably never reached his artistic maturity: his career was cut short abruptly at the age of thirty-four by a sensational trial for murder shortly after Keaton had started making films on his own. But as Steve Massa argued in the program notes to a Museum of Modern Art retrospective of his work in 2006, Arbuckle showed a remarkable degree of ingenu-

ity in his films at Comique, moving quickly beyond the unfussy filmic mode
that was the studio standard at Keystone to become "an innovative comedy
creator and a sophisticated director."[36]

In fact, in Arbuckle's innovations we can begin to see the origins of Keaton's
film technique. Arbuckle was undoubtedly still indebted to Sennett in many
of his narrative and visual assumptions. A classic Arbuckle short like *Coney Island* (Comique, 1917) ends, in true Keystone style, in a "rally" in which nearly
all of the characters fall into the water. And Arbuckle sometimes maintains the
counterproductive tendency of the early Keystone shorts to break up the slapstick action of a single gag if it cannot be easily captured in a single medium
long shot. Trying to get a better view of a passing parade, Keaton's character
scurries up a lamppost with only his bare hands, but Arbuckle divides the shot
in two: a shot of him leaving his fellow parade watchers behind as he climbs
upward and a shot of Keaton reaching the top of the lamppost, when a single
long shot of the full action (surely how Keaton would have framed the action
once he became a director) would have made for a more impressive comic feat.
And of course some of the gags and bits carry over. A squabble over a park
bench in *Coney Island* looks for all the world like a moment out of *Twenty
Minutes of Love* or any of the other early Keystone park comedies.

Yet these holdovers pale in comparison with the techniques that Arbuckle
introduced that went beyond standard working method at Keystone. For one,
Arbuckle was far more comfortable intermixing both long shots and close-ups
in his work than were the directors working under Sennett during the same
time period. Keaton's first short with Arbuckle, *Butcher Boy* (Comique, 1917),
is a case in point. For its first scene in a country general store, Arbuckle readily switches between a long shot of the cavernous, two-story store interior and
medium shots that direct us to particular moments of action within the space.
He frames most of the comic bits in medium or medium long shots that subdivide the sections of the store, but he does not hesitate to introduce key characters in close-up and he uses an iris to direct our attention to the love interest.
At one point, Arbuckle even uses a ninety-degree cut-in-action to show us
two perspectives on a dog that has been placed on a treadmill to run a pepper-
corn grinder. Arbuckle returns to the long shot of the full store interior for the
scene's climactic flour-bag fight, as the space and everything within it become
drenched in white powder. His technique generally holds to Keystone's tradition of unbroken shots from a fixed distance, but these are placed within
a context of cinematographic attention-grabbing devices like the close-up or
iris, guiding us from one character or specific bit to the next. Arbuckle was not
afraid to flirt with classical technique if it helped him to tell his story. *Butcher
Boy* is a far cry from the climactic football game in *The Freshman,* but nei-

ther is it a matter of shot-as-scene Keystone construction. Arbuckle's work, like much of the slapstick of the 1910s, stands distinctly outside the dominant trend toward classical consolidation insofar as its construction is not entirely driven by classical imperatives, but it also exists in more active dialogue with classical technique than most of the work of his peers.

At the same time that he flirts with the features of classical style, Arbuckle also does not shy away from the long shot or the extreme long shot, moves that have a relatively small place in classical style as compared to the medium shot and close-up. In *Butcher Boy,* Arbuckle uses a long shot to encompass the entire two-story set, not just to present the initial location but to capture the whole of the flour-bag fight in all its extensive mayhem. The long shot is here an extrapolation on the principle of unbroken space behind the Keystone medium long shot taken to an exaggerated height; it encompasses not just a human scale of action but a scale beyond the human—an entire two stories of action within a single frame. Arbuckle will take this approach even further in his short *Out West* (Comique, 1918), using the long shot and extreme long shot in ways that specifically foreshadow moments in Keaton's work. Here, Arbuckle begins the short with a chase atop a moving train, filming the sequence from afar so that we can take in at once the small human figures and the colossal train on which their actions unfold (as well as the monumental vistas of the Western landscape behind them). He ends the short by besting his own initial device, showing in an extreme long shot two characters pushing an entire house off a ledge so that it slides down a gorge and shatters at the bottom. Arbuckle expands the slapstick universe to a scale that it had never known in his days at Keystone, a world where even the occasional long shot will no longer suffice and only the extreme long shot can properly capture the entire gag—a gag that has grown far beyond the scale of the human body, a gag that now involves the world itself. It is an explosive move—and also a dangerous one. *Out West* is one of the few slapstick films of the era to break the contract laid out so explicitly at the start of *Safety Last:* that death shall have no place in this tale of peril. Instead, Arbuckle makes death an active part of his comedy. Keaton as the saloon owner shoots a number of characters in an early bar scene; he even has a special trapdoor in the floor for disposing of all the dead bodies, one of the era's more macabre slapstick gags. When the film culminates in a requisite chase across the Western landscape, we are a long way from the innocence of *The Curtain Pole.* Characters get shot and die during the chase, their bodies becoming obstacles to those still engaged in the pursuit. In the new comedic realm in which Arbuckle begins to experiment, there is no longer any guarantee of safety, as there will be none in the comic universe that Keaton would come to create. An Arbuckle short like *Out West* gestures toward a new visual and thematic mode in slapstick—an epic mode, one that will be most fully realized in Keaton's work.

Of course, Keaton did more than simply continue the trajectory that Arbuckle began and in which he was abruptly cut short. Keaton brought to his shorts and features a background and acumen in comic performance that was second to none, an overall level of physical mastery that has scarcely been matched in the century since. He was quite literally born into show business. His parents were traveling vaudeville performers who used to keep baby Buster in the wings of the theater while they performed and who brought him into their act from an extraordinarily young age. In Keaton's recollection:

> Having no baby sitter, my mother parked me in the till of a wardrobe trunk while she worked on the stage with Pop. According to him, the moment I could crawl I headed for the foot-lights. "And when Buster learned to walk," he always proudly explained to all who were interested and many who weren't, "there was no holding him. He would jump up and down in the wings, make plenty of noise, and get in everyone's way. It seemed easier to let him come out with us on the stage where we could keep an eye on him."[37]

They called themselves "The Three Keatons" and Buster's specialty in the act was a kind of extreme physical comedy that even to audiences at the time seemed to border on cruelty. Buster's signature routine was called "The Human Mop" and it involved his father turning him upside down and sweeping the stage with his hair. Other routines involved an all-out brawl between father and son, with Buster being thrown across the stage and landing in the orchestra pit. On several occasions, the Three Keatons were investigated by the Society for the Prevention of Cruelty to Children and were partly prohibited from performing Buster's act in New York, but Buster had mostly fond memories of the experience.[38] "All little boys like to be roughhoused by their fathers," he would remember. "They are also natural tumblers and acrobats. Because I was also a born hambone, I ignored any bumps or bruises I may have got at first on hearing audiences gasp, laugh, and applaud."[39] He became a consummate physical performer, well practiced in all of the jumps and falls of the vaudeville comic acrobat.

More than a training in physical comedy, though, Keaton's background seemed to influence his vision of what slapstick might be. Keaton's father was a prodigious force in the young Buster's life, one that he and his mother would have to abandon when his alcoholism became too great for them to bear. It was, according to his biographer Rudi Blesh, a move from which the young Keaton never recovered and that informed his comedy from that point forward. At the age of twenty-two, after having spent nearly his entire life performing with his father, Keaton had to come up with solo acts to support himself. As Blesh writes, "He set up obstacles, with hotel chairs and tables as props, to stumble over and get tangled up with. He would think up a task for them to interfere with; but, more important, first he must create a fate for himself by setting up its inanimate pawns. Joe Keaton was gone. Someone—better, something—had to take his place."[40] Keaton's imperative as a comic performer would be forever to find a force great enough to equal the opposition he first met in his father, to re-create in outsized comic battles of man versus world the initial comic battle first waged between father and son—and, by extension, to find a visual means of containing and capturing this conflict.

KEATON'S EPIC MODE OF COMEDY

The result of this quest is the epic mode in which Keaton's films are often composed, a mode taken from Arbuckle but extended even further than Keaton's mentor might have imagined possible. While the monumental is only an element in Arbuckle's comedy—for example, most of *Out West* is composed on a more manageable human scale—with Keaton it will sometimes be the exclusive mode in which he works. His 1922 short *Cops* (Comique) may be the apotheosis of this epic drive, for nearly the entire short occurs in a series of spectacular long shots and extreme long shots—a rarity in film even to this day. Having interrupted a police parade and been mistaken for an anarchist, Keaton must somehow evade not just a few policemen but the entire Los Angeles police force, represented by a cast of hundreds of extras in uniform. *Cops* is composed like a Canaletto painting, with crowd scenes of tiny figures set against towering architecture that is in itself a study in large-form geometry. The classic shots in *Cops* proceed with Euclidean precision: Keaton evading two streets full of policemen by ducking into the entrance of a triangle-shaped building as the police lines converge in front; Keaton being chased by an army of police under a grand architectural arch at the top of the frame, then escaping through a miniature arch at the bottom of the frame created by the open legs of the one policeman standing in his path; Keaton forming a series of triangles as he balances atop a ladder on a fence that functions like a giant seesaw. Once the chase begins, Keaton never breaks to a close-up and hardly ever uses the medium shot. His interest is in the body in a broad environment of peril, not just a small radius of human action.

Keaton's approach is not that of Lloyd, who subdivides the massive feat of climbing a skyscraper into a series of medium and medium long shots, the extremity of the situation only indicated by what we can see in the background planes of the frame. But neither is Keaton's performing body that of Lloyd. Lloyd must show us the story of a particular man climbing a particular building, blanketed by a promise of no consequences, to allow for our laughter. Keaton needs no such techniques: his comedy lies in the motions of his body no matter what the distance of the shot and no matter what we may know of his character's backstory, his motivations, or his possible fate. For unlike Lloyd, who shows us his struggles with the terrifying task at hand, Keaton moves through the extreme environments of the short like a child on a playground. His movements on the ladder atop the fence are as expert as any trapeze artist's and even his running and ducking through the streets of the city is accomplished with an acrobat's flair. His body in motion is nearly unreal in its precision and control. There is no mistaking that this is not just any man in peril but a very particular man, and we need no medium shot to tell us so. If there is humor in the failure of the human body to achieve poise and control, Keaton's comedy is something of its opposite: it is the incredulous humor of a body that maintains poise and control even when it seems that it should not, a body defiant of its environment and situation.

Though you can hardly see it amid all the long shots in *Cops,* this is also the comedic principle behind Keaton's famous "stone face," his utterly unchanging visage maintained no matter what mishap may occur. In other words, Keaton's humor is the humor of self-control rather than its loss: he may not triumph over his environment but he will stubbornly and steadfastly refuse to be affected by it, even long past the point at which such a stance might be reasonable. And indeed, Keaton, like Arbuckle, gives us no guarantee of amiable consequences. *Cops* in fact ends with a morbid implication of suicide by execution: Keaton is rejected by his betrothed and so finally surrenders himself to the police, with the final image of the film being a tombstone with his trademark porkpie hat on top. Keaton can get away with such morbidity, even when inflicted upon the hero of his short, because his humor does not rely on the avoidance of consequences, merely their defiance. The consequences that all slapstick must keep at bay to achieve its comic ends are here held in abatement by Keaton's body itself.

Cops is an extremity in Keaton's career, the film that is perhaps most fully composed in his elemental style. More typical of Keaton's work is a mixture of the kind of grand stylistics of *Cops* with a series of borrowings from the storehouse of classical technique. Keaton is not averse to using basic classical shot composition when he has no greater filmic purpose in mind. The expositional moments of his films (unlike those of Chaplin) tend to look much like the expositional moments of any other film shot in the classic Hollywood style. Keaton readily subdivides the space of action, cycling through a series of repositioned medium shots interspersed with close-ups for emphasis, drawing freely on shot/reverse-shot technique and cuts-in-action. The domestic scenes in *Sherlock Jr.* and *The General* function mostly in this way, as does most of his first feature film, *Three Ages* (Buster Keaton, 1923), which relies on long strands of exposition interspersed with scenes of comic business.

Curiously, though, Keaton's reliance on subdivision and reframing moves at least one step beyond classical style; in particular, Keaton will frequently reposition his camera ever so slightly for no narrative gain whatsoever. It is not that Keaton engages in the mobile frame in these instances but that he simply cuts to a moderately different shot of what he is presenting, with the characters now just subtly repositioned. Such moments occur, innocuously enough, in *Sherlock Jr.* when Keaton's projector operator approaches the movie screen, in *The Navigator* when Keaton and his love interest are trying to climb the ship's ladder to escape from the cannibals, and in *The General* when Keaton's rebel train conductor is searching through a pile of Union shoes. These repositionings carry no clear narrative weight but seem instead to function like a kind of visual hiccup in the film. What they do, in fact, is keep the frame in constant motion, never letting the image become static for too long. In this sense, they are a kind of cinematic equivalent to the diegetic kinesis that Sennett created by undercranking and cutting out frames. Sennett wanted constant motion within the frame, and Keaton seems to want constant motion of the frame. But this is more than a demand for movement for its own sake (as it was in Sennett), for what Keaton also achieves is a constant, subtle reminder of the degree to which what we see before us is framed and placed into a particular perspective; it is as though Keaton is calling attention to the existence of the frame itself.

More specifically, he seems to be calling attention to the limitations of the frame and the possibility of perspective as a kind of counterbalance. Absent the long shot that is his favored mode, the action and environment of a scene are only ever presented in some small part. (Of course, even the extreme long shot only captures some small picture of the total environment, though the relevance of extreme scale seems eventually to suffer from diminishing returns.) In other words, Keaton's filmmaking seems impatient with anything other than the total picture and compensates for this lack with a constant but subtle reframing of the scene. This evinces a degree of comfort with the elements of classical technique not immediately apparent in a short like *Cops*. If he cannot shoot in long shot, Keaton wants to shoot from as many perspectives as possible—an imperative, to be sure, that overlaps with classical technique but adapts it to its own ends. Keaton's goal is not to subdivide the sequence for the purpose of advancing and clearly communicating the narrative per se, as his consistent repositioning of very simple shots serves no narrative ends. Rather, he is open to subdividing space as another means of getting at its totality through a series of its parts if it cannot be presented in its unbroken whole. Thus he takes the division and rearrangement of space even further than classical technique would seem to allow.

This imperative toward presenting action from a series of multiple perspectives would become a defining trope of Keaton's feature-length visual style. Keaton does not go so far in this regard as Sennett in a late short like *Lizzies of the Field,* where multiple perspectives on a car crash are presented for the sheer enjoyment of seeing the crash happen in as many ways as possible. Keaton's multiple perspectives are presented in the context of the film's narrative unfolding, not as a kind of excessive visual cadenza on top of that narrative. But the imperative to reshow the same event from a multiplicity of vantage points when a single long shot will simply not do is nonetheless a notable facet of many of Keaton's most iconic sequences. It is a device frequently used in *The General,* where the constant movement of the train precludes most of the major action that occurs on the train cars from being captured from a single, long-shot vantage point. Keaton's battle with a loaded cannon that he has trouble controlling is a case in point. Keaton begins the sequence with the camera positioned at a ninety-degree angle to the action, the train car and the cannon covering the left-right axis of the frame. He holds this position for most of the action of loading and pointing the cannon, but as the conductor's troubles with the object begin to mount and he finds the loaded cannon pointing straight ahead at the train car he is on, Keaton subtly repositions the camera, now showing the action from a forty-five-degree angle looking back on the cannon. As the conductor continues to struggle with the cannon, throwing wood at it to try to knock it off course and then simply fleeing the vicinity and moving to the front of the train, Keaton shifts to a head-on shot at the back of the cannon and then to another head-on shot facing the cannon. In a sequence of no more than a few minutes, Keaton's camera describes a 180-degree half circle around the point of focus. It is a move that exceeds the narrative demands of the moment. We gain a sense of the conductor's desperation as we see the cannon pointed at him in so many different ways, but we do not narratively need such a complete schematic. It is a compensation, a way for us to see the comic action in as full a view as possible and consider it in a kind of constructed totality to make up for the unified totality that cannot be achieved. It is as close as Keaton can come to showing us a full picture of man's battle with the total world around him in this situation.

Keaton makes a similarly premised, though visually distinct, move in the famous chase sequence from *Sherlock Jr.* Here, Keaton finds himself speeding after a criminal as he sits on the front of a motorcycle, holding the handlebars behind him. It is a spectacular scene with new obstacles and contrivances at every turn: a city street full of traffic, convicts shoveling dirt onto the road, a bridge with a gap in it that is filled at the very last moment by two trucks passing underneath. Yet one of the most remarkable features of the chase is that its most suspenseful moment is in fact presented twice. We watch at the very beginning of the chase in a long shot as Keaton navigates the motorcycle through a busy city street, just barely missing a series of cars coming at him at ninety-degree angles down a cross-street. Then, at the very end of the chase, Keaton doubles down on the stunt: now his character is on a country road and again misses several cars and a train coming at him from a ninety-degree angle, only this time we see the action in a tracking shot that follows Keaton's character in profile close at the shoulder so that we can see the oncoming traffic advancing directly at us. As the rest of the total sequence ably demonstrates, there is no lack of ingenuity in the construction of the chase; Keaton is not simply out of ideas. Rather, the repetition seems premised entirely around the issue of perspective. Here, Keaton's initial long shot of the motorcycle on the city street fully captures the action and the environment but it misses one crucial aspect of the scene: the experience as seen from Keaton's seat on the motorcycle and the vision of near miss that can only be achieved from that perspective. It is a problem easily solved in standard classical filmmaking: one need only cut from the long shot of the street to the close-up on the bike and back again, intermixing the objective and subjective points of view to tell the story of the chase and the characters involved in it. But Keaton does not seem concerned with the story of the chase as such; he seems more concerned with the action and the space in which it occurs, presenting each in as unbroken a manner as he can. Hence the doubling back to the initial stunt, a way of capturing the fullness of the picture over an elapsed stream of time.

Keaton makes a kind of reverse move in a very different chase sequence in *The Navigator.* Here, Keaton and his love interest, alone on an ocean liner that has been set adrift at sea, circle the decks of the boat searching for each other. Set amid the perfect right angles of the ship's three-level rectangular deck, the chase is a study in symmetry: as one character moves toward the camera on one level of the deck, the other moves away from the camera on another level of the deck; as one character turns a corner from right to left, the other turns an opposite corner from left to right; as one goes up a staircase to another deck, the other comes down to the deck just departed. Keaton composes the chase in a maddening series of medium long shots, teasing us with only limited pieces of the total space so that we can never exactly tell where the characters stand in relation to one another. But he culminates the chase in a cathartic extreme long shot with all three levels of the deck in frame at once; at last we can see the exact pattern of movement as the characters continue in their series of symmetrical near misses. Here, Keaton combines the accumulated space of shifting perspectives—the floor plan of the ship that we mentally reconstruct through the combination of all those individual shots—with the revelation of the total space seen all at once, offering a complete vision of the action of the chase through both the perspective of its component parts and the perspective of its unbroken whole. It is among the most thorough presentations of a single action sequence in Keaton's career, and it points to the heterodox variation on classical technique that he has crafted for himself. In standard classical style, the long shot stands in opposition to the close-up; it is the most impersonal and imprecise of shot distances, used mostly (though not exclusively) to establish tone and location and rarely to serve any serious narrative function. Yet in Keaton's visual approach, the long shot is near cousin to the close-up. Just as the close-up is used to place narrative emphasis and to draw the viewer's attention to a specific person or item in the action, so too for Keaton is the long shot actually a tool of visual emphasis and a means of drawing the viewer's attention not inward but outward. What Keaton means to emphasize—what is most important in his visual and narrative schema—is the total picture of the action that is unfolding. He prompts us to better understand what is going on not by zooming in but by zooming out, by considering not the isolated image of a moment important to the action but the total image of the total action. Keaton asks us to understand not in specificity but in totality. He is telling a story but it is a story of the human figure in an all-encompassing environment, a story that is not aided so much by images of the human figure in isolation as it is by images of the human figure in as much of his or her environs as the camera can capture, shot from afar.

The Limits of Keaton's Classical Compromise

Keaton's variation on classical technique would represent the best compromise that he could devise between the visual needs of his variety of slapstick and the cinematic demands of effective storytelling, as his stories would typically be composed not at the interpersonal level of human to human but at the elemental level of human to world. As stories of people, Keaton's narratives are shockingly banal, a far cry from the nuance achieved by Chaplin or even by

Lloyd. In Moews's description, "Basic to the Keaton heroes is a psychological dynamic of essentially adolescent transformation. They always make some traditional move from youth to maturity, from being a novice in life to being an expert. They invariably begin as despised raw rookies and wind up as seasoned and respected pros."[41] The only other people with whom Keaton's characters would ever truly interact, the succession of love interests in his films, were typically little more than a series of human props. "Though the Keaton hero invariably loves a heroine, she generally remains a somewhat distant and dramatically underdeveloped figure," Moews writes. "She is used in a stylized and simplified way to provide a primary motivation for him, an initial impetus for his subsequent actions. . . . If the films are all love stories, the major focus still remains exclusively on the hero."[42] Classical technique would prove ill adapted to stories that cared hardly at all about people beyond the hero and perhaps too much about the world in which the action would occur. And so Keaton had to adapt classical technique to his demands.

But Keaton's manner of constructing films was not just a variation on the usual classical means of presenting a cinematic story; his technique would prove actively hostile to any kind of story that was not set at the level of the purely elemental. Placed inside a world of standard social relationships, where the enemies are flesh and blood more than they are objects and monuments, Keaton's visual and comic approach can look downright strange. *College* (Buster Keaton, 1927) is a case in point. A kind of penance paid after the spiraling budgets of *The General,* which proved hard to make back at the box office, *College* was Keaton's attempt to craft a film on a smaller, more intimate scale; the film was in fact an almost brazen attempt to copy, in its setting and its general story, Lloyd's success with *The Freshman.* But Keaton cannot adapt his slapstick or his camera to the standard narrative world of a film like Lloyd's. Unlike Lloyd, Keaton elides nothing: his narrative exists in service of his gags and not the other way around. In contrast to Lloyd's efficient football training sequence and his narratively driven climactic football game, we have in *College* prolonged sequences like Keaton's attempt to make the track team. For nearly ten minutes, the narrative all but stops as we watch Keaton attempt again and again to succeed at a series of track and field events: trying to perform a high jump with an uncooperative bar, knocking over the hurdles one after another in the hurdling event, being thrown in circles down the field by failing to release a shot put in time. All of the bodily contortion and humiliation that Lloyd avoided in his football training sequence—or that he offered only in discrete, narratively necessary quantities in his football game—is here in spades, filmed mostly in long shot with Keaton alone in the frame or with only a few other figures in the background for balance.

There is a narrative purpose to all this: the sequence helps to set up the film's comic finale, when Keaton will use his newfound track and field skills to rescue the heroine. Yet the sheer extent of the sequence borders on the counterproductive: what we need to know of Keaton's determination and abilities we learn in the first few minutes; everything else merely buries his character deeper under a weight of seeming physical incompetence that is hard to convincingly emerge from later in the film, all while the supposed need for social acceptance and love in his life—the driving force in Keaton's film as in Lloyd's—is further undermined by the extreme visual isolation of Keaton's long shots and sparse shot composition. There is a significant disconnect between the narrative drive of the film and Keaton's comic drive, both in its content and its visual style. And, indeed, it is this extreme level of disconnect that would prompt none other than Luis Buñuel to declare *College* to be an exemplary model of the surrealist vision, a world where logic and necessity have been cast aside and replaced by the improbable and the discontinuous such that Keaton can "give lessons to reality itself, with or without the technique of reality."[43] Left to his natural comic landscape—the grander the environment and the greater the physical object at its center, the better—Keaton can craft as clear and compelling a cinematic vision as any filmic craftsman; but forced into a world of classical narrative and visual logic, a box of social relationships with little outlet to the world of inanimate opposition, his style becomes confused and counterproductive. There is no shame in crafting a surrealist masterpiece, but it is not exactly what Keaton had in mind.

Keaton was able to master the camera—but only on his terms. The compromise he struck with classical technique was as far as his comic body and his comic vision would allow him to go; he had no room left for further negotiation. There is, not surprisingly then, a recurring strain of frustration with the camera, at least in its traditional classical mode, that recurs throughout Keaton's career. The negotiation between comedy and camera is a delicate one and it can easily go awry. Keaton gives us a glimpse of this process in what would be one of his greatest cinematic tricks: the collage of changing locations toward the beginning of *Sherlock Jr.* Here, Keaton's character steps into a movie screen, and he is utterly overwhelmed by the experience. Trying to engage with the action on screen, he finds himself immobilized by a series of changing backgrounds. Each time he tries to move—to walk, run, climb, or even swim to safety—the background environment changes and he is thwarted in his effort to progress or to escape. There might be no clearer image of a person subsumed by the world of film, the unlimited scope of the cinematic medium proving not only liberating but also limiting to the figure who cannot be in control of it. Thrust into a film with no means of affecting the organization of its images, Keaton's character is made impotent almost immediately.

The irony is that Keaton's point about the impossible situation of the comic figure left alone in the world of film is made through a bit of screencraft that showed an almost uncanny mastery of the cinematic form. In an age of limited trick photography, the ability to reproduce Keaton's image in exact replica across a series of different backgrounds, each shot far apart on location, seemed like an all but impossible feat of editing. When the film came out, cameramen and directors from across Hollywood would talk to one another about how many times they had seen it, trying to figure out how Keaton achieved his trick. Years later, Keaton revealed that it was not a trick of the camera at all but a careful symbiosis of camera and performer. Shooting one part of the sequence in a given location, Keaton would develop the film from that shoot and then place the last celluloid frame inside the viewfinder of the camera at the next location so that his cameraman could help him to achieve the exact same bodily posture as in the shot before. It is, in other words, a camera trick that relies on a body trick, the ability of Keaton the performer to exactly replicate his prior stances with the guidance of the cameraman. Keaton the director, unlike Keaton the character inside the film, could achieve unheard of tricks of cinematic imagery, but only when he was left to his own devices.

Keaton's *Sherlock Jr.* sequence was in part a kind of manifesto on the necessity of visual independence for cinematic comedy, but it was also a kind of tragic foreshadowing of the effective end of his silent career, one that would be repeated even more poignantly in a similarly purposed sequence in his last great silent feature, *The Cameraman* (Metro-Goldwyn-Mayer, 1928). The first film that Keaton made after an ill-fated move to Metro-Goldwyn-Mayer, *The Cameraman* tells the story of a newsreel photographer struggling to win a job with a major newsreel company. Offering to screen his first newsreel footage for the studio heads, Keaton's character is mortified to see that he has mishandled the camera and produced an embarrassing visual cacophony. He has double-exposed the film and the result is a sequence as surrealist as anything Buñuel might hope to see: ocean liners floating down the main street of the city, cars driving into the ocean, a city intersection that looks like something from an M. C. Escher drawing. The irony is that the cameraman's "mistake" is an incredibly complex piece of cinematic craftsmanship. The cameraman's work exceeds the visual imagination of the newsreel heads; needless to say, it is not what the producers are looking for. Keaton's character eventually does learn how to make films in the proper manner, managing to capture a newsworthy event with the proper attention to clear imagery and organization. But the irony of this success is that he has only shot half of the footage that he shows. The other half was shot by a pet monkey he acquired, who simply stood by the camera and cranked it. Keaton's character can master traditional film technique to be sure. But so, in the end, can a monkey. It is no tombstone with a hat, but it is hardly the stuff of a happy ending.

And it was, for Keaton, a sad harbinger of what was to come in his career. Among the great silent clowns, only Chaplin made it out of the silent era with his artistic independence and cheering fan base intact. Lloyd was befuddled by the transition to sound: he made talkies through the early 1930s but he realized before the end of the decade that his heyday had passed and chose to retire with dignity, living out his last decades in his luxurious estate and occasionally issuing compilations of the film sequences that once made him famous. But the end of Keaton's career was something else entirely: it was ended not by the transition to sound per se but quite literally by the avenging angel of classical technique. *The Cameraman* was Keaton's first film at Metro-Goldwyn-Mayer, and though it was monetarily successful the studio heads were horrified by Keaton's improvisational working method and lack of a clearly defined production plan. Irving Thalberg, one of the great producers of the era of classic Hollywood, saw to it that the license granted to Keaton with *The Cameraman* was never repeated. Thalberg demanded an end to improvisation-based story construction and took away Keaton's control over key production decisions, provisions that effectively ended Keaton's creative output. He never made another film that might truly be called his own or that could match the artistry of his earlier works, and he spent most of the rest of his career making low-budget shorts and serving as a gag writer for hire.

Keaton's work was literally stamped out by the gatekeepers of classical Hollywood style, figures who saw in his heterodox approach too great a deviation from the visual and narrative system that had for so long proved conducive to the studios' bottom line. In Keaton's own words on Thalberg:

> Like any man who must concern himself with mass production, he was seeking a pattern, a format. Slapstick comedy has a format, but it is hard to detect in its early stages unless you are one of those who can create it. The unexpected was our staple product, the unusual our object, and the unique was the ideal we were always hoping to achieve. Brilliant though he was, Irving Thalberg could not accept the way a comedian like me built his stories. . . . Our way of operating would have seemed hopelessly mad to him. But, believe me, it was the only way.[44]

Keaton, like Lloyd, had found in the 1920s an effective point of compromise between the slapstick tradition and the newly consolidated classical system. But in the end, classical style brooked no compromise: almost as soon as Keaton entered the formal studio system he was forced to change his filmmaking style to the point of unrecognizability. Only Chaplin maintained the stubbornness and, most crucially, the independence necessary to sustain his work in the face of classical style's ultimate ascendancy after the rise of sound. Or, put another way, only Chaplin had the freedom to continue to discover, to promote, and to refine a visual mode suited to his particular cinematic vision, one that might stand in contrast to classical technique long after his fellow silent clowns had seen their own careers end.

PART II

THE SILENT ERA

Chaplin's Filmmaking Technique

In an interview with the London *Times* in 1925, Charlie Chaplin predicted that the filmmaking industry, which had changed considerably since he first entered it in 1914, would continue to undergo substantial developments. "We're only just beginning," he told the interviewer in response to a criticism of the lack of "beauty" in the recent motion pictures put out by Hollywood. "Try to intimate to the public that our medium is new, that we are young at the game, and that we'd be grateful if those who can help to educate people to see this new sort of beauty—if it is beauty—would do so. . . . We can't make progress unless we get credit for trying. . . . Give us credit, and we hope to do better."[1] Chaplin had no way of knowing how prescient his words would be: the cinema was young, technologically speaking, and with the coming of synchronized sound in 1927, Hollywood would indeed be forever transformed. But technological change was not what Chaplin had in mind. "People blather of 'talking films,'" he told the interviewer, but "the screen we have is quite enough."[2] The change he predicted was stylistic, concerned with how filmmakers might order, compose, and present the world: what he calls in the interview the "architecture-in-motion" of the screen.[3] In this regard, Chaplin could hardly have been more mistaken. While specific filmmaking techniques might alter and filmmakers' individual styles would develop and evolve, the fundamental "architecture" of what Tom Gunning calls film's "system of narrative integration"—the core set of assumptions as to how narrative film should organize and interpret its material—was well in place by the time of Chaplin's interview.[4] Coalesced into the classical system of filmmaking, these assumptions retained a kind of aesthetic hegemony in the film industry for decades, still to this day defining what David Bordwell calls a basic series of "extrinsic norms" that "have remained in force since 1917."[5] Chaplin made his greatest shorts and silent features not during a moment of stylistic indeterminacy, but during the period of the classical system's great ascendancy, a reign that would prove remarkably resistant to transformation. More than fifty years after Chaplin's interview, Stanley Cavell would wonder at the sheer persistence and stability of basic filmmaking technique, asking "how the movie for so long could have remained traditional."[6]

Chaplin can be forgiven for thinking that the evolution of filmic style might still be far from completion, for its development had largely left him aside. Chaplin would clearly rather play an as-yet-unacknowledged antithesis to the dominant thesis of classical style, both still awaiting their final synthesis, than accept the status that many critics had already assigned him: an outlier to the classical system. The view that Chaplin was, for all of his performative gifts, at best a merely serviceable director—and at worst an unoriginal, untalented, or even lazy one—emerged early, one of the few points of discord in the torrent of critical praise that accompanied his rise to fame.[7] It was, to be sure, far from a universal criticism in the early stages of his career. Not only his comedy but also his filmmaking ability more generally was often lauded by major critical outlets in their reviews throughout the 1910s and 1920s. In 1923 *Photoplay* declared him "one of the greatest of all directors," and as late as 1932 Alfred H. Barr Jr., the first director of New York's Museum of Modern Art, specifically credited "Chaplin (as director)" alongside such luminaries as Sergei Eisenstein and Vsevolod Pudovkin in helping to create "the only great art peculiar to the twentieth century."[8] But censure of Chaplin's directing style (along with, separately, criticism of the violence and amorality in his earliest shorts) was one of the only persistent points of disapproval in early writings on his work. As early as 1919, in an article titled "Is the Charlie Chaplin Vogue Passing?" *Theatre Magazine* declared Chaplin a "phenomenally successful comedian" but doubted his filmmaking abilities and "strenuously object[ed] to incompetent persons styling Charles Chaplin a great artist, when he's nothing of the sort."[9] In 1934 George Jean Nathan declared Chaplin merely a "competent but certainly not great" director and responded to the claim that Chaplin was a genius with one word: "bosh."[10]

But it wasn't just individual critics who were hostile to his filmic style. Many of the most important early attempts at formulating a theory of film took no note of Chaplin's technique, revolving, instead, around the same stylistic approaches—largely centered on editing and cinematography—that have occupied generations of film theorists since, constituting what Bordwell calls, with deliberate capital letters, the "Standard Version of stylistic history."[11] As he describes it:

> In cinematography and editing many writers thought they had found
> the answer to the problem of defining film as a distinct art. For these

techniques unmistakably mediated between what was put in front of the lens and what the viewer eventually saw. They shaped and stylized photographed reality in order to create an artistic effect. No wonder that, confronted with the virtuosic camera movements and editing of the 1920s canon, many observers believed that the silent cinema had finally begun to display its full creative possibilities.[12]

Those possibilities, as Bordwell makes clear, were specifically construed as techniques of the camera and the editing knife that inevitably rendered Chaplin as an "'uncinematic' director" to many early theorists for his notably restrained use of both.[13] The most famous such theorist, of course, was Eisenstein, who in the early iterations of his theory of montage took D. W. Griffith as his model and chastened those who used a different approach. "There is no such thing as cinema without cinematography . . . [and] cinematography is, first and foremost, montage," he declared in 1929.[14] But Eisenstein was not alone. All the major figures of what might be considered the first great generation of film theorists in the 1920s and 1930s—Jean Epstein, Vsevolod Pudovkin, Rudolf Arnheim, Béla Balázs—centered their analyses on stylistic elements and techniques that were simply not central to Chaplin's toolbox. Editing (in particular montage) and the close-up were the typical points to which they returned again and again in their writing, searching for what Jean Mitry calls those "fundamental principles" of the art that would be enough to "explain the whole of cinema."[15]

Chaplin simply did not fit into such systems. Insofar as his filmic technique was considered by critics and theorists, it was typically deemed, in his own words from his 1964 autobiography, "old-fashioned."[16] But "old-fashioned," frequent as the charge was, does not fully capture the degree of Chaplin's outdatedness. It is not just that Chaplin's technique is stodgy; it is that it seems to participate in a system antecedent to the development of classical style, one that takes its methods and assumptions from a time before filmmakers supposedly came to understand the potential of the new medium—a time of rough experimentation and aesthetic infancy. Indeed, Arnheim and Balázs were both great admirers of Chaplin's films, but to reconcile their attraction to his work with their theoretical formulations on the nature of cinematic language they essentially had to exempt him from the modern history of film. Arnheim links Chaplin to "a film style before the 'discovery' of the camera and montage" and considers him—though the two were contemporaries—as though he were a specimen from the past.[17] Balázs likewise gives Chaplin a kind of aesthetic pass for first developing as a filmmaker "*before* the specific new method of film art and the new form-language of the film was developed."[18] Wes Gehring labels these explanations a kind of "forgiven primitivism," but if they ultimately render Chaplin unevolved they did not mean to do so in disparagement to his achievements.[19] Arnheim and Balázs could find no other way to categorize a body of work that seemed so uninterested in the core tenets of filmmaking technique that came to dominate the industry by the 1920s.

Chaplin nonetheless bristled at such charges as insults to his artistry. "I am surprised that some critics say that my camera technique is old-fashioned, that I have not kept up with the times," he writes in his autobiography. "What times? My technique is the outcome of thinking for myself, of my own logic and approach; it is not borrowed from what others are doing. If in art one must keep up with the times, then Rembrandt would be a back number compared to Van Gogh."[20] And he was not without his defenders. One of the most eloquent was fellow screen comedian Max Linder, who could perhaps bring a more practical perspective to the issue than the typical film critic or theorist. Linder, an early star of the Pathé slapstick films, is largely credited today with being the first of the great slapstick artists, and to Chaplin's mind he was a venerable predecessor: when Linder visited Hollywood for the first time in 1917, Chaplin invited him to his studios and presented him with a photograph inscribed "To the one and only Max, The Professor, From his Disciple Charlie Chaplin."[21] In Linder's perspective, the tendency of critics to praise Chaplin's performative abilities while at the same time discrediting his directorial capacities was an attempt to sustain an unworkable contradiction. The two matters were for Linder inseparable, and it was Chaplin's skill behind the camera that distinguished him from the throngs of imitators who sought to replicate his trademark performances in everything from street-corner busking to B-grade slapstick reels.[22] Chaplin's performative gifts, Linder notes, "have to be translated into this special language of the screen, the effects reduced to their elements, their range accurately estimated, their exposition set out by careful stages. The imitators of Chaplin succeed to perfection in executing the same tricks as he does, but why do they not provoke the same laughter? Let the scoffers try a few of these 'capers' before the camera lens. They will soon see if one is as good as another."[23] In Linder's estimation, Chaplin's artistry relied absolutely on the camera. But what is made clear by Linder's brief list of supposedly filmic elements in Chaplin's work—"the effects reduced to their elements, their range accurately estimated, their exposition set out by careful stages"—is that Chaplin did not rely on the camera in the same manner as classical style would dictate. Linder's perspective is that of a man whose own career peaked before Chaplin's, in the early 1910s when elements of what would become classical style existed but were far from dominant. Chaplin's ascendancy in the later 1910s and into the 1920s can obscure how tied he is to that same world of early film that claims Linder: the degree to which he was not so much "old-fashioned" as simply out of time, come to maturity in an industry that had wholly changed from the one in which he first learned how to make films. Chaplin first learned his craft in a genre (slapstick), in a studio (Keystone), and in a moment (the "transitionary phase") when classical technique was anything but given.[24] That his filmmaking would not conform to a series of techniques that crystallized after he had already become a star is perhaps not surprising.[25]

Chaplin's attitude toward the evolution of filmic style in his *Times* interview can be viewed as both a product of this condition and a response to charges of primitivism in his work; it is not so much his particular brand of filmmaking that is primitive, he says, as the whole business of filmmaking itself, classical and preclassical technique alike. Chaplin refuses to acknowledge that the tenets of the classical style might actually have a lock on what it means to properly make a film. Hence his later comparison in his autobiography to Rembrandt and Van Gogh: art evolves, finds new approaches to basic concerns and new ways of representing and refining the same set of properties. If early film theorists like Arnheim regarded the development of classical technique and its focus on cinematography and editing as a fundamental transformation of the medium, akin to the introduction of perspective in Western art, Chaplin insisted it was more like the movement between the Dutch golden age and the postimpressionist era—a significant transformation, to be sure, but one that was ultimately based in style and aesthetic choice and had nothing to do with a sudden discovery of fundamental principles or foundational properties. It is an important point. Regardless of how fundamental a change it might ultimately represent, what would become known as classical technique was at bottom a series of particular responses to specific artistic problems, largely having to do with the issue of conveying narrative. Thus, as much as it was a "discovery" of the medium, to use Arnheim's term, it was also a catalog of answers on how to handle issues like clarity, complexity, length, and a host of other narrative matters. It was, in Thompson's description, a series of "guidelines, which had reached the status of rules" and which in turn would later become seen as "basic principles."[26]

Like any filmmaker, Chaplin confronted those same problems of narrative clarity and stylistic choice. But he developed different solutions from those laid out in the classical "guidelines." Against critics who charged him with being uninterested in the properties of film as such, Chaplin was always adamant in his fidelity to the medium. He compares himself in his autobiography to Eisenstein and Griffith, and he expounds there on his commitment to the basic "tools of the trade" and the medium's "technical essentials."[27] He is committed to film itself, he insists, but not to what he calls the "arid dogma" that eventually grew up around specific film techniques.[28] He demands as his artistic right a "complete freedom to do the unorthodox" and to "use his own art sense about dramatic effects."[29] He insists, in other words, that his filmmaking style relies as absolutely on the camera as anything that Eisenstein or Griffith might do—just not on the specific techniques of the camera that classical style would privilege and ultimately elevate to dogma. Or, put another way, what some critics saw as an absence in his stylistic approach was actually a sign of the presence of something else: a different filmic toolbox, a new set of aesthetic assumptions, an alternate way of making films. Insofar as there is a system of filmmaking that stands apart from the classical paradigm, Chaplin stands as perhaps its first great expression, hidden in plain sight.

Chaplin's Relation to Narrative

Chaplin's conflict with classical technique did not stem from any fundamentally different position over the place of narrative in film. Chaplin was in fact arguably more aligned with the drive for using film as, in Gunning's words, an "expression of characterization and story" that motivated a classical pioneer like Griffith than were many of his slapstick cohorts.[30] As the 1915 series of *Photoplay* articles on Chaplin's nascent career makes clear, he was in his own day credited with single-handedly bringing a stronger focus on narrative into the slapstick tradition by insisting that "comedy should be more subtle and have more real story."[31] At the height of his popularity in the 1920s, Chaplin himself told an interviewer from *Motion Picture Magazine* that he hoped his pictures would influence Hollywood filmmaking to become even more narratively driven. "The next course that pictures will take is narrative," he said, contrasting the intertwining of stories and "character studies" in his own work—what Chaplin means by the term narrative here—to the tightly crafted but empty scenarios that he felt were worn "threadbare" by Hollywood.[32]

This is not, of course, the standard slapstick position. Classic Harold Lloyd and Buster Keaton films like *Safety Last* or *The General* are many things, but they are not anything we might call a character study. The difference in narrative approach is significant, and it can easily be seen in the very different nature of Chaplin's imagery as compared to other slapstick masters. The most famous images created by Lloyd or Keaton contain a kind of immediate iconic status that can be conveyed in a still frame—Lloyd dangling from a skyscraper, Keaton standing astride a thundering locomotive. The significance of these daredevil gag-images is immediately apparent, whatever other questions they may raise. But it is in fact very difficult to isolate the same kind of image from any of Chaplin's films. There are, to be sure, classic depictions of the Tramp wandering alone down an empty road, but this relies mostly on the status that the Tramp himself has attained over time in the culture. To convey the essence of an actual comic sequence from one of Chaplin's films in a single isolated image is remarkably difficult. More than encapsulating an isolatable gag, still images from Chaplin's films tend to press us with a series of questions that can be answered only in motion: Who is this figure? What is his relationship to the people and objects around him? What is he trying to get? What is he trying to avoid? They present us, that is, with questions of narrative—of the figure in sequence rather than stasis. To a far greater degree than most other slapstick clowns (Lloyd in his highly narrative romantic phase being the great exception), Chaplin's comedy unfolds not in a series of individuated comic set-pieces but in a stream of ongoing movements and interactions—with objects, with other figures, with the world around him. Rarely is Chaplin's comic persona trying to *do* something as monumental as those feats accomplished in the worlds of Lloyd, Keaton, or the classic Keystones—climb a building, build a house, commandeer a train, crash a car. The universe of these figures is one in which the action to be accomplished quite often overshadows the goal to be achieved; figures like Lloyd and Keaton must surmount (or simply survive) the extraordinary to reach what are often relatively modest narrative goals—the hand of a nondescript sweetheart perhaps. For Chaplin, the task hardly ever eclipses the objective. His actions are frequently modest—perform a dance, hold down a job, make a meal—while his goals are often outsized: cure the girl, protect the child, save himself from starvation. The narrative interest in Chaplin's work typically comes less from an isolatable visual curiosity about what he must *do* than from a continuous emotional concern about what he must *get*. His slapstick is often inseparable from his narratives.

This tendency in Chaplin's filmmaking is a product of his training in the pantomime tradition of the British music hall, one of the most narrative-driven subsets of variety theater comedy. Compared to the only minimally motivated comedy of Buster Keaton's act with the Three Keatons, where the smallest pretense for a fight unleashed a torrent of physical acrobatics and body gags, the typical pantomime sequence relied on a kind of micronarrative that ran throughout the routine. The act that made Chaplin's name as a stage performer in one of Fred Karno's traveling comedy troupes is a case in point. Chaplin first appeared on American stages in a touring production of *A Night in an English Music Hall* (or *Mumming Birds,* when it played in Europe), where he played the part of the "Inebriated Swell," a drunken patron trying to take his place in a theater box. It is, in one sense, just a sequence of physical gags like anything the Three Keatons might perform: Chaplin takes off one of his gloves and hands it to the usher as a tip; he tries to take off the same glove again by pulling on his bare fingers; he tries to light his cigarette on a lightbulb in his box, thinking it is a gaslight; he tries to get a light from a patron in another box but tumbles down onto the stage instead; he becomes a nuisance to the show-within-a-show, chasing bad performers off the stage and trying to seduce the pretty ones. A battery of gags, to be sure, but marked by a greater consideration of protonarrative elements than the trademark routines of a comic acrobat like Keaton. Chaplin's stage persona is not just any figure fighting and tumbling onstage. This is an upper-class man who came to the theater drunk—someone with a specific social status, with an implied past that predates the appearance onstage (getting drunk) and, most important, a defined objective that super-sedes and organizes the individual gags: he wants to enjoy a night out at the theater. In the logic of the routine, Chaplin's character does not exist simply to go through physical gags without context. Rather, he wants to perform the normal actions of going to the theater in a dignified fashion (taking his seat, lighting his cigarette, reacting to the players on the stage), he is impaired by his drunkenness, and the gags result as he attempts to reconcile his condition with his goals. It is hardly the stuff of great storytelling, but neither is it a sequence of gags for their own sake. The gags here are subordinated and made intrinsic to a micronarrative that organizes and justifies their deployment.

This sense of the gag as subordinate to character and objective—to the ru-diments of story—would stay with Chaplin throughout his filmic career, even in what are arguably his least narrative works. *One A.M.* (Mutual, 1916), for instance, is essentially an explosion of his old Karno routine: for nearly thirty minutes, Chaplin works alone, playing a hopeless drunk trying desperately to get into his house and into bed. It is as close to a pure gag-reel as Chaplin would ever come: he surfs along a slippery throw rug, gets caught on top of a spinning table, climbs and falls back down the stairs some ten different times, does battle with an intractable Murphy bed. But as in the Karno routine, each of these individual gags exists only as an expression of the conflict between Chaplin's inebriated state and his basic desire to get to bed, the smallest of nar-rative quests. Compared to other gag-heavy shorts from similar points in the careers of Keaton and Lloyd, the degree of Chaplin's commitment to the narra-tive elements of character and objective stands in stark relief. In *The Balloonatic* (Buster Keaton, 1923), for instance, Keaton crafts an exceedingly peripatetic work: a character of indeterminate social status and background spends a day at the amusement park, rides a hot air balloon, lands in the wilderness, and at-tempts to live in the forest, undergoing a series of adventures there. The short includes some classic gags—Keaton dangling from a hot air balloon, fighting a black bear, falling from a waterfall—but as a story it seems like a deliberate subversion of narrative. Keaton's character reacts to events but never exhibits any kind of explicit drive, and the short itself wanders into a kind of narrative wilderness to parallel its central character's predicament. In a different vein, Lloyd's *Never Weaken* utterly breaks down when it comes time to balance narrative and slapstick gags. Typical of his comedic approach, Lloyd's comic figure is highly embedded in a specific narrative scenario far more elaborate than Chaplin's *One A.M.* drunk: he is a young professional trying to win the heart of the girl in the office next door. Yet the short's central comic sequence is almost entirely disconnected from this narrative setup. Blindfolding himself in a suicide attempt after thinking that the girl has betrayed him, Lloyd is unaware as a construction beam from the building site across the street comes in through his window and lifts him into the air. Thereafter, the short revolves around Lloyd trying to get down from the high-rise construction platform. The narrative serves as a springboard to the slapstick instead of as a part of an inseparable whole. Linked only by the thread of the blindfold itself, narrative and slapstick are contiguous but unconnected. It would take Lloyd and Keaton time to master the kind of intrinsic connection of narrative and gag that Chaplin showed from the very beginning of his career; far more frequently than Chaplin they would chafe at the linkage.

Yet, while Chaplin's contention with classical technique did not stem from a fundamental discomfort with narrative itself (as was the case with his fellow slapstick filmmakers), storytelling was still a stylistic sticking point for him. In the end, the fundamental question over which Chaplin diverged from the tenets of classical style had little to do with *whether* one should convey narrative within the fictive film and everything to do with *how* one should convey it. It is far more than a technical concern. Indeed, the question of how one conveys narrative in film is, in Gunning's analysis, the basic problem over which classical technique originally emerges. "The style of narrativity" that is first seen with Griffith, Gunning writes, was designed to address a problem that other filmic styles were not able to surmount: "the creation of a complete and coherent dramatic whole, founded . . . on characterization and comprehensible to the audience even in a nonverbal presentation."[33] Or, put in more practical terms, it is the problem of *Those Awful Hats,* where the attempt to depict the interior of a rowdy nickelodeon results in utter narrative confusion. To present only a sequence of isolated incidents in the nickelodeon hall is to miss one of the aesthetic goals of the short: a total demonstration of the ebullient chaos that is the modern movie hall. But to present the hall's activities all at once seems to sacrifice the ability to tell a story with any kind of direction and coherence: we are left unable to isolate the narratively important moments of chaos—the disruption caused by the ladies with those awful hats—from the cacophony of movement all around them. Griffith's ultimate solution, and the solution around which the film industry would eventually reorient itself, was

to sacrifice the unity of space of that full hall and to use the camera—a mechanism external to the actual content of the film—to narrate that content to us:
to direct our attention within the space first to one element, then to another,
building over time a sequence for us to follow.

Griffith's solution is an end run around the problems of filmic space, a declaration that the minimally edited, static camera, shot-as-scene constructions of
unbroken space from which narrative film emerged were incapable of the kind
of sequencing and development that narrative ultimately required, let alone
the level of characterization and individuation that might be possible with his
technique. Chaplin's solution, equal parts elegant and radical, is to be more
deliberate about the composition of that space. It is a version of what Bordwell
calls the "long-take, 'scenic' method" of film construction that predominated
in much of early cinema and that allowed filmmakers to create visual emphasis
by developing visual schemes and staging practices within the mise-en-scène,
a forerunner to later cinema's practices of "staging in depth."[34] Largely alone
among the major filmmakers operating in Hollywood during the moment of
classical consolidation, Chaplin would pursue this kind of composition within
the frame as his primary working method. Though there are multiple aspects
to Chaplin's differentiation from classical presumptions, this is at bottom the
fundamental point of departure between his approach and the classical style:
a conviction that, to appropriate a term from Siegfried Kracauer, unbroken
filmic space can be redeemed, that it can be made capable of complex narrative
without the active intervention of the camera.

HARNESSING SPACE TO NARRATIVE ENDS:
DIRECTION AND ATTENTION IN CHAPLIN'S FRAME

Chaplin's approach relies on a highly purposeful arrangement of the filmed
space itself. Of course, all competent filmmakers arrange and compose the
spaces that they capture, but arguably no filmmaker before Chaplin and few
since have arranged their filmed spaces with such painstaking attention to the
demands of storytelling. The result is that there is almost no such thing as
undifferentiated space in a Chaplin shot. The space itself is organized according to narrative dictates. That is to say, it is typically broken into a series of
separate units such that the progress of figures on screen through those units
corresponds to the narrative direction we are meant to follow. In this way, the
space literally arranges itself for us the way the camera might try to arrange it
in a more typically classical construction.

Chaplin's long shots of tenement life in his early short *Easy Street* (Mutual,
1917) exemplify this approach. In one sequence, a neighborhood ruffian leads

an unruly mob of slum dwellers in targeting and beating up the police officers trying to keep peace in the neighborhood. It is the kind of raucous large-
crowd sequence that seems impossible to parse narratively using a preclassical
shot-as-scene construction—the problem of *Those Awful Hats* writ large.[35] But
Chaplin deliberately organizes the mise-en-scène to aid us in following the sequence, dividing the filmed street space into an implied nine-part grid. Along
the front-back axis of the frame he clearly demarcates the three planes of space,
using a carefully arranged sequence of shadows cast by the buildings to separate the background, middle ground, and foreground, each plane in the shot
outlined in alternating stripes of sunlight and darkness; a prominent lamppost
even emphasizes the division of middle ground and background, separating
out the middle ground and foreground as the main playing areas of the frame.
Without conscious effort, the viewer's eye can easily determine which figures
stand in close proximity to the camera, which stand farther away, and which
stand in the background. In addition to this clear delineation of planes, Chaplin marks another layer of organization along the left-right axis of the frame.
Two raised sidewalks flank the leftmost and rightmost limits of the shot, with
a lowered street running through the middle. At any given point in the sequence, viewers can immediately tell where a figure stands within this system:
back-center, middle-left, front-right, and so on. (As an added level of demarcation, Chaplin marks off the top of the playable space with clotheslines that
obscure the upper reaches of the frame and direct our attention downward.)

As the scene unfolds, Chaplin ensures that the figure of narrative focus—
the neighborhood ruffian—always remains in the most conspicuous position
in this system relative to the other characters when his actions are meant to be
watched. At the start of the scene he is placed in the foremost plane of space
compared to the other figures in the shot, assaulting a police officer while the
rest of the crowd fights among themselves in the street behind him. A few moments later, he decides to chase down a new police officer and begins to trace
the perimeter of playable space: moving first down the raised left axis, disappearing behind the crowd in the street, reappearing again on the right axis,
and finally overtaking his prey in the foremost plane of the frame. Only when
the ruffian disappears behind the crowd does he vacate the most visible position in the shot relative to the other figures, allowing us to easily understand
when we are meant to keep our focus on his pursuit and when we should look
back at the crowd still tussling in the center of the frame. When toward the
end of the scene the ruffian corners his man, Chaplin places the confrontation
along the leftmost axis of the frame in the same middle plane as the brawling
crowd with no one in the foreground space. Positioned on the raised sidewalk
above the other figures in the street, with no one visible on the opposite raised

sidewalk to counterbalance his position, the ruffian naturally draws our eye. Chaplin cuts within the sequence, but he does so only sparingly, beginning with an extreme long shot that establishes the total filmic terrain and cutting to a closer long shot that maintains the same layout and spatial arrangements. Throughout the sequence, he also occasionally cuts back to the police at their headquarters, recovering from the beatings that they've taken in the streets. Yet such jumps serve for inflection and interest only—they hold no clarifying or directive function. All of the information that we need to know about the street brawl is conveyed through Chaplin's careful staging in the frame. Indeed, when Chaplin changes the shot of the street in a slightly later sequence that has a closer framing, he employs a similar compositional arrangement: the raised sidewalks remain visible and now within the tighter playing space two lampposts alone can demarcate the separation points of foreground, middle ground, and background. Without any need for continuous cutting or other intrusive aspects of analytical technique, Chaplin ensures that there is never any question as to where our attention within the frame should be focused even as the scene descends into mayhem.

Of course, the organization of landscape in *Easy Street* is particularly convenient; rarely are tenement streets so well arranged. *Easy Street* is visually outlined with a kind of cartoonish simplicity, a fact acknowledged by a humorous series of shots that cap the brawling sequence where the ruffian stands alone in the center of the frame and relates to entire masses of slum dwellers as a kind of single, panicked collective—faking first in one direction to make everyone to the right of the frame run away in unison, then faking left to make everyone on that side flee together as well. Here, Chaplin seems to be calling attention to the highly schematic way in which he has organized the visual space of the film and divided the filmic universe between central and background characters: the crowd might as well be treated en masse narratively as well as visually. But it is a thoughtful simplicity, a deliberate visual counterpoint to and amelioration of a narrative world that is far darker and less cartoonish than its visual organization implies, involving at various points scenes of vicious spousal abuse, inner-city lawlessness, and on-screen heroin use. (In one of the more disturbing moments of the film, Chaplin's otherwise defenseless Tramp even defeats the neighborhood ruffian by poisoning him with gas from a broken streetlight.)

But Chaplin proved equally capable of far more subtle visual systems when they might better serve the aesthetic of the film. *The Rink* (Mutual, 1916) is a case in point. The central set-piece of the short, a crowded skating rink, seems on the surface a poor environment for directing narrative attention, as it is marked by the endless circles of a seemingly undifferentiated crowd of skaters.

Central scenes of confrontation are handled easily enough, of course. When Chaplin's Tramp begins to challenge Eric Campbell's obnoxious rink patron, the other skaters retreat to the background plane against the edges of the rink while Chaplin and Campbell move to the center foreground space, an area clearly marked by the edges of a large doorway in the background of the frame. But within his long shots of the rink Chaplin also handles narrative business more complicated than a fight. Prior to the confrontation, he must establish that Campbell has bothered Edna Purviance's skater, who then turns to the Tramp for help. Rather than cut to medium shots or close-ups of these more subtle confrontations, Chaplin frames them in long shot with the other patrons still busily circling the rink. Chaplin isolates the narratively important interactions visually within the frame by placing a long pole in the bottom left corner of the shot, diegetically construed as a rod for skittish skaters to grab onto for support but also serving double duty as a visual magnet for the attention of the film's viewers. Campbell is a poor skater, and his interactions with Purviance all happen as he grabs onto this eye-catching pole for support. Even as the other skaters continue to circle around the rink, our eyes are naturally drawn to these figures clutching to the pole in the bottom left of the frame. In contrast to the extreme symmetry of the *Easy Street* streetscape, Chaplin uses a strategic asymmetry in the rink to draw our eye to a specific location and then places the pivotal action of the scene neatly in the same spot to which our eyes are already attracted.

This kind of narrative organization of space is a key technique for taming crowd scenes, but it holds a much broader and more ubiquitous place in Chaplin's filmmaking style than that, helping even to organize intimate sequences that involve only two characters. The first meeting between the Tramp and Purviance's kidnapped girl in *The Vagabond* (Mutual, 1916) is a pertinent example. Though they are the only two figures in the shot, Chaplin here uses the same nine-point spatial organization as in the crowd sequences of *Easy Street,* even if it is much more subtly masked within the scene. A fence marks the backmost plane of playable space on the screen, reducing the area of focus for the viewer while allowing the scene to retain the depth of an open field behind the fence. A large water bucket in the back right of the playable space marks out the same backmost plane as well as the right side of the coordinate space, while a laundry basin in the front left of the frame marks out the foreground plane and the left side of the coordinate space. The empty space between the edges of these two set-pieces defines the center axis of the frame.

Deciding to play his violin for Purviance, Chaplin proceeds to the center of the frame into the position at the middle of the implied grid. Purviance is sitting in the foremost left segment, closer to the camera than Chaplin but

seated and set to the side. Each figure occupies a unique and defined portion
of the space, and while Chaplin's is the more conspicuous position it is only
barely so—Purviance is closer to the camera. Thus, while we focus primarily
on Chaplin's violin playing in the center of the frame, our attention occasionally vacillates to Purviance's reactions in the foreground plane. There is a pull
for dominance between their two spatial positions in the shot, one that reinforces the thematics of the sequence. Chaplin is meant to be the center of
attention—he is the free artist giving us a virtuosic performance on the violin,
she is a prisoner forced to do laundry—but Purviance has a subtle pull on him
and us; he will duly fall in love with her in a matter of minutes. Indeed, when
Chaplin's violin performance concludes he tumbles backward into the water
bucket in the back right section of the frame. His position has become a visual
corollary to hers—he seated in the back right while she is seated in the front
left—and in this newfound equivalency it is she who has more importance.
The sudden spatial rebalancing foretells a sudden narrative shift: almost immediately he will seek to equalize their social status, determining to release
her from the gypsies and give her the freedom that he himself possesses. Just
as she holds a slight dominance within the frame, it is she who will be in the
slightly more dominant position in this new relationship when Chaplin tries
to woo her as the object of his affections (with only limited success) after they
have reached safety. More than just clarifying the narrative, Chaplin's spatial
arrangements here serve to emphasize and orient the thematic direction of the
film as well.

Where to Place the Camera: Space, Style, and Theme

Chaplin reflected on the spatial aspects of his composition in his interview
with the *Times,* where he elegantly contrasts filmmaking to the demands of
the theater that he knew so well: "On the stage we already have a perfect three
dimensions. Why, we lose half our quality if we lose our limitations! Motion,
two planes, and a suggestion of depth: that is our chaos from which we will
fashion our universe."[36] It is more than a flippant distinction—three dimensions versus two—for unlike what is viewed in the theater, in the cinematic image issues like depth are only illusory and must be carefully constructed by the
way in which the filmed space is presented. Chaplin's three-dimensional organization of space is designed therefore only for the two-dimensional world of
the screen, not the three-dimensional world of the stage. As a consequence,
Chaplin feels able to sum up much of his visual technique in a single decision:
where to place the camera. It is not a minor point, for in Chaplin's universe it is

this decision that determines everything else about the arrangement of a shot and the action that happens within it—how the space is divided, how objects are placed, where people move. In Chaplin's words, "the placing of a camera . . . was the basis of cinematic style. If the camera is a little too near, or too far, it can enhance or spoil an effect. . . . Placement of camera is cinematic inflection."[37] Chaplin's extreme attention to the whereabouts of his camera denotes just how connected he was to it, even if his use of it substantially differed from the prescriptions of classical technique.

Chaplin's visual style is a manner of filmmaking that is absolutely concerned with the camera. In fact, his technique of dividing the filmic space within a shot and basing everything else on this division is an extreme extrapolation from one of the earliest cinematic techniques for dealing with narrative development in the shot-as-scene constructions of preclassical film—the alignment of separate narrative points with separate filmic spaces. As a style, it parallels the working method of early narrative films like Griffith's *The Sealed Room* or the Kalem Company's 1907 *Ben Hur,* where a movement between clearly defined (and usually contiguous) spaces was used diegetically to marry narrative development and spatial organization.[38] For obvious reasons, such films in their most primitive form can be oppressively stilted, forced to tell their narratives in broad, physically separated sections with very little narrative development happening within a single space. But Chaplin's approach, though it is dispositionally aligned with this preclassical form of arrangement, is infinitely more refined. His innovation is to transpose the overly obvious separation of rooms into the highly subtle separation of sections within a single filmed space, allowing the narrative to progress through distinct spaces that help to carry it along without forcing a change of scene. In Chaplin's compositional scheme, any space can be narratively tamed by an arrangement into parts, and those parts can be dealt with in sequence as a way of guiding us through the progression of the story itself.

Chaplin elevates this form of composition into an intricate and highly aestheticized visual style, establishing motifs of space where other directors might establish a motif of cinematography. This tendency is evident even in the first of Chaplin's Mutual shorts, *The Floorwalker* (1916), a film which helps mark his transition from the more Sennett-styled work of his Keystone and Essanay shorts into something closer to his mature works. Set in a large department store, the film is typical Chaplin in its central theme: a study of the conflict between the freedom of the outcast and the responsibility of socialized man, here rendered spatially in a series of visual patterns. After an accidental run-in, Chaplin's Tramp switches places with a store employee who looks remarkably like him. The employee has embezzled money from the store and needs a way out of his identity. The Tramp, who has been falsely accused of stealing from the store, is trying to avoid the undercover detective who wants to arrest him; he needs a way into the socially acceptable world of commerce and employment. (In the language of the film's intertitle when the two decide to switch places, "You need a job—I need a change.")[39] Chaplin's Tramp escapes "in" to the world of the store while the store's floorwalker escapes "out" of that world. Or, viewed in a different metaphor of movement, the Tramp moves socially "up" to the level of the respectable floorwalker—literalized in the trip up the escalator that takes him to the management offices—while the floorwalker moves "down" to the level of the indigent Tramp—epitomized in his journey down in the store's elevator to escape from the building. But the irony of the exchange is that spatial and social movements like in and out and up and down ultimately matter not at all in the world of the film. No matter which direction the Tramp goes, he is always boxed in. Visually, the film is a triumph of spatial organization as an expression of theme.

The entirety of *The Floorwalker* takes place in a department store that is spatially divided into a series of boxes. The cavernous two-level main hall of the store (itself a large rectangle) is subdivided by the camera into four equal-sized rectangular shots—top left, top right, bottom right, and bottom left—and is only ever shown in one of these four perspectives. It is a box built of boxes. To the left of the main hall is another rectangular room, to the right another still. One room sells luggage—rows and rows of rectangular trunks and suitcases; the other sells shoes—walls covered from floor to ceiling with equal-sized rectangular shoeboxes. A large elevator at the right of the main hall, on the same side as the shoe room, is shaped like a visual analog to the luggage trunks; an escalator at the left of the main hall, on the side of the luggage room, looks from afar like a series of stacked shoeboxes. On the upper, management level, a long rectangular balcony leads to two more right-angled rooms: an antechamber and an executive office, a collection of desks and tables recessing into the inner reaches of the store. Not only has Chaplin subdivided the space of the gargantuan department store, but he has also turned it into an incessant, M. C. Escher–like regression of boxes, cubes, and rectangles.

This compositional scheme is three things at once: an effective organizational system—a way of taming the large, confusing space of the department store into narratively workable subsections; a kind of parody (through excess) of the room-to-room constructions of early narrative film, where all the world was divided into one rectangular interior space after another; and an effective thematic visual motif, the Tramp's attempts to become incorporated into the realm of respectable commerce leading him to a world in which he is literally "boxed in" and seemingly cannot escape. Pursued by the store manager, who thinks the Tramp is the floorwalker who betrayed him, Chaplin never does make it out of the store: the short ends with him trapped in the elevator, merely moving from one level of boxes to another. Even the real floorwalker never manages to escape: he is arrested on the way out of the store by the detective looking for the Tramp, dragged off to his own confined future in a jail cell. It is highly effective as slapstick comedy, but it is also a stylistic triumph: a declaration that filmic space, properly organized, can be as much the origin point of thematics as the camera itself. What other directors might try to achieve cinematographically, Chaplin achieves through his diegetic construction of an otherwise uninflected space.

An even more sophisticated recurring spatial motif occurs in *The Vaga-bond*. Chaplin opens this short with a startling visual arrangement: the Tramp proceeds away from the camera and tucks himself into the background plane of the shot at the far left of the frame—it is a space that lies at the end of a long wall which begins in a corner close to the camera and stretches back from the foreground. Chaplin is a traveling violin player, and as he sets up to play his instrument in the far background, a brass band takes up residence around the corner from him in the foreground of the frame. No one inside the saloon can hear his music. It is an effective visual demonstration of the Tramp's outsider status—he is both at a distance from and around the corner from the main action—but the strength of the arrangement is amplified by the way in which it becomes a dominant motif of the film. In the very next scene, we see an echo of this visual arrangement: we are inside an opulent mansion with an open entryway mirroring the saloon doors at the center of the prior shot. There is a woman doing needlework in the bottom left corner, evoking the original placement of the Tramp. Only this time, the camera pans left to reorient itself so that the woman moves to the center of the frame: here, the visual world of the film readjusts to accommodate the wealthy, whereas it happily left Chaplin squeezed into an obscure corner in the background of the previous shot.

The motif occurs again, reversed, later in the film when Chaplin has at last established his own domain. With the Tramp having taken up residence in a gypsy wagon where he lives with Purviance's character, Chaplin sets up his shots of the domestic space around the wagon in an analog to the original shots of the bar: the back wall of the wagon dominates the foreground space with a set of open doors in the middle while the side of the wagon forms a corner at the far left of the frame with only a little stretch of road visible in the background plane of the shot. Chaplin is now at last on the dominant side of that pervasive corner, occupying the open foreground space in front of the wagon doors—the equivalent space to where the brass band once stood in front of the saloon doors—as he cooks and cleans and conducts a happy domestic life in his open-air home. Yet the world again accommodates the wealthy. From the depths of the background space—the outcast position that Chaplin occupied in the opening shot of the film—a small car eventually emerges, growing larger as it approaches the foreground plane of the frame. It is Purviance's wealthy parents come to take her back: the civilized world that Chaplin had relegated to the distant corner space he once held has come foreground again to reassert the rightful social order. If the Tramp manages to flip the spatial arrangement that made him an outsider at the film's opening, he cannot compete with the way in which the world seems to reorient itself to serve the powerful.

Chaplin emphasizes this point differently earlier in the film when he draws a striking contrast between the world of the Tramp and the world of the wealthy in a jarring tracking shot set in an ornate museum gallery. Starting in tight focus on a painting of Purviance—a portrait that was completed by a wealthy artist who met her in the wilderness where she was living with the Tramp—the camera pulls back slowly as the artist enters the frame along with three con-test judges who have awarded the painting first prize; with their backs to the camera, they observe the picture and then, as the camera continues to track backward, turn in unison to walk through the gallery toward the front of the frame, Purviance's once-giant portrait receding into the background. The world of the wealthy is organized, coordinated, mobile, and almost wholly inverted from the world that the Tramp occupies. The only corner to be found in this shot is turned inside out: it is the corner of interior walls in the back right of the frame that stands in counterpoint to the corner of exterior walls at the front left of the frame in prior scenes. The artist and the gallery judges are on the inside of the dividing walls that define the film's visual motif, and they are in complete lockstep with their environment. But for all of their refinement, they have none of the individuality of the Tramp—they are dressed alike and move in unison—and their world will only diminish Purviance; her seemingly gargantuan por-trait turns out to be a small part of a gallery filled with myriad paintings. This shot stands in remarkable counterpoint to the rest of the film: a rare instance of self-conscious cinematography in Chaplin's work, a proto-Wellesian combi-nation of composition and camera movement. But it is used here as a point of contrast, almost of disparagement. The precise control of the shot is emblematic of the controlling world it depicts, a world that will destroy the happiness of the girl it will reclaim and of the Tramp who lives on its margins.

CHAPLIN'S CINEMATOGRAPHY OF THE BODY

Chaplin's mastery of cinematic space arguably constitutes the core of his de-parture from classical visual technique, but it is only one half of the system he developed for conveying narrative within the components of the frame itself. If Chaplin's filmic world was marked by a precise control and demarcation of the space within the frame, it was also marked by an unprecedented level of control of the bodies in that space. Insofar as critics have considered this aspect of Chaplin's work, it has mostly been in the context of his own performance style. Commentators from Chaplin's day to our own have noted the preternatural bodily control that formed the hallmark of his physical technique. It is largely on the basis of this acute physical mastery that no less a figure than John Barrymore declared him one of the greatest actors in the world.[40] As Dan Kamin notes, Chaplin evinced a remarkable ability to isolate individual parts of his body in movement, holding the rest of his frame still:

> The secret lies in the extraordinary articulation of his body. His movement is hypnotic to watch both because it flows so well and because it is so selective. Quite often, only one part of Chaplin's body moves at a time. When he shakes his head, for example, recovering from a blow or a fall, his head is the only thing that moves, and it moves like a washing machine agitator, rapidly rotating left and right, rather than wobbling around. Far from making him look stiff, such machinelike precision is highly amusing, directing the eye of the viewer.[41]

This ability helps account for some of the most virtuosic moments of performance in Chaplin's films. In *The Rink,* for example, Chaplin holds the viewer enthralled as he performs the simple act of preparing a cocktail: keeping his trunk entirely still, he turns and twists his arms through a series of precise contortions, occasionally allowing a particular shaking motion to reverberate up through his arms, into his shoulders, and into his head as though sending shock waves through his body. Similarly, in *The Immigrant* (Mutual, 1917) the act of throwing dice becomes a kind of full-body performance art. Chaplin gets ready for his throw like a baseball player preparing to pitch, freezing his full body and moving only his hands or arms through a variety of extreme postures throughout the windup and release.

Where observers have found a larger filmic purpose to masterful performative moments like these, it is typically in linking Chaplin's precise physical control of his body, so subtle and detailed that it would be lost in all but the most immediate of theater environments, to an overall sense of intimacy between actor and audience in Chaplin's films. Mack Sennett makes just this point in contrasting Chaplin's performance style to the typical Keystone output. "Anything that diverts the camera's eye from Chaplin himself," he writes, "is likely to be a waste of celluloid. His style is intimate, not panoramic—the one-shot instead of the crowd scene."[42] In that intimacy, moreover, Chaplin has found a way to communicate far more than his actions alone. It is, as Alex Clayton observes, the intimacy of a communication without words: a masterful transposition from mind to body, the subtle succession of the motions of the Tramp doing more to tell us about the intelligence and fervor that lie within that figure than any spoken confession ever could. "While the ontology of the silent film is already such that we grasp the mind *through* the body," Clayton writes, "few performers have achieved such lucidity of expression as Charlie Chaplin, and so few performers have so strikingly created the impression of the mind as perfectly *visible*."[43] We know at nearly all times in a Chaplin film where he stands emotionally, toward what end he might be scheming, when his perception of the world has shifted. The intricacy and precision of his actions serve as indicators of a soul and a mind active and alive to the world. Cavell calls this "the sublime comprehensibility of Chaplin's natural choreography."[44] It is in this light that we might properly understand Barrymore's description of Chaplin as the cinema's finest actor, for it is literally in his actions that he seems to lay bare for us his soul.

Telling as such observations might be, what they tend to obscure is the degree to which Chaplin used precise bodily movement not just as an aspect of his own acting but as an explicit compositional technique in his filmmaking. That is, Chaplin's bodily movements do not simply tell you something about his character, something about the "sublime comprehensibility" of his inner life; they also, on a much more basic visual level, tell you where to *look* within the frame. Nothing attracts the eye like movement, and Chaplin the director knew this. As noted, when Chaplin was once told that "his camera angles were not very interesting," he responded, "They don't have to be interesting—*I* am interesting."[45] As much as it is a statement on his performance, it is also a statement on his composition. Camera angles serve as tools of narrative direction and focus, but Chaplin was able to draw out those properties without recourse to the camera through his control of motion in the frame. It is, in fact, one of only three components that he cites as foundational to his approach to filmic composition—"motion, two planes, and a suggestion of depth."

Chaplin always claimed that he directed by "pure instinct," but modern studies of how and why we look suggest that behind such "instinct" was a grasp of a basic truth: the eye is drawn to moving things.[46] Neurological studies by Tim Smith, of the University of London and the Dynamic Images and Eye Movements Project, seem to confirm through experimentation what Chaplin knew instinctively: that on-screen movement attracts the attention of the viewer's gaze more than any other visual factor. Regardless of other compositional aspects—camera angle, lighting, editing (in other words, all the tools and techniques of the classical style)—the viewer's eye will nearly always be attracted to the point of movement on the screen in a process that Smith calls "attentional synchrony."[47] As Smith writes, "viewers' gazes are attracted by the sudden appearance of objects, moving hands, heads, and bodies. The greater the motion contrast between the point of motion and the static background, the more likely viewers will look at it."[48] Properly executed motion, according to Smith, can "command viewer attention as precisely as a rapidly edited sequence of close-up shots."[49]

Chaplin possessed an intuitive sense not only of this fact but also of its possibilities as an organizing visual principle of filmmaking. As he writes in his autobiography, his camera placement is always conceived in relationship to the motion on screen: "My own camera setup is based on facilitating choreography for the actor's movements."[50] Chaplin's control of the movement of bodies within his frame serves as a complement to his control of the space put on film. Just as one answer to the narrative unwieldiness of unbroken cinematic space is to become more deliberate about constructing that space, so too is the deliberate control of bodily motion an answer to the visual cacophony that impedes narrative clarity in early shot-as-scene constructions. By controlling the movement of bodies on screen, Chaplin can control the focus of the viewer; he can use the isolated movement of bodies and parts of bodies to tell you what to look at in a shot, creating a kind of corporeal analog to the classical imperatives on the camera. More important, Chaplin's bodily movement works in concert with his spatial differentiation: as his filmed bodies tell you where to focus, their positioning within the differentiated spaces of the frame help to isolate and clarify moments of narrative importance. Without cuts and without close-ups—without moving the camera at all—he is able to use the contents of the frame itself to create narrative focus and narrative movement. Chaplin uses the body in cooperation with the space that it inhabits to disintermediate the camera as a narrative apparatus.

It is this total control of motion-in-frame that helps make Chaplin's work so comprehensible where other shot-as-scene constructions prove obscure, a point illustrated even in an early and less sophisticated short like Chaplin's *Burlesque on Carmen* (Essanay, 1916). In one scene, Chaplin sets up a classic three-person shot that in its broad outlines is not unlike any number of other stand-in-a-row shots from the days of early slapstick. Purviance's Carmen has just seduced Chaplin's dragoon character, and as she leads him outside of the fortified gates of the city he must find a way to disperse another soldier who comes to rebuke him for leaving his post. The visual composition of the confrontation among the three characters is simple. With the gates blocking any visible depth or other visual interest in the frame, the three characters stand side by side in the foreground. It is a more-or-less identical setup to that used in the conclusion of Sennett's Biograph comedy *An Interrupted Elopement,* where the lovers, the minister, the kidnapped father, and the friends all stand in the foreground of the frame as the climax unfolds. But whereas a typical Sennett slapstick might have all the characters on screen gesticulating at once, each seeking to communicate their particular piece of the story line in the visual equivalent of having everyone talk over each other, Chaplin choreographs his scene quite precisely.

The main center of visual attention in Chaplin's *Carmen* scene is his eyebrows. Holding the rest of his body and his face almost entirely still, he makes a repeated series of exaggerated eyebrow contortions, broadcasting to the other soldier that he is trying to slip away with the alluring gypsy and would rather not be disturbed. Another director might cut to a close-up of Chaplin's face, but Chaplin focuses our attention without the intervention of the camera. As Chaplin gestures with his eyebrows, Carmen and the other soldier move almost as if in slow motion. They do not hold completely still such that their absence of motion might draw attention to itself for its unnaturalness, but they slowly and methodically repeat an appropriate motion for their disposition in the scene: Carmen moves her hand to her face and back to her hips in a gesture of impatience and disgust; the other soldier stares at Chaplin intently and very slowly shifts his weight. Only when Chaplin has concluded his eyebrow ballet does the soldier gesture again for them to return inside, during which time Chaplin holds almost entirely still except for subtle shifts in his weight; he then recommences his eyebrow antics when the soldier has finished his gesticulating. To watch the scene with an eye toward the movement of all the characters is to witness something quite surreal: those who are not the center of attention move as if they are in fact slow-motion windup dolls, giving the scene an eerie and unnatural quality. But this is not what the viewer actually sees. Watching the scene holistically and in context, as it is intended to be viewed, the slow-motion choreography is effectively invisible. We watch Chaplin's comic eyebrow gestures, then the soldier motioning for him to return inside, then Chaplin's eyebrow gestures once again—our attention passing easily from one figure to the next with no sense of anything unnatural in the frame. With the camera holding perfectly still, the characters themselves have told us what to watch.

Chaplin uses a similar technique to even greater effect in one of the pivotal confrontations in *The Vagabond.* Here, Chaplin's Tramp has prepared a special meal for himself and Purviance's character, but she arrives for the meal with the wealthy artist in tow. They met in the woods and are clearly smitten with each other. As the meal unfolds, the scene might as well be shot in a close-up of the Tramp: our entire focus is on the heartbreak and anxiety he feels at seeing the woman with whom he has fallen in love enamored of another man. But the scene is shot in Chaplin's typical medium long shot, with all three characters fully in view; the focus is a matter of composition and movement, not camera work. The three sit in a triangle, with the artist's back positioned toward the camera. Purviance sits opposite the artist, her body partially obscured by his figure. Only Chaplin is in full view, his face and body cheating toward the camera. As the meal begins, he pulls a checkered napkin up to his collar and tucks it in. In addition to drawing further visual focus to his person—the checkered pattern reads quite clearly against the monochromatic clothing of the other characters—it also helps to obscure almost everything but his arms and his face. As Chaplin engages his arms in meaningless business on the table—moving the food, pouring the coffee—he holds his trunk still and subtly moves his eyes from Purviance to the artist and back; we cannot help but be drawn to the details of his face, to watch the meal unfold through his eyes. The artist moves hardly at all in the shot, his stillness naturalized by the fact that we see him only from behind. Similar to her movements in the *Burlesque on Carmen,* Purviance performs a series of repetitive motions appropriate to her situation and character—she intermittently nods and smiles at things the artist is saying, making her movements slowly and sporadically enough to discourage our attention. The focus of the scene is clearly on the Tramp, but at the same time we never lose sight of that which is causing him so much pain. It is a carefully controlled and coordinated way of bringing our attention to Chaplin's body in the frame, even as we remain always aware of the world around him.

Chaplin is often just as willing to use these techniques to draw attention away from himself. In *The Pawn Shop* (Mutual, 1916), for example, he uses his precise control of bodily motion to cast attention onto the other character in the scene, drawing it back to himself only in brief moments. Here, an old man enters the pawnshop where Chaplin is working and tries to get money for a wedding ring that he says is the last remaining token of his deceased wife. The old man is a histrio par excellence, gesticulating grandly as he tells the sad story of the ring, and Chaplin hands the focus of the scene entirely over to him. Chaplin, for his part, leans against the store counter and slowly eats a cracker, moving hardly at all as he bites into it and chews. But he also uses the cracker to suddenly and sharply draw attention back to himself during the tale. At key moments in the old man's performance, he spits out a mouthful, sending an explosion of food flying over the counter. Our attention is immediately pulled back to him, and the old man freezes momentarily in surprise to allow our gaze to shift. But the rebalancing in attention lasts only a moment before the old man returns to his terrible tale and his exaggerated gestures and Chaplin quietly returns to his snack. The cracker gag functions like a reaction shot without the cutting. Each time Chaplin spits it out, we register his changing reaction to the story: incredulous at first, then increasingly sad with each succeeding spit-up until by the end of the story he is both crying and spitting up uncontrollably at the same time. Without ever losing focus on the storyteller and listener together in the same frame, Chaplin effectively "cuts" from one to the other, showing us with the motion of the bodies how we are meant to follow the exchange.

To no less a figure than Eisenstein, Chaplin's technique was a revelation. In his 1938 revision to his theory of montage, Eisenstein went so far as to make an exception for Chaplin's approach. Redefining montage to encompass not just the work of editing in film but any circumstance in film by which "two film pieces of any kind, placed together, inevitably combine into a new concept, a new quality, arising out of that juxtaposition," Eisenstein found he now had room to accommodate Chaplin's technique.[51] He took Chaplin as an explicit model of how montage might work in the absence of other cinematographic forms of emphasis, quoting George Arliss in saying "the art of restraint and suggestion on the screen may any time be studied by watching the acting of the inimitable Charlie Chaplin."[52] Eisenstein extrapolates here from the level of performance to the level of composition, asking "What is 'suggestion' if it not be an element, a detail of actuality, a 'close-up' of actuality, which, in juxtaposition with other details, serves as a determination of the entire fragment of actuality?"[53] The actor himself, he thus claims, may emphasize individual elements of the screen and place them in sequence, generating not "a flat representation" but "a genuine image according to the method he uses to construct his performance."[54] It is a montage made entirely in the diegetic interior of the frame, a montage composed of bodies that can exist even in the absence of editing: "Even though his performance be shot entirely from a single set-up (or even from a single seat in a theatre auditorium), none the less—in a felicitous case—the performance itself be 'montage' in character."[55] If, in other words, the aim of montage is to drive us through a series of states of awareness so as to help us arrive in the end at a new understanding of the images presented, then at last Chaplin's filmmaking, regardless of its relationship to cinematography or editing proper, would fit into Eisenstein's scheme. It was in part a personal validation. The two filmmakers met and became friends during Eisenstein's stint in Hollywood in 1930, with Eisenstein frequently joining Luis Buñuel for tennis and dinner at Chaplin's estate. Eisenstein's revision was a way to bring his friend Chaplin into the fold of acknowledged film technique. But it was also an admission that there was something new at work in Chaplin's approach: a different way of accomplishing the standard narratological and thematic ends of montage theory while at the same time clearing the way for forms of visual construction not available to standard classical composition.[56]

As Eisenstein seemed to recognize in his revision, there is something more than just idiosyncrasy or stubbornness in Chaplin's approach to filmic composition, something that approaches a kind of visual grandeur not easily available in other forms of construction. At the height of his abilities, Chaplin is able to commute his mastery of space and movement into images of extraordinary power, as exemplified in the iconic dance hall sequence at the center of *The Gold Rush* (United Artists, 1925).[57] Entering civilization for the first time since his arrival in Alaska, Chaplin's Tramp visits a bustling dance hall looking to make some kind of human connection. With the camera set in a long shot at the back of the hall, we see a large crowd of patrons filling the screen, the Tramp almost indistinguishable among them. Suddenly and all at once, the men and women in the crowd pair off and head to the dance floor, leaving Chaplin alone in space, cast in silhouette as he looks out toward the dancers on the floor. Chaplin's composition of the cavernous dance hall space is impeccable. A balcony with a crowd of people on it occupies the far back plane of the shot. The dance floor, open and full of light, marks the middle ground. And the entry section of the hall, where Chaplin is left alone, defines the foreground space, delineated by a low-hanging ceiling and a pair of wooden pillars that set the borders of the playable space and frame the Tramp with proscenium-like clarity. Likewise, the front-back axis of the frame is clearly defined by two pillars in the balcony that define the midpoint of the screen and clearly mark Chaplin's character as standing in the center foreground of the shot. Spatially, there is never any question as to the relative distances between the characters. We know when Chaplin is part of the crowd, and we know when he is separated. What's more, when the dancers move to the middle plane of the shot we know how relatively far they are from Chaplin: it is clear to us that they have not moved to the far back plane delimited by the balcony—they are still in proximity to Chaplin, though he is separated from them. And this movement from one defined space to another clearly and elegantly tracks and defines the central narrative of the sequence: Chaplin is lost in the crowd, marked by the events in one plane of the space; then he is left alone as the crowd abandons him, marked by its movement into another plane of space.

But the heart of the sequence comes in the way that Chaplin intermingles the movement of his body and his treatment of the space. When the crowd moves to the dance floor and leaves Chaplin alone in silhouette, an immediate spatial tension is put into play. Chaplin is in the center of the shot in the plane closest to the camera, occupying the most vital part of the frame. But, at the same time, his back is turned toward the camera and the entire middle plane is taken up with a cacophony of movement and activity. There is an immediate push and pull between the individual and the crowd, and though our attention mostly resolves in favor of the overwhelming crowd of dancers, Chaplin upends this dynamic at three specific moments in the sequence. First, as he stands and watches the crowd, he demonstratively shifts his weight. Then, a few seconds later, he leans and rests on his cane. Then, a few more seconds after that, he drums his fingers on his leg. In each of these moments, our attention is drawn to Chaplin's silhouetted body. The motions are tiny, but Chaplin's single figure is so disproportionately larger than the other figures on the dance floor (owing to his proximity to the camera) that even these micro-adjustments draw our attention. As soon as each motion is finished, however, Chaplin returns to a bodily state of rest, and our attention goes back to the mass of dancers on the floor. Without ever breaking the single shot that allows us to envision the whole of the dance hall and all of its occupants at once, Chaplin brings our attention into tight focus on his body, as if in a reaction shot, and then back to the large-scale focus on the dance hall, controlling our gaze with something as minuscule as the movement of his fingers. We witness the totality of the dance hall and Chaplin's individual experience of the dance hall all at the same time without ever losing sight of either.

TURNING PEOPLE INTO CAMERAS: THE ROOTS OF CHAPLIN'S PROCESS

If Chaplin's focus on the composition of filmic space for narrative ends can be linked to early film techniques of marrying narrative to changes in location, his attention to bodily motion within the frame can be seen as an outgrowth of his work with Karno. It was there that he honed his skills as a pantomime artist—a form of performance at which he was clearly gifted but also one that Karno was famous for perfecting in the members of his troupe. The Karno training regimen was intensive. Cast members had to memorize approximately a dozen shows to be part of the company, and, in Chaplin's words, "each man working for Karno had to have perfect timing and had to know the peculiarities of everyone else in the cast so that we could, collectively, achieve a cast tempo."[58] It is no surprise that the other great film comedian to emerge from the Karno company, Stan Laurel, was widely regarded by his peers as equal or superior to Chaplin in the precision of his comic technique, though in general he wore it less openly than Chaplin in his films.[59] But even more important for Chaplin's development as a filmmaker than his own technical training was the Karno tradition of having every player in a traveling company learn multiple roles in every show that the company performed, all with the same level of precision as his or her own assigned part. The point, according to Chaplin, was "so that the players could be interchanged. When one left the company it was like taking a screw or a pin out of a very delicate piece of machinery."[60] Each Karno show—as many as eighteen on the road at once across Europe and America—was meant to function like a machine.

For Karno, such rigorous standards were a means of industrializing and standardizing the intensely uncertain world of the theater. He demanded that his players achieve a uniform level of technical ability and that they know how to substitute for one another: as actors came and went, he could substitute one player for another without worrying that the show-machine might cease to function. In this way, with multiple companies touring multiple countries, he could turn a profit no matter what might happen on the road. But what Chaplin imported from this process into his own work was almost the opposite of industrial; it was, we might say, intensely artisanal, especially in its shocking inefficiencies and time-consuming drive for perfection. For Chaplin, all the pieces of a given scene ultimately had to fit together as perfectly as they were meant to with Karno: each actor in sync with the others on the screen, all of them working with extreme precision and careful timing. The mechanical interlocking of the cast that functioned as a kind of overarching insurance for Karno becomes, when translated into the filmic medium, an astounding production liability for Chaplin and a major contributor to the shockingly high costs for his films. It was also regularly a source of tension on the set, as actors unfamiliar with Chaplin's working methods joined the company and were horrified to see the degree to which their performances would be controlled. His was not a benign directorial hand, prodding his actors on to their own discoveries. Chaplin's approach was something else entirely, an effort essentially to commandeer the bodies of his cast members and harness them to the execution of his own particular vision. It was not an easy approach for anyone involved. Chaplin was a legendary perfectionist, and the numbers that are typically recounted about the amount of footage that he shot or the length of time he spent on a film never quite convey the depth of his exactitude or his obsessive management of the production process. Linder, for instance, recalls that when he visited Chaplin's studio, he witnessed a film Chaplin was making (he does not say which one) on which he spent a total of two months, conducted fifty rehearsals, shot each scene twenty times, and used about 36,000 feet of negative to arrive at a picture of 1,800 feet. More telling perhaps, however, are the relative cost figures for some of these films. Chaplin spent approximately $100,000 on each of his two-reel shorts for Mutual—almost as much money per short as Griffith spent on the entire twelve-reel *The Birth of a Nation*, the most expensive film ever made to that time. In a similar comparison, *The Kid,* coming in at six reels, cost more to make than Keaton's eight-reel *The General,* which is also perhaps the most technically elaborate slapstick film ever attempted. Especially for films that were fairly limited in their technical scope, Chaplin's production figures tell the story of a level of repetition and reshooting that has perhaps never been matched.

To be fair, much of Chaplin's production time and production costs were spent on improvisation and experimentation, often on material he had already successfully shot but had since reconceived. As his secretary Elsie Codd recounts of Chaplin's working method, "Sometimes he is struck with a sudden new idea when the cameras have finished recording a scene. . . . Quite often after a day of five or six hours' work he has 'shot' the spool length of a whole comedy. But as a matter of fact he has merely recorded a certain number of variations on a single theme."[61] And yet, improvisation and reshooting cannot account for the whole of Chaplin's tremendous expenses. Improvisation was a standard working method among slapstick comedians at the time, none of whom would match the levels of time or expenditure that Chaplin would put into a single film. (Indeed, part of Keaton's loss of independence at Metro-Goldwyn-Mayer came from the studio management's disgust with the amount of improvisation on his film shoots. And yet, his costs were almost always lower than Chaplin's, despite the much more extensive technical requirements of his films.) More than a matter of improvisation, the time and money that went into Chaplin's films seem to be in large part a product of the visual and compositional system that he developed in contrast to the working methods of typical classical technique. For a typical Chaplin take—far longer than the typical take by almost any other filmmaker at the time—was, once it had been settled on through a series of improvisations, not so much planned or rehearsed as carefully choreographed. As a director, Chaplin was famous for acting out all the parts in his films, demonstrating how they should be performed and demanding exact copying from his actors rather than coaxing them into performances of their own creation. As Codd recounts, "Chaplin makes the actors rehearse their parts one by one, having previously tried the business himself. Without exaggeration I think I can say that he has played every character in every one of his comedies."[62] Many of his actors balked at this approach, declaring that it wasn't acting at all that he was demanding of them so much as mimicry. (Virginia Cherrill, who costarred with Chaplin in *City Lights,* claimed in interviews to have learned nothing about acting from Chaplin.)[63] But if we think of Chaplin less as a typical film director working with actors to either find a performance or simply get out of the way of the star and more as a choreographer demonstrating the new steps to all of the members of his company, the approach becomes more clear. Because he relied so little on the camera and so heavily on the composition within the frame, Chaplin needed to ensure precision among his actors. It was part and parcel of his working method. They didn't need to know who to be so much as they needed to know where, how, and when to move; they were not so much actors as they were parts of a bigger machine of filmic composition, all of them together operating as part of a collective storytelling apparatus.

Hence Linder's commentary that, despite Chaplin's use of improvisation early in the process of shooting each scene, he ultimately "leaves nothing to the chance of improvisation. He goes over and over scenes until he is satisfied. He 'shoots' every single rehearsal and has them thrown on the screen several times, so that he may find just the flaw which spoils the effect he is striving after. He keeps on starting again until he is content, and he is harder to please than his most harshly critical spectator."[64] But this is not just perfectionism for its own sake. Chaplin was almost never trying to get only one thing right in a given take: a nuanced reaction shot, a proper entrance. Rather, he was trying to get everything right, all at once, all in the same take. Every single person on screen—and especially the people whom the audience was *not* supposed to look at—had to master compositional choreography across the whole take, all in the same take, and all with some of the longest takes yet attempted on film. Thus, each take in a Chaplin film was like a miniature theatrical performance—and all of those performances had to have the exacting precision of a Karno performance.

To call Chaplin a perfectionist is to ignore the degree to which he was not simply trying to be exacting in an established mode of filmic composition. He was inventing a new mode—one with different strictures, grounded in different expectations, and premised on different techniques. And one, ultimately, that aimed for a different aesthetic experience than classical technique could allow, even a different philosophy of what it might mean to make a film. But the grand aspirations of Chaplin's technique began not in theories but in hard realities: in spaces and in the bodies that filled those spaces. In Chaplin's filmic method, the people on screen were more than just actors. They were, collectively, the camera itself.

Chaplin's Filmmaking Philosophy

When the French film director Robert Florey took a job assisting Charlie Chaplin late in Chaplin's career, he expected to learn a great deal from one of the world's most famous filmmakers. But he was shocked by what he saw when he began to work on set. In a typical anecdote from one of Florey's later accounts, Chaplin makes a series of what seem like bizarre and irreconcilable demands. He wants his "head in the foreground in the whole scene" but at the same time "he also wants to show the little cat on the ground and the female actress in the back, and the table at the left" and then again he wants everything framed so that the audience can "see my feet" throughout the entire scene.[1] Florey, an accomplished technician who instinctively conceived of shots in terms of lenses, recounts how he listened to Chaplin's changing demands and tried to parse them into a series of lens sizes that would meet those wants, running the gamut from twenty-five millimeters to two inches, as a way to assist the cameraman. But Florey is ultimately stymied. "He doesn't see with a photographic eye," Florey puts it at one point.[2] Or, in a less charitable revision: Chaplin is the "irreconcilable enemy of all that is photographic composition."[3] To hear Florey tell it, Chaplin's conception of camera angles and apertures was basically that they weren't much more than "Hollywood chi-chi."[4] Whenever Florey tried to introduce some greater cinematographic attention into the planning of a scene, Chaplin insisted that he knew what he was doing as a director. "I have been in this business for 20—for 30 years. . . . I have been cutting this scene in my mind for the past three years," he exclaimed when challenged.[5] But Chaplin's methods were almost entirely impenetrable to his assistant. When Florey at one point pressed Chaplin about his insistence on framing his full figure in almost every shot, he found Chaplin's response simply puzzling: "I act with my feet as much as my head."[6]

Of course, acting with one's feet—if most performers would even know how to do such a thing—is no call in itself to capture the full figure of the actor in shot after shot. What Chaplin leaves unsaid is a small but pivotal component of his performance technique: that he acts with his feet and with the rest of his body all at the same time. It would seem to be hardly any effort at all—and certainly more in keeping with the expectations of a director steeped in classical assumptions like Florey—to determine those moments at which one part of Chaplin's performing body conveyed the central point of communication and to aim the camera toward that section of his person, whether feet or hands or face. It might still mark Chaplin's performance style as unique—few screen actors would need to choose between so many different parts of their body in isolating where the emotion of the shot was most conveyed—but at least it would do so in a manner more comprehensible to the arbiters of classical style. It would return a degree of agency to the camera and force on Chaplin the kind of cinematographic choice that he normally eschewed: a question not of how to frame a scene in toto but of how to use the camera to focus the viewer's attention within that scene. For once, he would have to seriously consider lenses. But it would also, as Chaplin well knew, unmake almost everything that most defined his manner of performance. To disaggregate Chaplin's performing body, as Florey would have preferred, is effectively to erase it. Even Chaplin's signature ability to move only one component part of his body at a time, for comic effect or dramatic emphasis, becomes meaningless if the rest of his unmoving frame cannot be seen in the shot. Chaplin needs to be seen in whole, or he cannot truly be seen at all. In Gilles Deleuze's description, his work is marked by "an irreducible simultaneity."[7]

Simultaneity and the Irreducible Body

The issue of simultaneity is a constant refrain among Chaplin's defenders. Insofar as theorists have recognized a unique cinematographic style in his works, it has largely centered on the idea of simultaneity as a foundational property of his aesthetic and, in particular, of his performances. In André Bazin's analysis, Chaplin's body of work is one of a relative few given to a unique "law of aesthetics" that so much of classical cinema has ignored: "When the essence of a scene demands the simultaneous presence of two or more factors in the action, montage is ruled out."[8] Bazin does not entirely eschew montage as a legitimate cinematic technique, but he makes its usage conditional: "It can reclaim its right to be used . . . whenever the import of the action no longer depends on physical contiguity even though this may be implied."[9] For Bazin, Chaplin's adherence to these ideas stems from the nature of his performances themselves. His manner of comic acting almost always depends on "the simultaneous presence of two or more factors in the action," almost always depends on "physical contiguity" within his body itself. "Chaplin's gags are often of such short duration that they allow just enough time for you to 'get it,'" Bazin writes. "Although he was brought up in the school of the music hall, Charlie has refined down its comedy. . . . This need for simplicity and effectiveness requires of the gag the greatest elliptical clarity."[10] Chaplin's performance is so precise, in other words, as to constitute a kind of simultaneity in itself, standing in clear opposition to classical dictates. It is a point that Deleuze would explicitly pick up on and continue in his lengthy readings of Chaplin's work in *Cinema 1*. Though Deleuze would ultimately place Chaplin within the general period of classical film construction—within the paradigm of the movement-image, in his terminology—he would be positioned within that period in a kind of perpetually critical stance. Classical film technique is necessarily based on an aesthetic of sequencing—of isolating actions, placing them in succession with one another, and drawing linkages between them. But as Deleuze observes, Chaplin's unique art of performance has nothing to sequence in this manner. The very idea of sequencing is rendered impossible within his acting style: his bodily action is "so compressed," Deleuze writes, that it "rebels against any montage."[11] For Deleuze, Chaplin is concerned with action not as part of an instrumental sequence but ultimately only "for itself."[12] He appears in his films as a force bound by laws known only to him, the unceasing kinesis of his body seemingly operating without any cause in or concern for the laws of this world, physical or social. He offers an explosion of movement fully formed, to which the world around *him* must react and reconcile itself; he is both organizing and challenging the world at the same time. Chaplin's actions, in other words, are always already complete, and when the world responds or changes around him, he responds with whole action once again. The essence of Chaplin's work, according to Deleuze, is thus: "Charlie caught in the instant, moving from one instant to the next, each requiring his full powers of improvisation" until, in his jump from point of action to point of action, he fully describes "the line of the universe" that he has made, his actions re-creating the world in their wake.[13]

This tendency is epitomized in the alarm clock scene from *The Pawn Shop*, one of the most frequently examined sequences in the whole of Chaplin's oeuvre. Chaplin's disregard for the rules of our world is on full display, but so too is the degree to which his actions spring to life in full form within his films. Here, a customer brings an alarm clock to pawn at the shop where Chaplin's Tramp is working. Chaplin's inspection of the clock, shot in two of the longest takes of his career thus far, is a kind of riot of surrealistic responses to a simple physical object. Chaplin examines it with a stethoscope, taps its joints, bangs on it with a hammer, applies a can opener, smells it, magnifies its innards like a jeweler, applies oil, extracts its gears like a dentist removing a tooth, smells it again, measures it, dumps all of its parts onto the counter, holds it up to his ear. More remarkable than the series of actions themselves, however, is the rapid and seamless transitions that Chaplin makes between his various handlings of the clock. Chaplin's various actions unfold as if they were all part of some single greater means of handling the object—one that seems perfectly sensible and natural to the logic of Chaplin's personal universe, though it appears comically incomprehensible to our own. To film the sequence in anything but the long takes that Chaplin uses, his camera positioned to capture his entire upper body at once, would be to change the nature of the scene itself. Cutting, for instance, first to a close-up of the clock, then to Chaplin's face, then to the customer's reaction, then back to a medium shot of the two of them—this would be to break what appears as one continuous collage of actions into a series of smaller, discrete, comprehensible movements and, more important, to imply some degree of development or change between them: the customer is displeased, so Chaplin tries something else; or, Chaplin has hit a dead end in examining the clock in one way and must move on to another approach. As bizarre as his treatment of the alarm clock may be, it is in Chaplin's aesthetic universe ultimately a kind of single, fundamentally indivisible action. The one reaction shot that Chaplin gives us of the customer is positioned about halfway into the nearly four-minute segment: it is a reaction to the extreme duration of Chaplin's bizarre behavior—a testament to its indissolubility—as much as a stupefaction at the actions themselves. Such is the nature of Chaplin's particular brand of movement: his actions emerge fully formed and force us to reconcile ourselves to them, for they take no account of how we think the world should work.

SIMULTANEITY AND
THE IRREDUCIBLE WORLD

The kind of virtuosic kinesis that marks a sequence like the alarm clock bit from *The Pawn Shop*—or the dice throwing from *The Immigrant* or the skating in *The Rink,* or many other similar moments in Chaplin's work—is not the only kind of event that happens in a Chaplin film. It may be the most memorable event in the film; by some readings, it may even be the most important event in the film. But Chaplin's physical virtuosity is always embedded in a narrative that exceeds any of its individual sequences and that contains any number of moments that might not need to rely on an aesthetic of simultaneity and ir-reducibility. Indeed, were those moments where Chaplin presents us with a spectacle of fluid bodily movement the only ones in which he departed from classical prerogatives, his visual style might not seem so far afield of classical technique. He might look in fact much closer to Buster Keaton, who was per-fectly willing to conform to classical shot construction in mundane and expo-sitional moments and only broached serious challenges to classical orthodoxy in those sequences where he presented some of his most pivotal comic action. Keaton took issue in his films with classical technique as a means of properly presenting and communicating physical comedy. Chaplin seems to have taken issue with it as a means of representing the world at all. Despite the tribute that theorists like Bazin and Deleuze pay to the irreducible simultaneity of action in a Chaplin film, there is at least as much material in his films that seems not to fit this rubric at all—that seems in fact eminently divisible but that he simply refuses to divide. As a matter of course, Chaplin will routinely group within the same shot actions that seem unrelated to one another, characters that are not central to the moment at hand, even bits of business that might seem to distract from the central purpose of the scene. Unlike aspects of his own vir-tuosic performances, there is nothing irreducible about these moments. They are not outside of the ability of classical technique to capture, as is so much of Chaplin's own full body performance. They are moments and actions that Chaplin should be able to reduce, that he should be able to divide. But he does not. It is not so much that his own motions and actions are composed of an irreducible simultaneity, as Bazin and Deleuze emphasize. It is not even that he follows Bazin's prescriptions and eschews montage when "the essence of a scene demands the simultaneous presence of two or more factors" but not when "the action no longer depends on physical contiguity." It is that he be-lieves the world to be composed in a kind of necessary simultaneity no matter how divisible it may seem. For Chaplin, everything—the whole world, every-thing that can be captured on film—is ultimately irreducible.

If Chaplin's technical divergence from the classical school rests on a number of stylistic points—his deliberate approach to spatial composition, his care-ful choreography of bodies in the frame—the philosophical divergence that underlies these techniques stems almost entirely from a profound doubt that the world can or should be rendered as divisible as the classical style would require. Or, put another way, Chaplin's filmmaking actively wonders, and asks us to call into question, what is missed in the division of the world imposed by classical technique and what might be deliberately hidden. Bazin comes closest to describing Chaplin's filmic philosophy (though he does not attri-bute it directly to him) in his own criticism of montage, specifically in the way that it "presupposes of its very nature the unity of meaning of the dramatic event."[14] Chaplin refuses to make such a presupposition, at least to any absolute degree, and he frequently uses his filmmaking to call this kind of an assumption—what might be considered the fundamental philosophical assumption of classical technique—into question. Chaplin does not include too much in the frame as his critics often claim. (He does not simply include the feet when he should really cut off the frame before the legs, to use Florey's contention.) He uses his frame to show us the artificiality, even the danger, of the presumed unity of meaning to which classical film has inured us; he asks us to wonder whether the world can be so easily and uniformly described as traditional film would make it seem and whether there is not something vital in our awareness of the world that is lost in such a presumption.

The basic dynamics of Chaplin's approach are epitomized in an abrupt and shocking compositional choice in his dramatic directorial debut, *A Woman of Paris* (United Artists, 1923), one of only two films that he directed but in which he did not star. Here, Chaplin follows a scene—the emotional climax of the film—in which the young artist, Jean Millet, commits suicide with a scene in which the film's heroine and the woman for whom he killed himself, Marie St. Claire, is shown nearly passed out in the background of the frame while her wealthy new lover and the cause of Jean's anguish, Pierre Revel, is positioned on the telephone in the foreground. The point of emphasis is clear within the frame. A table and an entryway mark the separation points of background, middle ground, and foreground planes; the arch of the entryway defines the center of the frame. Pierre is positioned in the center foreground of the frame, looking out toward the camera as he desperately dials the phone. Marie is collapsed at the edge of a couch on the right side of the middle plane, blocked from the camera by a table, almost unmoving throughout the scene. Chaplin essentially refuses to provide his viewers with the point of focus that they have every right to expect. The relationship between Marie and Jean has been at the center of the film from its very first frames, and we know full well that the suicide must be devastating to the young woman. Everything, including the scene of the suicide itself, in which Marie figures prominently, has led us to believe that she should be the focus of this sequence and that her anguish should be the sole point of focus when we see it. But we have been watching a film, like almost any film, with more than two characters, each with his or her own set of priorities and concerns, each of whom might rightly serve as the protagonist in a different film based on the same events.

What Chaplin does in this post-suicide scene is essentially posit a shift: for this one moment, he turns our protagonist into the secondary character and our secondary character into the lead. We never learn whom Pierre is calling or what he is trying to achieve with that call; perhaps he is trying to reach help for Marie, but we cannot even be sure of that. He storms out when he is finished, disgusted and distracted, and we never see him again in the film except for a few brief frames at the very end. Nor do we ever get a better perspective on the physical suffering that Marie endures as she tries to come to terms with the suicide: she never moves from her position tucked into the back of the frame. We see only what the frame allows us to see, and we cannot know what it will not allow us to know. In capturing Marie and Pierre at once in the same frame while upending the expected balance of focus between them within that frame, Chaplin gives us a short glimpse into a different story, a story in which Pierre is positioned as the protagonist—a story that we must assume has been running parallel to the main story of the film the whole time but that we have never quite seen. And in this moment Chaplin reminds us, forcefully and uncomfortably, that the stories films tell us are defined as much by what they leave out as by what they include. Any one of the characters on screen might properly be the protagonist of another version of this same story; any one of them might be the protagonist of another new story altogether.[15]

This jarring message in *A Woman of Paris* is made even more stark when it is accomplished with the beloved Tramp. Hence the uncanny moment in the 1925 version of *The Gold Rush* where the Tramp briefly becomes a secondary character in his own film.[16] Chaplin would say in interviews that the scene was his favorite of the picture—a seemingly minor interaction where the Tramp enters a frontier dance hall in a town where he knows no one, thinks that Georgia, a pretty young dancer, is coming over to greet him, and goes to take her hand only to realize she is greeting the handsome man standing directly behind him.[17] It is in one sense a classic instance of missed connection, an encapsulation of the Tramp's hopeful but lonely place in the world. But it also touches on the idea of film as a housing place of a multiplicity of narratives out of which we can select just one that we might follow. The Tramp's assumption that he is the one being greeted by the girl is innocent enough diegetically— his back is turned to the man behind him. But insofar as we fall for the gag it is also an exposition of our hard-wired narrative assumptions. We can see the tall, handsome frontiersman standing behind the tiny Tramp easily within the frame. If we pay attention, we can see that as the Tramp smiles and shifts his weight a little to greet the girl he does not know, the frontiersman makes the same expression and movements almost as though he is mirroring the Tramp—though his smile has the confidence of someone reconnecting with an old friend in contrast to the Tramp's bashful grin. And yet we are conditioned to believe like the Tramp that Georgia must be waving at him: he is our protagonist, he must be the point of focus, it must be his story that we are following. Chaplin's shot sequence even seems to "trick" us into this assumption: when we first see Georgia in the scene it is from the Tramp's point of view (indistinguishable, of course, from the frontiersman's point of view), then the shot reverses to show her advancing toward the Tramp (and frontiersman) with her back to the camera. Surely the film must be communicating a narrative point about the Tramp's personal story to us; it does not even occur to us that the film might encompass a moment from the story line of someone unconnected to the Tramp. What would such a person even be doing in this world and in this space, one that is supposed to be carefully organized to show us only what it deems important for us to see? It is a surprising reconfiguration when we realize that the Tramp is in fact the extra in this shot, and it is a statement on the world in which the Tramp exists—one that does not necessarily accommodate itself easily to his needs or, more important, to the needs of the narrative we think that we are following. The frontiersman in our story is only a minor character; but in his own story he is the lead, and the Tramp may be no more than the kind of nondescript extra whom we originally assumed the frontiersman to be. Chaplin's filmic world acknowledges this multiplicity.

This too, then, is a kind of simultaneity, though it is hardly irreducible. It is a statement on narrative simultaneity: a reminder that every story comes at the price of another story happening right alongside of it, that every protagonist comes at the cost of the possible protagonist standing quite literally next to him or her. The very job of narrative is explicitly to "reduce" this simultaneity: to isolate and emphasize one story among many, to raise some characters to starring roles and consign others to supporting parts. The job of narrative is to choose, and the job of classical construction is to support and emphasize those choices. But Chaplin often declines to make such calls: he refuses to close off the narratives of his film, to preclude and predetermine their meaning. He instead leaves his films radically open to intersecting and interacting with other narrative lines or points of focus that exist beyond or in excess of the particular story that he has chosen. And so he likewise leaves them open to ignoring, reappropriating, or subverting the tactics of classical composition that are meant to help filmmakers isolate and emphasize within the total universe of narrative possibilities. That Chaplin sees these techniques as tools of reduction is evident from the very first sequence of A Woman of Paris. Here, Chaplin focuses on Marie staring out of her bedroom window, longing for a life beyond her provincial home. He moves in on her image through a series of jarring reductions: a long shot of Marie's home bounded by the other village houses; an abrupt dissolve to a closer shot that leaves out some of the village context; a dissolve to another shot that brings us closer still; and so on until we are tightly focused on Marie in the bedroom window. With each shot, Chaplin shows us how he is taking away more and more of the world. We can become closer to Marie, but we can only do so by cutting away everything that surrounds her; to emphasize and study her unique place in the world, we must literally cut her out of the world in which she naturally exists and look at her, unnaturally, alone.

We cannot help but lose something vital in the process, Chaplin seems to say—a point that he confirms through the contrast of a scene shortly after the introduction. Here, Jean is battling with his parents, who do not want him to run away to Paris and marry Marie. At the start of the scene, the boy's father plants himself firmly in the center of the living room. Jean argues with him, calls down his mother, ushers Marie in from the other room, and paces across the space in an impassioned confrontation with his father. Chaplin films the entire scene in a medium long shot, all the characters in the room always on screen together. And in this extended shot we can see that once the father has positioned himself in his chosen spot in the room, he does not move an inch for the remainder of the scene. He stands close to the center of the frame, just to the left: when Jean comes to confront him face-to-face, the space between their bodies defines the exact center of the shot. The father's resolution is such that he will not give any physical ground to his son, and no degree of editing work or crosscutting or close-ups could convey his unchanging stance so well as Chaplin's unmoving shot. Only by seeing the scene unfold in its total context, all the participants visible at all times, can we understand what is at stake in this conversation and the degree of resistance against which Jean must rebel—a state of affairs told far more eloquently through the father's stubborn body than in any fragmented shot composition crafted in the name of narrative.

Bazin's descriptions of non-montage technique are apt here. It is what he would call a scene that is allowed to unfold "before the camera in its physical and spatial reality."[18] For Bazin, this type of scene presented in the traditional classical style "would have had the impact only of a story and not of a real event. There would have been no difference between the scene as shot and the chapter in a novel which recounted the same imaginary episode."[19] The unbroken frame of Chaplin's composition is, paradoxically, film at its most cinematic—its most highly open and receptive state to the world. If cinema is meant to capture for us a vision of the world rendered on screen, then in some sense all the stylistics of classical technique are a rejection of this role because they do not show us the world whole; they only show it to us in its pieces. In Bazin's terms, "there are cases in which montage far from being the essence of cinema is indeed its negation."[20] There is something to be gained by showing not the parts but the thing itself.

REAPPROPRIATING CLASSICAL STYLE: CHAPLIN'S CLOSE-UP

That is not to say that Chaplin could not or does not draw upon aspects of standard classical technique. In nearly all of his mature works, he does so at some point. But because his filmic style is not based in these techniques—because they are not fundamentally constitutive of how he communicates his narrative, which is most typically handled within the frame itself—he is free to repurpose them, to treat them as flourishes to be manipulated more than component parts of a necessary whole. Thus when Chaplin does use the traditional techniques of emphasis of standard classical style—when he turns to the close-up or to shot/reaction-shot editing, for example—it is often in a kind of subversion of the aesthetic assumptions that these techniques most typically convey. Hence the close-ups that Chaplin uses during a massage sequence in *A Woman of Paris*. Here, Marie learns from a friend that she has been betrayed by another friend of hers who has secretly gone out to dinner with Pierre. It is a pivotal scene of disclosure in the plot, so we may be forgiven for thinking that some kind of intimate picture of Marie's reactions is in order. That is, if there were to be a close-up in the exchange, we would expect it to be of Marie. But Chaplin never gives this to us. Instead, he stages the scene with Marie receiving a massage in her bedroom, effectively cut out of the frame for decency's sake except at the start of the scene. The close-ups that we see are almost entirely of the masseuse who is working on her back. As Marie's friend tells her gossipy story of betrayal and deceit, Chaplin intercuts her story with a series of medium close-ups of the masseuse and her incredulity at the tale. He essentially stages a shot/reaction-shot sequence between a minor character and an extra. There is a degree to which the masseuse stands as a simple surrogate for Marie, transposing her reactions of disgust into her own person and countenance. Yet there is no compelling narrative reason why Chaplin would need to set up a surrogate for Marie here. She does not need to be receiving a massage in this scene; her reactions do not need to be so gratuitously masked by a figure who appears nowhere else in the film. To a degree even more radical than his framing of the scene in which Marie reacts to her lover's suicide, Chaplin seems to be placing his main story line in the background of the film. We learn nothing of this masseuse beyond what we see in this scene, yet we are asked to intimately watch her reaction to the news from Marie's friend.

It is a flagrant reversal of what we might typically expect from a close-up or shot/reaction-shot composition. Rather than place us on intimate terms with a character central to the scene, the close-up is used to direct our attention away from the pivotal characters—to stand in contrast to the film's narrative rather than in support of it. Chaplin's close-up does not serve to emphasize so much as to distract, to open our attention to that which stands in the background of this story. The masseuse is a mere underling in this world, an unacknowledged functionary in the lives of the Parisian rich. But as a human being she has as much interiority as any other character on the screen; she would be as worthy of a close-up as any of them were this her story. And so for a moment, Chaplin makes it so. Who knows what personal betrayals she has undergone, what loyalties she might feel, what deceptions she herself might be in the midst of perpetuating. Chaplin gives us no answers. But what he does do is radically unsettle our complacency that the narrative we are seeing is the only narrative to be told and that the characters we are asked to care about are the only ones who exist. The close-up is a tool of emphasis—a "silent soliloquy," in Béla Balázs's famous phrase[21]—and while Chaplin has only limited use for it in telling his own stories, he is happy to harness it to draw our attention to unusual points of focus, to drive home the degree to which the story we are told is always constructed by a process of exclusion. With a series of different narrative choices, it might have been the masseuse whose close-up we wanted or expected to see or whose soliloquy we wanted to hear; it might have been her world and her experiences that the film chose to tell us about.

Indeed, even in his most seemingly standard and straightforward uses of the close-up—those instances that are not directly subversive to the film—something of this narrative skepticism remains in Chaplin's technique. Chaplin is not entirely averse to using the close-up to emphasize an established character in his films (to deploy the technique properly, from a classical perspective), but he will typically use it as a means of stressing isolation more than intimacy. Chaplin's close-ups do not tend to bring us closer to the characters that they depict so much as they move those characters farther away from the world around them. As in the opening sequence of *A Woman of Paris,* the close-up is most often for Chaplin a tool of exclusion and extraction. It tends to emblematize a retreat from the world and an absence of connection: it is not a window to some intimate aspect of the self so much as a picture of a figure lost in himself or herself, a closing-in on the self and separation from one's environment.

Hence the dynamics of what is perhaps Chaplin's most famous use of the close-up in the "Oceana Roll Dance" in *The Gold Rush.* Here, Chaplin is imagining himself entertaining Georgia and her dance hall friends on New Year's Eve, and he punctuates his dream fantasy with a moment of virtuosic performance where he transforms two dinner rolls on forks into legs that he holds up to his torso for an elaborate dance, seemingly shrinking his total frame and turning himself into a dancing man-bread hybrid. The shot is a straightforward medium close-up, and it is literally positioned as a kind of "silent soliloquy," though Balázs hadn't yet coined the phrase: the dancers demand a speech from Chaplin, but when he is choked up with emotion and cannot get the words out he decides to offer them a dance instead. Within the context of the fantasy itself, it is a moment of extreme connection and attention; the dance ends with the girls shouting "he's wonderful."[22] It is the moment where classical technique might most demand that we see the character in close-up, the better to understand his subjective experience of this high point in his narrative. But within the context of the film's full narrative, the sequence is delusional: Chaplin is in fantasy land and he is making himself the absolute center of attention at the exact moment that he is actually entirely alone. Only a few moments after the dance ends, the frame widens and the girls fade away to reveal Chaplin sleeping alone at the table he has set, his dinner guests having stood him up. What looks like a moment of extreme connection is actually a moment of total isolation; what looks like attachment to the world is actually a complete withdrawal from it. And Chaplin dramatizes this tension within the shot itself, for though the shot is technically a close-up, it is also a close-up and a full-body medium long shot at one and the same time. It is a close-up of Chaplin's face and upper torso, but he has transformed that face and upper torso into what looks like his entire body through the use of the dancing fork-roll legs. (He focuses the camera just on his face and yet still manages to get his "feet" into the shot—Florey would be flabbergasted.) Chaplin is the center of attention and he is entirely alone, he is connected to the world and he is living inside his own head—all at the same time. Of course Chaplin places himself in close-up and medium shot at once: there is no other way to capture the simultaneity of such disparate psychological states.

The Oceana Roll sequence is a masterful instance of Chaplin's reinvention of the close-up as a signifier of emotional isolation, but his most elaborate and sustained application of this technique comes in the kidnapping scene from *The Kid*—one of the few sequences in Chaplin's body of work that seems to conform easily to classical demands. Chaplin begins the scene in his typical sequence of middle-distance shots. Two child custody officers enter the Tramp's apartment and begin a comical three-person bit where one of the officers mediates a conversation between his superior and Chaplin, even though they are all huddled together in the tight quarters of the flat. But as soon as the officers decide that they need to take away Chaplin's boy, famously played by Jackie Coogan, the shot sequencing changes to something quite unusual for Chaplin's work. Interspersed with the medium and medium long shots of physical struggle, we see a series of close-ups, some of them even framed in irises: the boy huddling scared and alone, the Tramp and the boy backed into a corner, the boy crying out for his father from the back of the officers' truck,

Chaplin staring painfully at the camera as the officers hold him down. The scene, in other words, is told in pieces—a far cry from the unmoving camera work in the confrontation between Jean and his parents in *A Woman of Paris.* D. W. Griffith could not have set the confrontation better; the scene even bears a kind of basic compositional similarity to Griffith's own scene of child kidnapping in *Intolerance,* where medium long shots of the struggle over the baby are interspersed with close-ups of the mother fighting for her child or being overpowered by the women who have come to take him.

But what is most striking about Chaplin's scene from a compositional standpoint is that this level of conformity to classical technique occurs almost nowhere else in the film. Far more typical are the confrontations shown in long shot, the movements of the bodies on screen weaving elaborate patterns that would be untraceable in the broken and divided style of the kidnapping scene. This is the approach that Chaplin uses in the film's first great confrontation with the police, where Chaplin's Tramp and Coogan's boy exist in total harmony with the landscape around them. Fleeing an off-duty police officer who has discovered their scam to sell window repair services, Chaplin and Coogan duck into a tenement alleyway. In a single long shot, we watch an impressive display of evasion: Chaplin and Coogan run halfway down the alleyway, trip the police officer with their window repair equipment, run back to the entrance of the alleyway, then take off in opposite directions like a pair of synchronized figure skaters so that the policeman tumbles past them. In a different scene of confrontation, Coogan beats up a neighborhood bully while the bully's much tougher older brother eyes Chaplin for revenge. Like the escape from the police officer, Chaplin's escape from the brother is played in long shot such that the movement of both their bodies is always visible at once. Having taken advantage of the distraction provided by a charity worker, Chaplin disables the ruffian with a few blows to the head with a brick. Nearly assured of victory, he calmly makes his way back to his tenement, with the ruffian stopping him every few feet to try to position him for a punch to the face; Chaplin accepts the positioning each time but ducks the punch and gives the bully another hit to the head with his brick. The process takes on a highly choreographed feel, as though Chaplin and the ruffian were performing an elaborate dance from the background to the foreground of the frame.

Chaplin could have composed these sequences in a manner similar to the kidnapping scene with no loss of narrative clarity. As the Tramp and the boy flee from the police officer, he could have cut in shots of each of them running alone, of the two of them communicating or signaling to each other, of the police officer exasperated in pursuit. Or as the Tramp evades the bully's brother in the later sequence, he could have cut between the brother's dazed expression and the Tramp's masterful ducks and parries, interspersed the reaction or worry of the boy, shown us more closely the Tramp scheming his escape. (To continue the comparison to Griffith, one might think here of the cutting in the climactic battle sequence in *The Musketeers of Pig Alley,* where medium shots and the occasional close-up are interspersed with a recurring long shot of the alleyway confrontation.) But such an approach would lose the impressive synchronicity of action in these scenes: the honeybee patterns of the movements of father and son, the way in which they so elegantly and fluidly command the tenement street while escaping the policeman, or the careful ballet that Chaplin measures out as he slowly escapes from the ruffian. In these moments, Chaplin and Coogan are both in obvious command of their environments, in sync with the world around them and nimbly able to navigate its pathways and escape routes. They are connected to the world.

And this is precisely the difference between the kidnapping scene and these earlier confrontations. Chaplin's and Coogan's navigation of their world is flawless in the earlier scenes, but the kidnapping scene is a study in defeat. Every effort Chaplin makes to stop the police is blocked, and every attempt that Coogan makes to escape his captors is foiled. The close-ups in the sequence are images of despair and impotence and isolation: Coogan huddled in a corner, Chaplin desperately trying to hold off the attackers with a bowl full of flour, Coogan distraught in the back of the truck, Chaplin held down and defeated by the officers. They are literally images of Chaplin and Coogan unable to take command of the world around them. It is acceptable then if the close-up cuts out the environment and shows them in an artificial visual isolation, for they are themselves cut off from each other and the world. They are disconnected and they are alone, a state that they are forced into by external forces. They are living the situation of the close-up itself; it is, for this moment, the perfect tool for emphasizing the nature of their sad defeat. And it is ultimately a cinematographic style from which they must escape as much as they must escape the police themselves.

It is no coincidence that as Chaplin's Tramp determines how to overcome the orphanage officers and win back his son, the film's cinematic style also returns to form. Following the truck that is taking Coogan away, Chaplin climbs up to the top of his building and races across the tenement roofs to intercept the vehicle. The sequence is shown in a series of medium and medium long shots that culminate in one of the widest shots used in the film—a view of the Tramp on the roof and the truck in the street below together from the same vantage point. When Chaplin at last jumps from the roof onto the truck bed, it is now the officers who are shown in close-up, their expressions of surprise and fear at Chaplin's reappearance clearly indicating the shift in fortunes in this new chapter of their conflict. Chaplin allows the Tramp and the boy a hug in medium close-up when they are first reunited—a fleeting moment in which they might be said to forget about the world around them—but it lasts only an instant before Chaplin is back in action. Throwing one officer from the truck in a medium tracking shot, Chaplin manages to scare off the other simply by making furious gestures toward him, shown in an extreme long shot that encompasses nearly the whole city block. The Tramp is in control of his environment once more, and he is in sync with the world around him. The close-up is for Chaplin a visual register of pain or isolation or retreat; it is not the proper means to frame a return to agency, no matter how joyous or personal or intimate. In this way, Chaplin's visual aesthetic is almost Brechtian in its insistence that the human figure can only properly be regarded when placed inside its context, set within a specific social network and a particular physical situation. The close-up is an artificial isolation from these contexts; the only thing it can properly show us is the state of isolation itself. In Chaplin's own words, "There is no set rule that a close-up gives more emphasis than a long shot. A close-up is a question of feeling; in some instances a long shot can effect greater emphasis."[23]

NARRATIVE MULTIPLICITY AND THE EVER-WIDENING FRAME

What is at issue in Chaplin's bias toward the wider frame, as in so much of his aesthetic, is a dedication to preserving a kind of simultaneity: the simultaneity of the world itself as it unfolds in space. To understand a family fight, we must see all three family members fighting together; to understand a triumph over enemies, we must see both the victor and the vanquished in relation to each other. We must see it, in Bazin's terms, "in its physical and spatial reality."[24] Chaplin's aversion to the close-up—his sequestering of it to moments of narrative subterfuge or emotional isolation—is based on the idea that it takes too far the necessary elisions and omissions that any narrative storytelling requires, reducing the world to too small a picture. In Chaplin's view, narrative itself may hide too much; classical techniques of narrative emphasis like the close-up insist on hiding it even more. Chaplin's drive is the opposite: it is to widen the frame of the shot as much as possible, to widen the frame of the narrative as much as possible, to recognize the ways that "a long shot can effect greater emphasis." The more that he can encompass in his frame, the truer that frame will be—even if it widens so far as to take him practically into other films.

Chaplin does, on occasion, take his drive toward inclusion to almost epic extremes, as in an unusual narrative sequence at the center of *A Woman of*

Paris. Here, in a fight with Pierre over the possibilities for their future together, Marie looks outside her ritzy Parisian apartment and gestures to the world beyond: it is a world that looks remarkably like the universe of Chaplin's slapstick films. Talking about how she wants to settle down and have children, her attention is drawn to children and parents passing by on the street. The children are dressed like slum dwellers, as though they could be extras from *The Kid*: shoddy garments, mismatched stockings, shoes that don't quite fit. As the argument progresses, Marie throws a pearl necklace into the street in anger—at just the moment that a disheveled tramp character happens to be passing by her opulent building. She determines that she does not want to lose the necklace after all and must race outside to wrangle it back from the confused vagrant. The man is not dressed like Chaplin's Tramp per se, but he is clearly of a piece with the universe of characters in Chaplin's slapstick world.[25] As if for good measure, Marie is chased by a stray dog (reminiscent of the pooch in *A Dog's Life*) as she returns, passing along the way a French gendarme—as common a figure in French slapstick shorts as there could be—strolling alone along the sidewalk and eyeing her suspiciously, as though he had just emerged from one of Max Linder's Pathé films and knew how to do nothing else.

On one level, Marie's intersections with the children, the tramp, the dog, and the gendarme form a kind of in-joke for the audience: a quick nod to the kinds of films that made Chaplin famous and a brief return to the slapstick environment from which he was now departing in this, his first dramatic picture. But there is also a more serious purpose behind such non sequiturs: an acknowledgment that just as no story is the only story, no world is the only world. The world of leisure and riches that Marie inhabits does not just momentarily intersect with the world of poverty and violence that is Chaplin's usual milieu; it exists alongside it at every moment, bound together in an encompassing simultaneity that goes beyond the ability of any single frame to capture, no matter how wide. As Marie's story unfolds in the chambers of an expensive Paris apartment building, the story of the tramp's deprivation unfolds on the street, the story of the family's struggles unfolds in the home they are going to or coming from, and the story of the gendarme's responsibilities unfolds on the route of his patrol. That the stories occurring outside of the apartment building belong to the world of slapstick and not to the world of melodrama only serves to further emphasize the insurmountable limitations and foreclosures that storytelling imposes. No story, no aesthetic, and no genre can be complete; they only approach completeness, ever so slightly, when placed in combination, in ever-widening their frame and their aesthetic. But they are all shackled with blinders—blinders that they need so that they might exist at all, but blinders nonetheless. And, for Chaplin, all storytelling structures are maddeningly dishonest insofar as they refuse to acknowledge the acute degree of their limitations, the degree to which they presuppose a "unity of meaning," the degree to which, ultimately, one story can tell us hardly anything at all.

A *Woman of Paris* ends by accenting this note. Having left Paris to work at an orphanage in the countryside, Marie finishes the film riding on a wagon down a humble country road. Unbeknownst to her, Pierre is driving in a car only a few feet away. The film ends with the two former intimates passing each other unawares, traveling in opposite directions. Story lines that were once joined have diverged, worlds that were once shared have separated. The contrivance of narrative itself has unraveled, and a world that asserted a kind of singular direction and purpose as its rightful prerogative, as any story must, has broken into its component parts. Two lovers have become strangers living now in different worlds, bound together only by the simultaneity of their lives and stories, which is the simultaneity of all lives and stories. Yet as much as the ending of *A Woman of Paris* is a narrative critique, it is also a kind of visual triumph of Chaplin's widening frame. It is a means of both capturing and acknowledging a multiplicity of stories within a single filmic moment, the closest thing to aesthetic honesty that the cinema can achieve in Chaplin's philosophy. It is also a sister moment to scenes like the one where Marie reacts to her lover's suicide in the background of the frame or where the Tramp becomes an unexpected extra in *The Gold Rush*. For Chaplin, the ideal frame is wide enough to tell multiple stories at once, to capture something of the simultaneity of the world.

And when he is at his strongest, Chaplin is able to create and to sustain a kind of narrative and visual interlacing of stories within his films that classical technique might never allow, turning the visual cacophony and simultaneity of a short like *Those Awful Hats* into something precise, controlled, and harmonious even without breaking up the space and time of the sequence. The fuguelike restaurant scene from *The Immigrant* is a case in point and is perhaps the greatest example of Chaplin's narrative simultaneity at work. The scene is duly famous for the precision of Chaplin's pantomime, but equally virtuosic is the composition of the sequence itself. By the scene's end no fewer than five separate story lines have played out to greater or lesser degrees of emphasis, all without the typical techniques of classical editing, and all of them coming together in the scene's final moments. Functioning as the baseline and driving force of the scene is the story line of Chaplin's Tramp, here a recent immigrant who realizes he has lost the money that he found on the street just as he witnesses the restaurant's policy of physically beating any customer who cannot pay. Another tramp enters the restaurant and takes the table next to Chaplin, examining a coin that he seems to have found serendipitously. Chaplin suspects that it is his own lost coin and means to reclaim it, but he is inadvertently blocked by the waiter at every turn; the other tramp buys himself some coffee before Chaplin can intervene. Chaplin thinks he has found relief, however, when the waiter drops the coin from the other tramp and Chaplin picks it up to pay for his own meal. But the coin turns out to be counterfeit, and Chaplin must deflect the waiter's attention (and his wrath) by ordering more coffee until he can figure out another strategy. Layered on top of this narrative is the story line of Edna Purviance's character, another immigrant who is mourning the recent loss of her mother and whom Chaplin is determined to both impress and protect. She knows that he lost the coin, but she nevertheless trusts Chaplin to take care of the check and of her. Chaplin introduces a third story line in the deus ex machina of an artist who determines that Chaplin and Purviance make the ideal picturesque subject for his next painting and who joins their table, offering to pay for their meal. Added to this trio is the tramp at the next table, who found the coin that Chaplin found first and who remains visible throughout most of the scene, and the physically imposing waiter, who is willing to wait for Chaplin to come up with payment but who is determined to receive his money nonetheless or have Chaplin suffer the consequences.

What separates the restaurant sequence from any typical scene of confusion and misunderstanding is the degree to which Chaplin elevates the idea of simultaneity to a kind of active working method. Once introduced, nearly all the characters are on screen together nearly all the time, and with the exception of the Tramp each remains unaware of the actions of the others, cocooned in his or her own needs and drives, in the particular reality of his or her own concerns. Chaplin emphasizes the narrative equivalency of the characters in the visual equivalencies that he establishes on screen. As always, Chaplin carefully defines the coordinates of space within the shot. A wall behind the Tramp's table defines the middle plane of space, a wide entryway leading to a pair of musicians in the next room of the restaurant defines the background space, and the empty space in front of the Tramp's table defines the foreground of the shot. The entryway in the center of the frame marks the front-back axis of the shot and clearly defines the exact middle of the frame. Yet despite this intensive differentiation of space, Chaplin places all of the characters in what is essentially a position of spatial equality: the foreground space is left bare, the background plane is left to the musicians, and all of the characters in the scene fill the middle plane from left to right. The Tramp is essentially centered, Purviance and the artist to the right and the waiter and the other tramp to the left, but whatever importance this central position might signal would seem to be compromised by the equivalent plane positioning of the other characters in the shot. What's more, the vertical beams on the back wall of the room, just behind the Tramp and the other characters, serve literally to segment each character's position, giving them each a defined section of the plane in which to operate, the waiter framed in his space by the opening of the doorway. Chaplin visually alerts us to the autonomy and equivalency of each character in the frame even before the action begins, inviting us to consider the scene from any of the perspectives offered by the figures on screen, even as he uses the arrangement of bodies and movements to emphasize the Tramp and his predicament as our main point of focus. Like the artist in the meal scene from *The Vagabond,* the artist here is positioned with his back mostly to the camera, and Purviance is partly obscured by his figure. The other tramp on the far left of the screen is partially cut off by the edge of the frame when he is included in the shot, while the waiter mostly stands sideways so as to face the Tramp's table. Unless interacting with the Tramp, all of the characters engage for the most part in the typical slow and repetitive motions of a Chaplin extra, creating a kind of blanket verisimilitude in the frame without drawing attention to themselves. Only Chaplin's Tramp looks outward from the scene and asks us with his hyperactive body to follow his machinations.

And some machinations they are. Having foolishly declined the artist's generous offer to pay for the meal in a gesture of false politeness that he does not expect to backfire, the Tramp must contrive a new way to pay for the meal. What transpires is a kind of three-card monte with coins. When the artist puts down money to pay for his portion of the meal with the intention of leaving the remainder as a generous tip, the Tramp quickly gets the idea to ask the waiter for his own check. Before the waiter can claim the artist's tip and before the artist can notice what is happening, the Tramp takes the coin from the artist's plate and hands it to the waiter to pay for his own bill. The waiter brings the Tramp his change in turn, the Tramp offers it back to him as a respectable tip, and he stands to leave along with Purviance and the artist. Behind them, the waiter looks at the artist waiting for his tip. He makes a gesture, but the artist thinks he is being thanked for the generosity of the tip and waves the waiter off. Eager to avoid discovery, the Tramp ushers Purviance and the artist out of the restaurant as the waiter seethes behind them and the other tramp remains just barely visible in the corner of the frame. What is remarkable about the sequence is the degree to which Chaplin is able to create so many independent perspectives on reality—so many independent story lines—from such a small series of actions presented in quick succession. As the party prepares to leave the restaurant, the perspective that each character has of the events that just transpired is worlds apart. To the artist, the Tramp has paid for his own meal, he himself has left a generous tip that has made the waiter happy, and there was never any dilemma. To Purviance, the artist has paid for his own meal, the Tramp has paid for their meal somehow, and there is no concern over tips at all. To the waiter, the artist has paid for his own meal, the Tramp has paid for his own meal (after trying first to pass off a counterfeit coin), the

Tramp has left him a respectable tip, and the artist has shortchanged him to the point of insult. To the other tramp, he found a perfectly legitimate coin on the street, used it to buy some coffee, and there was never any problem. And to the Tramp, the other tramp essentially stole his coin, the coin turned out to be counterfeit anyway, the artist paid for both meals, and he tricked the waiter into thinking the artist left him no tip.

The countenance of each character in the final moments of the scene reflects these divergent perceptions: the artist self-satisfied at his own generosity, the waiter furious, Purviance content at the happy resolution of the meal and diverted from her bereavement, the other tramp unsuspectingly sitting in the corner, and our own beloved Tramp hoping that they can all get out of the restaurant before his scheme is uncovered. None of the characters on screen is occupying the same perceptual reality, and none of them except for the Tramp is even aware of the degree of divergence between their realities. And yet all of these perceptual realities appear on screen at once. Indeed, they have been on screen together all along. Chaplin does not cut back and forth between members of the party; he does not give us close-ups of the artist or of Purviance to show their obliviousness; he does not cut to the other tramp to show us his perspective. These realities occur simultaneously and yet even in that simultaneity they diverge in the most basic of ways. And what's more, Chaplin lets us watch that simultaneity unfold in front of us, enabling us to track how and where and when each character's perception spins off into his or her own version of the truth. He directs our attention within the frame through his configuration of space and movement, but he does not foreclose our ability to disregard his direction. We can watch the artist through the entire sequence if we choose; we can watch the other tramp; we can watch Purviance. We can pick and choose our point of focus, and depending on our choices we can even become as ignorant of what just transpired as any of the characters on the screen. Just as Chaplin's composition demonstrates in real time the way in which a single, simultaneous reality can itself diverge into utterly separate stories and views, so too does he allow that divergence to emerge from his own presentation. Chaplin casts his frame radically wide to better capture the world as it unfolds, and in so doing he leaves it radically open to the ambiguities and contradictions of the world itself.

DANGEROUS AMBIGUITIES: QUESTIONING THE FRAME, QUESTIONING THE NARRATIVE

Chaplin's filmmaking moves in two aesthetic directions at once. In a positive sense, it opens itself toward ever-greater expressions of simultaneity, widening its frame to capture more of the world in both small moments and whole con-structions. But at the same time that it seeks to represent our world more fully, it also evinces a profound skepticism toward filmic representation itself. To a degree arguably unmatched by any other major filmmaker of his era, Chaplin distrusted any attempt to foreclose and determine meaning within a film, even within his own self-consciously expansive filmmaking style. Chaplin simply did not trust that anything framed into an image or ordered into a narrative might escape the limitations of those processes, that it might be able through exclusion and reduction to arrive at anything we might call truth, even in the most mundane sense of the word. Hence the constant questioning of the frame itself that permeates Chaplin's visual style. The frame for Chaplin is not a neu-tral or invisible device; it is a choice and should be acknowledged as such—a choice that might be deceitful or might support an agenda other than the clar-ity that is part of the grand bargain of classical style, that unspoken agreement by which viewers will allow the world to be reordered for them so long as that reordering offers them what Robert Ray calls "a constantly optimum vantage point."[26]

Quite often, for instance, Chaplin's framing of a given scene is simply wrong, and purposefully so. With relish, Chaplin will place the camera in an unsatisfactory position for gaining the most advantageous view of the action that unfolds, and the mistake of Chaplin's form is as much a part of the hu-mor as his content. Hence the comical moment in *Sunnyside* (First National, 1919) where the Tramp, here a rural laborer, is searching in town for a herd of cows that he has lost. As he investigates the background plane of space in the town's center, a cow suddenly appears in the middle plane, charging out of the window of a house. Just as the Tramp moves to where the cow emerged, we notice in the back left of the frame a crowd coming out of the local church. The Tramp joins the crowd, enters the church, and exits riding a bull. As he is about to ride off on his bull, yet another cow wanders across the empty foreground of the frame with no warning whatsoever. In each of these cases, the humor is as much in what is missed as what is seen: the shock of having the cows continu-ally appear in unexpected, unimportant sections of the frame coupled with the realization that Chaplin's camera has actually missed the better part of the gag altogether—the scene that would presumably show us the cows running wild through the church or through a house or something other than the empty town streets. We laugh at the scenario, but we also laugh at missing the better part of it. We laugh at our recognition of what the frame can leave out.

Elsewhere in Chaplin's work, the frame is not so much wrongly placed as it is deceptively positioned, designed not to miss the action but to actively hide it. It is a manifestation of what Deleuze calls in *Cinema 1* the "perception-image,"

a movement in the frame that is based around a realignment in our perception of the content of the frame itself.[27] It is a common technique in slapstick
comedy. Harold Lloyd was a frequent practitioner, as in the opening of *Safety
Last,* where what looks like a scene of execution turns out to be a farewell at a
train station. Keaton had used almost the same setup a year earlier in the opening of *Cops,* where the bars of an iron entry gate mimic the bars of a jail cell
until a camera readjustment allows us to re-recognize the object as innocuous. But Chaplin's variation on this format takes on a different valence; in two
classic examples from his work, the position of the frame actually forces us to
misperceive the actions of Chaplin's body. One, in *The Immigrant,* has Chaplin
gesticulating over the side of an ocean liner as though vomiting; only when he
turns around do we realize he has been fishing. Another, in *The Idle Class* (First
National, 1921), shows Chaplin from behind seemingly shuddering with tears
after reading a note that his wife has left him on account of his drinking problem; when Chaplin turns around, we realize he has simply been fixing himself
another cocktail. The humor in these moments is similar to that in the Lloyd
and Keaton examples, but the differences are significant. Lloyd and Keaton
can claim in their perception-gags a kind of put-on innocence. They begin in
a close-up of the central character and reveal to us our misperception of the
circumstance as they pull back to a wider shot; the mix-up is a product of our
assumptions based on limited information, and the frame actively helps us to
resolve our confusion. But Chaplin's version of the gag offers no sugarcoating
and no redemption of the frame. The misperception at the heart of the gag is
revealed not when the frame readjusts but when the body moves within the
frame: only when the Tramp turns to face the camera do we become cognizant
of our mistake. Chaplin's frame does not help us to understand our mistakes;
it does not move at all. In other words, the frame is not the resolution of the
problem but its source. Had Chaplin chosen to place his camera elsewhere—
say, on the other side of the Tramp's figure—there would have been no misperception, but neither would there have been any gag. Chaplin's perception-gag
is achieved only through deceit—through the self-conscious placement of the
camera in an unhelpful, misleading position. Chaplin all but tells us that his
frame—and, we may surmise, any frame—may not help to resolve our confusions; it may in fact work to actively create them if such confusion can serve
the purpose of the film.

In other scenarios, Chaplin's frame may not fail us and may not deceive us,
but neither does it give us sufficient information for our purposes, concealing
or deemphasizing important components of a scene. Such is the case in one of
the opening sequences of *The Kid.* Here, the first time that we see the Tramp he
approaches us from the far background of the frame, snaking his way through

a tenement alleyway littered with debris and carefully avoiding the garbage being dumped into the street by tenement dwellers above. By the time he makes it to the foreground of the frame, Chaplin seems to have successfully navigated the terrain, avoiding both the garbage on the ground and the garbage from above. Yet just as he seems to have made it all the way through, a mass of garbage falls on him from a point unseen above the upper reaches of the frame. The laugh is in the surprise appearance of this dumping and the irony of its timing, but both of these are products only of Chaplin's decision as to where to place the camera. Had he pulled the frame back a little farther we would have seen the source of the trash the same way that we saw and anticipated the other garbage being tossed earlier in the scene. It did not need to be a surprise, nor did it need to come at the very end of Chaplin's trek, an endpoint determined arbitrarily by the location of the camera within his path. These conditions are evidence—offered at the very start of Chaplin's first feature—of how the frame controls and limits our perception of the world to the best advantage of the film: in this case toward the end of the gag.

If there is any question as to the danger of this approach—metaphorically in an interpretive sense, but even literally within the diegesis of the film—it is answered by one of the more sinister examples in Chaplin's body of work. In *Sunnyside,* Chaplin wishes to win Purviance as his girlfriend and to rid her house of his pesky younger brother, who will not leave the two of them alone. He tricks the boy into a game of blindman's bluff and sets him outside to roam blindfolded toward the street. The house is on a quiet country road, yet as soon as the boy reaches the edge of the little lane a car comes racing by and nearly kills him. It is a sudden shock: the boy is almost at the very edge of the frame when the car appears as if from nowhere, just barely missing him within its first second in the shot. As viewers, we have no lead time to adjust to the presence of the car, and part of the humor of the scene (dark humor, to be sure) is the degree to which we are taken by surprise by the near-cataclysmic event. But this surprise is again utterly a construct of Chaplin's framing. There is no reason we should not be able to see a lone car coming down an empty country road, no reason we cannot anticipate and prepare ourselves for its near-collision with the boy—except for the fact that to anticipate the car is to lose the gag, which depends for its impact upon surprise. As in the sequence from *The Kid,* Chaplin's frame acts as an artificial limit on our perception and not a benign one. The very act of framing must always make us question what we are being shown and what is being hidden—what speeding cars may lie just beyond the reaches of the frame, what trash may be hanging over our heads just hidden from view. To frame is to exclude, and Chaplin asks us always to be aware of these exclusions and to regard the placement of the frame with a kind of skepticism.

In the end, of course, framing serves the interest of the film, which is to say the film's narrative. It is aimed in the typical case to help make the film's story line more clear and to dispel confusion and ambiguity. Yet the goal of narrative clarity is not one that Chaplin would necessarily support. He was a master narrative craftsman, to be sure—far more so than most other slapstick artists—but he was at the same time deeply skeptical of narrative as a means of organizing the world. Framing, editing, montage—all the standard tricks of classical technique—are usually applied quite explicitly to clarify and to naturalize narrative events, to make the unfolding of the story as seamless as possible. But to Chaplin there was nothing natural about narrative at all; it was an artificial process of selection, exclusion, and concision, and while it might be enjoyed as entertainment, it must always also be held in a kind of aesthetic abeyance. It can never be trusted.

In this respect, Chaplin's reputation as an unreconstructed sentimentalist is almost entirely undeserved. While he was quite happy to offer the most saccharine of narratives in his film, the structures of qualifications and cautions that he sets up around those narratives is almost always skeptical of them, even deeply—and sometimes disturbingly—cynical. There is almost never a happy ending in Chaplin that does not come with an asterisk attached—and if the ending of a saccharine tale cannot be trusted to ensure happiness, the whole of the tale that precedes it must descend into free fall. Such is the case in one of Chaplin's earliest and most flagrant happy endings, in *The Vagabond*. Here, Chaplin's Tramp is devastated when the wealthy girl whom he has rescued from gypsies and since tried to woo is taken away by her family and the wealthy artist with whom she seems to have fallen in love. Yet almost no sooner is the Tramp left alone than the car that has taken away Purviance returns. An intertitle during the girl's journey in the car alerts us to "the awakening of the real love," at which point she forces the car to turn around.[28] "You come too," the girl demands in the next intertitle, and she pulls the lonely Tramp into the limousine to speed off toward her mansion. It seems like a happy ending plain and simple, except that it takes no more than a few moments' thought to realize that nothing has been resolved at all; if anything, the situation has only been made more complicated. Purviance's girl has not renounced her affection for the artist. She asks the Tramp to come in addition, not instead. What resolution they will possibly find that can accommodate all three parties to this love triangle is a mystery, as is the question of how Chaplin's ragtag Tramp might adjust to life among the millionaires, whether he saved their daughter or not. As Walter Kerr puts it, "What is Charlie doing in the car? There is no answering that question. . . . The vagabond, the tramp, can be taken in. But there is no 'in,' really—not for him. The ambiguous ending, with emotion going one way and logic another, becomes the only valid ending for a Chaplin film."[29] The film's supposed resolution is no resolution at all; it is merely, and quite explicitly, a deferral. Chaplin has not solved the problems of the film—he has merely postponed the inevitable narrative collapse that they will cause until after the ostensible ending of the short. He has created a happy ending only by making it no ending at all.

If the cynicism of this ending is not clear enough (Chaplin in fact originally considered having the Tramp commit suicide at the end of the short), he essentially doubles down in a kind of revision to it in *The Kid*. Here, the Tramp again finds himself in a "you come too" position. Wandering lost and alone after his boy is taken away from him, the Tramp is picked up by a police officer and brought to the mansion where the boy's wealthy mother resides. The basic situation is dangerously similar to the scenario at the end of *The Vagabond*—the Tramp has been invited into a world of wealth but Purviance's character is again attached to another, a wealthy artist who in this case is the boy's biological father. Although they are not married, Purviance and the artist have a scene earlier in the film where they consider reuniting if they could find their lost child. Are we really to believe that the Tramp will suddenly take the artist's place as husband to a woman he has never met so that he can remain as a surrogate father to her child? Or perhaps that he should have some third role if Purviance and the artist do marry as they had implied earlier in the film?

Lest we have any doubt as to Chaplin's own position on this ending, he makes sure to precede it with another, much more literal, fantasy sequence. Lying asleep in a doorway after he has given up searching for the boy, the Tramp dreams of a world where everything is right. The tenement alleyways are transformed into a masquerade version of a heavenly paradise, the slum dwellers remade into angels with Christmas pageant robes and wings. And in this fantasy world, the boy returns to his surrogate father, dressed like a little angel. But the fantasy quickly descends from wish fulfillment to dark morality play. "Sin" enters the angelic world of the reborn slum, and within minutes the Tramp has not just fallen into a dispute with another winged slum dweller but has wound up dead, shot multiple times in the chest by an angelic policeman who leaves him lying upside down in a doorway. As if that were not gruesome enough, the sequence ends with the boy emerging from the crowd and running to his dead father, desperately hugging the Tramp's lifeless corpse. It is a remarkably grisly sequence, one that on its own should be enough to dispel complaints about Chaplin's sentimentality. There is no escape into happiness in this filmic universe: if the Tramp cannot survive even his own imagined resolution to the problems at hand, we have to wonder at the resolutions that the narrative presents. The starkness of Chaplin's fantasy sequence does more than just ask us to call the ending of the film into question; it demands that we regard it prima facie as a failure, possibly even a dangerous one. The Tramp is stepping dangerously out of his social milieu in the narrative's official ending—he is even brought to the millionaire woman's home by a police officer, a figure associated only with pain and degradation in the tenement world of the film. More than just worrying about the failure or success of this new iteration of the "you come too" arrangement, Chaplin suggests that we should perhaps even worry about the Tramp's very life.

There is, of course, one happy ending in Chaplin's silent features: Chaplin strikes gold, becomes a multimillionaire, and gets the girl—kisses her even!—at the conclusion of the 1925 version of *The Gold Rush*. It is an unusual turn of events for the downtrodden Tramp, and it is not surprisingly one of the most contextually problematic endings that Chaplin would ever create, at once a diegetic fairy-tale ending and a kind of metanarrative rebuttal to the idea that any filmic tale can ever end so neatly. More than a conclusion that follows naturally from the events of the narrative, it is an ending that is, almost literally, forced onto the story by the film itself. Chaplin actually begins the final stretch of the picture as if the film is already over, as if it had stopped when he and his prospecting partner had struck gold. Diegetically, he is on a ship traveling home, dressed not in his famous Tramp outfit but in a millionaire's finery—a sharply pressed suit, a rich overcoat, an expensive cane, and a top hat. But in a metanarrative sense, it looks like Chaplin himself—the filmmaker, not the Tramp character—has stepped onto the screen. "Make way for the multimillionaires," an intertitle reads to transition us into the finale, and it looks for all the world as if the film has ended and a documentary reel about Chaplin, a multimillionaire many times over by 1925, has been spliced in. Though Chaplin still wears the mustache, his gait has nothing of the Tramp in it. And everywhere he goes, he and his partner are followed by photographers and reporters recording their every move, as in much of Chaplin's own life. He might as well be on a boat going to the premiere of the film, were it not for a quick bit in which the Tramp instinctively tries to bum a half-used cigar off the ground, forgetting he and his partner now have pockets full of them. It is the media that demands that Chaplin become the Tramp again. A pair of journalists want to take a picture of him in his prospector's clothes to go with an article they are writing. We are thus witness to the strange spectacle of Chaplin in his stateroom beginning to remove his millionaire's outfit, helped by assistants and valets, and reemerging as the Tramp, at which point his physical mannerisms again resume in full. It is as though Chaplin is literally staging for us the process of reentering the film, re-creating a scene that must not look too much unlike the actual processes by which the millionaire Chaplin transformed himself into the impoverished Tramp every day on set.

And of course he must become the Tramp again at this point: there is unfin-ished narrative business to attend to. Just before he begins to remove his suit, Chaplin notices a picture he has put up in his cabin. "Everything but Georgia" the intertitle reads—a reminder of the one thing that the Tramp does not have in his newfound social position, but also, more provocatively, a statement of the one thing that has not been wrapped up in the narrative. Chaplin must become the Tramp again to finish the film. And it is in his returned Tramp state that he at last finds and wins the girl, literally pushed into doing so by a man with a camera. Getting ready to shoot a photo of Chaplin on the deck, the press photographer keeps asking him to step farther backward, eventually sending him tumbling down an open staircase. And at the bottom of those stairs is Georgia, who, unbeknownst to Chaplin, is also on the boat. Seeing the Tramp in his typical outfit, Georgia is convinced that he must be the stowaway that the ship's crew is looking for and she tries to help him avoid detection, first by hiding him and then by offering to pay for his fare. She essentially initiates the ending that the film might more logically contain were it not for the discovery of the gold. Of course, Chaplin smiles lovingly at Georgia as the misunderstanding unfolds, amused by the fact that she does not yet know of his newfound wealth yet also, it seems, because she does not realize the film is already over. He just needs to bring her into its resolution. With the confu-sion resolved, the journalists decide to have Georgia pose in the picture with Chaplin, carefully positioning them both in the frame. "Gee! This will make a wonderful story," an intertitle reads. Their faces close together as they pose, Chaplin ends the film by kissing his heroine. It is a tentative, even awkward kiss, yet it is also, in Kamin's words, "one of the most satisfying kisses in movie history."[30]

It does indeed "make a wonderful story," but it is also a complete lie. The last real interaction between Georgia and the Tramp in the film was when she stood him up for the New Year's Eve celebration he proposed. Chaplin thought she had apologized to him afterward and declared that she loved him, but it was a trick—a note she had written to her loutish boyfriend Jack apologizing for slapping him was given to the Tramp as a kind of prank. When the Tramp celebrates what he thinks is Georgia's declaration of love in the town's dance hall, Chaplin frames the shot so that it is possible to see Georgia in the upper-left corner of the frame on the balcony, collapsed and distraught at Jack's cal-lous disregard for her apology. It is one of the last times we see her in the film before the boat. Whatever kindness she shows to the Tramp on the steerage deck cannot be taken as a pure declaration of affection: she has shown the Tramp kindness and pity before, which he has consistently mistaken for signs of love. Clearly things have not worked out with Jack for Georgia to be on that ship, but there is no guarantee she is ready to fall in love with the Tramp.

The kiss is a wish fulfillment: it is how the Tramp wants to see the situation, and how the narrative does too. But it has no bearing on Georgia's emotional reality. Yet that kiss is not the final moment of the film. There is one last intertitle in the concluding seconds, conveying the dialogue of the disgruntled photographer who wasn't ready for the kiss: "Oh! You've spoilt the picture." It is certainly one of the stranger ways to end a film, with a statement that can so obviously be read as self-criticism. And it is an even stranger comment in light of the fact that Chaplin seems to have actually done nothing of the sort. Far from spoiling the picture in any traditional sense, he has saved it: he has brought Georgia into the narrative resolution, however improbably, and salvaged the possibility of a happy ending. It is exactly what Chaplin is supposed to do as a storyteller: he has brought all of the film's narrative lines to a final point of rest. Yet to offer such a pat resolution that so neatly ties up the film's narrative is, within Chaplin's own aesthetic, indeed to spoil it. Purposefully, the ending of *The Gold Rush* is nothing but a series of contrivances—which is to say that it is an ending which tries to close down and resolve the tensions of the picture, to bring them into order. Chaplin cannot offer such an ending without also commenting on its aesthetic failures and its dishonesty.[31]

In this sense, the ending of *The Circus* (United Artists, 1928) can be seen as a kind of answer to the ending of *The Gold Rush,* an open refusal to offer a perfect ending in contrast to the cynical acquiescence to narrative closure of his prior feature. Chaplin would return here to the "you come too" scenario one last time, rewriting it yet again to further emphasize its artificiality. Here, Chaplin plays a homeless vagabond turned circus clown who falls in love with the circus's beautiful equestrian performer; she in turn loves a handsome tightrope walker. Realizing the futility of his love and recognizing that a marriage to the tightrope walker will help protect the girl from her abusive stepfather, the Tramp arranges for them to be married. As the ceremony finishes, the circus is preparing to leave town and all must reboard their wagons. The girl and the tightrope walker do not want to leave the Tramp, who has been so kind to them, and they invite him into their wagon. "Come in with us," the starlet says to him, offering a variation on Purviance's line from *The Vagabond.* But here Chaplin literally rewrites his former ending. The Tramp refuses the offer: he holds up two fingers and then three fingers to the girl, indicating that it makes no sense for him to be a hanger-on, that a relationship between the three of them cannot work. But it is no great loss, he indicates; he will simply board his own wagon and see them in the next town.

But as soon as the Tramp turns down the offer of the happy ending—as soon as he literally closes the door on the girl and her new husband instead of accepting their offer to come inside, as he did in *The Vagabond* and *The*

Kid—something extraordinary happens. All of the circus wagons leave at once in a rush of dust and motion, leaving the Tramp behind despite the fact that he was meant to come along. In a stunning visual sequence, the Tramp stands in the middle of the thunderous caravan departure until the dust finally clears and he realizes he is now standing alone in an open field, the only remaining traces of the circus structure being a giant outline of the big-top ring in the dirt. The moment that the Tramp explicitly denies the requisite happy ending, as improbable as its demands might be, he is quite literally abandoned by the film: the whole apparatus of the narrative heads out of town and refuses to bring him along. Almost the whole of the story has unfolded in that big-top tent; now all that remains is the circular trace of it in the dirt, a trace of where the narrative once was. It is as powerful a metaphor for the narrative process as anything in Chaplin's work. Realistic or not, narrative demands resolution; it demands that it be made sense of. The narrative strains that have defined the story—the connections between the Tramp and the girl, the girl and the tightrope walker, the three of them and the girl's stepfather—must be set to rest, placed in a series of final relations, used up so that there is nowhere else for them to go. When the Tramp refuses the neat and tidy, if improbable, ending that the girl offers him—all three of them will be happy, all three of them will be reconciled to one another, all three of them will be unremorseful and on good terms—he essentially refuses the film itself. And so he is abandoned by the film and by the narrative, left to an empty, undefined locale, discarded to a field that once held edifices but now holds nothing. To question narrative, for Chaplin, is to question film itself.

The Unavailability of Meaning: Chaplin's Anti-Film

This sense of constant questioning—of narrative, of framing, of the basic assumptions of classical technique—lies at the heart of Chaplin's cinematic style not just as a product of his technique but as a fundamental part of his aesthetic. Chaplin's film functions, from a certain perspective, as a kind of anti-film: at once an effort to undo the limitations of classical prescription and a testament that those limits can never truly be undone. We must always limit, we must always choose, we must always excise: such are the conditions of making a film and of telling any kind of story at all. We must always force ourselves to pretend that we can define the filmic world with certainty and without contradiction, and yet we must always acknowledge that such meanings are never exclusive, never complete, always contingent. Chaplin ultimately thematizes the inevitable unavailability of meaning, the degree to which we can never really believe we have settled on a proper and complete representation of the thing we mean to show or the event we mean to capture.

And there is no more powerful example of this than the figure of the Tramp himself. Chaplin's Tramp is one of the most iconic personages ever presented on screen. In Bazin's words, as noted before, he is a "mythical figure . . . a hero like Ulysses or Roland in other civilizations."[32] But he is also, ultimately, one of the most unknowable. He seems even to resist the very idea of being known. For Bazin, the difference between the Tramp and the other heroes to whom he is compared is that "we know the heroes of old through literary works that are complete and have defined once and for all, their adventures and their various manifestations."[33] There is a sense, in other words, in which they might be considered knowable, closed, definable. Not so with the Tramp. Bazin links this sense of unknowability to Chaplin's own living person, arguing that "Charlie . . . is always free to appear in another film."[34] Hence his journey is necessarily open-ended, even though when Bazin wrote his essay the last Tramp film had come out over a decade earlier. But this sense would linger long after Chaplin himself could no longer serve as the "guarantor of Charlie the character," as Bazin puts it.[35]

For critics like Kerr, the sense of unfinishedness and unknowability that Bazin detects is embedded in the substance of the Tramp's very persona. The Tramp is well known as a protean figure, but for Kerr it is not just that he is changeable; it is that he is an embodiment of change itself. The Tramp is the ultimate social performer, but as a consequence he is unable to exist outside his exquisite performances. As Kerr writes:

> The secret of Chaplin, as a character, is that he can be anyone. . . . The moment he wishes to become a boxer, he becomes an extraordinarily deft one. The moment he wishes to put on roller skates, he becomes Nijinsky on wheels. . . . If he wishes to rescue a woman from a burning building, his skill and bravery are unexampled; if he wishes to walk a high-wire, he walks a high-wire superbly; if he wishes to set a table for dinner, he sets it with Cordon Bleu finesse.[36]

The tragedy of the Tramp, according to Kerr, is that as a consequence of his adaptability, he is condemned to have no self. "For the man who can, with the flick of a finger or the blink of an eyelash, instantly transform himself into absolutely anyone is a man who must, in his heart, remain no one."[37] The Tramp is designed so as to always foil our attempts to come to know him, to find a way to pin him down. We can say what he does, but we can never quite say who he is.

Yet even this may be too pat an explanation—even this may be too much definition and solidity for an artist as profoundly skeptical and cynical as Chaplin. Kerr himself admits that his anti-definition definition—the paradox of a figure only knowable in his unknowability—requires a conscious exclusion of a substantial portion of Chaplin's output. To say that the Tramp is a consummate performer, Kerr must exclude those moments where he cannot perform. To say that the Tramp is eminently adaptable, he must exclude those moments where he cannot adapt. It is no small matter. Kerr explicitly excludes everything in Chaplin's body of work prior to *Police* (1916), his last film at Essanay, deeming them experimentations that occurred before "Chaplin discovered for himself what his true, all-embracing, ultimate, and indivisible comic character was."[38] Never mind the fact that these experiments actually constitute more than half of all the films in which the Tramp appeared—some forty different shorts—or that it was on the basis of this body of work that Chaplin made his name before he ever left for Mutual, where Kerr's analysis essentially begins. And never mind the fact that the basic contours of the costume and the fundamental catalog of trademark gestures—the very features that so define the Tramp and mark him as the same character from film to film—were more or less settled within the body of these films and would change little through Chaplin's time at Mutual, First National, and United Artists, even as other elements of Chaplin's filmmaking style and ability evolved.[39] Even if these exclusions were not enough to call into question Kerr's definition, Kerr himself admits that to make his characterization work he must essentially exclude *The Circus,* one of only three feature films that Chaplin made with the Tramp during the silent era. For the central comic premise of *The Circus* relies on the Tramp's utter inability to perform: asked to work as a circus clown, he cannot get any of the routines right and is only able to make people laugh through his accidents and failures. If the essence of the Tramp is his ability to adapt and his capacity for performance, *The Circus* is a meditation on his failure to adapt, his failure to perform. This is not the real Tramp, according to Kerr, but a mistake or an impostor. "Whatever he is telling us about his 'character,' we know better, know that *he* knows better," Kerr writes.[40]

Or perhaps the idea of knowing better—of knowing at all—is all wrong. In this vein, Alan Dale puts forth another theory—even more of an anti-theory than Kerr's: the Tramp is simply unknowable. Like some mysterious quantum particle, to attempt to define him is to lose him. In Dale's words, he is "incoherent, unresolvable. . . . The silent Tramp was never all of a piece."[41] Or, to use a 1932 magazine profile of Chaplin that works just as well for the character he portrayed, "At no stage can one make a firm sketch and say: 'This is Charles Chaplin'; for by the time it is done the model has moved. One can only say:

'This is Charles Chaplin, wasn't it?' "[42] Even Chaplin would have trouble defining the character of the Tramp on the rare occasions that he tried to do so, settling in his autobiography not on any single definition but on a series of subjunctive presumptions and hopes and a kind of eternal suspension between opposites:

> You know this fellow is many-sided, a tramp, a gentleman, a poet, a dreamer, a lonely fellow, always hopeful of romance and adventure. He would have you believe he is a scientist, a musician, a duke, and a polo-player. However, he is not above picking up cigarette-butts or robbing a baby of its candy. And, of course, if the occasion warrants it, he will kick a lady in the rear—but only in extreme anger![43]

Chaplin claims that he used these words to describe the Tramp to Mack Sennett in the character's very first appearance on screen, but it is almost certainly a back-formation, perhaps even a very late one. It works not at all as a description of the Tramp as he appears in the first Keystone short filmed with him as a character, *Mabel's Strange Predicament* (1914). Here the Tramp is much more of a close variation on Chaplin's old Karno drunk (he keeps taking drinks from a flask surreptitiously throughout the film) than any kind of new comic invention sprung fully formed. But the description hardly works that much better for later iterations of the Tramp. As a catalog of characteristics meant to encompass the character over nearly seventy different films and shorts, it is simply not accurate. The Tramp is, at various points in Chaplin's long career, all of the things that his creator lists here. But he is also quite often none of them, sometimes he is their opposite, and he is rarely more than one or two of them in the same film.

There is a greater degree of unknowability in the Tramp than even Chaplin himself seems wont to admit. The Tramp is usually kind (*The Immigrant*) but sometimes wantonly cruel (*The Pawn Shop*); he is sometimes homeless (*A Dog's Life*) but more typically has a job (*The Bank* [Essanay, 1915]); he is usually poor (*The Kid*) but sometimes seems quite comfortable (*Pay Day* [First National, 1922]) and is even occasionally well-off (*One A.M.*); he sometimes fails in his endeavors (*The Circus*) and sometimes succeeds spectacularly (*The Gold Rush*); he is usually abused by people in power (*Behind the Screen*) but can sometimes be an authority figure himself (*Burlesque on Carmen*); he can be consigned to a life alone (*The Tramp* [Essanay, 1915]) or he can win the girl—questionably (*The Vagabond*) or unequivocally (*The Immigrant*); he can be a physical virtuoso (*The Rink*) or physically incompetent (*One A.M.*); he can successfully adapt to the hardest of roles (*The Pilgrim* [First National, 1923]) or fail at the easiest (*The Circus*). In fact, the only trait that is absolutely consistent across every film with the Tramp—even including his physical movements and characteristics—is the mustache. It is this tiny branding under the nose alone that "marks" a character as the Tramp, from *Mabel's Strange Predicament* to *Modern Times;* everything else is up for grabs. In fact, even to mark the Tramp as some kind of unitary figure, as Chaplin clearly does and as the public readily accepted, is in some ways to make a mockery of the idea of consistency, of the idea that we can define anything at all or be certain of anything. The Tramp is a parody of the very idea of knowability.

And in this way the Tramp is entirely of a piece with everything else in Chaplin's filmic universe, for beyond the presence of the Tramp—whoever he may be—the trademark of a Chaplin film is the endless series of transformations to which the physical world is subjected. Objects are repurposed, the body is repurposed, the environment itself is placed on its head. Chaplin, in Kerr's description, "fell in love with the interchangeability of things," his "awareness of instability in some way exhilarated him."[44] Though the gag with the alarm clock in *The Pawn Shop* is perhaps the quintessential example, it is actually almost impossible to give a proper accounting of these transformations as they are so pervasive in Chaplin's films. They are not so much a recurring element in his humor as a fundamental property of it. In trying to develop a catalog of these instances in Chaplin's work, Kamin has arrived at no fewer than eight transformational categories that make up Chaplin's filmic universe, and there are perhaps several more besides. They paint a picture of a world in perpetual flux: an object can be used like another (a wooden spoon is treated like a ukulele in *The Pawn Shop*); a setting can be treated like a different setting (the twelve-person choir in *The Pilgrim* turns the church into a courtroom in the mind of Chaplin's escaped convict); a human body can be turned into an object (Chaplin disguises himself as a tree in *Shoulder Arms* [First National, 1918] and disappears into a forest); an inanimate object can be turned into an animate one (Chaplin kissing an upturned mop like a girlfriend in *The Bank*); one living body can be turned into another (Chaplin becomes a giant chicken to his hungry companion in *The Gold Rush*); one body part can be treated like a different body part (in *The Kid*, Chaplin pretends that the boy's head is his knee as he hides him under the covers of his bed); the inorganic can become organic (Chaplin eating his shoe in *The Gold Rush*); one form of action can be turned into another (Chaplin's fight with his coworker in *The Pawn Shop* transforms into an attempt to clean the floor when their boss walks in); a relationship between individuals can be turned into another relationship (in *The Kid* Chaplin goes from encouraging his boy like a boxing coach to scolding him like a father when he notices the local ruffian is watching him).[45]

In other words, almost nothing fits a single definition in Chaplin's universe; almost everything is subject to change, open to a new functionality, capable even of a new ontology. In Bazin's description, "In our world, things are tools, some more some less efficient, but all directed toward a specific purpose. However, they do not serve Charlie as they serve us. . . . Every time that Charlie wants to use something for the purpose for which it was made . . . either he goes about it in an extremely awkward fashion . . . or the things themselves refused to be used."[46] For Chaplin, almost anything can be made into something else, and almost anything can demand to be seen (and used) anew. It is for this reason that Raoul Sobel and David Francis connect Chaplin's comic perspective on objects and identities to the much more serious philosophical skepticism of a figure like David Hume, who writes in the *Treatise on Human Nature* that "objects have no discoverable connection together; nor is it from any other principle but custom operating upon the imagination, that we can draw any inference from the appearance of one to the experience of another."[47] In his constant transpositions and uncertainties, Chaplin has essentially discovered an escape clause in our own natural law: a way to undo our understanding of the world, to render it null and void. In other words, what we think of as constitutive of the fundamental being of a thing, Chaplin shows us to be perceptual, based not in that thing but in our reading of it—our own exclusion and limitation of other possibilities.

Chaplin, then, takes it as his mission to open us to a multiplicity of perspectives, to widen our own frames, to show us multiple realities at once. It is, in some sense, a project of de-mediation: an attempt to return us to a place before perspective, a place of all perspectives, to take us to a version of the world where nothing is limited or defined; or, put another way, where everything is in doubt and everything can change.[48] In Chaplin's own words about his filmmaking philosophy, "I believe in suspended judgment, and try to put across the philosophic doubt I feel about things and people."[49] It is what he calls "a little gentle skepticism" in his films.[50] But it is often more than gentle; there is also something intensely antisocial, even sinister, about it, and Chaplin does not shy away from the more pathological side of his perspective. Chaplin may pull his punches just a little—he may die a bloody death only in his fantasies, he may forestall the inevitable collapse of unworkable narrative arrangements until just after the short has ended, the incessant instability of the worlds that he creates may all be in good fun—but it is not hard to see the darkness just beneath the surface of these ameliorative gestures. It is in many ways a position of trauma, of a profound loss of faith that any structure—whether physical, social, or emotional—can truly hold, that it will not always eventually collapse, change, or transform.

Chaplin's approach to filmmaking undoubtedly stems from and expresses a particular aesthetic position. Yet it is also, arguably, the product of an emotional position. That is, it is difficult not to view the tenets of Chaplin's filmmaking approach as at least in part an expression of the experiences of his own life. It is no secret that Chaplin lived much of what he put on film either literally or figuratively and that he explored the poverty of his early life again and again in his filmmaking career. But more than just a life of poverty, he lived a life of constant—and painful—transformation. He spent his early years in and out of orphanages as his mother battled with insanity. When she seemed at last to have recovered—when she took an apartment with the young Chaplin and found work as a seamstress—it turned out to be an illusion. She became permanently insane in 1903 with the fourteen-year-old boy as her only caretaker; he came home to find her speaking to people who were not present and was told she took lumps of coal and went door to door in the tenement where they lived to distribute them as "birthday presents" for the children. She later told a doctor who examined her that "the floor is the River Jordan and she cannot cross it."[51] She was Chaplin's only family at the time—his father had since abandoned them and died of alcoholism, his half brother Sydney was in the navy and away at sea—and she utterly transformed the world on him, unmade whatever stability or solace he thought that he might have at last achieved. When she was institutionalized, Chaplin was left entirely alone. Having tasted workhouse life before, he pretended to have another relative to live with and spent the next several weeks essentially homeless, sometimes sneaking back to the empty apartment where he had lived with his mother, sometimes sleeping on the street. There was nothing in Chaplin's young life that could not be taken away: no love, no structure, no promise, no reality at all that could not just as easily disappear.

Reflecting on his troubled childhood in one interview, Chaplin encapsulated his experience—and the philosophy of life that it produced in him—in a single anecdote. He was seven years old, an "inmate" in a London orphanage while his mother was institutionalized with an earlier bout of insanity, and he was standing in line to select a Christmas present from a collection of trinkets laid out for the children:

> I had picked out with my eye a big, fat red apple for my present. It was the biggest apple I had ever seen outside of a picture book. . . . When the line had moved up so that I was fifth from the table a housekeeper, or somebody in authority, pounced on me, pushed me out of line and took me back to my room with the brutal words, "No Christmas present for you this year, Charlie—you keep the

other boys awake by telling pirate stories." I have always found that red apple of happiness just within reach of my hand when some invisible presence or force drags me away just as I am about to grab it.[52]

According to Chaplin, even after he had achieved worldwide success and tremendous wealth, the incident still encapsulated what "life is like."[53]

It is perhaps little wonder, then, that Chaplin might be among the most aesthetically skeptical of filmmakers—that he would not trust any system that purported to hold a perfect perspective on anything, even something so small as how best to divide up and reorder the space of a scene. But he was also in some ways among the most aesthetically humble of filmmakers, inclined to have his scenes unfold before us with as little forced direction of our attention as possible, asking us even to question what little direction he might give us—to always question his frame, always question his story, never hold anything as safe or certain. It would take an international trauma before the filmmaking industry would truly catch up to the skepticism that Chaplin seemed to draw from his own personal traumas. Eventually, in the postwar era, the unchallenged dominance of the classical system would collapse. In *Cinema 2*, Deleuze positions the Second World War as both the site and the cause of this break, a historical trauma that deeply affected the aesthetic assumptions on which the classical system rested. "In Europe," he writes, "the post-war period has greatly increased the situations which we no longer know how to react to, in spaces which we no longer know how to describe."[54] The world, in other words, could no longer be taken as solid. Bazin's "unity of meaning of the [classical] dramatic event" could no longer be presupposed. A new generation of filmmakers would "plunge the drama into a 'multiplicity of facts', none of which would be principal or secondary, so that it could only be reconstituted following a broken line lifted from among all the points and all the lines of the whole."[55] Chaplin was already there: he had already arrived at that position, already started from a place of trauma. But before that postwar era of filmmaking could emerge, a new challenge would have to be surmounted—one that seemed to push the film industry even further away from the ambiguity that Chaplin cherished, even further toward solidity and certainty. Chaplin would need to confront the advent of sound.

A Masterpiece of Mediation

City Lights

In 1973, when Charlie Chaplin was eighty-four years old, Peter Bogdanovich asked him if he had any personal favorites among his films. He replied quite simply: "Oh, yes. I have. I like *City Lights*."[1] Chaplin was not alone. The film has had its critics, but ever since its opening in 1931 praise for the picture has ranged from exuberance to extravagance. Alexander Woollcott was one of the first to offer fulsome support, declaring it Chaplin "at his incomparable best" in a contemporary review.[2] James Agee called its climax the "highest moment in movies."[3] Walter Kerr categorically declared it a "masterpiece" and an almost effortless one at that—a film that meets the criteria of masterpiece status "as if they were not requirements but afterthoughts."[4] Arthur Knight compared the film to "Michelangelo's works in the Sistine Chapel."[5] What is perhaps most remarkable about such praise, aside from its ubiquity and its ardor, is that it rests on a film that was made at the same moment that Chaplin's peers in the world of slapstick were suffering their period of greatest decline. *City Lights,* with its avowed refusal to include spoken dialogue, premiered four years after *The Jazz Singer* (Warner Brothers, 1927) first introduced synchronized sound to a mass audience and three years after *Lights of New York* (Warner Brothers, 1928) marked the industry's first all-talking picture. By 1930, all of Hollywood had gone over to the talkies in what Alexander Walker calls the unprecedented "lightning retooling of an entire industry."[6] It was a retooling that marked the end for almost all of the other great slapstick artists who could be considered Chaplin's peers. A new wave of comedians was flooding Hollywood—verbal comedians from the vaudeville circuit who had either been floundering in silent films like W. C. Fields or had remained until that point onstage like the Marx Brothers. These were artists for whom dialogue had always been a natural comic tool, and they brought a facility with jokes and puns that was as well developed as Chaplin's and Keaton's facility with pantomime and acrobatics when they first stepped from the variety stage to the screen.

Around the time that *City Lights* premiered, Buster Keaton was being forced into films like *The Passionate Plumber* (Metro-Goldwyn-Mayer, 1932), where he had to play second fiddle to Jimmy Durante, a verbal comedian who could make better use of audiences' new fascination with sound. Harold Lloyd had originally fared somewhat better by making the move to sound extraordinarily quickly—in 1929 he delayed the release of his newest silent picture, *Welcome Danger* (Harold Lloyd, 1929), so that he could finish filming it with sound and dub in a soundtrack and dialogue over the half of the film that was already shot. It turned out to be the second-highest-grossing picture of his career, but the success was short lived. While Chaplin was feted as a genius at the premiere of *City Lights* and undertook a celebratory worldwide promotional tour, Lloyd was making less money on each successive film after *Welcome Danger*. By 1935, he had to give up running his own studio and hire himself out as an actor, and by 1938 he settled into a dignified but unwelcome retirement.

The paradox of *City Lights* is that it marks an apotheosis of Chaplin's cinematic vision at the very moment when both his genre and manner of filmmaking should have been most in disarray. For the coming of sound was more than just a change in the nature of film comedy; it was the last step in the consolidation of the classical system. In Tom Gunning's reading, the "cinema of narrative integration" was designed to afford some means of presenting the same degree of characterization and narrative clarity that dialogue allowed on the stage, to offer "a new set of signifiers to fill the void left by the spoken text."[7] Classical Hollywood was thus not undone by sound; it was in some sense waiting for it. Exempting the early years of the initial transition and the technological challenges they presented, the basic techniques of classical composition almost all remained in place before and after the coming of *The Jazz Singer* and *Lights of New York*. Close-ups, cuts-in-action, shot/reaction-shot compositions, montage, and process editing remained entirely in use, almost unchanged, after filmmakers overcame the transition's original mechanical limitations and uncertainties. By the early 1930s, in David Bordwell's words, "shooting a sound film came to mean shooting a silent film with sound."[8]

In fact, the coming of sound seemed to command an adherence to the classical approach. If the basic promise of classical style was, in Robert Ray's words, "a constantly optimum vantage point," then sound forced another clause to that original contract.[9] Now audiences had to be assured not just of seeing the most important aspects of the action but of hearing them as well. Sound was thus a redoubling of classical prerogatives. This new, audio-enabled world would be recorded for us in all its multiplicity of sounds, yet none would ever get in the way of our ability to hear what we would need to hear to make the story comprehensible.[10] In this way, the coming of sound was more than a technical problem for Chaplin's filmmaking; it was also a philosophical affront. It was not only a matter of whether or not to include dialogue or what voice Chaplin might possibly give to the Tramp, which is where most critical attention on Chaplin's relationship to sound has focused. More than a question of dialogue and voice, it was, more fundamentally, a movement away from ambiguity toward certainty and specificity—if Chaplin asks us to question the frame and the narrative, sound asks us to accept them with even greater ease. Sound in classical film was almost from the beginning used in what Jean Epstein calls a "superabundant banality,"[11] a way of naturalizing the filmic world by masking classical processes of exclusion and concision—hiding compositional choices and elisions beneath a wash of diegetic noises that purport to be reality, naturalizing narrative through the explicit confusion of real speech with speech directed toward narrative ends. It became a key support of what Mary Ann Doane calls the "illusion of uncodified flow," a way to further "hide the work of the production" and "promote a sense of the effortlessness and ease of capturing the natural."[12]

For Chaplin, then, sound would have to come to mean something else, something more aligned with the skepticism of his filmmaking philosophy. The story of the success of *City Lights*—all the more unlikely not just for the era in which it was made but even for the simple fact that it was the first sound-enabled effort of a director who had been working in the silent mode for nearly twenty years—is in large part the story of how Chaplin came to manipulate sound into a complement to his well-honed visual style, how he turned a moment of aesthetic challenge into a springboard toward an artistic culmination of his vision. It did not come easily—he composed the film originally as a fully silent picture and was only corralled into adding sound and music by the officers at United Artists—but the film would not be the same without it. Chaplin may not have known it, but his manner of filmmaking was in its own way waiting for sound every bit as much as the classical system; he would use it as a means of shadowing and counterpointing and contradicting his visual apparatus and of putting his imagery in play with other communicative elements in the same way that it was in play with itself.

Chaplin's ultimate approach to sound, as it manifested in *City Lights,* was purposefully contradictory, even paradoxical. If his visual style was marked by an ever-widening frame and an insistence on an always irreducible visual simultaneity, he would stand this in counterpoint to a highly constrictive use of sound—a focus so tight that within an encompassing long shot he might highlight only a single tiny noise. In contrast to Epstein's "superabundant banality," he would rely on a kind of precision unthinkable to his classical counterparts, a philosophy of sonic isolation that seemed to stand even against his own visual and intellectual focus on simultaneity and multiplicity. But if its methods were different, its objective was the same. Chaplin consistently uses sound in *City Lights* to magnify or draw attention to a particular aspect of a shot or sequence, to highlight one reality within many—without ever losing sight of the many. Chaplin reinforces his commitment to visual simultaneity not by matching it to an undifferentiated soundscape, one that in the absence of classical means of visual focus and exclusion would simply return him to the cacophony of undifferentiated space; he reinforces simultaneity by moving our attention in and around the space of the frame through his use of sound, drawing our attention in ways that work to foreground rather than conceal his manipulations. Sound, for Chaplin, is like lighting in the theater: it casts color onto simultaneous space, it spotlights our attention to portions of that space, it illuminates or obscures aspects of the space without ever actually changing it at all or taking it out of view.

The status of *City Lights* as perhaps the premier example of Chaplin at the height of his artistry—a status reaffirmed by each generation of critics over again—is due in no small part to its incorporation of sound. In confronting the greatest threat to his film sensibility, Chaplin realized how to reemphasize its greatest strengths. In this regard, the fact that *City Lights* is yet another Chaplin film *without* dialogue—clearly the biggest story when the film premiered well into the talkie era in 1931 but also the biggest story in any number of critical commentaries since—is of less importance than the fact that this is the first Chaplin film *with* sound. Chaplin's refusal to include dialogue within his film is significant, to be sure, but it is not actually the foundation of his approach to sound in the film; it is an outgrowth of it, a declaration of one of the limit points of his approach rather than its centerpiece. (Chaplin's true confrontations with dialogue would come later, first in *Modern Times* and then in *The Great Dictator,* when he found it inescapable and when, correspondingly, the seams of his filmmaking began to come undone.) In *City Lights,* sound is a vehicle for turning his stylistic and philosophical concerns into thematic aspects of the film itself. Uncertainty, ambiguity, suspension of meaning, malleability, multiplicity, even sight and sound and action themselves—all of these had been a part of Chaplin's filmmaking from very early in his career. In *City Lights,* however, they would become not just aspects of his film but the very subject; it is a film about the challenges of knowing, the necessity of action, the dangers of seeing and hearing. It is about the very skepticism and ambiguity that had always defined Chaplin's work. *City Lights* would be a better expression of Chaplin's technique than almost any film before it, and it would take as its subject the foundations of that expression. It would be, brilliantly, a film about itself.

CHAPLIN'S SONIC FRAME: SOUND AS CINEMATOGRAPHIC ACCOMPLICE

Even if Chaplin had pursued his plans of making *City Lights* a fully silent film, it would have been a consummate effort. Chaplin is here at the height of his visual powers, able to compose images as subtly structured but visually broad as any he had yet created—and, as often as not, totally untrustworthy. *City Lights* is Chaplin's most disbelieving cinematographic work, more pervasively skeptical of its own technique than any other. There is, for example, the camera work during the nightclub sequence, a kind of apotheosis to the destabilized frame seen in earlier works from *Sunnyside* to *The Kid*. Here, as the Tramp enters the club, he slips on the well-polished dance floor, nearly falling entirely out of the frame as the camera tracks toward the table at which he is to be seated. He remains in the shot only when he is pulled back into the frame by the Millionaire and the maître d' just as the camera is about to track past him. It is a sophisticated joke on the excisions of cinematography: the main character of the film nearly falls out of his own frame because he interrupts the narrative flow with a pratfall. Such is the single-mindedness with which the camera pursues narrative drive and narrative clarity—even in Chaplin's universe—that it is willing to push onward to the next point of the story and leave the main character floundering on the floor.

In true Chaplin style, of course, what is inside the frame is not entirely to be trusted either, and many of the shots within *City Lights* are comically unwilling to disclose to us their most salient points of interest. The epitome of this technique occurs in an innocuous establishing shot that immediately precedes the film's famous boxing match. For a few seconds, Chaplin shows us a long shot of the Tramp's challenger entering the arena and marching toward the ring. The frame is clearly centered on the boxing ring itself, which looms large in the exact middle of the shot, the approaching fighter contained in the bottom third of the frame until he ascends to the ring. Yet within that bottom third of the frame, a tiny micronarrative unfolds with no filmic emphasis whatsoever. Just as the challenger enters the frame, a heckler in the audience shouts something to him and makes a disparaging gesture. Without skipping a beat, the challenger punches him in the face and the heckler falls over, unconscious. The exchange is more than just easy to miss; it is almost impossible to see if you are not looking for it. There is nothing in the framing of the shot, in the motions of the characters, in the positioning of the camera, or in the progress of the narrative that would make a viewer notice it—nothing within the whole retinue of techniques that Chaplin developed to supplant classical means of emphasis and focus. And the entire exchange transpires in less than two seconds.

But it is clearly not an accidental or off-the-cuff inclusion. Several minutes later, when the boxing sequence has concluded, Chaplin presents a copy of the earlier establishing shot, this time with the challenger leaving the ring and returning to the locker room. In a much more elaborate micronarrative that continues the story of the first marginalized encounter, the same heckler appears at the bottom center of the frame, sees the fearsome boxer coming, and runs out of the frame as he approaches; the boxer pauses for a moment in the center of the foreground of the frame and considers following the heckler before deciding to simply return to the locker room. As soon as the boxer leaves the frame, the heckler momentarily reappears to look for the boxer and make sure he is gone. This latter sequence could still quite easily be missed, occurring at the end of what seems like a simple transitional shot to move us from one scene to the next. But it is much more elaborately staged than the first encounter: it lasts around five seconds and takes place conspicuously at the center of the frame's bottom third with the boxer facing the camera, inviting our attention to his actions. Yet the latter sequence, subtly emphasized, makes no sense without having paid attention to the former, which was entirely deemphasized. Here, Chaplin's frame seems not to know its own mind: it calls on viewers to recall a moment that it neglected to properly show them when it actually occurred. More than that, it seems momentarily unable or unwilling to function. It neither openly emphasizes the business with the heckler as relevant nor works to exclude it as irrelevant; in fact, it seems to act as no proper guide to the action at all. To notice such moments in the film is to see the idea of narrative itself in its negative reflection; through the failure of the frame in these instances we are reminded of the ways in which, in almost all other moments, it seeks to carefully control and deploy only that which it wants us to see, even in a filmmaking style as open to ambiguity as Chaplin's.

The success of sound in *City Lights* comes from the way that it serves as both handmaiden to and critic of narrative emphasis. In eschewing a total sonic diegesis in favor of a highly selective use of sound effects, Chaplin calls attention to specific points within a frame, asking us to focus in a certain direction for narrative development even as he foregrounds the fact that he is doing so. Some critics, George Jean Nathan first and foremost among them, have found Chaplin's use of selective sound effects "stale and obvious."[13] But they are not so much obvious as they are simply made apparent. They are unmasked and unadorned—nakedly in contrast to a system of filmmaking that has conditioned us to prefer our narrative manipulation subtle and naturalized. In his use of sound, Chaplin wants us to see not just the item to which he is pointing but the finger that is itself doing the pointing. When, for instance, the Tramp indecorously slurps spaghetti in the fancy nightclub where the Millionaire has brought him as a guest, we do not hear the party and commotion that can be seen in the frame all around him, the club-goers talking and laughing. We hear only a slide whistle, a fanciful sonic reinforcement of the visual point of emphasis in the frame. It cannot be mistaken for a real sound. It is almost literally the sound of the film redoubling itself, reemphasizing its own main point of focus within the frame, the humor coming as much from the nakedness of the ploy as the comic nature of the sound itself. Or when the Tramp and the Millionaire speed home in a racing car, we do not hear the thundering motor or the screeching tires. We hear only another slide whistle flourish when the car veers off the street and onto the sidewalk. It is supposed to be an aural point of emphasis on the more comically destructive aspects of the car's fast careening.[14] But it is also an obvious and dangerous elision of the uncontrolled manner in which the car is being driven even when the sound effect is not in place. The selection of only a few perilous points for sonic emphasis is almost a kind of whitewashing of the recklessness of the rest of the trip. The effects even skip one of the car's most risky moves, the second time it runs up onto the sidewalk. The Tramp himself offers a kind of correction to the sound effects within the diegesis of the film. "Be careful how you're driving," he warns the Millionaire in an intertitle after cues for the last two sound effects have been missed. The Millionaire, still quite drunk, replies "Am I driving?"—at which point the Tramp desperately grabs the wheel and very seriously steadies the car, rescuing the film equally from the Millionaire's drunk driving and the soundtrack's attempt at comic amelioration.[15]

Such selective sonic enhancement, though always readily apparent, need not be purely for comic emphasis. It is in many cases simply another way to attract attention within an already crowded visual system, its very obviousness meant to reinforce its specific function rather than allowing it to become naturalized within the shot or sequence. The most elaborate example is in the film's famous boxing scene, one of Chaplin's most beloved set-pieces. The sequence is awash in activity: managers and coaches on the sidelines, a rowdy crowd all around the ring. But Chaplin controls our attention and focuses us on both the action and the narrative at hand through a careful combination of visual and aural elements. His framing of the scene is ingenious. He constructs the boxing arena with a notably low ceiling, a series of beams blocking off all visual interest just above the heads of the boxers. At the same time, the ropes of the boxing ring are placed in the foreground of the frame, with the top of the ropes stretching just below the upper torsos of the Tramp and his opponent. There is a visual cacophony of bobbing heads among the spectators in the background, but they are placed at the bottom of the frame and mostly obscured by the ropes of the ring. The only clear plane of visual space—that which lies between the top of the ropes and the bottom of the ceiling beams—exactly encompasses the heads and upper torsos of the boxers, the target area of the fighters in the ring. Though we can see the bodies of the boxers in full throughout almost the entire scene, we watch the match as though it were framed in a medium close-up of their heads and shoulders—the places where almost all the punches land. In other words, we are focused throughout on the most important part of the frame and on the most important part of the match.

And Chaplin's use of sound in the scene serves to further underscore this effect. We do not hear the crowd in the background or the shuffling feet of the boxers. We do not hear the punches landing. There is nothing of Epstein's "superabundant banality" or "all-purpose sound."[16] The only sound we hear is the ringing of the bell that starts and stops each round. It is artificially isolated to be sure, but it is also absolutely the most important sound in the scene. The Tramp knows that his opponent is much stronger and more fearsome; his only hope is to last through as many rounds as he can, to wear down his opponent and get in the occasional hit. The bell is essentially his lifeline; everything else can be conveyed visually. We do not need to hear the crowd to know that it is restless, and we do not need to hear the punches to know they are painful—that can be easily conveyed within the visual line of focus within the frame. The bell, of course, could be conveyed visually as well, but to do so would be to constantly interrupt the fight itself. There would be no way to make us focus on the ringing of the bell without inserting a close-up in the middle of the action or crafting the movement of the scene to emphasize whoever was ringing the bell at that moment. Through the focused and isolated use of sound, however, Chaplin is able to effectively interrupt the action of the scene without having to interrupt the movement: he can start and stop the fighting without having to break up the choreography of the fight itself with visual interruptions. The resulting scene is one of the most cherished in Chaplin's body of work in part because it is so tightly crafted to marry sight and sound. Each time the bell rings—whether to mark the legitimate end of a round, by accident, or when the Tramp cheats and pulls it as a way of moving the fight along a little faster—we are reminded of the Tramp's dire circumstance, and we watch the fight unfold wondering when the bell will ring again. In other words, each time the bell rings it is another step toward success. We are entertained by the gags, but we are kept focused on the narrative. Without ever having to break from his long shot of the total boxing ring, Chaplin is able to convey both elaborate physical stunts and narrative drive all at once. Sound has become, along with movement and space, yet another means of directing viewers' attention within the scene without ever having to sacrifice or even challenge the unbroken space and expansive simultaneity that stand at the core of Chaplin's approach.

In a similar vein, Chaplin is also able to use a strategically isolated deployment of sound not just in a narrative sense but also to isolate and highlight particular psychological states or emotional registers within a much broader unbroken scene. The most familiar example occurs at a party at the Millionaire's estate, where the Tramp accidentally swallows a whistle that is offered to him as a party favor. It gives him the world's worst case of the hiccups—just at the very moment that a singer is about to entertain the assembled guests. Of course, we hear nothing of the ebullient party happening all around the Tramp, nothing of the piano player as he begins the accompaniment, nothing of the song itself as the performer begins his aria. What we hear is only the whistle: a raspy, grating, tiny tin sound that bursts forth each time the Tramp hiccups with an upper-body contortion. Some critics have found the scene disorienting in its intensely isolated use of sound, explicitly privileging exactly one sound over all of the other much larger and more obvious sources within the frame. Dan Kamin, for one, notes it as a break even with Chaplin's limited approach to "naturalistic, synchronized sound effects" because we hear the interruption but not what is actually being interrupted, the "pretentious classical singer . . . whose singing we *don't* hear on the soundtrack."[17] But it is only disorienting in the context of a filmmaking system that demands that each visual element on screen come with a corresponding sound with no obvious, non-diegetic isolation or emphasis among them. Yet this same filmmaking system has no trouble artificially isolating and emphasizing visual elements on the screen, breaking the unity of space to cut to a close-up of a person or an object as though such a shift were not itself a tremendous break from the way in which the world visually operates.

What Chaplin achieves in the whistle scene is a kind of aural close-up—a way to spotlight our attention on a small aspect of a larger scene without breaking the unity and simultaneity of that scene. Chaplin begins the sequence in a medium shot that encompasses the Tramp and several other party guests around him, and he even goes on to show us the whole of the party at once—from the singer and piano accompanist to the assembled guests; but in both cases our attention is unmistakably drawn to the Tramp and to the whistling sound that accompanies his movements no matter where he is in the frame. Through the device of the whistle, we are drawn into his isolated experience of the party without ever having to leave the full breadth of the festivities; we see him in his own world of embarrassment and in his relationship to all those around him at one and the same time. That is to say we see him, in a way, closer to the way in which he might see himself at that moment—tremendously embarrassed and tuned in to himself, yet as visually and spatially connected to everything around him as he would be at any other moment of his life. It is an artificial isolation to be sure—we could never literally only hear the whistle without also hearing the singer and the background noise of the party, though emotionally it might feel like it if we were in the Tramp's position. But Chaplin's aural close-up never seeks to naturalize or erase itself in the manner of the visual close-up. The fact that the technique asks us to hold two perspectives at once—the isolated sound and the encompassing visuals—foregrounds its own artificiality to us, alienates us, and allows us to remain aware at all times of the way in which the world is being presented. Here we laugh not just at the event but at the supreme importance the film seems to place on the small sound of the whistle.

Scoring Simultaneity, Underscoring Skepticism

In contrast to that tiny, isolated whistle sound stands Chaplin's fulsome use of orchestral music in the film. Chaplin had actually created scores for several of his films before *City Lights,* at least after a fashion. Unlike most silent-era directors, he worked directly with professional arrangers to develop suggested scores for each of his United Artists features, combining and building off established classical and operatic works (he had a particular fondness for Tchaikovsky, Wagner, and Brahms) and placing them alongside popular tunes and dance music. There was no guarantee, of course, that local theaters would use his score suggestions when the film was distributed, and Chaplin was perpetually critical of the effect that "feeble vamping on a piano or the excruciating efforts of an incompetent or ill-led orchestra" could have on his pictures.[18] He supported from early in his career "the efforts being made to provide music by mechanical systems," and the opportunity to finally provide a definitive score for one of his films was a welcome development.[19]

In fact, of all the elements of Chaplin's filmmaking technique, his musical scores seem most in line with standard cinematic practice and can be seen almost as a kind of compromise with classical technique. In its close marriage to the events on screen and its omnipresence in the film, his score in *City Lights* seems particularly to fit within classical standards and even to stand in rebuke to his highly subtle, selective, and isolated use of diegetic sound. Theodore Huff goes so far as to compare Chaplin's work in *City Lights* to the work of some of the great film composers of the classical era. He concedes that "by strict musical standards Chaplin's score may not equal those of Virgil Thompson, Max Steiner, Georges Auric, or William Walton," but he declares that "the haunting and pleasant Chaplin melodies in *City Lights* are pleasing in themselves" and calls the film "one of the few extant examples of the silent medium's power when wedded to a musical score which properly interprets the action and heightens the emotion."[20] But interpreting action and heightening emotion, while certainly legitimate enterprises for most film scores, sound like the kind of overdetermination that Chaplin meant always to avoid. Chaplin's use of music within the film is more in line with his general philosophy of sound than it may at first appear, however. Chaplin's score interprets and heightens, sometimes brilliantly, as Huff describes. But it also in doing so chooses to highlight very specific aspects of the action and very specific elements of a scene's emotion; it cannot and does not attempt to capture the multitude of actions and valences that Chaplin includes within a frame. To interpret action and heighten emotion within a classically arranged film, one that presumes André Bazin's "unity of meaning of the dramatic event," is one thing.[21] But to do so within a framework that purposefully overstocks the frame and often deliberately undercuts its own attempts at "unity of meaning" is to craft a musical score that is ultimately as baldly selective as Chaplin's use of sound effects.

At times, in fact, Chaplin's score seems comically unaware of what is happening within the film; just like Chaplin's frame and Chaplin's sound effects, Chaplin's score in *City Lights* can serve to ignore, conceal, or leave unemphasized seemingly important aspects of his scenes. Such is the case in one of the film's earliest gags, where the Millionaire pours the Tramp a glass of alcohol and raises his own glass in a toast. As the two raised glasses and upward-looking faces of the Millionaire and the Tramp draw our attention to the upper reaches of the frame, the Millionaire absentmindedly empties the bottle of alcohol into the Tramp's ill-fitting pants in the lower third of the frame. Our eyes are drawn upward in the shot (there's even an intertitle to make us focus on the toast), and the music does nothing to countermand this direction. The music continues in a pleasant, lilting melody that gives no indication of trouble or accident; it remains unchanging throughout the scene. It is not until Chaplin breaks up the action of the scene to insert a close-up of the bottle pouring into the Tramp's pants that the viewer is even likely to notice the comic business. In this way, music will not always prove a reliable guide. In fact, after showing us the gag in action and returning us to the medium shot where it continues in the bottom third of the frame, Chaplin reemphasizes the untrustworthiness of his own compositions. About a minute after the first gag, the comic business repeats: the Millionaire goes to fetch another bottle of alcohol (the first is now mysteriously empty), raises another toast, draws our attention upward in the frame, and then proceeds to pour the new bottle down the Tramp's pants all over again while the music continues on in comic ignorance. Only this time, there is no insert to force us to attention. Chaplin's world unfolds as it will, and we cannot always rely on being told exactly where to look.

More than being a matter of actual exclusion, however, the misdirections of Chaplin's score are as often as not a product of the layering of meaning within his visual and narrative compositions. Chaplin's music may try to legitimately emphasize and heighten one aspect of a scene, but in doing so it can leave itself comically open to its own discrediting as other aspects of the same scene come to the fore. It can, in other words, serve as a flagrant confirmation of the degree to which Chaplin's filmmaking subscribes to no single unity of meaning. The Tramp's famous quasi ballet near the opening of the film is an exemplary case. It is one of the first examples of the kind of composition that Chaplin would repeat throughout the sound era—the creation of a scene that depends fundamentally for its humor and its interest primarily on its relationship to the music playing underneath. It is a scene that essentially amounts to a dance sequence with the music serving as a kind of accompaniment, but it also contains in plain view an explicit point of challenge to its own pretentions and interpretive foreclosures. In this sequence, the Tramp stands in front of a window display at an art gallery, ostensibly regarding a statue of a horse and rider but stealing surreptitious glances at the full-body nude next to it. Positioning the camera behind the window of the art gallery, Chaplin frames the Tramp squarely between the horse and the nude, the entryway of the building across the street centering the frame; the space between the window and the edge of the sidewalk becomes his stage. As the scene unfolds, the Tramp moves backward and forward, angling for a better view, all to the melodic strains of a slow, lilting waltz. The music is timed to the actions on screen—it stops when the Tramp stops, it starts when he starts—but it also seems to follow its own independent melodic line, as though the movements were choreographed to the music instead of the other way around. It is on one level a masterful confirmation of the critics who had so long likened Chaplin's movements to those of a dancer. (Vaslav Nijinsky himself told Chaplin "your comedy is *balletique,* you are a dancer.")[22] But Chaplin does not actually dance like a ballerina, as he had tried to do—to relatively little comic effect—in *Sunnyside;* instead, his most mundane motions are elevated to the level of ballet by the total composition of the scene.

In fact, the Tramp is not only unaware of this elevation but also actively working against it. Even as the music turns his unadorned actions into art, he is trying at the same time to turn art into something unadorned—to turn a nude sculpture into pornography, angling for an illicit glance even as he pretends to be considering it like a connoisseur. In this moment, Chaplin's score is both perfectly matched to the scene and perfectly inappropriate. It has captured the grace of Chaplin's actions and in the process has made an artful ballet out of sexual prurience. Here, the score has proved as selective as any of Chaplin's sound effects and has only served to reemphasize the degree to which any single interpretive stance cannot properly encompass Chaplin's filmic art. In fact, Chaplin stages within the scene a kind of parallel to this interpretive ignorance as a diegetic instance of ignorance within the frame itself. As Chaplin moves backward and forward along the sidewalk, the ground just behind him disappears—it is no sidewalk at all but the top of an elevator platform leading to a work space below the street. (If you look closely in the shots before the gallery sequence, you can see the Tramp passing a sign that reads "Danger," deemphasized in the frame and totally ignored by the Tramp.) The Tramp avoids falling into the elevator shaft only by happenstance, moving backward just as the platform realigns with the street, moving forward just as it disappears again. The music serves to emphasize the Tramp's precarious position, pausing every time he seems about to fall into the open shaft, restarting just as he moves back to safety. But these emphases too seem to occur by happenstance. The music starts and stops to its own internal melodic logic, and its coincidence with Chaplin's moments of danger give the comic appearance of being accidental; both the Tramp and the music are so absorbed in their own realities that they simply miss anything outside their respective interpretive spheres of attention. The total comedy of the scene is the comedy of ignoring what is right below your feet, of not considering the possibility that it might be in flux, that it might even be two things at once. If the Tramp misses the sign that says "Danger" just before he enters the frame, so too does the score itself: the music fails to recognize that almost nothing is so solid in Chaplin's world that it can sustain only one interpretive register.

In this sequence Chaplin's score ignores such multiple registers at its own peril, but elsewhere in the film Chaplin uses his score to directly emphasize the multiplicity of emotions and events that might exist within a single frame. As often as the score will settle on one interpretive stance and find itself comically out of touch with the shifting reality within the frame, it will with equal frequency—and much greater success—move between aspects of simultaneous realities within a scene as a way of drawing our attention not toward any one of them but toward the fact of their convergence. In the film's robbery sequence, for instance, Chaplin's score must perform double duty across two contiguous but obviously nonconvergent realities: in the foreground of the frame sit the Tramp and the Millionaire discussing the troubles of the flower girl, while in the background of the frame, separated by a couch and table that occupy the middle plane of space, a burglar—part of a pair of villains attempting to rob the house—moves in and out of plain sight, waiting for the right moment to club the Millionaire in the head. It is more than just a matter of comic unawareness, for what happens in the foreground is something far beyond the kind of idle business that might act simply as a placeholder while the frame asks us to truly focus on the dangers of the burglar. Just before the sequence begins, the Millionaire tells the Tramp not to worry about the blind flower girl he is courting and hands over a thousand dollars to pay for an operation to restore her sight. On a purely narrative level, it is perhaps the Tramp's greatest triumph in the film so far, a total resolution to the monetary problems that have driven the last third or so of the picture. Thus, when the dual-reality sequence begins, the Tramp and the Millionaire are doing more than idly taking up space; they are discussing this act of extreme generosity, which leads almost immediately to a return of the Millionaire's suicidal streak, originally caused when his wife left him. In the foreground of the frame, the Tramp must dissuade from suicide the man who has just given him the means to restore sight to the woman he loves. In the background of the frame lurks a figure who puts them both in mortal danger. Chaplin's music must make an almost impossible choice for a typical film score—it must either underscore the highly emotional and narratively relevant moment in the foreground, or it must underscore the danger lurking just behind. Chaplin refuses to present these items in quick visual sequence as a more typical classical composition might, thereby allowing the score an opportunity to alternate between them. He presents them simultaneously, and he essentially renders the moment impossible to score.

The music is purposefully divided: Chaplin scores the exchange of money and the discussion that follows with an ominous timpani beat, focusing on the danger that moves into the background of the frame with the burglar. But not long after the burglar is established visually, Chaplin begins to score the discussion in the foreground, focusing on the thwarted suicide and ignoring the immediate threat behind our two protagonists. Nothing Chaplin can do will capture both sides of the scene at once, and the drastic movements of the music back and forth only serve to emphasize the simultaneity he has constructed. The scene is rendered musically irreducible—it cannot be constrained to one component part—in a clear parallel to the visual irreducibility that is Chaplin's primary working method. Indeed, even when the scene seems to resolve into a single point of focus, this turns out not to be the case. When the Tramp at last discovers the burglar and his accomplice, after the Millionaire has been knocked out, the score switches to a fast-paced string melody for their chase. There seem to be no complexities or internal contradictions in the scene at this point: yet strangely, ominously, the same music continues even after the Tramp has chased the villains away. The music has in fact not been scoring the literal danger in the scene but a bigger danger that is at play. The Millionaire, untrustworthy to begin with, is the only figure who is welcoming to the Tramp; almost everyone else in the film, from his butler to the police, believes the Tramp has no place inside a mansion. Only a few moments after the burglars have been chased off, the Tramp will be mistaken for a criminal and it will be assumed that he injured the Millionaire to take his money. The melody that seemed to define the danger of the burglars as the main point of emphasis in the frame was in fact designed to emphasize a different kind of danger for the Tramp: the imminent threat of misrecognition and the persecution that comes with it. That too was also always in the frame, hiding behind the couch alongside the burglar, so to speak. The music here has drawn our attention to a danger that lies beyond sight but that exists simultaneously with the one that we can literally see in the frame.

TURNING SPEECH INTO SOUND AND SOUND INTO SPEECH

Sound effects and music in *City Lights* are in keeping with Chaplin's overall philosophy of filmmaking. Just as they direct attention within a scene, they are open to ambiguity and imprecision; they can just as easily cast doubt on other aspects of the frame or be cast into doubt themselves. They reaffirm Chaplin's core technique and its basic principles. In Chaplin's perspective, this was the only way that sound could work. And it is only with this idea of workability in mind that we can understand what Chaplin believed would not be workable within his system, what he literally casts out of the film in its very opening sequence: that is, speech. Chaplin's mockery of speech in *City Lights* is perhaps the clearest manifesto on filmmaking within his films. And it is essentially a reaffirmation of his core beliefs on how film should function. That is not to say that the scene, which depicts a series of public speeches at the unveiling of a civic monument that are all voiced by differently timbered kazoo-like sounds (Chaplin produced them himself by speaking through a saxophone mouthpiece), is not many things. For one, it is an obvious joke on the idea of the talkies and the relationship of Chaplin's film to Hollywood at the time. If anyone happened to enter the theater with any doubt as to how Chaplin would partake of the new technology of synchronized sound, this sequence provides an unequivocal answer: there will be sound—comic sound—but decidedly no speech. It is also a joke on the technical reality of talkies. Early sound recording equipment was so poor that the actual dialogue in full-fledged talkies was often no more comprehensible than the saxophone mouthpiece sounds in Chaplin's opening. And it is of course a joke on officialdom and public sanctimoniousness more generally, on the kind of public speechifying and moralizing that all sounds alike anyway. In Gerald Mast's words, the "saxophone squawks and squeaks . . . perfectly reveal the speeches' content without a single word."[23]

But for all its layers of humor, the sequence also presents a kind of philosophical stance against the filmic scenarios perpetuated by dialogue. The voices in the sequence are all voices of authority—they are voices of those who literally get to stand onstage and dictate to the unspeaking crowd what the art behind them means. They are, in this scenario, smug civic officials, but in a broader sense they could be any characters that the world of talking film privileges with speech. All characters who speak, in other words, are reducible to the position of these haughty, controlling, exclusionary voices. Speech in film is always just that—speech; or rather, *a* speech. It is unidirectional, monovocal, overdetermined, and overdetermining; it is all those things we know the public orations to be without ever actually having to hear them. Within this framework, speech is just another means of controlling film's narrative presentation, of excluding and excising and eliding; it is the opposite of simultaneous or multiplicitous. Thus, Chaplin positions himself in the opening sequence as the literal excess to the public officials' declamations. When the work of art is unveiled, the Tramp is the one who disrupts the sanctimoniousness—repurposing the statue (as a bed on which to pass the night) and interrupting the monovocal declaration of what the art is supposed to mean or what it is supposed to do. As he tries to dislodge himself from the sculpture, the Tramp ends up with his nose pressed against the open palm of one of the statuary figures. Here, he literally thumbs his nose at the righteous civic pillars who demand that he vacate their statue to "peace and prosperity" but also at the whole apparatus and philosophy of sound film—at a world that places certain people onstage to talk us into a unified understanding while actively trying to exclude and hide anything that does not fit into a prescribed meaning. Dialogue for Chaplin, at this point in his career, is the very opposite of the skepticism that he sought in his work.

That is not to say Chaplin found no place whatsoever for speech-like elements within *City Lights*. It might be more accurate to say he found no place for spoken words. In fact, much of Chaplin's film is scored in a quasi-operatic manner that uses music as a direct replacement for speech. Throughout the film—and in much more than the comic saxophone squawks of the opening scene—Chaplin supplants dialogue with orchestral emphasis. The film's suicide sequence, where the Tramp rescues the Millionaire from drowning, is a perfect case in point. When the Tramp gives his speech to the Millionaire to dissuade him from what is his first attempt at taking his own life, the orchestra follows both figures as if scoring a duet: sweeping strings for the Tramp's gentler encouragements—"Tomorrow the birds will sing!" as the intertitle reads—and a sharp string crescendo as he changes to a sterner approach—"Be brave! Face life!" What follows is a blunt emphasis with the brass section as the Millionaire declares "No, I'll end it all!" The content of their dialogue is told quite literally through the orchestra; the characters might as well be singing in Italian for all the correspondence that Chaplin insists on between dialogue and melody. (Huff calls the scene "an amusing burlesque of opera" wherein "the music 'tells' what he is saying.")[24] This approach is repeated in almost all the major exchanges of the film (and Chaplin would use it again in similar scenarios throughout *Modern Times*).

It is perhaps a surprising turn to specificity for an artist who in the film's very opening seems to condemn speech on the basis of its irresolvable tendency toward overdetermination. But there is a world of difference between the emotionally legible but literally unintelligible emphasis of a brass section and an actual instance of speech. The latter demands attention above and beyond any other element of filmic composition, renders itself central, and casts everything else in the frame as only so much background information. We *follow* speech: its absence in silent film was the founding motivation for creating a system of storytelling that would allow us to follow a kind of visual narration as we would the literal narration of spoken dialogue. (Hence Gunning's preference for terms like "system of narrative integration" or the even more specific "narrator system" over the more generic terminology of classical technique or classical system.)[25] But for Chaplin, the nonexistence of speech was not so much a challenge to overcome as an opportunity to exploit. Chaplin's technique in the silent era was premised on making an artistic point of the instability and indeterminacy that the absence of speech allowed without sacrificing a basic clarity of narrative and action. The operatic strains of Chaplin's score for *City Lights*—which function separately from the more melodic aspects of the score and are often placed separately within a scene on top of such melodies—are only just a shadow to that action, a highlighting of the narrative line running through the film. These musical motifs serve to underscore without overdetermining, to highlight without overspecifying, and allow for a clarity of narrative action without rendering themselves ontologically above any other aspects of a given scene. More important, they do not demand our attention and loyalty the way that speech does; they do not insist that we discard the freedom and indeterminacy that was so central to Chaplin's filmmaking style.

SEEING, HEARING, AND THE
CONSTRUCTION OF MEANING

If there is any film in Chaplin's body of work from which dialogue would need to be so carefully and explicitly excluded, it would be *City Lights*. There is perhaps no other Chaplin piece that more directly explores the anxieties that underlay his manner of filmmaking—the very concerns that made him cast dialogue aside. It is as though what Chaplin perceived as the unpardonable certainty of sound prompted him to create a film that is itself about uncertainty: of relationships, of status, of the body, of love itself. The foundation of Chaplin's technique has become his very subject. Kerr is explicit on this point:

> Whether consciously or unconsciously, he was about to embark on his most exhaustive exploration of the instability of the very concept of structure, private or public. Even the incidental sight-gags work over the theme of 'instability' obsessively throughout the film. . . . A man may be toasting you with a wine glass, spilling the contents of a martini pitcher down your trousers at the same time. You may actually light a cigar in your mouth three times; it is always someone else's cigar. Reproving his drunken companion for driving so wildly through the early-morning streets, Charlie gets his answer: "Am I driving?" What is fortunate is unfortunate. During the boxing match, the bell-rope becomes wrapped about Charlie's torso. Each time he is hit, his stagger rings the bell, luckily, for the end of the round. Each time he gratefully turns to his corner, the movement rings the bell again to start the next round. . . . These philosophical instabilities are not belabored in the film; they simply exist like the multiple, maze-like, imprisoning refractions of Charlie's fun house in *The Circus* have existed. All those repeated, reversed images, and no way out.[26]

Almost nothing in Chaplin's world, whether central to the story or inconsequential to it, is exactly as it seems, and almost nothing is resistant to change: an avowed friend can become a complete stranger, a gift can become an act of theft, a rescuer can be seen as a burglar, a Tramp can be mistaken for a millionaire, a poor girl can become a well-to-do entrepreneur, a blind girl can regain her sight, the love of your life can become an unrecognized passerby, a civic statue can become a private bed, a sidewalk can become an elevator, a work of art can become a piece of pornography—even a beloved, winsome Tramp can become a defeated, disheveled shell of a man, as happens in the last scenes of the film when the Tramp emerges from jail utterly broken, more desperate and dejected than we have ever before seen him in almost seventy different films. Instability is not just a feature of this film. *City Lights* is about instability and the impossibility of knowing anything for certain.

And, as such, it is about seeing and hearing—about the ways in which we try to come to or create stable knowledge in this world and about how those processes can deceive us. Thus, it is about the processes that define Chaplin's filmmaking itself. In both the plotline with the Millionaire and the plotline with the blind flower girl, questions of sight are of the utmost importance. We wonder at every encounter whether the Tramp will "be seen" by the Millionaire—whether he will welcome him into his home, as he does when he is drunk, or whether the Millionaire will retreat into his sober depression and refuse to "see" anyone—"I'm out to everybody!" and "Whoever he is, get rid of him!" in the words of the film's intertitles. And once the Tramp is seen, we must wonder if he will be recognized by the Millionaire—whether sight will actually yield knowledge. "Who is this man?" the Millionaire demands when he awakens from being hit over the head by the burglar. The Millionaire can see the Tramp perfectly—the Tramp is one of the few figures or objects that remains unchanging in the film, at least until the very end. But sight brings with it no certainty of recognition or knowledge. Yet hearing is even more suspect: it is always imperfect, always incomplete—and almost always, actually, a means of deception, well-intentioned though it may be. Chaplin crafts the Tramp's interactions with the flower girl to be an almost perfect inversion of the audience's own relationship to the Tramp. The flower girl is blind—she cannot see him; she can only hear him. We can see him without impediment, but in the world of silent film we are totally deaf to him. We can never hear what the flower girl hears. And with the exception of a few intertitles, we can never know what it is that he says to her in their scenes together—what his voice sounds like, how he manages to convince her with his pitch or with his diction that he truly is the millionaire he pretends to be. What we do know is that the deception he weaves with his voice is effective. The girl swoons for him, she believes in the money that he hands her and the expensive car he seems to own, and she senses no conflict between his person and the objects and items that he shares with her, as she would if only she could see him. When she has regained her sight, she thinks nothing of eyeing a well-dressed, moneyed young man who enters her flower shop, thinking he might be the one—the only kind of visual that could possibly match the voice that she heard, the only kind of character who could fit into the stories she was told to justify and explain the actions that were performed. Since the slamming of the car door when the Tramp and the girl first meet, she has misread every sound cue she has been given and misimagined every story that was told to her. And her misunderstanding has been orchestrated throughout by the Tramp, who has carefully controlled her sonic world. The Tramp has crafted a false reality for her, easily done when there is no recourse to sight.

What is left when both sight and sound are compromised would seem to be action. We may know someone not by what they look like or say but by what they do. Yet even here Chaplin's film proves deeply skeptical. The Millionaire's actions are objectively the most generous in the film, even if that generosity comes at no great cost to himself. He takes the Tramp out for nights on the town, throws him a party, gives him a Rolls-Royce, hands him a thousand dollars. And then he takes it all back: forgets the nightclub, forgets the party, takes back the Rolls-Royce, essentially accuses the Tramp of stealing the money. Even the Tramp's actions, almost saintly in the film, function as a kind of deception and as a way to hide himself. The Tramp could have corrected the flower girl's mistake when she first took him for a millionaire and performed his gallantries as himself. But on some level he wanted to hide from her and escape from himself, and thus his actions become a kind of mask. Getting a job, buying groceries, risking life and limb to win the prize money for her rent—as much as these are acts of generosity, they are also used in the film as acts of deception, of reconfirming to the blind girl an identity that the Tramp does not rightfully possess. They are as much instances of exclusion and misdirection as any story that the Tramp tells to the girl; in their extremity they seek to obscure the very poverty that makes them so generous. These actions are no surer a path toward knowledge than anything seen or heard within the film.

Sight, sound, action—they are the basic elements of composition in the new world of the talkies: the visual imagery of the frame, the audio track that accompanies it, the narrative action that they both present to us. And they are the basic elements put into play within *City Lights*. The genius of Chaplin's ending—one of the most famous ever put on film, Agee's "highest moment in movies"—is in no small part based on the collision of these imperfect means of knowing in a moment of joint suspension: a dramatization of the unresolvability of meaning that Chaplin's filmmaking had been emphasizing all along. The meeting is a perfect chain reaction of action, sight, and hearing that would in almost any other film lead to a simple happy ending. Meeting the Tramp on the street, the now fully sighted flower girl takes him by the hand and the action leads to a spark of recognition in his touch. She feels his arm and shoulder. She sees him now as we see him, with nothing hidden. When the grave disjunction between the recognizability of the touch and the utter unrecognizability of the impoverished man before her proves too great to bear, she asks for some kind of confirmation. "You?" she asks, with no need to specify the question any further. He answers with an action—he nods—and then he asks her in turn,

"You can see now?" She must recognize his voice. It should be enough. Sight, sound, action—all have come together to make the Tramp finally known to her. But it is all, tragically, perhaps not enough. The question that has dogged the Millionaire throughout the film has now become the flower girl's own, and their separate narratives have thematically converged. She can see the Tramp, she can hear him, she can be present to his actions. But will she recognize him? Will she be able to understand him—to know him—as the man who helped her, as the handsome millionaire of her imagination?

The film brilliantly ends before this question can be answered, but Chaplin's cinematographic choices help clue us into the deep impossibility of a reconciliation. Throughout the picture, Chaplin has filmed much of the interaction of the Tramp and the flower girl in a series of close-ups or medium close-ups: when she thinks of him after returning home the day they meet, when he glimpses her at the window of her apartment, when she stands in her doorway and wonders at his kindness to her, when he tells her he must depart and leave her for a time. It might be a sign of intimate connection for another filmmaker, but not so for the director who declared "there is no set rule that a close-up gives more emphasis than a long shot."[27] As in Chaplin's earlier uses of the technique, the close-up here is a manifestation of isolation and inwardness, a turning away from the world and a turning into the self rather than a moment of emotional connection or collaboration. We do not know it until later in the film, but when the flower girl swoons in her romantic isolation, she is not thinking of the Tramp as we know him; she is thinking of someone like the rich young man in the flower shop. She is thinking of a version of her suitor that she has constructed in her own mind, cut off from the world. The Tramp, for his part, can only be thinking of a connection intensely private to himself. He does not want to be seen or recognized; he does not want to be known. Part of the beauty of the relationship for him is that he remains hidden within it and remains unknown and unconnected to the woman he loves. She is his way to escape himself, and he is embarrassed to be known to her.[28] It is not just that he tries to run away when he meets the girl again at the end of the film at the point where she tries to come around the glass window that separates them, him on the street and her in the shop. Earlier in the film, there is a brief moment where we see his fear of being seen and his expectation at the impossibility of a full connection. When he reads to the girl a newspaper article about a foreign doctor with a cure for blindness, she shouts excitedly, "Wonderful! Then I'll be able to see you!" In a tiny gesture, Chaplin looks forlornly toward the camera after she says it before quickly picking up with his millionaire act again. He believes they are ultimately isolated from each other, and he does not believe that true connection can be established. Indeed, almost all of the shots of the Tramp swooning over the flower girl are doused with cold reality. When he stares at her drawing water from a fountain, he gets a cold splash in the face. When he stares longingly at the window of her apartment, he gets a flowerpot on the head. Nearly every moment of communion that he attempts is broken. Hers never are, but then they are based purely in imagination.

In this way, Chaplin prepares us for the final series of close-ups that will mark the unresolved reunion of the Tramp and the flower girl at the end of the film. Their meeting is in fact doubled, their moments of recognition rendered separate. There is one exchange where the Tramp recognizes the girl through the shop window; another where she comes to recognize him on the street. The composition of their bodies in the frame in these two exchanges is almost exactly reversed. In the first, the shots of the Tramp include the back of the flower girl's upper torso and head. He is recognizing her and she is rendered part of his world. The reaction shots of the girl, however, show her alone; the Tramp is entirely excluded. He is not recognized, and he is not part of her world. Indeed, even though the girl looks in these shots as though she is placed directly in front of the camera, she is actually separated from it within the diegesis of the film by the glass window of the shop; there is literally an invisible barrier that keeps her from the Tramp even when he is in plain sight. In the exchange on the street, this setup is reversed. In the shots of the girl, we can see the back of the Tramp's upper torso and the back of his head. She has seen him now and by remembering the feel of his hand she has identified who he is. As she wonders what to do with this new knowledge—as she struggles with the process of actually recognizing him even after she has identified him—he remains, tentatively and partially, part of her world. But she is no longer part of his. The Tramp knows he has been seen and identified, and he retreats into complete isolation. There is no chance for them together once he is recognized. In his close-ups, it is now the girl who cannot be seen; she is outside the frame, sometimes just barely inside to the smallest degree. The framing is essentially of him alone—although, tantalizingly, not absolutely so.

But the two figures are kept, undoubtedly, separate. And to emphasize this separation, Chaplin allows into his frames one of the most famous continuity errors ever to pass final cut. The jumps between the Tramp and the girl are supposed to be instantaneous, as in traditional shot/reaction-shot sequences, but in the shots of the Tramp he holds a flower to his mouth; in the shots of the girl, we can clearly see that he is holding the flower down and away from his face. It is, in Jonathan Rosenbaum's words, a sequence that is "flagrantly mismatched" but that in the end might not even really constitute "a lapse when the emotion and ambiguity of these shots are all that finally register and matter."[29] It is, he says, "a sequence that should be shown and described to every film student who has ever believed that eyeline matches count for very much outside of routine filmmaking."[30] As Rosenbaum argues, the sequence works despite the continuity error. But it can perhaps also be said to work in no small part because of it. Chaplin was famously cavalier about continuity errors as a director, consistently refusing to take them seriously as an artistic concern. When, late in his career, his assistant director asked an aide to interrupt a shot "if anything goes wrong technically," Chaplin corrected him and said, "We'll stop if anything is *esthetically* wrong."[31] The clear implication here is that a technical error is not the same as an aesthetic one, and that sometimes what is technically an error can still be aesthetically correct. Such is the case in the shot/reaction-shot sequence that ends *City Lights*. On the one hand, there is the simple matter of framing. Holding the flower to his face in his own close-ups allows Chaplin to effectively block the lower half of his face and draw the viewer's attention to his eyes. In a miniature version of the way in which he carefully composes much larger shots—the way that he turns the long shot of the boxing ring into a medium close-up of the fighters' heads and torsos, for instance—Chaplin here turns a standard close-up of his face into an extreme close-up of his eyes, without having to actually shoot anything so extreme or disorienting. Yet if he were to continue to hold the flower to his face in the same position in the reverse-shot of the flower girl, the flower itself would be partially blocking her face. Technical correctness would get in the way of aesthetic clarity.

On a much broader level, though, the continuity error that Chaplin allows in this sequence helps to cement the impossible thematics of the scene itself. The Tramp and the girl quite literally inhabit different, irreconcilable worlds. Even in a sequence that is supposed to be continuous, their realities are entirely incompatible. Chaplin is predisposing us against the idea that they might actually connect. And indeed, his narrative seeks to confirm this idea of separate worlds. The moment in which the flower girl identifies the Tramp as her former suitor is preceded by one of the cruelest intertitles in Chaplin's body of work. Noticing this strange, homeless man staring at her through the window of her flower shop—staring at her with the same love he has always shown her, though she was never able to see it—she turns to a fellow worker and declares "I've made a conquest!" The off-handed joke perfectly encapsulates the new social world into which the now well-to-do flower girl has moved. The sarcasm of the very word "conquest" points out the comic impossibility of the romance; it is unthinkable that a woman like her might start a relationship with a man like that. Indeed, when the Tramp is trying to fend off the newspaper boys who are assaulting him in the shot just before his encounter with the girl, we can see her through the shop window laughing at him from the background of the frame. His suffering makes good theater. Of course, the flower girl is kind enough. After she makes the joke about a conquest, she offers a free flower and a coin to the vagrant who is gawking at her. She sees his plight, and she wants to give him a little something and send him on his way. It is more kindness than almost anyone else in the film has shown him. But it is worlds apart from the kindness that the Tramp showed to her when she was poor and alone. He saw her plight and he gave her everything that he had: first all the money in his pocket, then a hundred dollars for all her flowers, then bags of food, then a thousand dollars for her operation. Where she wants to give him a little something, he wanted to give her everything and ultimately change her life. It is unlikely that she will now try to repay the favor. Every gift that the Tramp has been given in the film has been taken away when the gift-giver finally *sees* him. The Millionaire—blind drunk, we might say—gives the Tramp his Rolls-Royce, then takes it back when he wakes up sober in the morning and sees the Tramp not as his friend but as just another bum. Later he gives the Tramp the thousand dollars to give to the girl, only to charge the Tramp with stealing it when he awakens from the burglar's blow to the head and sees the Tramp next to him. The flower girl's final instance of gift-giving followed by an act of seeing may be different, but there is nothing in the film to prepare us for it.

But the brilliance of Chaplin's ending is that he does not tell us for sure. Endings had always been tricky for Chaplin. In Kerr's analysis, "The ambiguous ending, with emotion going one way and logic another, becomes the only valid ending for a Chaplin film."[32] But in this case, the impossibility of an ending is actually the only possible ending. The ending is a statement of impossibility, a reaffirmation of everything to which his approach to filmmaking had always committed itself, here rendered in the moment of that filmmaking's greatest peril. Chaplin's final sequence is not just about whether the flower girl will recognize the Tramp, whether she will accept him—within the narrative at least this could be answered definitively if he would just hold the shot a little longer. The ending is also about what happens when what we see is combined with what we hear, when the stories that we are told and the stories that we see finally come together, when action meets the worlds of sight and sound at once. The ending asks us to consider what knowledge might come from that encounter, whether we might come any closer to truth or certainty or whether we will be left in the same position of suspended meaning as we always were. It is, in Slavoj Žižek's reading, one of the supreme moments of epistemological encounter in all of film, one that directly asks whether perfect knowledge is possible. Here at last we see "the moment when the tramp exposes himself to the gaze of the other, offering himself without any support in ideal identification, reduced to his bare existence of objectal remainder."[33] The Tramp is at last only "being itself, the object in us that resists symbolization."[34] And the question that his body poses in this moment—the question of whether he can truly be recognized—is the same question that Chaplin's filmmaking has always asked. Chaplin cannot answer this question. He can only hold it in abeyance, the same abeyance in which he has always held all attempts at final meaning and resolution in his films. Chaplin's approach to filmmaking, forced to confront speech, would quickly begin to change after this film. The ambiguity so rapturously captured in the final moments of *City Lights* would soon be placed in jeopardy. But as a capstone and apotheosis to the filmmaking style that he had been perfecting since his days on the Keystone lot, the ending of *City Lights* would serve as a kind of living memorial to a manner of filmmaking that resisted all certainty. It would take the suspension of meaning in Chaplin's filmic philosophy and render it eternal. In Chaplin's own beautiful defense of his aesthetic, "The final motions of the soul are speechless."[35]

Figure 1. A confrontation between the Tramp and the lovers in Chaplin's directorial debut, *Twenty Minutes of Love* (1914).

Figure 2. Disruptive audience members in D. W. Griffith's early Biograph short *Those Awful Hats* (1909).

Figure 3. Iconic imagery of the body in peril from Buster Keaton's *Steamboat Bill Jr.* (1928), *top;* and Harold Lloyd's *Safety Last* (1923), *bottom.* Copyright © United Artists / The Kobal Collection (*top*); copyright © Harold Lloyd Entertainment, Inc. (*bottom*).

Figure 4. The climax of the building climb in Harold Lloyd's *Safety Last* (1923).
Copyright © Harold Lloyd Entertainment, Inc.

Figure 5. The cannon sequence in Buster Keaton's *The General* (1926).

Figure 6. The neighborhood ruffian (Eric Campbell) in *Easy Street* (1917).

Figure 7. Spatial motifs in *The Vagabond* (1916).

Figure 8. The restaurant scene from *The Immigrant* (1917).

Figure 9. The dance hall sequence from *The Gold Rush* (1925). Copyright © Roy Export S.A.S. All rights reserved.

Figure 10. Displacing the protagonist within the frame in *A Woman of Paris* (1923), *top left; The Gold Rush* (1925), *top right;* and *Monsieur Verdoux* (1947), *bottom left and bottom right.* Copyright © Roy Export S.A.S. All rights reserved.

Figure 11. Troublesome endings in *The Kid* (1921), *top;* and *The Circus* (1928), *bottom.* Copyright © Roy Export S.A.S. All rights reserved.

Figure 12. Framing shots within shots in *The Gold Rush* (1925), *top;* and *City Lights* (1931), *bottom.* Copyright © Roy Export S.A.S. All rights reserved.

Figure 13. Shot/reaction-shot sequences in the conclusion of *City Lights* (1931). Copyright
© Roy Export S.A.S. All rights reserved.

Figure 14. "Ballet" sequences from *City Lights* (1931), *top;* and *Modern Times* (1936), *bottom*. Copyright © Roy Export S.A.S. All rights reserved.

Figure 15. Problems of speech in *Modern Times* (1936), *top;* and *The Great Dictator* (1940), *bottom.* Copyright © Roy Export S.A.S. All rights reserved.

Figure 16. Thereza's audition sequence from *Limelight* (1952). Copyright © Roy Export S.A.S. All rights reserved.

Figure 17. Chaplin getting tangled up with himself, literally and figuratively, in *Limelight* (1952), *top;* and *A King in New York* (1957), *bottom.* Copyright © Roy Export S.A.S. All rights reserved.

Figure 18. The return to simultaneous action in *A Countess from Hong Kong* (1967). Courtesy of Universal Studios Licensing, LLC.

PART III

THE SOUND ERA

7

Dangerous Voices

Modern Times and *The Great Dictator*

odern Times may be the only film in history that reversed its course creatively and changed, mid-production, from a sound picture to an essentially silent film—the opposite of Harold Lloyd's silent-to-sound film *Welcome Danger.* Despite the critical fanfare and financial triumph of the dialogue-less *City Lights,* Chaplin was originally convinced that he could not repeat the trick, and in 1934 he began shooting his next film as a talkie. Gone was the bravado of the artist who had declared in a 1931 *New York Times* editorial that "because the silent or nondialogue picture has been temporarily pushed aside in the hysteria attending the introduction of speech by no means indicates that it is extinct or that the motion picture screen has seen the last of it."[1] In his place stood Chaplin the worried studio head, who told one reporter, "The talking films have come. They have come to stay, I believe. They have vitality—more vitality than the silent film, though less of beauty."[2] It was no small matter. To shoot *Modern Times* in the new style, he had to finally enclose his studios—the last open-air stages in Hollywood—at great expense. He had to purchase new technology and bring in new technicians. He and his new costar Paulette Goddard had to submit to voice testing. And he had to find a way for his famous Tramp to speak. The prospect of a speaking Tramp had worried Chaplin since the days when synchronized sound was just a matter of experiment and speculation. "If I did make a talking picture, no matter how good I was I could never surpass the artistry of my pantomime. . . . If I talked I would become like any other comedian," he recalled in his autobiography.[3] Yet Chaplin, thinking he was facing the inevitable, dutifully composed a screenplay for his next film that covered the opening factory segment through the department store sequence and that had at its center a speaking Tramp—a soft-spoken, somewhat aloof man, not unlike the barber figure who would take the Tramp's place in

The Great Dictator. But Chaplin could not follow through on the commitment: one day he told his crew that they would begin the film's fantasized domestic sequence with dialogue and sound as planned; by the next day, the film had become a silent picture. It was an agonizing decision, perhaps even more so than his calculations about *City Lights.* It was now almost ten years since *The Jazz Singer* had premiered. As Chaplin's son would later recall, "Every day he was forcefully reminded of how he was sticking his neck out. His silent picture making was the gossip of the town. There were lugubrious headshakes from his fellow producers and friends and tongue-in-cheek speculations by columnists. Sometimes he must have been appalled himself at his own conservatism."[4]

In fact, *Modern Times* would not truly be a silent film or even a sound film without dialogue like *City Lights;* more than sound effects and music, the soundtrack would actually have spoken words. But neither would it be a talkie. At no point would a character utter a spoken word to another character. Intertitles, the coin of the realm in silent film, would be used for that purpose. They would actually in some scenes exist side by side with audible voices, producing a kind of palimpsest of cinematic approaches to dialogue. From a sonic perspective, *Modern Times* is actually one of the most sui generis works ever produced by Hollywood, almost avant-garde in the degree of its singularity and unclassifiability. As much as it is about anything, it is about sound itself: the struggle of how to present it and specifically the destruction it can wreak, the way that it invades and controls and forecloses. If in *City Lights* Chaplin manages to hold back sound and all the surety that it brings—to negotiate with sound and incorporate it into his existing technique as a kind of natural extension and enhancement—then *Modern Times* shows his first signs of aesthetic collapse, the world of speech penetrating and reordering the universe of "gentle skepticism" that he had so carefully been crafting almost from the moment he first stepped behind the camera. In this way, the film is of a piece in its aesthetics and philosophy with Chaplin's final capitulation in *The Great Dictator:* his first full-fledged talkie and his fullest statement on the dangers of a monovocal world. Speech, as Chaplin sees it, stands in opposition to multiplicity and simultaneity, to the multifaceted and multivalent. If the sight of unbroken space can hold within it many individual realities presented at once, speech demands that those realities be presented, at best, one at a time, succession replacing simultaneity as the fundamental ordering principle. More typically, though, it demands not even succession but singularism: one story, one voice. In Siegfried Kracauer's description, the person speaking must almost always in some way "take the lead," as dialogue will "automatically turn the spotlight on the actor, featuring him as an insoluble entity."[5] If speech is disruptive and oppressive in *Modern Times,* it becomes downright dangerous in *The Great Dictator*. Speech itself can control; speech itself can harm. And the Tramp, for all his resourcefulness and charm, is ultimately ill equipped to contend with it. If the Tramp had always been not actually voiceless but a living embodiment of voicelessness—even unvoiceability—in *Modern Times* and *The Great Dictator* he would be placed against the very figures of the modern world (industrial titans, capitalist advertisers, political dictators) whose voices were loudest of all. The voiceless Tramp would finally confront the voices of the powerful. And Chaplin himself finally would have to confront speech and the changes it would bring to his working methodology.

EXPANDING THE EXPERIMENTS OF *CITY LIGHTS:*
MEDIATING SIGHT THROUGH SOUND

Modern Times is far from a total collapse of Chaplin's system of filmmaking. In fact, in many of its tactics it is a refinement and a further development of the work that he began in *City Lights* of bringing sound into his retinue of tools and making of it a powerful means of enabling and emphasizing simultaneity. Having abandoned the notion that the film would be a full-fledged talkie, Chaplin continues his experiments with sound as a complementary compositional tool. He in fact goes a good deal further in developing a system of sound effects that not only self-consciously draws attention to actions in the frame but also now works even to ontologically transform such actions. The Tramp and the Gamine's entry into their hovel of a home is a case in point. The physical assaults that the Tramp undergoes in this sequence are brutal: a heavy wooden beam falls from the ceiling and sends him reeling across the room, a table he is leaning on gives way and he falls to the floor, the roof nearly collapses on top of him, a door falls off and sends him tumbling into the waters outside. Yet the dangerous, poverty-ridden structure that attacks him more violently than almost anything else in the film is also a place of warmth and hope. "I've got a surprise for you. I've found a home," the Gamine tells him when she announces their new quarters.[6] "It's paradise," the Tramp declares when he enters the forlorn shack and sees how carefully the Gamine has adorned it with flowers and doilies. The hovel is about as structurally sound as the Tramp's frontier cabin in *The Gold Rush* (and about as scenically located as a hut in the middle of the New Jersey Meadowlands, complete with mucky waters and factories in the background). But in the care with which it is decorated for him and the sincerity with which it is presented to him, it is also a kind of heartbreaking, impoverished parody of the modern home as domestic oasis. When the cabin effectively assaults him, the sounds are far less drastic than the actual physical violence would indicate they should be. The soundscape participates in a reality distinct from (but simultaneous with) the visuals in the frame. The falling ceiling plank is marked by little more than a tap; the collapsed table sounds like crumpling cardboard; the collapse of the ceiling sounds like paper being torn; the collapsed door and the fall into the water produce nothing more than the sound of a little splash. Meaning here is conveyed not so much in the sounds themselves as in the gap between those sounds and the visuals with which they are paired. If the sonic representation of the scene is too easy, the visual reality that we see before us is perhaps too rough to fully convey the experiences of the Tramp, for whom such physical assaults are tempered by warmth and affection. Sound here is simultaneous to without being contingent upon what occurs within the frame, and in that gap of the aural and the visual Chaplin literally softens the blows of the diegesis and reminds us of the ways in which human connection can make light of even the worst hardships.

Elsewhere in the film, Chaplin doubles down on the idea that sound might highlight particular points of reality within a simultaneous visual construction, a notion he first develops in the soundscape of *City Lights*. The film's famous "gurgling" scene—perhaps the ur-text of sound-based bathroom humor on screen—is a brilliant extension of the juxtaposition of aural close-up and visual long shot that Chaplin first used with the whistle scene in *City Lights*. Left alone in the prison warden's office with the stern-looking wife of a visiting minister, the Tramp sits alongside her uncomfortably and embarrassedly sipping tea. In a scene that is otherwise silent, a distinctly ungraceful—and comically long—gurgling noise suddenly occurs. The minister's wife is having stomach trouble, and so too a moment later is the Tramp himself, his own stomach producing an unlovely, extended echo of the previous sound. Neither figure acknowledges the impolite noise. The Tramp smiles distressedly; the minister's wife stares straight ahead. They are living in double the embarrassment of the whistle scene, unable to escape themselves. If the previous party scene gave us a sonic close-up within a visual long shot, Chaplin here builds to two sonic close-ups within the space of a single medium long shot. When Chaplin frames the Tramp and the minister's wife together, we are equally cast into the isolated, inward experiences of the Tramp and of the minister's wife even while we are kept in awareness of their physical colocation and shared experience. Chaplin effectively draws us into three simultaneous realities: the world of the Tramp; the world of the minister's wife; and the world of the two together. To reemphasize the distinctness of these three overlapping spheres of reality, Chaplin concludes the sequence by setting all three even farther apart while still holding them together in the frame. Hoping to cure her stomach trouble, the minister's wife reaches for a bottle of seltzer water to help her take a pill. The Tramp meanwhile reaches for a newspaper to try to hide from the embarrassing encounter. We, watching both of them together, can see the joke coming. The minister's wife unleashes the spray from the seltzer bottle, and the Tramp sits up with a start—thinking for a moment that the sound is not seltzer but something far more impolite. Turning around, he looks from spray bottle to woman and back again, just to make sure he has properly placed the sound as innocuous. It is a version in miniature of the simultaneous but distinct realities shown at the end of *The Immigrant*—the minister's wife thinking the spray is totally harmless, the Tramp thinking the spray is something disgusting, and the viewer given access to both realms of awareness at once. Sound has given Chaplin a whole new facility for exploring such moments of simultaneous but distinct awarenesses of the world.

SYNCHRONY AND EVASION IN CHAPLIN'S FACTORY BALLET

In a similar vein, Chaplin's use of music in *Modern Times* is a further development and extrapolation from the approach that he cultivates in *City Lights*. As before, Chaplin's score offers a careful parallel to and enhancement of the action on screen, and this serves only to reemphasize the irreducibility of the action, clearly countermanding or excluding salient interpretive registers in its attempts to find and highlight a single unity of meaning in Chaplin's frame. But Chaplin's imagination has grown significantly. If Chaplin composed a short solo dance for the Tramp in the art gallery window sequence of *City Lights,* here he creates something close to a five-act ballet in the opening factory scene: a light fantasia for strings to begin the ballet on the factory floor; an accelerating cancan as Chaplin's antics move outside to the street where he chases a woman passing by and then is chased in turn by a police officer; a call-and-response for piano and orchestra as he disrupts the central control room of the factory; an extrapolation on the call-and-response theme as he returns to accost the other workers in the factory; and finally a bombastic tune for brass that echoes the opening strains of the film as his breakdown culminates in him dangling from a chain atop the factory floor. In the careful pairing of action and music and in the clarity of its act structure, it is the clearest run-up in his body of work to the actual two-act ballet that he will choreograph, score, and put on film in its entirety much later in *Limelight*. It is, moreover, the closest Chaplin had yet come to putting actual choreography on screen, a product of his growing confidence and ability as a composer. More than simply a parallel to the events of the film, his score now traces the microlevel actions of his performing body. According to Timothy Brock, a composer who has worked with the Chaplin estate and whose specialty is historical score restoration, Chaplin's musical construction is remarkably complex. Describing only one small passage from the music, he recounts that "this sequence contains 14 tempo changes, 9 meter changes, 27 synch points (places where the music sharply mimics the precise movement of the actors or their actions) all within the span of 68 seconds. Each of these 27 synch points had been meticulously laid out to not only narrate the action, but by the benefit of linear musical construction, every shot flowed with a natural consequence."[7] Chaplin is offering his score as a kind of shadow of his body, one that seeks to capture nearly every twist and turn of his frame.

It is an impressive technical feat, but it is equally important for its powerful aesthetic limitations. What the delicacies of the score seek to obviate is the terror Chaplin wreaks on the factory and on those around him during this sequence. He not only interrupts production—in itself a crime in the world of the film—but he assaults other workers, men and women alike, throughout. This is not the kindhearted Tramp of *City Lights* so much as it is, for this sequence at least, the devilish and sometimes wantonly violent Tramp of early shorts like *His New Profession* (Keystone, 1914) or even a few later instances like *The Pawn Shop*. It is all typical slapstick foolery, yes, but in case we needed any reminder of the way in which such antics could have very real consequences, Chaplin has the Tramp in the control room mischievously cause enormous, frightening balls of fire to erupt from the giant machine behind him; he nearly sets the factory ablaze, with all the workers still inside. It is hard, perhaps, to think of the Tramp in these moments as being connected to the Keystone and Essanay Tramp who prompted so many protests against his violence and amorality. We are on the Tramp's side throughout the sequence: his actions read as liberating more than as destructive. But that is in no small part because of Chaplin's score, which paints the Tramp's breakdown for us as a kind of masterful artistic expression of his body in a world that has denied him any organic mobility. It is perhaps the closest that Chaplin had yet come to predetermining the meaning of a scene for us. But it is not so much a slide toward the foreclosure of meaning as it is a remarkably sophisticated example of the inadequacies of any such attempt. As much as it is a brilliant instance of near ballet, it is also an inoculation against how we might interpret the same actions in that music's absence. The Tramp is not just attacking the inhuman machinery that has enslaved him; he is attacking the other workers trapped by the same system. And he comes close to putting them in real danger. Those balls of flame that the Tramp causes are alienating; they seem dangerous even with the lighthearted music playing over them. The Tramp is perhaps on the verge of doing something terrible. In one and the same moment that Chaplin reaches new heights in choreographing sight and sound, he asks us to consider whether this artistry isn't also a kind of evasion.

Systems of Communication:
Speech and Song

Little wonder that Chaplin begins *Modern Times* with the Tramp suffering a total breakdown from which he just barely recovers, for the film itself goes through much the same process. The near incineration of the mise-en-scène within the first two reels seems as much a rebellion against the total film as it is an act of protest against a particular diegetic element. Despite its development of certain aspects of sound from *City Lights,* Chaplin's first semi-talkie also marks a significant schism with his prior technique, self-consciously showing signs of breakdown where his previous films had shown composure. If one strength of *City Lights* lies in how it directly explores some of Chaplin's most basic artistic concerns, the power of *Modern Times* lies in its depiction of a realm where Chaplin's artistic prerogatives are under threat; it is a place from which the Tramp (not surprisingly) desperately wants to escape. The world of the film is one that seeks to replace ambiguity with top-down certainty, turn multiplicity into monovocality, and transform widening simultaneity into tightly controlled sequencing. It is a universe of institutions—factory, hospital, jail, department store—and it is only those at the top of those institutions who are ever literally given a voice in the film. Just as the first people to near-speak in a Chaplin film were the civic officials in *City Lights,* the first person actually to speak in a Chaplin film is a company president, played by Allan Garcia, who also (not coincidentally) played the officious butler in *City Lights* tasked with keeping the Tramp out of the Millionaire's home. To the powerful goes the voice. Indeed, the *only* speaking voices heard in the film are from individuals tied to systems of power and capital (the company president, the industrial salesman, the radio advertiser), and when they speak they do only one of two things—give orders or try to sell something. That is, they try to shape the world and the people around them to their agenda and their goals. More than that, though, they only ever speak when they are mediated in such a way that there can be no possibility of a response. The company president speaks into a video intercom system that he uses to order the workers around and through which they have no equal ability to communicate. The salesmen who come to sell the company president a feeding machine play for him a recorded speech from a "sales talk transcription company" that leaves him no ability to interrupt or ask questions of the speaker. The radio advertisement that the Tramp hears in the prison warden's office—a highly embarrassing ad for gastritis medication—is totally canned; he cannot chose whether it will come on or not (he's deeply embarrassed by the fact that it does), and he cannot interact with it or change it. The best he can do is shut down the contraption that allows for its dissemination—

just as the best that he can do with the company president is break the machinery that allows for his speech, even if it means possibly burning down the film in the process.

It is no small fact that all of the "dialogue" in Chaplin's first talking picture is actually a series of monologues. As with the civic orations in *City Lights*, these speeches serve as a model for how Chaplin views speech in film more generally—as well as how he views speech in the related media from which film was now borrowing. Screen, phonograph, radio—these are the devices that transmit speech in the filmic world of *Modern Times*, and they are all dangerous: dangerously one-sided and dangerously unconnected to the action around them. The video screens that give the workers no chance to respond allow the company president to increase production speed to the point at which it causes the Tramp's breakdown. The phonograph sales pitch that extols the wonders of the "Billows Feeding Machine" is dangerously out of touch with the actual operations of that machine, as the Tramp is quick to discover. If the radio ad on gastritis is not quite so literally dangerous, it is dangerously inappropriate, flagrantly and comically out of touch with the action happening in the same room. The common filmmaking logic of the time was that dialogue made characters on screen "more present" for the audience.[8] This truth is literalized in a certain way in *Modern Times*: the omnipresent image of the company president is undoubtedly quite real for the factory workers he scolds. But Chaplin offers a correction to this idea. If dialogue makes characters more present to the audience, it makes them less present to the world around them in the film. This is not just a matter of narrative construction within a film; it is the nature of speech as a compositional element in filmmaking. In a dialogue film, the visual world capable of holding within a single frame so many simultaneous stories runs a significant risk of being rendered only so much set dressing to the speeches that hog the audience's attention; in Kracauer's phrase, dialogue can "exile inanimate nature to the background."[9] If the sonic world of film is no longer flat—if certain characters' voices demand our attention as much or more than their visual images, as much or more than diegetic sound—then the power of Chaplin's skeptical camera and widening frame is severely constrained. Dialogue demands singular attention and effectively erases itself at the moment when it is challenged by any countervailing element; it is always like what we hear through the video screen, on the phonograph, or from the radio—always set apart from everything else, always demanding that it be isolated from the other elements of the world around it. On the most mundane level, we simply cannot hear dialogue and any other significant noise at one and the same time in the way that we can see two visuals at once. We cannot even necessarily hear two people speaking at once and understand what is happening.

Unless they are singing, of course. Song is the only unmediated form of the human voice to appear in *Modern Times,* and with good reason: it is not just another version of speech but a totally different system of communication, one that fits easily and wholly within Chaplin's established method of filmmaking. Singing, unlike speech, functions in a manner much closer to the visual elements Chaplin is more typically used to arranging: it can capture multiple individual voices simultaneously without any loss of meaning; it can be moved to a place of background attention in a scene without either disappearing entirely or overpowering the foreground attention; and it can be combined with silent-era visuals of dialogue—title cards and muted speech, Chaplin's traditional and more familiar tools—with no severe disjunction. It can, in other words, become part of the simultaneity of a scene. Hence the masterfully constructed sequence toward the end of *Modern Times* where singing voices, silent-style dialogue, intertitles, and (as if for good measure) prepared written texts and the actual process of writing coexist within the scene. Chaplin begins in the dining hall of the club where the Tramp has been hired as a singing waiter and allows us to watch as the other waiters begin their song and dance act, their four-part harmony fully audible. The song continues in the background as Chaplin cuts to an antechamber off the dining hall wherein the Tramp reads the text of the song he is meant to sing in order to keep his new job. The Gamine tells him in an intertitle that they should rehearse his song together, but Chaplin cannot remember the words as he goes through the motions of his performance. As a solution, the Gamine writes them on the cuff of the Tramp's sleeve—Chaplin uses a cut-in so that we can see what she is writing—and the rest of the Tramp's rehearsal goes off splendidly.

It is a relatively minor scene in the total narrative, but it is actually a little masterpiece of sonic and visual compositing. Only by allowing sound and silence to coexist can Chaplin achieve the strange feat of letting the other waiters' song waft in from the main dining room while the Tramp practices his own song in the antechamber. And only with the use of intertitles (rather than spoken dialogue) could Chaplin ensure that the waiters' song remains the main sonic point of attention while the Tramp and the Gamine discuss what to do about his flailing rehearsal. "I forget the words," he tells her in one intertitle; "I'll write them on your cuff," she responds—all while the very professional strains of the other waiters' song impress us without any breakage, their voices representing the standard that the Tramp must achieve in order to maintain this job. With the lyrics now written on his cuff—also a clever visual means to cue the audience in on the basic content of his song, without interrupting the unceasing pressure of the other waiters' crooning—the Tramp's rehearsal is triumphant. And it's a good thing: as we can hear from the other room, the waiters' song ends with a combination of applause and catcalls from the unruly crowd. The Tramp will need to not only meet their level of performance but exceed it if he hopes to be successful.

If before Chaplin had been able to hold two visually contiguous realities together in the frame, he is now able to hold discontiguous realities together at once through a combination of sight and sound. We see not just the Tramp and the Gamine together in a single long shot, his performance and her reaction happening before us always at once. We also hear the reality of the other room as it permeates this set-apart space, a constant reminder of the performance that the Tramp must match. Chaplin could not achieve the same effect with pure dialogue. To have the Tramp and Gamine actually speak would be to thrust the song into the background of the audio track, at least momentarily, instead of having it remain the only sonic point of focus throughout the scene. Conversely, to hear spoken words coming from the other room instead of a song would be to ask us to follow precisely what is happening there even as we try to follow the title-card dialogue between the Tramp and the Gamine. Actual speech either demands our full attention or requires our willful disregard. Song registers differently. We can casually pay attention without losing the gist; we can turn easily and at our own will between the mouthed words of the Tramp and Gamine and the presence of the song. In other words, we can absorb it in the same way that we do the multiple visual stimuli of Chaplin's frames. In this scene, Chaplin reaches a kind of technical peak. There is room for almost every form of human communication in Chaplin's filmic world in this instant—singing, reading, writing, muted dialogue. Everything, that is, except speech.

It is fitting then that when the Tramp finally "speaks" for the first time on film, he sings. It is an evasion of speech. Rendering the Tramp's first aural communication as a musical performance takes it outside the narrative development of the film itself. Nothing the Tramp sings will move the story forward; the act of singing itself is what is relevant—the narrative interest of the scene is about whether he performs well, not what he says in the performance. (The song, in fact, holds the same gratuitous position in relationship to narrative as Donald Crafton says of the gag itself in early slapstick, a moment of "excess" that can "contain its own microscopic narrative system that may be irrelevant to the larger narrative.")[10] Thus, the Tramp is exempted from the kind of narrative foreclosure and reduction of meaning that marks all other instances of speech within the film. Rather than shaping what we focus on and what we think about regarding the action of a scene, the Tramp's "speech" is rendered irrelevant to the action. It is also rendered incomprehensible. The actions of the Tramp's body literally divest him of the script he is supposed to follow—he flings away the cuffs on which his song is written when he thrusts his arms out in his preparatory dance steps—and he responds by telling his musical story in a pidgin language known to no one else in the world. "Sing!! Never mind the words," the Gamine tells him in an intertitle that might be taken as a kind of manifesto on Chaplin's relationship to speech within the film. Chaplin has no trouble with sound as such in his filmmaking, no trouble even with language—so long as it is stripped of its meaning and turned into just another form of sound. What he cannot find a way to accommodate is the kind of language that demands our unfailing attention and commandeers our comprehension, placing itself above everything else happening within a scene.

And in this way, the fact that the Tramp sings is not only an evasion of speech but an exploration of an alternative to it. What he offers us through song in this, the last set-piece of the Tramp's long film career, is an apotheosis of the interpretive uncertainty that has always been part of his filmmaking. Rather than foreclose meaning, the Tramp's song opens itself to multiple levels of meaning at the same time. It is, in Dan Kamin's phrase, "a tidy little tale of prostitution"—but one wherein both the jauntiness of the music and the sordidness of the story are equally active without being contradictory.[11] The song that the Tramp sings is buoyant and ebullient. The story that he pantomimes underneath—arguably his greatest act of physical storytelling since his famous sermon in pantomime in *The Pilgrim*—is sordid and debauched, a tale of a fat old man who lures a young woman of the streets into bed by offering her his diamond ring. But, as Kamin explores, to most viewers the song is not quite either of these things, a jaunty tune or a sordid tale.[12] It is simply a masterful act of performance, more beloved for how it is told than for what it communicates—"a charming but essentially meaningless demonstration of Chaplin's mime skills."[13] Though the nonsense language in which the song is sung helps to create a deeper chasm between the dark story and the playful music, the song could function in essentially the same way even if the lyrics were comprehensible. There would still exist a gulf between the content of the story and the manner of the music, and both would still be encompassed within Chaplin's masterful act of performance. Song is for Chaplin a form of communicative speech that allows for simultaneity, permits contradiction, and marries itself to action, working in concert with it. Song is, after silence, the natural aural medium of the Tramp and the natural verbal mode of Chaplin's filmmaking. It is a model for how Chaplin might possibly have begun to resolve the problems and disruptions caused by the introduction of the spoken word.

FEATURE-LENGTH FEVER DREAM: *MODERN TIMES* AS A MODEL OF SYSTEMIC BREAKDOWN

But the filmmaking model of *Modern Times* is one that Chaplin would never use again, a prototype for a machine that would never be built. If *Modern Times* exists at a kind of halfway point between silent film and the talkies, Chaplin seems to have known that it was also the farthest point he could reach before acquiescing to sound.[14] Quite simply, no one would ever go again to see a silent film—or even a semi-silent film—and Chaplin sensed this at the time. "The whole of Hollywood had deserted silent pictures and I was the only one left," he recalled; his entire experience while making the picture was marked by a grave "feeling that the art of pantomime was gradually becoming obsolete."[15] *Modern Times* is therefore perhaps the most perfect instance of planned obsolescence ever filmed, defined equally by a pervasive sense of looking backward and a sense of breakdown. Even the title *Modern Times* is perhaps the most ironic of Chaplin's career, an extreme and deliberate misnomer not least of all for the film's radical disavowal of modern filmmaking technology and practice. Chaplin seems to mark this irony in the film's visuals themselves within the first few frames of the picture. As much as *Modern Times* may borrow from René Clair's images of factory work and automation in *Liberty for Us* (Films Sonoris Tobis, 1931), it also deliberately takes its opening mise-en-scène from Fritz Lang's *Metropolis* (UFA, 1927). The factory equipment on which the Tramp and his fellows are hard at work as the film opens looks like no factory equipment in the real world so much as it looks like the byzantine art-deco contraptions of Lang's science-fiction fairy tale. Indeed, the scene in *Metropolis* where Freder enters the underworld and sees workers desperately pulling levers and turning dials on a giant machine to keep it from exploding in smoke and steam seems to specifically anticipate the central control room of *Modern Times,* where the Tramp nearly sets the factory ablaze by pulling on the wrong levers. The connection is not insignificant. In the fanciful factory setting of *Modern Times,* we are suddenly a long way from the gritty realities that marked Chaplin's mise-en-scène construction from *A Dog's Life* onward—what Walter Kerr calls a world in which dirt has become "real dirt, hard, soiling, transparently uncomfortable" and where "the comedy and a certain harshness of fact are being welded."[16] The world of *Metropolis* was not a world of modernity so much as faux modernity, a fairy tale involving sorcerer-inventors, modern-day princes, and virtuous maidens grafted onto a fantastical imagining of what the future might be like. For Chaplin to mark his work in connection to *Metropolis* was to make a joke of its connection to the modern world: it was a connection to the modern world as a fairy tale, the modern world as a fanciful reimagination of the facts. It was, in other words, not to connect it to the modern world at all. The film only pretended to look forward; where it was really looking was behind.

Indeed, much of what happens in *Modern Times* has very little to do with "modern times" and very much to do with old-time slapstick. In the words of

Otis Ferguson's influential review from the *New Republic,* "*Modern Times* is about the last thing they should have called the Chaplin picture. . . . All the old gags are brought out and dusted off for use."[17] Chaplin, like all slapstick artists, had always recycled and repurposed gags and scenarios from film to film. But no film he had yet made would offer such a complete catalog of his prior work. The picture seems deliberately reminiscent of past triumphs, the likes of which were likely never to be seen on screen again. If the Tramp's mental breakdown ballet reminds us of a more destructive and mischievous Tramp from the Keystone and Essanay years, his bout of cocaine-induced heroism in the prison sequence reminds us of his heroin-induced heroism in *Easy Street;* his explorations of the department store remind us of *The Floorwalker;* his figure skating reminds us of the graceful antics of *The Rink;* his shack of a home with the Gamine reminds us of his cabin home in *The Gold Rush;* the Gamine's dancing-girl getup reminds us of Merna Kennedy in *The Circus;* even the plotline with child welfare authorities coming to take the Gamine to an orphanage specifically recalls the plotline and orphanage authority figures from *The Kid.* Some commentators have taken this kind of self-cataloging as a sign of Chaplin's declining creativity in the age when all other slapstick artists had passed from prominence. In Kerr's assessment, Chaplin is working "late in the day and with no competing clowns to spur him on."[18] But it seems more apt to see it as a way for Chaplin to deliberately mark the film as a moment of slapstick's final passing.

Chaplin even goes so far as to purposefully include gags in the film that he himself had long ago discarded as old-fashioned. No one in a Chaplin film had received a pie in the face in almost twenty years, not since the 1916 Mutual short *Behind the Screen*—and even then it was marked diegetically within the film as an antiquated technique, a sure sign of the lack of inspiration at the two-bit movie studio where the Tramp is working as a prop man. Yet *Modern Times* contains two pies in the face, both ironically tied to modern machinery: one where the feeding machine pushes a pie into the Tramp's face with a mechanical arm, another where the Tramp accidentally pushes a pie into the face of his boss, who is trapped in one of the factory's machines, as he tries to feed him. Those pies are pushed as much in tribute to a passing art form as in humor. And, even more tellingly, the person into whose face that second pie is pushed is none other than Chester Conklin. Conklin was one of the stars at Keystone when Chaplin first arrived there, and he made more than a dozen films with Chaplin while they were both at the studio. He played alongside Chaplin in his very first Keystone film, *Making a Living,* and was one of the major players in his directorial debut, *Twenty Minutes of Love.* But Chaplin left Conklin behind when he departed for Essanay in 1915; by 1936, the two had not worked together in more than twenty years. Yet there he is in *Modern Times,* his very bodily presence—and unmistakable mustache—standing as a kind of totem to a world of filmmaking that was now gone. As much as the second factory in *Modern Times* is marked diegetically in the film as a welcome site of employment for the masses who have been thrown out of work, so too is it marked in a metanarrative sense as a site of employment for another kind of worker displaced by modern times. Yet almost as soon as the factory is opened, it is closed again, with the Chaplin and Conklin characters both thrown out of work. Like the filmmaking style of *Modern Times* itself, the new opportunity that the factory represents cannot be sustained.

Thus, Chaplin inscribes into the structure of *Modern Times* a sense of the breakdown that the picture itself would represent in his filmmaking approach. The film has been roundly criticized, in Chaplin's day and by later commentators, as perhaps the least narratively coherent of his major works. In Ferguson's words, *Modern Times* "is a feature picture made up of several one- or two-reel shorts, proposed titles being *The Shop, The Jailbird, The Watchman, The Singing Waiter.*"[19] Chaplin's half brother and sometime collaborator Sydney was perhaps most adamant in his critique, writing his brother a lengthy private letter about the film's narrative shortcomings, saying that Chaplin had started the picture "with a fast tempo then faded away. You gave them the best first instead of saving it until last."[20] In one of his many post hoc suggestions for how the film could have been improved, Sydney explains that the audience needed to see the tangible results of the Tramp's breakdown in the factory—the ravages that modern production can inflict upon itself. The factory should have made cars, and the Tramp's breakdown would have resulted in a "freak car."[21] But, in a way, that "freak car" is included in Chaplin's film: it is the film itself. *Modern Times* does not so much suffer from poor narrative construction as it seems purposefully resistant to it, deliberately misproportioned and struggling to support the weight of what narrative structure it does have. Though it opens with the image of a ticking clock, time itself is irrevocably out of joint in *Modern Times.* In contrast to the carefulness of *City Lights,* in which the time of day is very precisely enumerated throughout the film in a series of helpful intertitles that serve as narrative guideposts, the very length and order of the parts of the day seem totally undone in *Modern Times.* Take, for example, the bizarre sequence of events in which, in a single stretch of early morning, the Tramp tries to save the Gamine from getting arrested for stealing bread; tries to get arrested himself by ordering and eating two trays of food at a busy cafeteria without being able to pay; gets arrested; escapes from the police with the Gamine; and then finally seeks refuge on a suburban street where a typical suburban husband is just leaving for work as his typical suburban wife waves good-bye. Either this typical suburban husband has an atypical workday that starts closer to noon, or time itself seems to contract and expand at will within the film. It is, of course, no great harm to the story line and nothing of which any number of other films, slapstick and otherwise, wouldn't also be guilty, but it is atypical for Chaplin at this point in his career, evidence of a film whose narrative springs are coming loose.[22]

What we are left with in the place of proper time and proper sequencing—the requisite conditions for proper development of story—is ultimately less of a feature-length narrative than a kind of feature-length fever dream of human needs and social institutions. Chaplin had always crafted his stories and his comedy around a search for basic human needs—food, shelter, work if you can find it—usually laced with a deep skepticism toward almost all social institutions. Hence the scenes of domestic homemaking in *The Kid* or the evil orphanage officials and policemen in that film, the struggle for food and warmth in *The Gold Rush,* the groceries and rent payments in *City Lights,* or the unjust jail sentence that the Tramp suffers there. But these elements had always formed a kind of cradle in which Chaplin could place his narrative, building a comprehensible story inside these concerns. In *Modern Times,* the concerns essentially become the story itself. Like the factory conveyor belt in the opening segments, the narrative seems to have been sped up to the point where it is little more than a blur of Chaplin's obsessions with institutional structures and human needs: factory, hospital, orphanage, jail, food, shelter, food, food, shelter, food, shelter, jail, shelter, factory, food.[23] The concerns seem to flash by so fast that they begin to blur together—for instance, institutionalization becomes equated with food and shelter in the jail, shelter and job are combined in the department store, work and food become one and the same at the restaurant. The narrative structure that used to hold such obsessions together has been flung apart and only the substructure remains.

Hence the strange double-vision of the film's ending, perhaps the greatest mark of the degree to which its narrative has purposefully come apart. *Modern Times* has become so canonical within Chaplin's body of work that it can be hard to remember how strange its ending is within that canon. Chaplin's films had ended with some version of the iconic image of the Tramp traveling alone down an empty road many times before—in *Police, The Tramp, The Pilgrim,* and *The Circus.* Or they had ended with him getting the girl and finding some degree of human connection, whether confidently or contingently—as in *The Vagabond, The Immigrant, A Dog's Life, The Kid,* or *The Gold Rush.* The suspension at the end of *City Lights* is essentially the suspension between these two possible endings. But like some "freak car," *Modern Times* includes neither one ending nor the other nor the point of suspension that lies between them.

It includes both endings grafted onto each other. The Tramp gets the girl and walks alone with her down the road as if in some kind of narrative double exposure. In fact, the ending seems to be doubly doubled, insofar as the Tramp seems to be walking with another version of himself down that empty road; it is almost as though he has simply joined forces with his female mirror, a common reading of the Gamine's character. More than any other female figure in Chaplin's body of work, she shares his temperament and disposition—not only his obsession with fulfilling basic material needs but also his pluck and cunning in trying to meet those needs. She is nearly as much a copy of him as is little Jackie Coogan in *The Kid*. The dysfunctional narrative machine of the film has produced two Tramps: the figure walking down the road with him at the film's end is as much his doppelgänger as his romantic partner. Indeed, she is never even really courted in the film, unlike nearly every other female lead in Chaplin's work. It takes no more than about three-and-a-half total minutes of screen time together before the Tramp and the Gamine are fantasizing about a domestic life in the suburbs. It is as though the scenes of courtship were knocked out of the film in an industrial accident, leaving the Tramp and the Gamine to jump almost directly from meeting to imagining being married. The film's famous ending is a touching testament to love and commitment in the face of unceasing adversity, perhaps. But it is also evidence of a kind of narrative and structural dysfunction within the standards of Chaplin's own body of work. His manner of filmmaking is not just coming to an end; it is self-evidently breaking down.

A TALKIE ABOUT THE TALKIES: REFLEXIVITY AND REFUSAL IN *THE GREAT DICTATOR*

The Great Dictator, Chaplin's first full-fledged entry to the world of talkies, would be both the product of the stylistic collapse predicted in *Modern Times* as well as a careful diagnosis of its causes. The overwhelming force of politics in the film has tended to obscure the degree to which the picture is also one of Chaplin's most explicit films about film, absolutely invested in understanding and showing how film works and under what conditions it might break down. As much as the film offers a series of caustic parodies of politics and world events, it also offers a succession of parodies of filmmaking technique. Hence the remarkable moment in the film where Chaplin essentially stages in abridged form the last fifteen or so years of film history in a series of three short successive scenes. Apropos of nothing, Chaplin's Adenoid Hynkel walks alone across an empty hallway and trips over himself. Then, in the next scene, he walks alone into a room and begins to play a piano. Rising from the piano, he moves into another part of the room, approaches a bowl of fruit on the table, and speaks directly into it to call one of his officers into the room—the intercom is hidden in the fruit bowl. This is all, on one level, simply evidence of Hynkel's clumsiness and minuscule attention span. On another level, however, it is the history of the transition to sound writ small: the sequence begins with silent slapstick, moves on to a man at a piano (the advent of synchronized sound embodied in Al Jolson at his keyboard), and resolves with synchronized speech and a winking reference to the way in which primitive microphones were awkwardly hidden within the mise-en-scène of early talkies, with all the actors leaning into flower pots or fruit bowls or light fixtures as they spoke. Elsewhere in the film, Chaplin offers a kind of wry comparison of modern filmmaking styles. In an early running gag, Hynkel occasionally pops into an antechamber off his main command room, where he keeps two artists waiting, a painter and a sculptor. The artists snap to work on a portrait and a bust whenever he appears, but after no more than a few seconds of posing, Hynkel shouts "Enough!" and storms out of the room again, off to his next appointment.[24] The artist and the sculptor throw up their hands—how can they be expected to make art in such short bursts? Yet Chaplin is essentially staging a parody of classical film technique here, where art is in fact supposed to be composed in snippets of only a few seconds at a time. We would not expect painters and sculptors to work under these conditions; why should we expect it of our filmmakers?

But Chaplin's own approach to filmmaking fares no better when it comes up for self-parody later in the film. Attempting to stage a one-on-one encounter with Benzino Napaloni, the rival dictator of neighboring Bacteria, Hynkel must ensure that he always remains the most powerful figure in the room. In describing his plans for the meeting, Hynkel's advisor Garbitsch might as well be describing the composition of a Chaplin frame—the arrangement of space, the movement of bodies, and the objects of the mise-en-scène all precisely choreographed and considered:

> I have so arranged that he will always be looking up at you, you looking down at him. At all times the position will be inferior. . . . Then again, we shall seat him here, beside your bust, so that if you relax, that will always be glaring at him. . . . When he arrives, I have arranged he shall enter from the far end of the room—another psychological triumph. He will have the embarrassment of walking the entire length of the floor toward you.

Inevitably, when Napaloni comes into the room, he throws the whole scheme asunder: he enters through the wrong door, slaps Hynkel on the back and knocks him out of his chair, sits on the table, belittles and makes demands of Hynkel at every turn. The plan is a wreck. Napaloni was played by Jack Oakie, one of the new breed of verbal comedians who had transformed the nature of Hollywood comedy in the 1930s. He was part and parcel of the era of the talkies, fully immersed in the restrengthening of classical principles of division and emphasis that the sound era represented both for filmmaking in general and for film comedy in particular.[25] Of course Garbitsch's Chaplinesque idea of staging would no longer work. Chaplin was in a new moment of film history, and the old techniques could no longer be relied upon.

Indeed, one of the running gags throughout the film is the way that Chaplin's Jewish barber character, the new stand-in for the Tramp, cannot adjust to the world of the talkies. He is positioned within the film as a kind of holdover from the era of the First World War. Knocked unconscious in 1918, he finally returns home in the late 1930s with no knowledge of how the world has changed. He, like a kind of parody of Chaplin himself in the 1930s, thinks that everything is the same as it was years ago, and he has trouble adjusting to new realities. And more often than not, the Barber's troubles are linked metanarratively to the new world of sound. In one of the film's most explicit jokes about the transition from silents to talkies, the Barber runs into a room where his friend Commander Schultz is hiding and "tells" him in an agitated pantomime that the storm troopers are coming to get him. Diegetically within the film, it looks like the Barber is so agitated that he cannot get the words out. But metanarratively, it looks for all the world like a scene from a silent film, the Barber frantically mouthing words to his friend and gesticulating with no sound produced. Schultz just stares blankly at the warning, but the Barber seems to think he has communicated actual information. When his love interest, Hannah, comes into the room and asks the Barber if he has given Schultz the warning, he responds with a confident (and verbalized) "Yes." He keeps forgetting that the world now has sound, a point conveyed again in another gag that immediately follows. Attempting to hide any trace of Schultz's presence from the storm troopers, the Barber helps to gather his belongings from the room where he was hiding. If the need to collect these objects seems a tad obsessive—they begin with a suitcase and valise but move on to include a hatbox, golf clubs, a canteen, and yet another suitcase—it is in part because the Barber and his friends are thinking from the perspective of a silent film, where an individual's presence is often conveyed in representative objects and items of clothing. Chaplin was a master of the technique: the dropped shirt collar in the bedroom in *A Woman of Paris,* the small gifts on the table in *The Gold Rush,* the flower found in the gutter in *City Lights*—all are classic instances of objects serving as a visual marker of a particular human presence. But removing the visual traces of presence in *The Great Dictator* is not enough. The Barber successfully gets everything out of the room, cumbersome as the objects might be, but when he reaches the rooftops on which he and Schultz will make their escape, he proceeds to accidentally drop the objects one by one, each one landing with a muffled thud. (In fact, he drops them specifically because he has become disoriented at not being allowed to *see:* an inverted hatbox has been placed over his head as he and Schultz make their escape.) Visual erasure is simply not enough anymore. The Barber—like Chaplin himself—is in a different world now, and it functions by different rules. Only when he is captured by the enemy will his old techniques possibly serve him at all; as Schultz says to him in a bid to stop him from disclosing any information to his captors, "Remember, your silence will be appreciated."

Dangerous Voices: Monovocality and the End of Simultaneity

There is a way in which all of Chaplin's clever jokes about the new world of sound and speech in *The Great Dictator* might be considered quaint, were it not for the fact that this world is so explicitly positioned as dangerous within the film. It is, after all, equated with the world created by the Nazis. It is no coincidence that the Chaplin film most obsessed with literally staging a struggle between sound technique and silent technique is also obsessed with demanding that the world pay attention to the dangers posed by fascism. The two concerns are not, of course, the same for Chaplin, but they are deeply related. For Chaplin, the road that ends in a state that "makes men torture and imprison innocent people" begins in the highly controlled and restricted use of speech.[26] Speech itself is rendered dangerous in *The Great Dictator*. In one of the film's most famous sequences, Hynkel's microphones bend away from him to try to escape his vitriol. In another moment, the Barber literally runs and ducks to try to escape Hynkel's words as they are blasted from a loudspeaker on the street. Speech itself can harm, and speech itself can control. Chaplin's positioning of speech in *The Great Dictator* is in fact remarkably in line with his predictions in *Modern Times*. In *Modern Times*, speech is only ever unidirectional, never allowing for an interplay with other voices. At best it is only ever mediated, transmitting itself over great distances yet never connecting to the world around it. And it is only ever used to persuade or to control. Such are the same conditions of speech in Chaplin's version of Nazi Germany. It is a state where, in the words of the film's narrator, "free speech was suppressed and only the voice of Hynkel was heard." It is a state where that voice is transmitted through microphones and loudspeakers to every corner of the country. And it is a voice, as the Barber says in his own climactic speech, that can only ever "tell you what to do—what to think and what to feel." The perils of Chaplin's totalitarian state are the perils of speech itself writ large.

This is not only a political problem in the film; it is also a problem of filmic composition. The monovocality of speech, its disconnection from immediate interaction and simultaneity, its demands for our attention and our adherence—all of these are directly dramatized in the film's grand argument between Hynkel and Napaloni. The metasubject of the scene is the problem of filmmaking in the sound era itself, and it renders explicit the implied criticism that Chaplin had been making on the limitations of dialogue ever since *City Lights*. On a narrative level, the scene is a failed negotiation between the two great dictators of Europe, both of whom want to either invade Osterlich themselves or receive an assurance that the other will not. Trying to resolve their differences through a rational conversation, the two quickly descend into sheer cacophony, each trying simply to scream the loudest as they talk over each other and their advisers. The scene is a parodic put-down of the childishness of these petulant leaders, complete with a food fight; dealing with them is quite literally like dealing with children. But it is also one of the clearest statements that Chaplin would ever make on the limitations of synchronized speech. In theory, the scene is a perfect instance of simultaneity: the whole point is that Hynkel and Napaloni want to talk at exactly the same time. In this way, it is narratively no different from the restaurant scene in *The Immigrant* or the cabaret anteroom scene at the end of *Modern Times*. Chaplin was once a master at capturing such scenes of simultaneity. But now, in the sound era, his frame is held completely captive to the two bickering infants on the screen. Mute the sound and the scene could be freed to become a little masterpiece of the widened frame, the movements and gesticulations of Hynkel and Napaloni paralleling or countermanding one another in a kind of awful dance, our attention free to move from one detail of the frame to another. The Chaplin of *City Lights* or *Modern Times* could even compose a quasi-operatic score to accompany the scene, representing the bombast of each character in a sequence of complementary melody lines that could blend together even as they struggled against one another. But in the era of the talkie, the scene is almost nothing but noise. There are elements of Chaplin's silent-era approach hidden in the scene as it exists, traces of an earlier era of filmmaking. As Hynkel and Napaloni argue, they subconsciously engage in a series of hand gestures that render them something like two back-to-back figures from a cuckoo clock, inadvertent parodies of their own overwrought gestural systems of salutes and countersalutes. But these are visual traces only. No matter what else is happening in the frame, the main point of attention is in the awful discord of Hynkel's and Napaloni's simultaneous shouting. Everything else is simply background to this aural contest. Because, at bottom, Hynkel and Napaloni are basically right: only one voice can be heard at a time and there is no such thing as simultaneity in a world governed by dialogue. The best that one can hope for is orderly succession, first one speaks and then the other; it is a sequence of tiny dictatorships, only one voice allowed at a time. Indeed, in order to advance the scene forward narratively, Chaplin must break his unified frame and show us comprehensible side conversations in which first Hynkel talks to Garbitsch, then Napaloni talks to his ambassador. The idea of simultaneity—of a world irreducible to any one element—no longer truly exists. This, in Chaplin's view, is the world that the coming of sound has wrought and the final culmination of classical technique.

RECALIBRATING WORD AND ACTION

It is a dark fact that Chaplin's first talkie is absolutely obsessed with the dangers of speech and with a world controlled by speech. But it is perhaps darker still that Chaplin seems unable to find any alternative or antidote to this world within his film. Writing, for instance, is figured in the film as nothing but a different form of speech. There is a running gag where Hynkel can almost never manage to get any kind of writing implement to work: his pens always get stuck in their holders as if they are refusing to be used. And it is little wonder, for almost every document to which he signs his name is torn up in anger an instant later. Hynkel's promises and contracts are meaningless, but in a bigger sense the written word itself is rendered worthless. It is just as subject as anything that Hynkel says to design and manipulation, lies and falsehood. Hynkel's pens try to get away from him in the same way as his microphones, but it is a fruitless act of resistance in both cases. More despairing, however, is the degree to which action is rendered impotent within the film. "Actions speak louder than words," a character says early in the film. It is a direct quotation from *Modern Times,* where the phrase is used in the sales pitch for the Billows Feeding Machine. There is still a certain kind of truth to the statement in that film: the feeding machine goes haywire when it is put to use, and its actions quickly give the lie to all the exaggerated claims of the recorded sales pitch. But the same sentiment is rendered both morbid and ineffectual when it is recycled in *The Great Dictator.* It appears in the film in more or less the same context—an inventor making a sales pitch, this time for a new bulletproof uniform. He offers to have the dictator shoot a gun at him to test it, Hynkel does, and the inventor falls down dead. We have learned that the inventor is a liar and that the vest is a dud ("Far from perfect," in Hynkel's summation), but we have ultimately gained very little besides.

Throughout the film, action is effectively neutered: capable of communication perhaps but incapable of effecting any change. *The Great Dictator* in fact contains two of the greatest sequences of pure action that Chaplin would put on film. One is Hynkel's now iconic dance with the inflatable globe—a languid, bizarre, oddly sexualized, and infantile pas de deux between dictator and world, the quest for world domination rendered as a total regression of the human psyche, little more than a child playing strangely with a balloon. The other is its immediate partner in the film, the Barber's crisp, quick, and dexterous shave, played out to Brahms's *Hungarian Dance Number 5*. It is everything that Hynkel's globe dance is not: accomplished, professional, adult, grounded in the world of reality and responsibility instead of personal fantasy. (It is also a subtle nod to Chaplin's own performing past: barbershop routines were a staple of the British music hall, and the Tramp's supposed inability to properly perform one is a major plot point in *The Circus*.) These moments of pure action are as deftly composed and executed as anything that Chaplin would ever put on film. Yet they are also functionally useless. They may give us some greater insight into Hynkel's perversity or the Barber's quiet admirability, but they do nothing to affect Hynkel's ascension within the film's narrative or to change the film's compositional limitations. They are flourishes that effectively lie outside the film's narrative development as well as outside its basic stylistic approach, which is no closer to effectively handling the screaming match between Hynkel and Napaloni after these sequences than it was before. Narratively, these scenes are as futile as any individual act of resistance to the storm troopers; it is all too little too late. Action changes nothing once a system of totalitarian control is already in place, politically or artistically.

Indeed, action can become just as subject to lies and manipulation within the world of the film as any form of speech. Hynkel actually uses action as a means of lying in a pivotal juncture of the story. Hoping to win a loan from a foreign Jewish banker to finance his invasion of Osterlich, he commands that "all persecution of the Jews must cease. . . . At least, until I've negotiated this loan." The actions of his storm troopers henceforth become a kind of embodied lying. Instead of attacking and beating Hannah as they did at the beginning of the film, the troops help her up when she falls, pick up the vegetables she has dropped, and escort her kindly back home. It is such a shift that Hannah wonders if there might not be some truth in it, some reality to the thought that "things are looking brighter now." She wonders, in other words, if actions might truly speak louder than words and if the newfound kindness of the soldiers might outweigh all the vitriol that Hynkel has been speaking. In fact,

Hynkel entirely stops making speeches during this period of false appeasement. He withholds his greatest source of control and manipulation and allows a new world to be created where action supplants words, where speech—his speech—is rendered silent. But it is just another kind of lie. When the loan falls through, Hynkel rescinds his order; he makes his most hateful speech yet and allows his storm troopers to return to their terrible deeds, worse than before. Now instead of just attacking individuals, they overwhelm the streets, set off explosives, and send the whole Jewish ghetto up in smoke. Action has told us nothing.

Chaplin allows for the possibility that one might believe in a cliché like "actions speak louder than words," and he even presents the idea that belief in it might constitute a kind of nobility—but he does not make it a functionally tenable position all the same. Schultz is the exemplary case. Originally a member of Hynkel's government, he learns to rethink his assumptions about the Jews in part through the virtuous actions of the Barber, who saved his life during the First World War. "I always thought of you as an Aryan," he says in shock when he meets the Barber again, and he ultimately upends his entire system of beliefs to accommodate the new reality that his recognition of the Barber's actions has impressed upon him. But as much as he is a kind of hero, Schultz is also a figure to be mocked within Chaplin's film, a gross sentimentalist who is given to cliché. When he believes that he is dying during the First World War scenes early in the film, he becomes a kind of living fount of cinematic bromides: he speaks of "spring in Tomania" and how his wife Hilda "will be in the garden now, tending the daffodils. How she loves daffodils. She would never cut them for fear of hurting them. It was like taking a life, to cut a daffodil. Sweet, gentle Hilda. A beautiful soul. And she loved animals. And little children too." This, all while the Barber is hanging upside down from their plane as they hurtle toward the ground. The idea that "actions speak louder than words" is just one more cliché that people like Schultz might believe regardless of what is appropriate in the circumstance. Chaplin allows that Schultz might even be noble for his beliefs, but that makes them no less useless or untrue.

GOOD SPEECH, BAD SPEECH: THE IMPOSSIBILITY OF RESOLUTION IN *THE GREAT DICTATOR*

There is, of course, a possible counterweight to the oppressive world of speech within Chaplin's film. If speech utterly reorders the world to its own image—if it imposes on film the same kind of totalitarian conditions that it imposes on political states—then perhaps the only means to counteract it is with more speech: good speech to bad, liberating speech to oppressive speech, one reordering of the world to another. Hence the seeming solution that Chaplin works toward in *The Great Dictator*, where the last five minutes of the film are entirely given over to the speech that the Barber delivers in Hynkel's stead, as utterly opposed to Hynkel in its worldview as the Barber is to Hynkel in his character. "I'm sorry, but I don't want to be an emperor," the Barber begins. "That's not my business. I don't want to rule or conquer anyone. I should like to help everyone—if possible—Jew, Gentile—black men—white." It is, for all its good intentions, perhaps the most hated moment in Chaplin's entire body of work, the object of more critical vitriol than almost any other scene that Chaplin would ever create. For Gerald Mast, "The abstractions of language, the poetic failure of the words to add up to the grand concepts they attempt to express, represent a severe stylistic disruption in the film."[27] Kerr is even more blunt in his assessment: "The speech is dreadful. It is a hoary collection of disorganized platitudes, belligerently delivered. Not only the barber has disappeared. Chaplin the artist has disappeared. The film has disappeared."[28]

But the critical opprobrium directed against the speech is arguably deeply misplaced, for as much as the speech is a collection of vacuous platitudes, it is also one of the most internally problematic climaxes to appear in any of Chaplin's films. The Barber's attempt at delivering an alternate world program to Hynkel's homicidal mania is in fact no escape from the conditions of that mania whatsoever. The Barber has literally taken Hynkel's place—assumed his costume and his appearance, taken his position onstage in front of all the senior officials of his party, placed himself before Tomania's armies and zealots. The Barber does not tear off his disguise and announce his true identity. He delivers his speech *as Hynkel*. And in his own way he is merely replicating Hynkel's approach. He condemns those who "tell you . . . what to think and what to feel," then commands his audiences as to what they should think and feel. "With the love of humanity in your hearts! Don't hate!" he demands. When he condemns the way that Hynkel tries to "tell you what to do," he goes on immediately to do the same. "Soldiers! Don't fight for slavery! Fight for liberty!" When the Tomanian masses cheer in unison for the Barber-as-Hynkel, what are they cheering for? A sudden liberation or just a sudden ideological substitution? Or when Chaplin intercuts actual footage of cheering crowds from a Nazi rally, as he has at several other points in the film, are we to assume that this is a sign that they have been somehow suddenly liberated by the Barber or that this is an ominous portent for what the Barber is actually doing? For the only thing that the Barber has changed between himself and Hynkel is the literal content of his speech. In every other respect, what he is doing now and what Hynkel has done throughout the film is identical. It is just as monovocal, it is just as mediated and disconnected, it is just as unopen to question or interruption as anything that Hynkel has said or anything that any of the speaking characters in *Modern Times* might say. The Barber has done nothing to change the fundamental conditions of speech itself; indeed, he has only served to reinforce them and assert on no real evidence that they can be considered the allies of peace and liberation. We have to wonder whether the Barber has really changed anything at all.

Considered from this perspective, *The Great Dictator* can seem like one of Chaplin's most despairing works, the inevitable fulfillment of the systemic collapse predicted by those first few instances of speech in *Modern Times*. Speech, with all the assumptions of certainty that come with it, has emerged triumphant over other means of filmic representation, and it seems almost impossible to unseat or to change. The system cannot be co-opted; it will only replicate itself. If there is any hope at all it seems to rest only in the idea of breaking down all systems, of abandoning any structure whatsoever and taking something like a scorched earth approach to cinematic form. It might be an approach that was philosophically aligned with Chaplin's increasingly dark worldview, at least as he admitted to it in his more candid moments. "I'm an anarchist," he told one reporter almost twenty years later. "I hate governments and rules and—fetters."[29] Even democracy was perhaps too much order for him. Asked why he had never voted, Chaplin responded, "I don't believe in making any divisions of people. I think that any division . . . is very dangerous. I think that leads to fascism."[30] Yet Chaplin would never quite be willing to fully accept the despair—the anguish at the impossibility of breaking free from controlling structures—that seems so obvious in *The Great Dictator*. He brought himself artistically to the edge of the abyss, but looking out he convinced himself that what he saw was a new horizon. Despite all of the careful caveating to which the final speech would be subject within the film itself, Chaplin would go on in his public life to hold it up as an exemplary statement of principle. He would deliver it—as himself, without irony—over the radio during the Second World War to commemorate Roosevelt's third inauguration. He would reprint it in its entirety in his autobiography. He would come, in other words, to actually believe in it. And in a more general sense, he would come to believe in the power and possibility of speech as an aspect of film technique, turning his back on so much of what defined his style during the silent era and the early transition to sound in favor of the new path forward that he thought he found in the final moments of *The Great Dictator*. He would come to regard the breakdown that he foretold in *Modern Times* and that he dramatized in *The Great Dictator* as no breakdown at all but a chance to rebuild. It was a belief that he would hold almost until the end of his life. And it would almost destroy his art.

Substituting Speech for Style

Monsieur Verdoux, Limelight, and *A King in New York*

For an artist who made his reputation in a silent medium, Charlie Chaplin loved to talk. More specifically, he loved to hold forth on serious thinkers and serious ideas. Chaplin had little formal education, but he was remarkably (and somewhat ostentatiously) well read. Even from his Karno days, he was known to keep well-placed copies of Schopenhauer or Emerson in his dressing room, turning to them between shows. In an interview from 1920, he claimed that philosophy was for him a kind of relaxation from comedy: "Solitude is the only relief. . . . I go to my library and live with the great abstract thinkers—Spinoza, Schopenhauer, Nietzsche."[1] How much time Chaplin actually spent with these volumes is unclear; his friend Thomas Burke claimed that he "appears a very well-read and cultivated man when, in fact, his acquaintance with books is slight."[2] But what is certain is that he loved to talk about books and ideas. As Burke describes, "His mind is extraordinarily quick and receptive; retentive, too. . . . With a few elementary facts on a highly technical subject, his mind can so work upon them that he can talk with an expert on that subject in such a way as to make the expert think."[3] Hence the catalog of intellectual luminaries whom he made a point of visiting on his triumphant 1931–32 promotional world tour for *City Lights:* John Maynard Keynes, George Bernard Shaw, Winston Churchill, Albert Einstein, even Mahatma Gandhi. (He was also supposed to meet Sigmund Freud while he was in Vienna but had to leave the city early.) These were not social calls in any normal sense; they were more like friendly debates and private lectures. To Gandhi, he declared, "I would like to know why you're opposed to machinery. After all, it's the natural outcome of man's genius and is part of his evolutionary progress."[4] To Einstein, he explained, "These two mediums of exchange—credit and gold—will never stabilize prices, for credit is more elastic than gold."[5] (Einstein's somewhat bemused response was to tell Chaplin, "You're not a comedian. You're an economist.")[6] To Chaplin's own mind, at least by the time of *City Lights*, he was as much thinker as filmmaker. In David Robinson's words, summarizing Chaplin's critics at the time, Chaplin "was getting above his station. The clown was setting himself up as a statesman and a philosopher. He had mingled so much with world leaders . . . that he had begun to think of himself as one."[7]

Chaplin had long been aware of a kind of subtle philosophical purpose in his comedy. Hence his description, offered in an interview on the 1925 version of *The Gold Rush,* of how he tries in his films "to put across the philosophic doubt I feel about things and people."[8] Or, in a similar vein, his explication of the visual and storytelling techniques he developed in *A Woman of Paris,* which he describes as a kind of metaphysical exercise, an attempt to unmask as "absurd, antiquated, and unfair to humanity" the idea that there exists "a cosmos where humans were held responsible for their actions or the results of their actions."[9] But with the coming of sound, there was a temptation to turn philosophical overtone into a direct statement of principles, literalized in the culminating speech of *The Great Dictator.* Chaplin had resisted this temptation in *City Lights;* he had argued against it and demonstrated its dangers in *Modern Times.* And he had even still equivocated in *The Great Dictator* itself, crafting a film whose overall construction was as darkly cynical about the new world of speech as the content of that final address was hopeful about how it might be used. But no matter how much the film's concluding sermon was compromised within the context of the story itself, believing in its content and putting stock in its power became for Chaplin a kind of moral necessity. A muted philosophy of "gentle skepticism," as he called it—or even, more strongly and perhaps more accurately, a quasi-anarchistic philosophy of radical uncertainty—was hardly a counterweight to the unyielding absolutes of fascism.[10] As much as the film was a comic exercise, it was also quite plainly, in his words, an expression of his "hate and contempt for the Nazi system," and he desperately wanted to make that contempt clear.[11] As his costar Jack Oakie famously put it, "Chaplin only made that movie so he could deliver that long speech at the end."[12] The mute comedian who had for so long been a loquacious armchair philosopher off screen finally felt driven to speak out in the public medium of his films, to stake the full power of his international stardom on an openly articulated political stance. But more than an isolated instance born of the particular historical circumstances of the war, it would mark the beginning of a sea change in Chaplin's artistic direction. Chaplin would not just make more talkies after *The Great Dictator;* he would go on *talking*—discoursing on issues of morality, psychology, and metaphysics, filling his films with theories and postulations and aphorisms. It was as if he was making up for lost time. As

Siegfried Kracauer speculates, "Perhaps Chaplin's desire to speak his mind has also something to do with his lifelong silence as a pantomime."[13]

There are filmmakers for whom philosophizing is a conscious artistic choice and filmmaking styles that pay deference to the primacy of discourse. Even in the silent era, such models existed. For all the brilliance of its imagery, Fritz Lang's *Metropolis* is essentially a *film-à-thèse* that could easily accommodate a lengthy speech or two on its central conceit of the head, hands, and heart as the metaphoric anatomy points of modern society. But Chaplin's filmmaking had always stood in contrast to such approaches; it had always undercut or scoffed at the kind of intellectual and aesthetic stability that they needed to assume. If accommodating sound was difficult enough for Chaplin's style of cinema, accommodating philosophical discourse should have been all but impossible. Thus, most commentators have seen Chaplin's transition to an overtly verbal form of filmmaking as a kind of renunciation to his earlier artistry, setting it in direct opposition to his pre-*Dictator* efforts. Walter Kerr, in a contemporary review of *Limelight,* declares Chaplin's new artistic fascination with dialogue in the films after *The Great Dictator* to be an unseemly inverse of the works that made him famous:

> From being that genius who brought the form of the motion picture to its purest realization, Mr. Chaplin has moved to the logical opposite: he is no longer a man interested in making a *motion* picture at all. An inspired visual scenarist has become an indifferent playwright. . . . From the first reel of *Limelight* it is perfectly clear that Chaplin now wants to talk, that he *loves* to talk, that in this film he intends to do little *but* talk.[14]

Kerr reads *Limelight* as evidence of a transition not only in Chaplin's artistry but also in his chosen identity as an artist. The film, he says, is proof of "Chaplin's image of himself as a philosopher," and he cites a line from the film where Chaplin's character, the aging music hall performer Calvero, is told "To hear you talk no one would ever think you were a comedian."[15]

It is an easy line for a reviewer to pick on, but Kerr reads it quite seriously as a self-conscious attempt at erasure on Chaplin's part, a confirmation in the diegesis of the film of the change that the filmmaker's artistry had undergone and the new stage into which he had entered. After his first full entry into sound, Chaplin seemed to have become a new kind of filmmaker, one interested in deliberation and expostulation over and above his former fascination with irresolution and implication. And if he had excelled in one mode, it was all the more reason for many critics to expect he would fall short in the other. "The intuitive and the rational methods of getting at truth are antithetical methods which tend to fight one another," Kerr writes. "Rarely—very rarely—do we find the two highly developed, side by side, in a single personality. For Chaplin the switch-over was bound to be dangerous."[16] Or, as Allardyce Nicoll put it much more bluntly: "Everyone recognizes Charlie Chaplin's genius as a pantomime actor; everyone equally recognizes that his skill evaporates when he turns to dialogue."[17]

Yet the difference between the films before and after *The Great Dictator* is perhaps not quite so clear. On a stylistic level, it is not so much that Chaplin has clearly changed his approach to making films as it is that he seems to have lost hold of his own methods. The idea that Chaplin had carefully renounced his former artistic self is based in large part on the appearance of a new kind of imagery in his filmmaking by the 1940s, specifically an insistent stasis in his visual style. His new manner of cinematic construction, in Kerr's words, "speaks out its meaning in a series of logical equations which require no picture at all" and so his new imagery is "literal, explicit, and without esthetic life."[18] Kracauer says that Chaplin has "reverted to dialogue in theatrical fashion" and declares that "from the angle of the cinema this is undeniably a retrogression."[19] Even André Bazin, who looks much more kindly on Chaplin's later films than Kerr or Kracauer, similarly remarks on a newfound visual tedium in Chaplin's work. "I have seen *Limelight* three times and I admit I was bored three times," he writes, though he finds a redemptive purpose in this new cinematic monotony. "I never wished for any shortening of this period of boredom. It was rather a relaxing of attention that left my mind free to wander—a daydreaming about the images."[20] If these are the kinds of moments that have attracted the most attention in Chaplin's later films, they are not the only moments present on screen. Alongside the notable addition of such static on-screen interactions are flashes of inspired visual simultaneity wholly in keeping with Chaplin's earlier work. Yet alongside these again are flirtations with classical technique, some of the most elaborate of Chaplin's career. And alongside these again are moments that can only be described as halfway points between stasis and simultaneity or between the classical and the Chaplinesque.

The problem with the late films cannot simply be that Chaplin's approach to filmmaking has turned into something visually uninspiring. Chaplin's work had always stood in contrast to standard classical filmmaking technique; had he truly become an exponent of a new kind of radical stasis and unyielding stability in filmic imagery to consistently underline his new fascination with discourse—that is, had he actually found a visual style to match his speculative interests—then he might be credited with discovering a new and equally provocative point of contrast with classical style. As with so many artists, his late works might be different from his earlier efforts, but they would not be, ipso facto, symptoms of failure or decline. The problem with the late films might more accurately be said to lie in the fact that Chaplin's approach to filmmaking seems to be in free fall. As much as Chaplin himself may have succumbed to the spell of philosophical discourse, he is never able to find a coherent visual register to match his new fascination. Even the visual tedium that commentators have so often latched onto is not necessarily dominant within the films; it is new to Chaplin's style without being newly definitive to it. Mostly his visual style remains in a kind of rebellion to his ponderous content—not the productive rebellion of clear contrasts and counterpoints but the messy rebellion of mismatch and cross-purposes, a wanton insubordination more than a principled opposition.

It is perhaps fitting that Chaplin would begin his post-*Dictator* period with a reissue of *The Gold Rush* that he paired unevenly and imperfectly to a newly created narration; the story of the final decades of his career would be played out along this same axis of reconciling his old visual methods and his new verbal proclivities. The next three new films that Chaplin made after *The Great Dictator*—*Monsieur Verdoux, Limelight,* and *A King in New York*—are miles apart from one another in their tone and spheres of concern, ranging from dark comedy to high melodrama to broad satire. What they share is a level of visual incoherence and stylistic indeterminacy paired with a persistent and even obsessive backward glance, offering themselves as indexes to Chaplin's earlier self even as they lose their grasp on the unique visual style that underlay that comedy. It is this mixture of aesthetic disjuncture and persistent self-referentiality that is perhaps the defining mark of Chaplin's work in the period, a far cry from the films that preceded *Dictator.* Chaplin knew in *Modern Times* that dialogue might spell the end of his mode of filmmaking, and he staged the film as a kind of model of that breakdown. It could not have been a truer prediction of what was to come in his career. The films that immediately followed were not confined within inescapable constriction as *The Great Dictator* predicted they might be, wholly and unthinkingly subsumed into the classical hegemony. They were instead, like *Modern Times,* symptomatic of a stylistic breakdown in the face of sound and dialogue, though ultimately their collapse is of a very different sort. *Modern Times* is breakdown rendered as art. Chaplin's films of the 1940s and 1950s are, for all their flashes of brilliance, in many ways simply a mess. In their confusions, however, they shed light on what once made Chaplin's output so unique and demonstrate how far he still had to go to adjust his working method to the age of sound.

REWRITING SILENCE: CHAPLIN'S 1942
REISSUE OF *THE GOLD RUSH*

If *Modern Times* and *The Great Dictator* both portend the kinds of trouble that Chaplin would encounter in adjusting his working method to the era of sound, the actual seeds of those difficulties can first be seen in the reworked version of *The Gold Rush* that he released two years after *Dictator*. It was the first of many reissues that Chaplin would orchestrate throughout his later career, ensuring that new generations of filmgoers would be introduced to the Tramp in the era before film revivals or rentals. But it was also one of the most unusual experiments of Chaplin's sound-era work, every bit as sui generis as *Modern Times* in its attempts to reconcile silent film and recorded dialogue. Beyond adding an original musical score and occasional sound effects as he did with later rereleases, Chaplin also added extensive narration, read by himself, including several sections of dialogue spoken in his voice: the silent film as storybook session.[21] It was, in Jeffrey Vance's analysis, an attempt to "modernize the film" by showing its ability to be reconciled to audience expectations in the sound era, and it was indeed a tremendous success at the time—James Agee even declared it the best picture of the year.[22] But the reissue is also a kind of co-dex to the artistic problems that Chaplin would continue to confront over the final decades of his career. His visual compositions in the film, those that are unchanged from the 1925 version, are of course as vibrant and dynamic as ever. Yet they now would exist in tension with Chaplin's spoken words, which in many scenes seek precedence as the final arbiter of meaning and attempt to resolve some of the strategic ambiguities of the earlier print. Perhaps most surprisingly, though, Chaplin decided to go back and recut some of the film's most thoughtful and provocative visual compositions, substituting alternate takes from the original negatives that could more easily cohere with his new verbal additions. Though Chaplin (and later, his estate) would regard the 1942 reissue as the definitive version of the film, it is perhaps more accurately said to be definitive of the changes that were occurring in Chaplin's artistry as he formulated his engagement with the sound era rather than of the manner of filmmaking in which the picture was first composed.

To his credit, Chaplin does allow many of his most famous sequences of the film to play without any added description—the "Oceana Roll Dance" and the eating of the boiled shoe in particular both pass untouched. But elsewhere in the film he is content to let his voice overlay the visuals on screen and un-easily divide the viewer's attention: the masterful imagery of Chaplin fighting against a terrible wind that is keeping him from leaving the frontier cabin is unhelpfully echoed by Chaplin the narrator's disruptions of the scene with repeated interjections of "Get out" from the other character on screen, attempts to verbally reemphasize the Tramp's struggle that only serve to divert our attention from its masterful visual execution. Or later, the surprise of a moment in which the Tramp is suddenly driven out the back door of the cabin by another strong gale is almost lost as the narrator describes a newly interpolated exchange between the Tramp and a fellow prospector just before. The drollness of the Tramp's injunction to "bring home the bacon" as his associate leaves on a hunting trip simply cannot compare with the visual jocularity of the wind unexpectedly returning in full force a moment later.[23] In Dan Kamin's words, the film "sets up a parallel world in which Chaplin indulges his verbal wit at the expense of his visual storytelling," often creating moments where "our attention is distracted just enough by the comment that we don't see the movement as clearly."[24]

Yet the problem with such moments is arguably something even larger than an issue of distraction or of a new push and pull between verbal comedy and visual humor. There is an impulse, new in Chaplin's filmmaking, that lies behind many of these instances of tension: a new imperative to use language to clarify and, ultimately, to simplify—to render clear what was once provocatively ambiguous. In the narrated mode of filmmaking that Chaplin employs in the reissue, there is little room for the kind of simultaneity that once so defined his style, and many of the moments where Chaplin recut scenes and substituted alternate takes in the film serve ultimately to muffle this element of his silent-era craftsmanship. One of the Tramp's first encounters with Georgia in the dance hall is a case in point. The basic setup of the sequence is the same in both versions. Georgia looks forlorn and a fellow dancing girl asks her what's the matter. She indicates that she's looking for someone new in her life, then turns her body to scan the dance hall but completely ignores the heartsick Tramp standing next to her, looking right past him as if he isn't even there. In the 1925 version of the film, the moment is a masterfully intimate example of Chaplin's technique of simultaneous construction. Chaplin frames the encounter in a close-in medium shot of Georgia and the Tramp, showing only their upper bodies and almost completely balancing their positioning in the frame. They are thrust close to the camera in the foreground space of the shot and symmetrically distributed on the screen, a hanging rope in the background of the shot defining the exact center of the frame between their shoulders. The screen space is divided between them—and unlike most of Chaplin's compositions, as the moment proceeds there is no clear indication of where we should direct our attention. Slowly Georgia turns her body, facing outward toward the camera, one arm placed squarely on each hip, using her posture to invite our focus and to frame her most expressive features, her face and torso. Her eyes dart all around the room as she looks for a new man for her life. Usually the figure who is moving in a Chaplin frame is the one designed to attract our attention. Yet at the same time that Georgia turns around, Chaplin is competing for our focus. Though he stands perfectly still with arms tight at his sides, he too moves his eyes up and down and side to side in a fit of nervous distraction to rival the commanding eyebrow motions in *Burlesque on Carmen*. Within his compositional system of arranging bodies and motion in the frame, Chaplin has essentially given us two completely equal, symmetrical points of attention, purposefully refusing to unify his narrative center in this moment. The separate narratives and separate realities of Georgia and the Tramp are placed simultaneously before us, the visual tension within the frame reflecting the larger tension of trying to corral simultaneous lives and experiences into a single story line. The humor of the scene is the humor of a missed connection, but it is also the humor of a frame made to bear two equal narrative foci—elliptical in every sense.

And from this perspective, it is a completely different scene in the 1942 reissue, even if the basic content is the same. Here, Chaplin uses alternate footage and clear narration to erase any ambiguity from the frame. He stages the encounter in a three-quarters medium shot that allows him greater flexibility in differentiating between the postures of Georgia and the Tramp, and he ensures that the point of greatest attention in the shot is always clear. We must hold the Tramp's loneliness in suspension for this moment: it is Georgia who is our main focus, the humor of the scene stemming from her inability to see what is right before her eyes and not from the collision between her longing and the Tramp's own as in the silent version. Here the Tramp actually assumes the preternatural stillness of a secondary character in a standard Chaplin frame—he hardly moves at all for the duration of the shot; he is as still as in one of his statue gags. We are meant, visually at least, to discount him for a moment. With the crowd at the bar foreshortening the depth of the frame, he is tucked into the right side of the middle plane while Georgia stands clearly at the center in the foreground space. It is she who is undoubtedly our main focus. In fact, her posture is a kind of pastiche of Chaplin's own typical stance when he assumes command of a frame: she is turned out toward the camera, one arm placed squarely on her hip, the other touching her face. In Kamin's analysis of Chaplin's typical carriage when he means to take control of a scene: "He positions [his trunk] very carefully in relation to the camera . . . consistently playing scenes so that he includes us. He almost *never* crosses his arms over his chest; on the contrary, he'll sometimes frame it by making an 'L' shape with his arms, one hand on the side of his face, the other supporting his elbow."[25] Georgia has essentially assumed a feminine variation on Chaplin's dominant stance.

Chaplin, by contrast, stands straight as a board with no movement at all—his eyes are completely still and focused in this version, and there is nothing in his stature or his movement to draw our attention to him. Just to ensure total clarity, Chaplin's spoken narration reemphasizes the arrangement of the frame: "Then she turned and looked and looked and looked." Here, as elsewhere in the film, Chaplin's voice essentially takes over for and attempts to supplant the framing in the scene as our main source of information and of interest, streamlining any excess and ensuring that we follow the proper line of action in the sequence. It is, in the total context of the film, only a small change, but it is a harbinger of larger changes that were to come in Chaplin's filmmaking.

PERSISTENCE OF TECHNIQUE
IN THE LATE FILMS

What the reissue of *The Gold Rush* captures so well is a tension that would persist in Chaplin's work over the next several decades: not an erasure of his signature visual style in the age of sound so much as an inability to fully reconcile that style to new elements that were entering his filmmaking. In other words, works like *Monsieur Verdoux* and *Limelight* and even, to a certain extent, *A King in New York* are frustrating in part because they are not total failures. (In Kerr's phrase, "Chaplin *can* do wrong; but he cannot be uninteresting.")[26] Chaplin is still in these films sometimes a master craftsman, and they each include moments that echo or even expand upon the hallmarks of his visual style from his silent classics. *A King in New York* is weakest in this respect, though it is not without its flickers of inspiration. Stuck next to a loud jazz band at a New York restaurant, Chaplin's out-of-touch King Shadov tries to order caviar and turtle soup (items that are almost certainly not on the menu at a restaurant called the Cuba Club) first by pantomiming the entire process of a fish being killed and its eggs being removed and then by using table settings as props to indicate the turtle in the turtle soup. The "Oceana Roll Dance" it is not, but it is a charming pantomime cleverly justified within the diegesis and an effective moment of aural and visual simultaneity. The raucous jazz of the musicians seen in the background of the frame is in a communicative competition with Shadov's pantomimed visuals, each battling to be the dominant point of focus for the audience; and they are both as well in a kind of literal cultural competition—lively popular culture struggling with overly refined tastes, the music of the modern age struggling with the master of an antiquated form of entertainment, both of them trapped inside the same frame at once. Later in the film, Chaplin harks back to his classic simultaneous treatments of space and movement in a different way in an ingenious chase sequence in a hotel lobby. Shadov is fleeing a man he thinks is a government official and at the height of the chase they both arrive in the lobby separately but simultaneously, Shadov entering by the stairs and his pursuer exiting the elevator at the precise moment Shadov touches the lobby floor. Looking in different directions, they inadvertently mirror one another as they creep toward the main doorway, offering a kind of inverse of the mirror sequence in *The Floorwalker*. When they discover they are standing next to each other, Shadov escapes into a crowd of hotel guests and snakes his way through the bodies while his pursuer follows his same pattern of movements through the crowd, turned now from mirror reflection to visual echo. It looks like a Chaplin chase in slow motion—Chaplin must now film such sequences at the standard twenty-four frames per second of sound film instead of the eighteen frames per second of his silent works. But it is a Chaplin chase nonetheless, two independent realities placed side by side in space and then redoubled in exact sequence, one after the other. Even at sixty-seven years old, Chaplin still has touches of his visual flourish and is still grappling with issues of simultaneity within the frame and of bodies choreographed together in space.

Monsieur Verdoux, which is chronologically much closer to Chaplin's triumphs of the 1930s, contains far more than moments of visual flourish; it contains some of the most ingenious instances of composition that Chaplin would put on film. Verdoux's telephone seduction is an exemplary case in point, and it marks the director's fullest return to the framing techniques of *A Woman of Paris* in almost twenty-five years. Verdoux, seducing his latest victim and clearly the narrative focus of the shot, is placed disconcertingly in the middle spatial plane, demarcated in his position and separated from the foreground by an obtrusive telephone box. In the foreground of the shot, Chaplin places an utterly minor character, a flower shop girl who has served in the film only to take Verdoux's orders at the store. As Verdoux speaks on the phone, the flower girl turns her back to him and tends to some flowers in the foreground. They clearly occupy separate spaces and separate spheres of reality within the frame. In a kind of diegetic approximation of a split-screen technique, Chaplin even places the line of a prominent corner in the wall behind them down the center of the shot, sequestering their two regions of the frame from each other and accenting the spatial bifurcation with a series of floral decorations that come between them. They are meant to be kept apart within the same visual space, and the flower girl tries to abide by such separation within the diegesis by offering Verdoux a modicum of privacy in ignoring his phone conversation. But Verdoux has little use for distinctions of private and public—he makes a business of seducing (and then murdering) women, after all—and he offers his new prey the most extravagant sweet talk over the phone in easy earshot of the flower girl. As the conversation in the middle plane progresses, our attention is drawn visually to the girl's surprise and, ultimately, her own near seduction at Verdoux's passionate declarations.

In its setup and execution, the scene is essentially a juxtaposition of the fainting scene and the massage scene from *A Woman of Paris.* The obvious point of narrative attention is placed jarringly in a subordinate position within the frame while at the same time our attention is focused on a minor character, our exposure to Verdoux at the height of his romantic technique filtered through the reactions of a girl who is not his intended target and who will not appear in the film again. On one level, like the masseuse in *A Woman of Paris,* she serves as a stand-in for the other participant in the conversation, her own near seduction meant to indicate the swooning of Verdoux's victim on the other end of the phone. The scene is, in this sense, almost a kind of visual parody of split-screen technique, as though the corner that diegetically divides the frame were actually able to allow us to see both ends of the phone conversation at once. On another level, though, the flower girl is exemplary of a narrative unexplored, a character who is not our main focus thrust momentarily into the foreground of Chaplin's frame. Verdoux's entire operation is based on the idea of intersecting narratives: he turns women whom he happens to meet in passing—minor characters in his life—into full-fledged heroines, declaring them to be the objects of his obsession and devotion until such time as he can discard them from his life (and the world more generally) and move on to a new narrative. The flower girl is one such narrative never pursued, and as such she is a reminder of the simultaneity of lives lived outside Verdoux's many-branched narrative tree and a subtle cue to the concisions and exclusions to which all narrative is prone.

This reminder, almost nostalgic in its reminiscence of films like *A Woman of Paris,* is turned on its head in one of Chaplin's most brilliant and playful explorations of the distinction between protagonist and minor character later in the film. Here, Lena Couvais and Jean Couvais, the sister and nephew of one of Verdoux's victims, recognize the murderer in a Paris nightclub, but he does not know what they look like in turn. When they phone the police, Verdoux recognizes the detectives but now it is they who do not know what he looks like. It is as masterful a fugue of realities overlapping in ignorance of each other as anything Chaplin ever created, an inspired heir perhaps to the restaurant scene in *The Immigrant.* Chaplin begins the sequence with a series of encounters between Verdoux and Lena. Standing next to Verdoux's table in the nightclub, she recognizes him in horror. For her, in the left foreground of the frame, it is one of the most terrifying moments of her life; for Verdoux, a few feet away in the right middle plane of the frame, it is nothing whatsoever—he can clearly see her but she is no different to him than anyone else in the frame. A few moments later, when Verdoux happens to look in her direction as she sits at her table, Lena nearly chokes on her drink. His casual glance is her deathly stare. When he carelessly trips a little as he walks past her leaving the restaurant, she nearly falls out of her seat. Again, the harmless and the hideous coexist in full view and in full ignorance of one another, even occupying one and the same action and separated only by perception.

Later in the sequence, Verdoux grows wise to Lena and Jean—they have forfeited their status as unnoticed background figures by attaching themselves too firmly to his story line and following him wherever he goes—and he locks them in an anteroom at the club. Now, Verdoux assumes the position of knowledge as the police arrive and regard him as simply another extra in the frame. In one of his most inspired moments of visual irony, Chaplin shoots the unfolding scene from the position of the club's coat-check room, such that the curtains that drape over the coat-check window appear like the curtains that define a proscenium. Chaplin lays out the drama before us as if on a stage, yet in this drama the protagonist cannot be identified. Verdoux innocuously joins the growing crowd of patrons clamoring around the room where Lena and Jean are trapped, and he is literally pushed into the masses by a detective who does not know who he is and who forcibly removes him from his prominent position in the center of the frame. Moments later, when Lena has been released, she stands only a few feet away from Verdoux in the crowd, neither figure conscious of the other. When they do see each other, she faints and Verdoux catches her. Yet the police still regard him as an unimportant patron. His own body only a few feet from Verdoux, a detective asks Lena to identify where Verdoux went. Only when she stands and recognizes Verdoux as the man who caught her is he finally identified. The directionality of knowledge in the sequence is finally resolved: all the protagonists of the scene—Lena, Verdoux, and the detective—are finally able to recognize each other. Overall, the sequence is one of the most elaborate explorations of simultaneity in Chaplin's career. At every point in the sequence, at least two significant characters are present on screen at the same time, yet not until the very end do they all become aware of each other. Figures who seem like extras become protagonists, and the protagonist is forced into the role of an extra. The narrative climax of the film—the moment when Verdoux is finally caught—is culled together from an inconsequential sequence of routine business: a glance, a stumble, a man being pushed into a crowd. It is one of Chaplin's clearest explorations of the way in which narrative selects individuals out of the crowd of humanity to turn them into protagonists, the way it renders certain actions from the unfolding world significant; and, conversely, the way it leaves so many people out of its stories, rendering so many actions only so much inconsequential background movement. In the narrative confusion of the lead-up to Verdoux's capture, Chaplin dramatizes the very process of narrative selection and emphasis itself, laying bare to us the thin line that separates the main story and persons in a film from the countless other stories and persons in the unnoticed background of that world.

If *Verdoux* offers small masterpieces of simultaneity and overlapping realities, *Limelight* presents a kind of celebratory triumph of Chaplin's unmoving frame. Chaplin was joined on this film, as on *The Great Dictator,* by Karl Struss, one of the most prominent cinematographers of the silent era and one of the visual masterminds behind F. W. Murnau's legendary *Sunrise* (Fox, 1927). The collaboration resulted in some of the most gorgeous filmic imagery of Chaplin's career, his long-standing techniques of in-frame composition and arrangement turned here into a kind of artwork-in-motion. Thereza's dance audition on the empty stage of the Empire Theatre is a masterful example. Chaplin brazenly holds the camera unmoving for almost a minute and a half, capturing the entire audition from start to finish in a single take. The hallmarks of Chaplin's compositional technique are all in place. Though the camera is placed deep upstage in the theater in an extreme long shot that captures everything from the stage boards to the upper reaches of the balcony, our attention is focused within the shot on a single strip of space that approaches the frame-width of a more typical long shot. Two lines define the main area of focus within the frame, the top marked off by the bottom of the balcony platform and the bottom demarcated by the stage footlights. Nearly the entirety of Thereza's dance passes with her torso between these two lines, yet the expansiveness of the frame ably and beautifully captures the full breadth of the space she must be able to command with her dance. A diagonal shadow that runs across the stage provides a powerful contrast to the parallelism of the overall composition while at the same time serving to emphasize the extreme depth of the stage platform that Thereza must traverse. To complete the frame, Chaplin places a thin stage lamp just off-center in the middle plane. It is reminiscent of the off-center pole that he uses in *The Rink* to draw attention within a large and unwieldy space, but it serves no narrative function here; it is simply a means of destabilizing the otherwise extremely well-ordered composition. It is one of the most masterful visual moments of Chaplin's career, capturing at once the enormous feat of performing in such a space while at the same time subtly limiting and directing our attention, all within a setup that is simply in itself quite beautiful.

Such shots in *Limelight* stand in extreme contrast to the music hall sequences in the film, which are among the most austere images that Chaplin ever captured. As in Thereza's audition, Chaplin typically shoots the film's music hall acts in only one or two unmoving and unbroken shots, but instead of being elegant the framing is downright brutal. In each case, Chaplin shoots the scene head-on in long shot with almost nothing of visual interest in the construction of the frame. In Calvero's first music hall dream sequence, the shot is initially wide enough to capture some matters of visual interest—the bustling musicians in the pit—but it quickly tightens into a long shot that includes only the back and head of the band conductor, a thin strip of stage, and a generic painted backdrop. Halfway through Calvero's flea circus act, the frame becomes even more minimalist with nothing but Calvero himself, the box where his fleas supposedly perform, and a detail of the painted backdrop included in the shot. These shots, moreover, go on for small cinematic eternities: two and a half minutes in each case, with another one-minute shot similar to the first to finish out the routine. Such bare-bones framing seems to be a kind of negation of Chaplin's technique, an erasure of anything that looks like composition such that the frame does little more than telegraph the camera's lack of motion. Yet the nearly empty frame is also a kind of brilliant summary of the music hall world as experienced by the performer. Even though we are regarding Calvero from the position of the audience, we are actually in no vantage point that any real spectator would ever have; our sightline is too level with the stage to be coming from the orchestra, yet we are at the same time too close to the stage and to the performer to be looking on from the balcony or mezzanine. We are observing the scene from an idealized point of spectatorship that cannot exist in the real world, and what we see from that position is the unforgiving plainness of the music hall stage as it must be understood by the performer. Thereza may have the challenge of filling a grand hall with her movements, but at least there is an elegance and dignity in her surroundings that give her efforts a kind of aesthetic purpose and nobility. Calvero's natural environment is as cruel as his audiences turn out to be, plain and unadorned. The unrelenting, unbeautiful stasis of Chaplin's frame in the music hall bits calls out the extremity of the music hall performer's challenge: he must master this thin, undignified strip of stage through sheer force of his personality or he must abandon the effort altogether—as when Calvero walks off the stage in shame later in the film in his failed attempt at reviving his career. Here, even in its most austere moments, Chaplin's frame is still fully invested in clarifying the film's narrative and reinforcing its thematics. In a kind of triumph of his insistence on the power of the carefully considered camera, his frame has proven itself to be meaningfully composed even in the extreme absence of composition.

Technique Upended: Misapplications
and Misapprehensions

All of these later films, then, have moments where they show Chaplin at or near the height of his powers, almost every bit as visually inventive as in his heyday and in some instances even quite a bit more. Yet for almost every moment of visual triumph in the films there is a moment so unconsidered or disconcerting as to throw the efficacy of Chaplin's technique into question. *Limelight* is rife with such images. Critical attention has usually focused on what seems to be the utter lack of visual inspiration—even visual disinterest— of the numerous conversations that Chaplin stages between Calvero and Thereza during her long recuperation in his apartment. One character speaks and then the other; they sit in a bedroom, they sit in a living room. It is these scenes to which Kracauer refers most directly when he speaks of Chaplin's visual "retrogression" and his "dialogue in theatrical fashion." Yet the lack of inspiration in such scenes is relatively innocuous compared to what seems to be the misplaced inspiration of other shots in the film. As stunning as Chaplin's composition in Thereza's audition sequence is, the power of that imagery is undercut only a few moments later in the film when Chaplin tries to repeat the trick in an entirely different, and largely inappropriate, context. Now his point of focus is the choreographer, who describes in detail to the assembled cast the story of the new ballet they are to perform. Chaplin's shot setup is of a type with the audition sequence. The choreographer is positioned in the center foreground of the shot, the expansive audience chamber of the Empire Theatre spreading out into the deep space of the frame behind him, the rows of seats, the aisles of the auditorium, and the winding staircase at the far end of the theater creating an enchanting series of geometric patterns that dominate the space. And as in the audition sequence, Chaplin holds the shot steady—his camera remains unmoving for almost a full minute as the choreographer goes through the entire story line with only one short interjection from Calvero that briefly breaks up the sequence. But as compelling as the shot is, it begs the question of what exactly we are supposed to be looking at. Chaplin's framing of the audition piece was captivating in large part for its marriage of composition and action, the static artistry of the camera conjoined to the artistry-in-motion of Thereza's dancing. Here, the "action" in the frame consists entirely of the choreographer's lengthy description of the ballet that is to come. Chaplin frames the sequence as though the ballet master were delivering a powerful soliloquy instead of a perfunctory summary. The problem is not just that Chaplin has turned words themselves into the central focus of his masterful framing but that he has turned such totally pedestrian words into his point of focus, as though words in and of themselves—or, at least, any words that Chaplin might write—carried some kind of immediate power, producing instant poetry. Visually, he has equated an actual dance with a lengthy verbal outline of a dance and treated them both with gravitas. It seems to be a wanton misapplication of his own technique, and it serves to thoroughly dilute its power.

At least, though, the framing of the choreographer's monologue has some elegance, however misplaced it might be. In *Monsieur Verdoux,* Chaplin's traditional reliance on an unbroken frame has become at times almost a kind of handicap to his storytelling ability. Around the midpoint of the film, Verdoux has a lengthy conversation with an unnamed street waif whom he has brought into his home with the thought of testing out a new poison. The scene itself is a mildly disconcerting hodgepodge of cinematic approaches. Chaplin creates some long takes, some upward of a minute at a time, fluidly capturing without cuts such business as when Verdoux decides at the last minute to switch out the girl's poisoned wine glass for another without poison, the fatal sip only narrowly averted before our eyes. But he also creates some long takes of pure discourse, then intercuts to quick back and forths of classical shot/reaction-shot editing with standard eye-line matching, none of which seems to trace in any specific way the contours of the conversation. His shot sequencing is in a kind of stylistic disarray, all of which culminates in a jarring moment where Verdoux sends the waif on her way by escorting her to the back door of his apartment, which conveniently just happens to exist within the same space as their dinner table conversation, right there in the dining room. What is so alienating about the moment is its sudden and blatant contrivance: Verdoux has never mentioned or used the back door before, and it seems to suddenly exist in the universe of the film solely for the purpose of getting the waif out of the apartment without having to cut to a shot outside the dining room. Though he has shown no compunction about dividing and redividing the space of the dining room in his shot/reaction-shot sequencing, Chaplin has now subtly reordered his filmic world seemingly for the sole purpose of preserving the unbroken space of the shot and the temporal continuity of the thirty-second-long take that concludes the encounter. Chaplin's manipulation of space has always been full of contrivances—the masterful ending sequence where Verdoux is finally caught is itself rife with spatial coincidences that help to grease the wheels of the scene's narrative development. But they have never so blatantly disrupted the diegetic integrity of the film before. The waif's exit from Verdoux's apartment is, of course, a minuscule moment in the narrative and its disconcerting contrivance is quickly forgotten. But however inconsequential, it is a portentous indication of the degree to which Chaplin's traditional stylistic techniques, the commitment to unbroken space foremost among them, have become not so much a conscious and purposeful approach as an unthinking dogma—something to fall back on regardless of its appropriateness and a default way to organize the world on screen whether it supports that world or works at cross-purposes to it.

Chaplin will undoubtedly continue to show flashes of inspiration within his technique of using unbroken space. There is, for instance, the brilliant montage-in-simultaneous-space that represents Thereza's world tour in *Limelight:* against a single shot of her dancing onstage are superimposed the images of the places that she tours, from Paris to Rome. It is a kind of inverse to Buster Keaton's famous battle with the movie screen in *Sherlock Jr.,* where one action traverses multiple different spaces; here, multiple different spaces traverse a single action—one space becomes many, the whole world captured in Chaplin's unmoving frame. But just as frequently, Chaplin's use of the technique seems to serve no purpose at all, needlessly encumbering a simple scene that could more easily be handled with the same kind of classical shot construction that Chaplin uses elsewhere in these films. The bathroom scene from *A King in New York* is perhaps his greatest miscalculation in these terms. In the scene, Shadov helps Rupert Macabee, a young boy who has run away from home on a miserable and snowy day, into a warm bath so that he does not catch cold. In a thoroughly disconcerting choice, Chaplin shows the entire process of the boy undressing and getting into the bath on screen, his modesty preserved through a series of clever diegetic cover-ups: Shadov's body bending over at just the right angle, a piece of clothing held at just the right position. The scene seems to be a restaging of a sequence that Chaplin originally thought up for *Shoulder Arms* but never actually put on screen—a scene where the Tramp is stripped naked for a military physical and wanders through the military hospital in the buff, our view of him kept sanitized by a series of diegetic contrivances. (The gag would reappear almost eighty years later, and to great comic effect, in the *Austin Powers* franchise.) But to make use of the gag in the new context is to strip the sequence itself of any potential humor and to demonstrate the manipulation of diegetic space simply as an end in itself. There is nothing humorous about the possibility of a pathetic runaway being exposed to the audience, and we can take no delight in the clever ways that his nudity is hidden. Rather, the gag seems to touch on an uncomfortable thematic point in Chaplin's filmmaking, reminding us of the ways in which moments of extreme situational inequality and potential humiliation have been at the forefront of so many of his films, from the pairing of rich and poor in a work like *City Lights* to the pairing of small and large, weak and strong in a work like *The Gold Rush*. So long as the resourceful Tramp has been on the short end of these divisions, the humor has been largely intact: we trust the Tramp to outwit and avoid the social traumas

that are always hovering in the realm of possibility; or, failing that, we trust
him at least to recover quickly from his humiliations. Yet here it is Chaplin
himself in the position of power, the smart but ultimately unresourceful boy
placed in a position of unequal dependence. What might have been funny in
Shoulder Arms is rendered here comically moot; it is dexterous without being
humorous in the least. More than that, it all seems utterly superfluous: a simple
medium shot from the waist up would have thoroughly solved the problem of
modesty without the need for contortion. Chaplin's commitment to his traditional visual style has become not just unpurposeful but distracting, even
disruptive, to the film itself when set in the wrong context.

More disruptive still, however, are Chaplin's new accommodations to classical technique, moments where to no discernible advantage he opts to forgo
his usual visual approach and tries to translate some version of his standard
manner of filmmaking into a more classical setup. Hence the mix-up over
hydrogen peroxide in *Monsieur Verdoux*—a typical Chaplin exploration of
simultaneous reality rendered for the first time without the benefit of simultaneous space. The basic premise of the sequence is prime Chaplin material:
Verdoux brings a bottle of poison disguised as a bottle of peroxide to the home
of his latest victim, Annabella Bonheur, with a plan to spike her wine and kill
her. When Verdoux leaves the bottle in the bathroom for a moment, the maid
decides to take some to bleach her hair, accidentally breaks the bottle, and surreptitiously replaces it with another bottle of actual peroxide from the cabinet,
which Verdoux then mistakes for his poison when he returns to the bathroom.
He spikes Annabella's wine with peroxide, the maid does her hair with poison;
the uncultured Annabella decides she likes the dry taste, the maid's hair nearly
all falls out. Chaplin even adds a third layer to the sequence when Verdoux
himself accidentally drinks the wine and thinks he has now poisoned himself,
when in fact he is just drinking the same "dry" wine laced with peroxide that
he has accidentally given to Annabella. Rendered across a single unbroken
space, the simultaneous but disconnected realities at play might equal any of
Chaplin's other versions of similar scenarios. But in the new visual world of a
late film like *Monsieur Verdoux,* the action is presented as part of a narrative
sequence without being spatially simultaneous. Rather than finding a way to
configure the events and the spaces in which they occur so as to show us the
mix-up all at once, he cuts in quick succession between the component parts
of the confusion as it unfolds over four rooms and two different stories of the
house. Not until the very end of the sequence do the realities converge, when
the maid joins Annabella and Verdoux in the living room, her hair falling out
while Verdoux thinks that he is dying from poison.

Chaplin's camera is not perfectly aligned with the space of the action—it cannot be. And thus it does not reveal to us the events so much as it narrates them. It creates what David Bordwell calls "a process of hypothesis testing in a film's moment-by-moment unfolding," working to "retard the likeliest meaning" so that the "spectator adopts a wait-and-see strategy."[27] In other words, a sequence like this one asks us not to watch what is happening at once—for only one real event or action is happening within the frame at any given time—but instead to ask what might happen next. What would once have been a typically Chaplinesque exploration of space and simultaneity has become a typically classical exploration of time and sequencing. The scene is, in this sense, one of Chaplin's most extensive applications of classical visual storytelling, occurring at the complete expense of his usual focus on simultaneity of space and action and his camera's powerful ability to capture the world as it unfolds in multiple overlapping realities at once. Indeed, while there is humor in the sequence, there is very little visual mastery. It is rather, as in Jean Mitry's description of classical technique, as though the events are being told to us: first this happened, then this, then this. It is what Mitry describes as "the pictorialization of a story already written, the expression of an idea existing in itself independently of the medium which translates it."[28] There is no delight in the bombardment of disconnected worlds happening before us all at once, no fugue-like layering of different lines of reality intersecting and combining in a single filmic space. In short, there is very little of Chaplin in the sequence.

And there is even less of him in the comic conclusion of *A King in New York. King* is much closer to Chaplin's usual slapstick than either *Verdoux* or *Limelight,* but despite the ways in which he falls back on his typical treatment of space at moments within the film, Chaplin seems equally determined to demonstrate here that his comedy can still work in a world wholly won over to classical technique. The results are often unsuccessful. In one of his clearest returns to straightforward physical slapstick in decades, Chaplin has Shadov get his fingers stuck inside an emergency fire hose in the elevator at his lawyer's office building. Chaplin had not played with a fire hose since his early Mutual short *The Fireman* in 1916, but if he has retained any of the dexterity of his earlier self, we cannot really tell. Rather than show us Shadov's contortions in full view and in unbroken space, Chaplin divides his dance with the hose into a series of tiny component parts: we see him trying to disentangle his torso from the hose, then we cut to his legs, then to struggles with his finger, then to a medium long shot of his entire frame, and back again. The result is that we never really get to see the comedy, some kind of choreographed tango with the recalcitrant hose or some sequence of furious spinning and contorting.

We never see the gag unfold in space. We have a sense of Shadov's predicament, but beyond the basic scenario itself we are given nothing to make us laugh or wonder, only shots of legs and arms and fingers. It is telling perhaps that Chaplin staged the sequence inside an elevator, the constant opening and closing of the doors a perpetual reminder of the opening and closing of space itself in his cut-up construction of the sequence. Ironically, Shadov's lawyer complains that if the operator would only hold the elevator at a single floor for a few moments he and Shadov might be able to finally escape. It is as though he is complaining about the composition itself. But it is a fate that Chaplin has brought upon his own head. He seems to be trying to demonstrate with his shot construction the resiliency of his brand of comedy (and his own comedic body) even in the face of classical technique, but he has succeeded only in creating a kind of object lesson in how not to shoot a Chaplin comic sequence.

CHAPLIN'S PHILOSOPHICAL IMPERATIVE: DRAMATIZING DISCOURSE

It might be possible to redeem the wild variations and miscalculations of Chaplin's visual style in his films of the 1940s and 1950s as a kind of self-conscious breakdown and purposeful collapse—his anarchistic tendencies finally triumphing over his formal powers—were it not so clear in these films how much Chaplin is distracted from his camera and even from the idea of the motion picture as a primarily visual medium. Chaplin has added to his usual elements of space and visual composition another component that could exist only in the era of the talkie. It is not even dialogue so much as rational argumentation that Chaplin is now eager to put on screen—overt philosophizing, Kerr's "series of logical equations which require no picture at all." This is not just one element among many that Chaplin has added to his toolbox, something to be toyed with and carefully incorporated in the manner of his experiments with sound in *City Lights* or *Modern Times,* or even his careful qualification of dialogue itself in *The Great Dictator.* From *Verdoux* onward, argumentation has suddenly and almost immediately become a pervasive feature, even an organizing feature, of Chaplin's filmmaking, and certainly a feature to be treated with as much prominence as any visual arrangement of the frame.

Chaplin had often peppered his films in the past with subtle visual nods to the other great filmmakers of his age, from D. W. Griffith in *The Vagabond* and *A Dog's Life* to Fritz Lang and René Clair in *Modern Times.* Now he made a point to attach his dialogue to the great European thinkers: Verdoux and the waif discuss Schopenhauer in *Monsieur Verdoux,* Calvero name-drops Freud (twice) in *Limelight,* Marx is a prominent discussion point in *A King in New*

York. Chaplin had once sought through his visual references to declare his peership with other great film artists, but by his late films he seems to have lost interest in any kind of cinematic self-identification; his new self-markings, conveyed only in dialogue, are all intellectual and his new peer group grounded in the page rather than the screen. Even Chaplin's longtime cameraman and cinematographer, Rollie Totheroh, noticed the change. Totheroh worked with Chaplin for more than thirty-five years; he was involved with every shoot from the Mutual shorts through *Limelight*. But when it came time to film *Monsieur Verdoux,* he noticed something different. Chaplin, he felt, was changed "by his contact with the people who were deep thinkers, not the average public. . . . He wanted to be distinguished Chaplin now."[29] It was understandable to Totheroh, who had always known Chaplin's more loquacious side; but it was not necessarily an improvement to his artistry. "I really couldn't blame him," he recalled, "but it did hurt his pictures."[30]

It was no small change. The new moments of speechifying within Chaplin's films are more than just indicators of his own erudition used to add color to his works. They are more like grounding points from which Chaplin wishes us to understand the philosophical purpose of his films. The discussion of Schopenhauer in *Verdoux* centers on the philosopher's writings on suicide, the idea that a painless death might be preferable to "this drab existence."[31] Although it is not quoted directly in the film, Chaplin's whole story is in some ways an exegesis on the philosopher's statement that "as soon as a point is reached where the terrors of life outweigh those of death, man puts an end to his life."[32] Schopenhauer's phrase might be taken to underlie Verdoux's decision to commit his own suicide-by-execution after he has lost his family or, slightly later in the film, his justifications for his own cold murders as a kind of unbidden mercy killing in a modern world that has already blown "unsuspecting women and little children to pieces." In *Limelight,* Freud is similarly central to the actual story of the film. He is brought up both times in the context of the "psycho-anesthesia" that is keeping Thereza from life and from her dancing; "it's a case for a psychologist" to bring her back to the outside world and to her art, her doctor declares.[33] With this as its starting point, and with Calvero as the pseudo-psychologist on the case, the film offers itself as a kind of extended confirmation of Freudian connections between the work of art and the psychology of the artist. Thereza returns to dancing only after confronting the fact that she is ashamed of the way that, when she was a child, her sister worked as a prostitute to support her dance lessons after their mother died; her drive to dance becomes a drive to replace those memories of squalor and shame with something beautiful. (Freud himself considered Chaplin a prime contemporary example of his artistic theories at work, writing to a friend that the creator of the Tramp was "an exceptionally simple and transparent case [of] the idea that the achievements of artists are intimately bound up with their childhood memories, impressions, repressions and disappointments."[34] In a way, Chaplin uses *Limelight* to acknowledge this connection.) In *A King in New York,* Marx would not just be name-dropped but would haunt almost every major instance of social commentary made within the film. Shadov is at pains to declare that he is not a Communist when accused, but Chaplin still eagerly takes the excesses of capitalism as one of his main subjects. The New York of the film is a world where consumerism reigns supreme, where everything—including friendship—is for sale, where even a king can be bought and used to peddle products to the public, where even the body can be turned into a commodity in the plastic surgery that Shadov undergoes at great expense to become a better product-pusher. Chaplin's New York is a world where, in Marx's language, everything has been "reduced . . . to a mere money relation," always driven by "the need of a constantly expanding market."[35] "Do I have to be a communist to read Karl Marx?" Rupert asks defensively at one point, a question that Chaplin's film itself seems to pose to its audience.[36]

But Chaplin also saw himself as more than just a reader and cinematic interpreter of old philosophers. He saw himself as an original contributor to these selfsame discussions. *Monsieur Verdoux, Limelight,* and *A King in New York* are shot through with a distinctive brand of late Chaplin philosophical aphorism marked by an attempt to collapse grand ideas into quick summations. In *Monsieur Verdoux:* "This is a ruthless world and one must be ruthless to cope with it"; "Despair is a narcotic. It lulls the mind into indifference"; "Evil is the shadows cast from the sun." In *Limelight:* "Life is a desire, not a meaning"; "Time is the best author. It always writes the perfect ending"; "That's all any of us are: amateurs. We don't live long enough to be anything else." In *A King in New York:* "Political power is an official form of antagonizing the people"; "Monopoly is the menace of free enterprise"; "To part is to die a little." It is as though Chaplin were self-consciously preparing to be canonized in a published volume of his own thought, presumably titled something along the lines of *The Collected Wisdom of Charlie Chaplin.*

Perhaps most remarkable about many of these grand little phrases is their relative consistency of structure. They are frequently figured as equations, turning on the use of the word "is" as if it were some kind of intellectual fulcrum: despair *is* a narcotic, life *is* desire, something *is* something else. It is, surprisingly for Chaplin, a language of reduction and of certainty, a formulation in which large, abstract concepts can be reduced to a single central property. More often than not, his aphorisms are ontological, concerned with discovering the natural and essential properties of everything from emotional states to moral

judgments to life itself. There could perhaps be no more un-Chaplinesque manner of philosophizing. It is not just that such statements depend on a radical
degree of certainty to mean anything at all and leave no room for skepticism
and doubt. It is also that they consign grand ideas to a single typology, reducing meaning to one property and excluding all other possibilities. Chaplin was
once an artist for whom it was possible to classify no fewer than eight types
of transformations that regularly occurred within his films.[37] An alarm clock
could not merely be an alarm clock in Chaplin's world; it also had to be a sick
patient, a diamond, a can of sardines, a mouth full of teeth—or at least treated
as such, as in *The Pawn Shop*. It seems unthinkable in such a universe that "life"
itself might be so stable an idea as to be reducible only to "desire."

Yet this is the new filmic world that Chaplin has created, and from the tiny
certainties of these tiny aphorisms he manages to build grand schemes and
theses—expansive readings of society or even the cosmos. Hence the indict-
ments that Verdoux levels against all of modern society in the final two reels
of *Monsieur Verdoux*. "As for being a mass killer," he expounds during his trial,
"does not the world encourage it? Is it not building weapons of destruction for
the sole purpose of mass killing? Has it not blown unsuspecting women and
little children to pieces, and done it very scientifically? As a mass killer, I'm
an amateur by comparison." (In this final speech, the film actually becomes a
kind of perversely literal reading of Kenneth Burke's claim that "tragedy deals
sympathetically with crime. Even though the criminal is finally sentenced to be
punished, we are made to feel that his offense is our offense.")[38]

In *Limelight*, Chaplin's thesis is nothing so stark as in *Verdoux*, and the film
builds to no grand plan of the universe. For all of the wisdom that he so readily dispenses, Calvero is still a drunken, washed-up music hall performer who
never sustains his moral or cosmological argument for more than a few sentences at a time. But a kind of discursive thesis is embedded nevertheless in the
structure of the narrative itself. Calvero literally cures Thereza through talk,
conducting a series of discussions with her that are actually marked within the
film as psychoanalytic sessions, "a case for a psychologist." Calvero does not
explain an articulated theory of how the world works; instead, he presents the
idea that articulate explanation itself is how the world works, never mind his
statements about the "enigma" of "the heart and the mind." He is perhaps the
greatest exponent of the talking cure ever put on film. By explaining to Thereza
her shame over her sister's prostitution, he inspires her to see the causes of her
ailment; by explaining to her the nature of desire, he causes her to look toward
a future where she can seek beauty and love again. From these conversations,
the world is made anew. Thereza goes from a suicidal and quasi-paralytic invalid to a triumphant prima ballerina, all through the power of talk.

Indeed, in *A King in New York,* Chaplin diagnoses the failure to listen to grand theories and careful articulations as part of the problem of the modern world. Shadov comes to America with an elaborate plan to "revolutionize modern life and bring about a utopia undreamed of" through a new application of atomic energy, and he continues to stay in the country even after his life begins to crumble in hopes that the U.S. Atomic Commission will hear him out. But his plan never gets off the ground. Government officials finally look at his proposals but then dubiously claim they are already working on something similar themselves and so have no need for his ideas. Shadov is hounded as a Communist sympathizer—his dreams of an atomic-fueled utopia part and parcel of the accusations against him—and effectively forced to flee the country. His crime is the crime of having a theory, one that runs counter to the dominant ideologies of nuclear warmongering and capitalist acquisition. "I lost my throne because I didn't want atomic bombs," he explains, and he is driven for the same reason from the United States.

To his credit, Chaplin does not ever go so far as to present any grand theory in his films without dousing it with some kind of skepticism; his works are never entirely, or at least easily, reducible to a *film-à-thèse. Verdoux* comes closest to the form, but even here the main character's closing arguments are thoroughly qualified. They are, quite simply, the words of a serial killer delivered in his own defense. As much as they may be a grand explanation for modern society and modern morality, they may also be only so much self-serving sophistry. In fact, the degree to which Verdoux has never fully articulated such sentiments earlier in the film is part of the problem. His grand theory at the film's conclusion is built undoubtedly from some of his earlier philosophical musings on painless death and "drab existence," and he has hinted at some connection between his actions and a larger theory of society: when the waif tells him that her new husband is a munitions manufacturer, Verdoux declares "that's the business I should have been in." But Verdoux has never until his trial been much of a social theorist. He has, instead, been a great apologist for his own actions, even from the opening narration of the film where he describes his crimes as "liquidating members of the opposite sex . . . as a strictly business enterprise."

In Bazin's reading, Chaplin purposefully refuses to resolve the questions about the trustworthiness of Verdoux's social theory and instead constructs a scenario where to resolve such questions in any one direction is to lose something dear: we must either abandon Verdoux or we must abandon all notions of morality and social propriety, and we desperately want to hang on to both. "We go along with Verdoux, we are *for* Verdoux," Bazin writes. "It is the character that we love, not his qualities or his defects." Yet there is no question of

Verdoux's guilt. To "go along" with Verdoux, we must be willing to condemn "the condemnation of a man 'justly condemned by society.' " We must be willing to accept a world where "society no longer has any emotional claim on the public conscience."[39] Either existing social mores are correct, or we must rethink our system of morality on the basis of the final words of a convicted killer: for all our emotional connection to Verdoux, it is hardly a setup designed to encourage an easy intellectual conversion.

In a very different manner, Chaplin also renders as problematic the very idea of grand theorizing in at least one of the music hall segments from *Limelight*. Shortly after concluding one of the most cosmic conversations between Thereza and Calvero—the one that boasts such grand declarations as "Life is a desire, not a meaning"—Chaplin refigures the same conversation as broad comedy. Calvero has a dream of being in a music hall performance with Thereza as his sidekick, and their routine essentially consists of replaying their prior philosophical discussion as a series of comic flirtations. "At this moment, I'm beginning to grasp the meaning of life. Oh what a waste of energy," Calvero declares in his dream. "What is this urge that makes life go on and on and on?" "You're right," Thereza responds. "What does it all mean? Where are we going?" Calvero has a quick punch line: "You're going south, dear. Your hand's in my pocket." It is a powerful reconfiguration in the film: not only does Chaplin literally burlesque his own deep thinking, but he also throws into question the whole idea that Calvero and Thereza might be getting at anything more in their discourse than a kind of sublimated sexual desire. Perhaps, like their music hall equivalents in the dream, they are just performing for each other and with each other; perhaps they have no interest in anything more grand than their own bodies. Perhaps it is not talk at all that cures in the world of the film; perhaps it is passion.

Or perhaps, as Chaplin explores in *A King in New York,* any talk of serious ideas at all is only so much childishness. The film contains many direct statements of political principle—but they are almost all initially mouthed by Rupert, whom Shadov describes as an "obnoxious, offensive" little "brat." In fact, the film's most direct statements of principle are espoused in the middle of a food fight. As Jonathan Rosenbaum has observed in defense of the film:

> I would argue that those who reject *A King in New York* because they
> find Chaplin's ideas in it too obvious, simplistic, or bitter are likely to
> be overlooking the fact that he places many of his own most cherished
> leftist and anti-nationalist sentiments in the mouth of an obnoxiously
> self-righteous and hectoring brat . . . who often won't let Chaplin's title
> king get in a word edgewise when he holds forth. This implies a dialec-

tical as well as self-critical side to Chaplin—not to mention a certain intellectual depth—that few commentators are likely to concede about the man.[40]

There is for Rosenbaum more dialecticism than didacticism in Chaplin's late work.

Yet the various qualifications to which Chaplin dutifully submits the theorizing in these three late films seems more like an old reflex than a sincere form of skepticism. This is not the eternal suspension of *City Lights* applied to intellectual matters. Rather, it smacks strongly of a kind of questioning that is actually meant to resolve rather than to continue in perpetual ambiguity. The change in Chaplin's approach is conveyed most clearly in the matter of endings. Almost as much as the absence of the Tramp, what distinguishes *Monsieur Verdoux, Limelight,* and *A King in New York* most clearly from Chaplin's earlier works is the directness of their conclusions. This is a trend that begins even with the reissue of *The Gold Rush.* Chaplin famously simplified the role of Georgia in the story, changing a cut-in of a note she writes to her loutish boyfriend Jack apologizing for slapping him to a note that she writes to the Tramp, apologizing for missing the New Year's Eve celebration he had organized. The switch renders her an unattached romantic heroine for the Tramp to legitimately woo, and it allows for an unambiguously romantic conclusion to the film. Gone is the metanarrative commentary of the shipboard photographer at the original film's end—in fact, gone is the final kiss altogether, too tentative and awkward in the original version for a true romantic fulfillment between two legitimate romantic partners. Chaplin cuts the film off just before the final sequence, with the Tramp and Georgia headed up to the first-class deck for the journey back home together. The conclusiveness of the new *Gold Rush* ending, in contrast to the cynicism of the previous version, would form a template for his other sound-era films. Their endings would be definitive in a manner that was not generally seen in Chaplin's silent-era work: Verdoux is captured and executed, Calvero concludes a triumphant performance and dies, Shadov is cleared by the House Un-American Activities Committee and leaves the United States. Each of these stories actually ends; when Chaplin reaches the final frame, there is no more story to tell.

In a similar way, Chaplin's late films also seem to promise an intellectual resolution that is uncharacteristic of his earlier work. As much as Bazin sees a seesaw between Verdoux and the society that condemns him in that film's conclusion, he acknowledges that in the end "we go along with Verdoux, we are *for* Verdoux" and we are willing to reject "the condemnation of a man 'justly condemned by society.'" Indeed, Verdoux is even narratively marked within the final moments of the film as a kind of sage and martyr. When a priest says to him, "may the Lord have mercy on your soul," Verdoux subtly corrects him on his theology: "Why not. After all it belongs to him." When he is offered a final drink of rum, he is the brave bon vivant, committed to life until the end. He turns down the glass at first but then reconsiders: "Just a moment. I've never tasted rum," he says, moments away from execution. The camera zooms in to a medium close-up on him as he defiantly drinks the entire glass.[41] His final progression to the guillotine—set to grand, triumphant music—is the heroic death march of a political prisoner more than the final minutes of a cold-blooded killer. The ending of the film, in the words of one contemporary reviewer, carries with it "astonishingly enough, a grain or two of smugness."[42]

Limelight would not be so smug, but the ending seems no less determined to undercut any ambiguity Chaplin may have introduced earlier in the film. Calvero dies as he lived, talking and philosophizing—on a chaise lounge no less, almost a psychoanalyst's couch. The ending contains some of Calvero's choicest lines: "The heart and the mind. . . . What an enigma"; "I believe I'm dying, doctor. But then, I don't know. I've died so many times." He has switched places with Thereza now—he the invalid and she the performer—and he dies lying on that couch in the wings of the theater, watching his protégée take flight as he cedes his former glory to her. The heart and the mind may be an enigma at the end of the film, but there is little doubt that Calvero's mind has played some primary part in Thereza's restoration. He has given her the gift of his words, which she has internalized and turned into her art. Redemption has come through language. Indeed, in *A King in New York,* Shadov, the great utopian plan-maker, is practically the only character with any redeeming humanity left by the end of the film and is the only one who even thinks to comfort Rupert when the other adults in his life have forced him into naming names in front of the House Un-American Activities Committee to save his Communist parents. Rupert, the great espouser of bold political ideas, may now be silent and distraught, but only Shadov, the man with the detailed thesis on how to "bring about a utopia," has the humanity to offer him any solace.

LOSING STYLE, LOOKING BACKWARD: CHAPLIN'S RECURSIVE LOOP

Discourse may liberate the characters within Chaplin's later films: it may put them in touch with greater truths, lead them to great artistic heights, rescue them from the coldness and inhumanity of those around them. But if it has liberated Chaplin's art itself, it seems to have done so in all the wrong ways. Kenneth Tynan enigmatically praised the highly imperfect *A King in New York* in one review as " 'free cinema,' in which anything, within the limits of censorship, can happen. In every shot Chaplin speaks his mind. It is not a very subtle mind; but his naked outspokenness is something rare, if not unique in the English-speaking cinema."[43] There is a literal political truth to Tynan's assessment. Public sentiment against Chaplin had long been growing in the United States through the 1940s and early 1950s for his supposed Communist sympathies and for his refusal to take American citizenship even after living in the country for most of his life, and in 1952 he was denied reentry to the country after leaving for a short promotional tour for *Limelight*. *A King in New York* was his first film made in exile and an unchecked, often bitter, indictment of the mindless anti-Communist fervor that had cast him from his adopted country—an angry rebuke to the House Un-American Activities Committee from the one that got away.[44] But Tynan's comment is as much about style as politics. "The film shows little evidence of genius at work," he writes. "There are few sequences on which a scriptwriter of moderate skill could not have improved. And this, I think is the point: that no one has tried to improve them. . . . Nobody has subjected the script to 'a polishing job' which is the film industry's euphemism for the process whereby rough edges are planed away and sharp teeth blunted. . . . A crude free film is preferable, any day, to a smoothly fettered one."[45]

Tynan's reading can apply, in a way, to all of Chaplin's films of the 1940s and 1950s, for the crux of it goes even farther than his review is willing to admit. Chaplin in his late period does not just have "rough edges" so much as he seems to have no more organizing system or guiding philosophy to speak of in his filmmaking, at least nothing that can hold with any consistency throughout the entire length of a film. As much as Chaplin is free from political constraints and Hollywood polish, he is also free from his own self-imposed filmmaking structures. From *Monsieur Verdoux* onward his films grow more and more stylistically unstable: inspired instances of his old visual style mix with mundane moments of standard classical technique mix with moments of unfettered discourse mix with a subversion of discursive certainty mix with an insistence on discursive certainty. More than a master filmmaker at the culmination of his powers or even an aging filmmaker whose sure hand is starting to shake somewhat, Chaplin seems like a filmmaker set adrift, groping for a new way to make movies in a new world.

But if Chaplin is stumbling in his late films, it is in part because he is so committed to looking backward. It is fitting that he began this period by returning to one of his previous triumphs, resurrecting the Tramp for *The Gold Rush* reissue and transposing him to an era in which he no longer belonged. Insofar as critics have found much of interest in the late works, it is largely in terms of what they quite consciously say about Chaplin's previous work and specifically about the figure of the Tramp. "If *Verdoux* has a 'meaning,'" Bazin writes, "why look for it in terms of some moral, political, or social ideology or other . . . when it is so easy to discover it in Charlie?"[46] Or, as Gerald Mast writes of *Limelight,* it "is probably a better film in the light of the 40-year career that went before it . . . than it is as a single work of art."[47] As frequently as self-referentiality is cited, however, few commentators seem to take it as a potential artistic fault; it is seen as perfectly sensible and natural for Chaplin to conclude his career by becoming his own most extensive commentator. In Andrew Sarris's evaluation, Chaplin in his later years "used the screen as his personal diary," a tendency that made his late work "a study less in decline than in modal metamorphosis."[48]

But this quality of reflexivity also gives the films a strange, ghostly aspect that has little to do with anything else they might be trying to accomplish or present; the films from *Verdoux* to *King* are always haunted by a figure that does not actually appear in them. Whatever else it might be trying to say about systems of industrial morality or politically sanctioned murder, *Monsieur Verdoux* is also almost always read as staging a kind of execution of the Tramp, Jean Renoir's famous essay "Non, M. Verdoux n'a pas tué Charlie Chaplin!" ("No, Monsieur Verdoux did not kill Charlie Chaplin!") notwithstanding. Here in Verdoux is a figure who makes his life in performance; who constructs elaborate narratives one after another in which he is always essentially the same character; who finds, uses, and discards heroines with abandon; who inhabits, literally, the same body as the Tramp. And here, in the final frames, is that body that has always been the Tramp now being led to its execution. Noting a little shuffle in Chaplin's walk that evokes the Tramp's famous gait, Bazin calls it "the sublimest gag of all . . . the gag that resolves the whole film: Verdoux was Charlie! *They're going to guillotine Charlie!* The fools did not recognize him."[49] The film, in other words, is always on some level also about the Tramp. Whatever Verdoux says about society, he must also be saying about the Tramp. Whatever moral position he stakes must also in some way be staked in relation to the Tramp. "Charlie is always there as if superimposed on Verdoux, because Verdoux *is* Charlie," Bazin writes, using the familiar moniker "Charlie" ("Charlot," as he is known in France) to denote Chaplin's most famous creation. "There is no feature of the former character that is not turned inside out like the fingers of a glove. . . . By revising the character, the whole Chaplin universe is turned upside down at one stroke."[50] In other words, *Monsieur Verdoux* can make no statement that is not also a statement that casts its shadow backward, always coloring what came before it just as it is always colored by what preceded it. It is trapped in a filmic universe beyond that of its own immediate construction.

The same can be said even more so of *Limelight,* though here Chaplin seems to exalt in the connections. If *Monsieur Verdoux* stages the Tramp's execution, *Limelight* stages his glorious funeral. The movie commits to film the music hall world from which the Tramp emerged, celebrates the style of comedy that was his triumph, and merges that comedy into a grand ballet that is meant to exemplify the high art that the Tramp had finally achieved and to which Calvero's own performances are finally equated by the characters in the film. Almost everything that happens in the film seems like a celebration of a character who does not appear in it. The film even ends with the body which has always been the Tramp's body being carried off camera, as if its final frames morbidly picked up just where *Verdoux*'s left off. Inevitably, then, when the Tramp's body appears on screen again in *A King in New York,* it will be as though he has returned from the dead. As much as the film is about Chaplin's own immediate political and personal situation and a repudiation of those who sent him in exile from the United States, it is also inescapably a film yet again about the Tramp. Here, the body that is always the Tramp is appropriately placed in a new world that he does not know and does not understand, cast into an unreal landscape that makes no sense to him. He stands as if out of body *watching* other movies, even at one point *watching* other slapstick acts, always surrounded by comfort but always inescapably out of place and time, even outside himself. The Tramp now seems to be wandering through a kind of strange filmic afterlife.

There is a certain kind of pleasure in the constant backward glances of Chaplin's later films, yet there is also a degree to which their openness to self-referentiality becomes simply encumbering, constantly threatening to aesthetically capsize them. Whatever else they may try to do, *Monsieur Verdoux, Limelight,* and *A King in New York* must bear the weight of carrying a codex to Chaplin's earlier works. More than they are vehicles for storytelling or philosophical speculation or any other purpose Chaplin might have had for them, they are filmic repositories for Tramp references, a veritable Chaplin archive created in the form of narrative films. The level of indexing in these pictures goes far beyond the most obvious and most often cited references—*Verdoux*'s opening line while removing a caterpillar from his path, "Ooh la la, you'll be stepped on, my little fellow, if you're not careful," or Calvero's explanation that "There's something about working the streets I like. It's the tramp in me, I suppose." There are also object references: *Verdoux*'s conspicuous need to always have his hat when he goes out, the detective's remark that what Verdoux needs is "a pair of skates," Calvero's trademark hat and cane, Shadov's own distinctive hat that he is never without. There are situational references: the prominent flower shop in *Monsieur Verdoux,* the restaging of bits from *One A.M.* and *The*

Vagabond in *Limelight,* the reference to the mirror sequence from *The Floor-walker* in *A King in New York.* There are performance references: Verdoux's playful-cum-bashful smile and crossed arms in the boat scene taken directly from the Tramp and his somersault while holding a teacup taken from a similar gag in *Dough and Dynamite;* Calvero's foot-shuffling motion in his music hall act, taken from the song at the end of *Modern Times;* Shadov's classic Tramp moves and feints during the chase through the hotel lobby. There are even bodily references: the physical presence of Buster Keaton as Calvero's accompanist in the conclusion of *Limelight* creates a kind of walking archive in itself of an entire filmic world gone by, an exponential extension of the resonance marked by Chester Conklin's presence in *Modern Times.*

But Chaplin does far more than simply reference his past work in these films; he self-consciously crafts elaborate structures of doubling and redoubling that interlace the diegetic and the metafilmic and give his late films a deeply recursive quality. Numerous commentators have observed, for instance, the degree to which Chaplin's Verdoux resembles, both physically and dispositionally, the character of the wealthy womanizer Pierre Revel in *A Woman of Paris;* one contemporary critic even took it to be a direct parody.[51] The reference, once recognized, pushes the film toward the uncanny: it is as though Chaplin is playing a character who is also the Tramp who is also another Chaplin character, Chaplin-Verdoux-Tramp-Revel all at once. In *A King in New York,* Chaplin crafts a similarly uncanny scenario through another reference to a previous film. Here, we see the figure of the Chaplin-Shadov-Tramp not just watching another film within his own film but watching what seems to be a kind of parody of *Monsieur Verdoux,* a trailer for a film about "a killer with a soul." "I've gotta kill you, honey. It's for your own good" a man in a suit says as he points a gun at a woman in a well-appointed apartment. It is a parody of the noir craze on one level, but on another it is a kind of staging of the primal moment always left out of *Verdoux,* where the idea of mercy killing is discussed but never shown. More than simply watching a Chaplin film, we are now in the strange position of watching a Chaplin film in which Chaplin is watching a Chaplin film—in fact, the parts of the film that were never shown to anyone else; we are deep inside the hall of mirrors now.

But the deepest reaches of Chaplin's recursive impulse come in *Limelight.* Here, Chaplin as Calvero is playing not just another version of himself playing another version of the Tramp; he is also at the same time playing a version of his own father, who made his living on the English music hall stage writing and performing dirty nonsense songs of the same kind that Chaplin himself now writes and performs both diegetically within the film as Calvero and metafilmically as himself in creating it. He is, in other words, playing himself playing himself playing his father. Equally disconcerting is the way that Chaplin actually literalizes the idea of playing himself within the film. Calvero keeps an old publicity picture of himself as a young man on the wall of his apartment, and Chaplin frames himself standing directly underneath it during several points in the film—specifically, when he warns Thereza against "wasting her youth," or when he talks about "the few years I have left." As Chaplin says these lines, we can clearly see that the photo on the wall is in fact a well-known publicity photo of Chaplin himself from when he was much younger. It is on one level a jarring recognition of Chaplin entering his own movie not as a character but as himself. On another level, it is a dizzying redoubling of the idea of playing a part: old Chaplin pretending to be old Calvero is framed in the shot standing beneath a publicity photograph of young Chaplin pretending to be a publicity photograph of young Calvero, as though Chaplin had gone back in time to play Calvero across the full span of his life. Strangest of all, perhaps, is the manner of self-address that Chaplin manages to include within the film. Upon seeing Thereza's dance audition, Calvero tells her sincerely, "My dear, you are a true artist." It is sensible enough as a line within the diegesis of the film. But it is utterly bizarre when considered metanarratively. Chaplin is the one who actually wrote the music to which Thereza is dancing. He helped choreograph the dance she is performing. He is the one playing the character who compliments the work that she has done. Chaplin as Calvero is essentially complimenting the very works that Chaplin as director/composer/choreographer created, declaring them to be "true art." Chaplin is essentially filming himself talking to himself.

The extreme, almost Pirandelloesque recursiveness of Chaplin's late films is in itself a kind of heady achievement; there is very little else like it in the history of film outside the avant-garde. But it is also symptomatic of what Chaplin did not achieve in these late works—the project that he seemed to leave unfinished. Whatever its faults, *The Great Dictator* is a fascinating examination of the problem that speech had introduced to Chaplin's well-honed filmmaking style and a powerful argument against its easy and unthinking incorporation into modern filmmaking technique. It is a continuation of a project that began in *City Lights* and continued brilliantly in *Modern Times*. And in a larger sense, it is an extension of ideas and techniques that Chaplin had been exploring since his earliest days behind the camera: the visual potential of unified space, simultaneity and multiplicity, and the value of ambiguity, all of them facing existential challenges with the coming of sound. Chaplin's interest in these matters essentially ends with *The Great Dictator* in any kind of coherent sense. His next three films would circle around to look backward at his earlier career, caught in a recursive and self-referential loop.

Yet while Chaplin was busy becoming his own best archivist, other filmmakers were beginning to explore innovative ways of confronting the same aesthetic problems that Chaplin helped lay out during his work of the 1930s. As Kracauer recounts in his *Theory of Film,* there were filmmakers like Clair who chose to create dialogue that was "so casual in fact that their characters sometimes continue to converse while disappearing in a bar" and performers like Groucho Marx who "is given to talking" but whose "impossible delivery . . . tends to obstruct the sanctioned functions of speech" and "disintegrates speech all around him."[52] In making *Monsieur Verdoux, Limelight,* and *A King in New York* in the way that he did, Chaplin essentially exempted himself from these developments, and from ongoing film history itself; he had declared his own aesthetic endpoint and decided not to go any further. As early as 1936, some critics sensed the degree to which Chaplin might not follow through on the engagement with sound and the new techniques of filmmaking that films like *Modern Times,* and after it *The Great Dictator,* both promised and deferred. As one critic wrote at the time: "Some time ago Chaplin directed a picture, *A Woman of Paris,* as far ahead of the silent picture of its day as [John Ford's] *The Informer* [RKO, 1935] was ahead of *Modern Times.* Let Chaplin go back to directing his current love as a star, provided he combines his proven genius for picturization with normal use of sound."[53] If critics were looking for work as formally innovative as *A Woman of Paris,* as carefully crafted, and as firmly committed to Chaplin's own unique vision and philosophy of filmmaking but simply adjusted for the era of sound, films like *Monsieur Verdoux, Limelight,* and *A King in New York* were not those films. But Chaplin's last film, completed when he was seventy-seven years old, would finally respond to those expectations.

9

Return to Form

A Countess from Hong Kong

Countess from Hong Kong received, without exception, the worst reviews of any film that Charlie Chaplin ever made. "The nadir of one of the greatest figures in movie history," "not one trace of his former genius," "stiff and clumsy," and "a sad and bitter disappointment" are just a few of the most common critical reactions.[1] Bosley Crowther's review in the *New York Times* is sadly representative. After some initial throat-clearing about "how if an old fan of Mr. Chaplin's movies could have his charitable way, he would draw the curtain fast on this embarrassment and pretend it never occurred," Crowther gets down to it. "The dismal truth is it is awful," he writes. "It is so bad that I wondered, at one point, whether Mr. Chaplin, who wrote and directed it, might not be trying to put us on—trying to travesty the kind of hiding-in-the-closet comedies, where people banged on doors and those in the room dived for cover, that were popular as two-reel silent films."[2] The comedy has fared little better in the Chaplin scholarship. As if to protect their subject from unnecessary embarrassment, most books on Chaplin follow Crowther's advice and give the film only a few sentences, if they mention it at all. The film is taken only as evidence of a once-great filmmaker who has lost his way and become out of touch both with the times in which he is now living and the sources of his own once-formidable genius. "Clumsy, visually ugly, and leaden," in Gerald Mast's description.[3] Or, in Dan Kamin's accounting, a "sad postscript to Chaplin's career."[4]

The only aspect of the film that is generally given anything approaching real attention is the discord on set. Chaplin assembled a remarkable cast for his last effort, only the second film of his career in which he did not star. Marlon Brando and Sophia Loren played the leads, with supporting work by Margaret Rutherford and Patrick Cargill. By the end of filming, the aging director had managed to alienate practically all of them. Brando, who had worshipped Chaplin's work before beginning the film, fell out terribly with the director, later calling him "nasty" and "sadistic" and declaring his participation in the film to be a "terrible mistake."[5] The film even strained Chaplin's relations with his son Sydney, who had a significant supporting role and whom he regularly berated on set. Brando recalled that Sydney's hands would sweat whenever he arrived at the studio, though Sydney publicly excused the insults from his father by declaring "the old man is old and nervous, it's all right."[6] More than the usual Hollywood gossip, such accounts are assumed to be indicative of Chaplin's declining powers, his loss of artistic vision linked to a more general loss of control in his production process, giving the film what Eric Flom calls "a rushed and distinctly unpolished feel."[7] (Never mind the fact that Chaplin had always been hard to work with on set, that he regularly had fights with members of his cast and crew, or that he actually fired Virginia Cherrill from *City Lights* in the middle of filming when she left the set early one day for a hairdresser's appointment.) Insofar as *A Countess from Hong Kong* has any value for most Chaplin commentators, it is simply as a useful springboard for a closing metaphor on Chaplin's career, centered on a brief director's cameo that lasts no more than a few seconds in the film. "Appropriately, he exits films as he began, in eloquent silence," Kamin writes.[8]

In Chaplin's own opinion, however, the film was something much more than a farewell moment in a cameo. It was in his mind one of the most accomplished works of his career—"the best thing I've done," as he told the *Sunday Times* in London.[9] In some interviews around the time of the film's release, Chaplin even compares it directly to *City Lights* and implies that it may exceed that masterpiece. "Except for *A Countess,* I think I like *City Lights* the best of all my films," he told *Life* before the film opened.[10] He was downright puzzled by the critical response when it finally came, but he remained convinced that the critics were missing something important. "At first, when I read the reviews I wondered. Then I went again [to see it] the next day, and regained all my confidence. . . . Soon they'll come to their senses," he recounted.[11]

It is nothing new for an artist to be overly attached to his most recent work, to be blind to its faults and to treat it with kid gloves. And it is nothing new for an artist to be most protective of the work that receives the harshest treatment from critics. But such stances are actually not typical of Chaplin, who rarely offered direct praise of his own work in interviews and was usually at least somewhat open to criticism. As he told the critic Harry Carr in an interview with *Motion Picture Magazine* about *The Gold Rush,* "You said some hard things— and some good things about my picture. . . . You were exactly right—both times."[12] This disposition held true even late in his career, when he had all the more reason to sing his own artistic praises after so many others had stopped doing so. Chaplin would come to be deeply embarrassed by *A King in New York,* for instance, considering it ultimately beneath his talents and refusing to even mention it in his 1964 autobiography. Yet most later commentators have taken Chaplin's statements about *Countess* as further evidence of his decline in artistic judgment. Chaplin had given the world a perfectly adequate farewell in *Limelight,* as flawed as the film ultimately was, the logic goes. As Mast says, Chaplin should have known enough to "stay away after saying farewell."[13]

And yet, to view *Countess* in contrast to his other late works and in light of the struggle with sound that he explored between *City Lights* and *The Great Dictator* is to discover something surprising: Chaplin may have been right. A few isolated voices have come to this conclusion before. Almost alone among contemporary critics, Andrew Sarris called the film "the quintessence of everything Chaplin ever felt" and declared parts of the film "as comically exhilarating as anything Chaplin has ever done"; he even defiantly ranked it as one of the ten best films of 1967 in the *Village Voice.*[14] The British poet laureate (and former film critic) John Betjeman was so horrified at the critical backlash against the film that he wrote Chaplin privately to say that the film gives "the inner spirit . . . what it has been needing for years" and to declare the director simply "ahead of your time."[15] ("I wish I were a film critic again . . . so as to acclaim it to the public," he added.)[16] And a few of Chaplin's fellow filmmakers came to its defense: Jean Renoir and Éric Rohmer both defiantly found the film to be among Chaplin's best works.[17]

Far from being simply overzealous in their praise for a beloved film icon, these few affirmative voices have a point. *A Countess from Hong Kong* is arguably one of the strongest films of Chaplin's career—wholly in sync with the concerns and experiments that marked his filmmaking in the 1930s, fully in touch with the unique visual style and skeptical philosophy of his best shorts and features, and downright scornful of the works that he had produced in the 1940s and 1950s, which are surreptitiously mocked throughout the film. The work is both a late return to form and an unabashed critique of his own previous departures from it. In fact, the film is in many ways directly pulled from the decade of Chaplin's greatest artistic struggles and achievements, the epoch of *City Lights* and *Modern Times* and *The Great Dictator.* The screenplay is adapted from one that Chaplin wrote immediately after finishing *Modern Times;* it was at the time his first full dialogue-based screenplay, originally envisioned as a vehicle for Paulette Goddard and Gary Cooper. Most commentators regard the original 1936 script simply as a kind of dalliance, a trifling work designed to boost Goddard's Hollywood profile—a "light comedy vehicle" in Kamin's phrase.[18] But whatever else it might have done for Goddard's career, it would have also been, if it were made, Chaplin's first actual talkie, conceived almost four years before *The Great Dictator*. For a filmmaker who had refused for nearly ten years to make a proper sound film, it would have been a significant step in his artistry. It might best be regarded then as a kind of companion piece to *A Woman of Paris*, which was itself designed as a vehicle to help further Edna Purviance's career. But *Woman* was also far more than that: to Chaplin's mind, it was an important summation of his vision of filmic artistry composed at a pivotal inflection point in his career, the moment of his graduation from salaried artist at First National to full-fledged independent producer at United Artists, which is of course also the moment when he first becomes absolutely in control of his own pictures. Had he produced this screenplay in the moment when it was written, Chaplin's first real talkie would have come at no less pivotal an inflection point in his development, when his very ability to survive as an artist in the era of sound was still in question. There is every reason to believe he would want the film to serve not just as a career platform for Goddard but as a summation of what a sound film in the Chaplin style might properly look like.[19]

It would take him more than thirty years to make it, but *A Countess from Hong Kong* would finally be that film. Dialogue would finally be made subservient to the visual apparatus of Chaplin's filmmaking; the simultaneity of space would return as an organizing concern; every aspect of the film would be presented with skepticism; everything in Chaplin's world would again be untrustworthy. It was more than a new direction; it was a correction, as though Chaplin had hit the redo button on the last twenty-seven years of his career. Persistently, even obsessively, the film would seek to revise all the work that Chaplin had done since *Modern Times*—every talkie he had made, including *The Great Dictator*. Chaplin was in fact not wrong to compare *A Countess from Hong Kong* with *City Lights*. If *City Lights* was a culmination of everything Chaplin had achieved during the silent era, *A Countess from Hong Kong* would be a culmination of everything he should have done since.

DISCREDITING DISCOURSE: CHAPLIN'S SELF-CITATION

Perhaps the most immediately surprising aspect of *A Countess from Hong Kong* is the degree to which it openly marks itself in relation to Chaplin's other dialogue films. In fact, the idea that this may be just another philosophy-heavy work from a director who liked to hear himself talk provides the setup for the film's very first joke. The moment comes only three minutes into the film, almost as soon as the opening credits end. We see Brando as Ogden Mears standing in his cabin on a docked luxury liner, a man behind him sitting at a table before a typewriter. We know nothing of who he is or what the relationship between the two men might be, nothing of what the film will be about. And for those who have dreaded Chaplin's overt philosophizing and political stance-taking, Brando's first lines are not promising: "Every statesman, every minister and diplomat should dedicate himself to the cause of world peace."[20] It looks for a moment like Chaplin has gone off the deep end—now all his characters will do is spout philosophical and political positions from the first moments of the film; they will do it even while relaxing on luxury ocean liners. Yet as soon as Ogden is finished speaking, his words are immediately contextualized for us when the man at the table begins typing: Ogden is dictating a speech. It is actually a significant relief. Chaplin may still be committed to espousing clear political positions in his films, it seems, but at least the stilted manner of Ogden's speechifying is not supposed to pass for actual dialogue the way it did in parts of *Monsieur Verdoux* and *Limelight* and most of *A King in New York.* That is, at least there is hope that Chaplin's sense of the registers of spoken conversation is no longer entirely askew.

But Chaplin goes several steps further than this in the next line. Barging into the cabin at the same moment that the man at the table begins typing, Harvey Crothers—Mears's friend and adviser, played by Chaplin's son Sydney—chides Ogden for his words. "Oh, Ogden, are you still at that speech? Now here we are China, Hong Kong and you're still trying to save the world. Let's get out of here and see the town." Diegetically, the comment is one friend playfully harassing another. For anyone steeped in Chaplin's work from *The Great Dictator* onward, however, it is shocking. A character making a concerted statement of beliefs is being told to shut up—in favor of going to "see" something and simply having some fun. Even based on what little we know of Ogden's speech from the single sentence he utters, it seems a synecdoche for all of Chaplin's speechifying: it could be a sequel to the Barber's call for recommitting to a world that is "free and beautiful" in *The Great Dictator;* it could be the positive inverse to Verdoux's dark condemnation of militarism and warmongering in *Monsieur Verdoux;* it could even be an explanation of Shadov's plan for "a utopia undreamed of" in *A King in New York.* (Calvero, never one for formal platforms, is perhaps exempted from this club, though romantic statements like "Desire is the theme of all life—it's what makes a rose want to be a rose" are certainly in the same spirit.) It is as though Harvey has single-handedly cast out all of Chaplin's most cherished filmic moments from the past quarter century, declaring them inappropriate and misplaced. Instead, what is offered to us in the first moments of the film is a new variation on Chaplin's classic technique of object transformation. What sounds at first like normal spoken dialogue is transformed into a formal speech; what then sounds like a speech to be taken seriously—a heartfelt statement of principle—is transformed into just another form of work, something that is part of Ogden's job and that he can set aside to work on later. To Kamin's list of the eight types of object transformation in Chaplin's cinema, then, we could now add a ninth category: one form of speech for another. What once would have been a serious and straightforward statement in Chaplin's films has now instead become a very serious kind of joke, a testament not to the importance of world peace but to the persistence of instability. We are back in Chaplin's filmic universe.

More than that, though, we are definitely *not* in the universe of Chaplin's other talkies, a point Chaplin is careful to emphasize. Hence the ballroom sequence where the director offers a kind of "greatest hits" collection of the ponderous statements from his other late films. Chaplin begins the sequence with what seems like just another entry into the ever-growing Chaplin catalog of great thinkers referenced on film: it was Schopenhauer in *Verdoux,* Freud in *Limelight,* and Marx in *A King in New York;* here it is Aristotle. "I think dancing stimulates conversation. Wasn't it Aristotle who used to walk and lecture around the Lyceum and talk of the soul?" says a young socialite with whom Ogden is dancing. But there is clearly something different in this instance of philosopher name-dropping, as indicated by the manner in which Aristotle is brought up: the girl is shaking her body violently as she shows off a bizarre dance move, her voice trembling from the contortions as she speaks in an outrageously affected Kensington accent. She looks and sounds like an overprivileged fool. Aristotle is like a piece of jewelry to her, just something to show off. And so too is philosophizing itself, even a kind of philosophizing that intersects directly with Chaplin's own previous efforts. Still doing her ridiculous shimmy, she goes on to effectively paraphrase Calvero's insights from *Limelight:* "The soul is desire and . . . the whole of life is desire." Then, moments later, she essentially forces Ogden into replaying a sequence out of *The Great Dictator.* "Do you believe in the immortality of the soul?" she asks him as they spin around the dance floor. "Well," he begins to answer haltingly. She interrupts him to assert that she does and to explain her idea that "when we die our souls go on until they're reborn again through love." It is structurally analogous to an exchange between Hannah and the Barber, one of the most famous of that film, which also culminates in grand philosophical statements: "Do you believe in God?" / "Well . . ." / "I do. But if there wasn't one, would you live any different? I wouldn't."[21]

Such moments of deliberate self-parody are a far cry from the kind of self-indexing that Chaplin put into his films from *Monsieur Verdoux* through *A King in New York,* where visual quotations and other reminders of his past glories were included simply for their own sake, like filmic talismans. Here, Chaplin is systematically revisiting and revising his gravest offenses in pontification, even cutting down relatively beloved exchanges like the conversation from *Dictator*. What Chaplin once presented as heartfelt is now replayed as ridiculous. It is not an act of remembrance so much as an act of cleansing, a re-marking of such conversations as simply self-indulgent, derivative, and redundant. It is telling that Chaplin's philosophical socialite begins almost every one of her sentences with "Daddy says," as in "Daddy says [Aristotle] never had a clear idea of what the soul is. But Daddy has." She doesn't have an original thought in her head, yet still she goes on talking. It seems to be a winking reference to Chaplin's own prior ponderousness. (In fact, this cameo part was originally supposed to be played by Chaplin's daughter Geraldine, making the reference to Daddy all the more acerbic.) What's more, though, is that she isn't the only one with vacuous thoughts that she feels the need to express. When Ogden switches dancing partners, he quickly learns that deep thinking must be the trend among all the best society girls now. "I've been wondering about the immortality of the soul," his new partner says as they spin around. He smiles at her as though he is ready to bolt from the dance floor. He, like Chaplin himself, clearly wants to escape from this world of shallow deep thought. As the socialite says in perhaps her only sensible line in the film, "It's surprising what people will talk about to make themselves interesting."

Solving Sound: Turning Speech into Action

The socialite's statement might be taken as a kind of maxim for the film as a whole in its relationship to dialogue, as it touches on the crux of the solution that Chaplin has finally come to regarding the problem of speech. Speech in *A Countess from Hong Kong* is essentially evacuated of its meaning; it is simply another form of action. The ponderous statements of the dancing girls have no real content, they get no closer to any kind of truth simply by being articulated; they merely exist to make the girls seem interesting and attractive. Even Ogden's speech is meaningless from a content perspective: saying everyone "should dedicate himself to the cause of world peace" gets us no closer to understanding the nature of the world or how to live in it. Ogden may believe in these sentiments on one level (indeed, the film implies that he does), but in the end the speech is simply something Ogden has to *do* as part of his job as an ambassador. It doesn't mean; it *functions*—it marks him as a statesman, as someone who's supposed to think about things like world peace, regardless of whether that thinking leads anywhere. In fact, the film's comic climax specifically revolves around a supreme instance of language *doing* a great deal without actually *meaning* anything at all: a marriage of pure convenience, perhaps the "purest" of speech acts. Trying to get Natascha, the stowaway Russian prostitute played by Sophia Loren, legally into the United States, Ogden orders his valet Hudson to marry her on the ship so she can become a citizen. When the ship captain asks Hudson, who has had all of ten minutes to prepare for the impromptu wedding, the pivotal question, Hudson faints. "It was . . . those drastic words, 'til death do us part," he later explains—that is, the idea that the content of the question might truly mean something and that his answer might actually be taken as a real statement of affection and commitment. The mere thought of it is overwhelming. But the marriage is action only, designed to end in divorce in just a matter of days. When Hudson and Natascha ultimately answer yes to the question, they are not vocalizing an emotional truth; they are trying to pull off a scam. It is an extreme case of how speech functions in the film overall. The *act* of speaking is meaningful in the film. The *objective* of speaking may be important. But the actual *words* spoken are almost always irrelevant; they don't mean much at all.

In fact, while directing the film, Chaplin seemed markedly disinterested in anything that any of the characters had to say; he couldn't even seem to remember their lines as he directed them. Gloria Swanson visited the set on one occasion and recounted one of the most unusual forms of direction she had ever seen: "He tried to work out a way in which Loren could walk over to Brando, holding a glass. He paid no attention to dialogue. I heard him give only one dialogue direction. He may have written the words, but he could not remember them. 'So-and-so-and-so-and-so etcetera,' would be his delivery of an average line. The associate producer, Jerry Epstein, paced behind him, reading the correct lines from a script."[22] It was perhaps all the more puzzling for the fact that it did not seem to come from a lack of memory or from old age. As Swanson recounts, "He looked fit as a fiddle. He was bouncing in and out of his chair."[23] Chaplin's directorial technique was a matter of approach, based on the idea that the specific words that anyone says in the film simply do not really matter. What matters is how they hold a glass, how they cross the room, how they inflect their voice as they say "so-and-so." What matters, in other words, is simply what they *do,* which includes what they mean to *do* through their speech. And what does not matter is what they specifically say or what those words might mean beyond their particular function in the given moment.

For commentators like Wes Gehring, such an approach is simply evidence of a director who was never able to adjust to the world of sound, who continued to direct his actors as though they were in a silent film where the words they mouthed literally did not matter at all. "Chaplin's direction was just as it was in [Elsie] Codd's 1922 description," Gehring observes. "He tutored the performers' every action."[24] Kevin Brownlow's very inclusion of Swanson's recollections in his classic compendium on silent film *The Parade's Gone By . . .* essentially implies as much. But it is almost impossible to imagine Chaplin using a similar style of direction as he prepared to deliver his impassioned address against fascism at the end of *The Great Dictator*, his conversation on Schopenhauer in *Monsieur Verdoux*, Calvero and Thereza's lengthy discourses on life and desire in *Limelight*, even Shadov's food-fight arguments about Marx in *A King in New York*. Chaplin's directorial style in *A Countess from Hong Kong* is similar to how one might direct a silent film, yes, but that is because Chaplin had figured out a way, after more than thirty years, to return to this manner of filmmaking. If talking is just another form of action, then it is just another form of action to manipulate. By stripping dialogue of any real meaning, Chaplin has reduced the world to action once more, and he has turned his filmic world back into the one he has always known.

This is far more than a matter of aesthetic convenience. It is a shift with profound compositional implications, opening up to Chaplin the possibility of treating speech as just another action in the frame—presenting, in other words, possibilities for an exploration of simultaneity that incorporates speech as one of its many facets. Hence the scene in which Ogden finally delivers his full speech to an assembly of reporters on the ship. The content of the speech is a sly critique of Chaplin's concluding oration from *The Great Dictator*. "The solution for peace lies in man himself," Ogden begins, in a clear echo of the Barber's statement that "the kingdom of God is within man. . . . You, the people, have the power to make this life free and beautiful." Ogden then goes on to critique those sentiments on the same grounds as many of the film's harshest critics: "Liberty, freedom, and justice are generalities," he admits—echoing the kind of language used by Walter Kerr in his 1952 criticisms of the Barber's address, where he called it "a hoary collection of disorganized principles."[25] Yet he ultimately ends exactly where he began, as though Chaplin is admitting that such generalizations could never allow for more serious thought. "The solution for peace is in truth and tolerance and understanding," Ogden concludes, offering an equally vapid collection of generalities. In trying to circumvent the criticisms of the *Dictator* speech, Ogden instead offers convincing confirmation of the vacuity of thought behind the *Dictator* speech.

But what is most remarkable about this entire comic takedown of Chaplin's earlier oration is that it is delivered completely in excess of the main action of the scene—whatever Ogden actually says is entirely irrelevant. For as he is speaking, Harvey is standing behind him uncorking a bottle of champagne that spills all over a photographer kneeling at Ogden's side. Harvey goes to the bathroom to fetch a towel off-screen, where we know he will discover Natascha for the first time, wearing a pair of Ogden's pajamas that were accidentally torn apart when Ogden tried to get her to leave his cabin earlier. When Harvey returns to the room where Ogden is still speaking, his expression in the background of the frame is of utter disgust and disbelief. But Ogden, oblivious to all of this action, goes right on giving his address. It is a classic Chaplin moment of conflicting but simultaneous realities, only here for the first time the element of speech has been fully incorporated into the realities that overlap. In Ogden's version of reality, he is a respectable government official delivering a perfectly standard speech about modern political morality. In Harvey's version of reality, Ogden is a reckless adulterer spewing moral hypocrisies. The two realities, like the two friends, stand side by side yet worlds apart. But only by deemphasizing the content of Ogden's speech is this feat possible. Chaplin has essentially rendered Ogden's speech the equivalent of the waiters' song wafting into the restaurant anteroom in *Modern Times*: it is a sonic element whose presence and general features are essential for us to recognize but whose specific content is ultimately in excess of the focus of the scene. By minimizing the importance of content and turning speech mostly into sound, Chaplin has essentially solved the problems of dialogue that he first directly confronts in *The Great Dictator*. Yes, only one person on screen can speak at a time in any kind of comprehensible way. But if it doesn't matter what they are saying, then this isn't much of an obstacle. In other words, if speech is only an action anyway, then it is fundamentally equivalent to any other action; speech and silence have been rendered ontologically commensurate at last.

Chaplin's Belated Return to Form

It was for Chaplin a liberating discovery and a trigger for a kind of aesthetic restoration in his filmmaking. After more than a quarter of a century of making films that, from *The Great Dictator* onward, looked with each successive iteration less and less like the silent-era and transitional sound films that made his legacy, Chaplin finally returns in 1967 to a filmic universe that is his own—Rohmer calls it a Chaplinesque "mise-en-scène delivered to us here—as in the past in *A Woman of Paris*—in a pure state."[26] Here, space again is at the forefront of his composition—not in isolated, discrete instances like the theater scenes from *Limelight* but throughout the whole of the film, offering a colorized, wide-screen version of the kind of attention to spatial arrangement that marked classic shorts like *The Floorwalker* or *The Vagabond*. Chaplin's ocean liner is structured like a kind of beautiful prison, the ornate gold scoring on the walls of the luxury cabin where Natascha is essentially trapped repeating like so many prison bars, the beautiful recessive chambers of the first-class hallways always empty and tinged blue like some kind of luxurious cell block. In contrast to the framing in Ogden's cabin, where the ceiling cuts in just above the actors' heads and always holds the camera in a perpetual and eventually claustrophobic medium or medium long shot, the public chambers of the ship—the dance hall and grand staircase—extend upward far past the reach of the frame and demand sweeping extreme long shots, emphasized by soaring columns and tall decorative frescoes; it is the closest that Natascha comes throughout most of the film to the freedom she so desperately desires.

And in this restored world of spatial composition, Chaplin is finally able to return to some of his classic forms of shot construction, techniques long ago abandoned in his other talkies. Pursuing Natascha into a bar where one of her old johns has compelled her to have a drink, Ogden and Harvey take up seats on opposite ends of the couple to eavesdrop and interfere; they are intimates of Natascha but strangers to the john. It is a classic Chaplin shot of simultaneous but separated realities, visually reminiscent of the Tramp's table at the end of *The Immigrant:* all four figures are aligned in a row at the bar in the middle ground, Natascha and the john are framed within a decorative gold enclosure on the far back wall, two large decorative poles separate Ogden and Harvey from the couple on either end, and a lamp defines the exact center of the shot. The characters are physically divided in the frame in a spatial sequence of one figure / two figures / one figure, directly anticipating the interactions to come. As the john tries to woo Natascha, oblivious to the men sitting around him, Harvey and Ogden distract from either end, Harvey sprinkling water behind the man's ear and stealing his drink, Ogden leaning obtrusively to one side to listen to their words. Here, it is the gestures that count; specific words are irrelevant to the scene. Natascha and the john talk continually throughout the sequence, but the scene easily could have come from any of Chaplin's silent films; its humor is the humor of shared but discordant physical realities.

More so than in any of his films since *Modern Times,* in fact, Chaplin commits his camera to an ongoing and unbroken exploration of space. Though it has pockets of fast cutting and occasional elements of classical technique, *A Countess from Hong Kong* is filmed for the most part in some of the longest and most elegant takes of Chaplin's career, shots that regularly run forty-five seconds or even a minute at a time as a matter of course. Chaplin's camera seems to inhabit not so much the story of the film as the spaces of the film, showing us the world rather than describing it to us. Jean Mitry's description of Chaplin's standard camera technique undoubtedly applies here. Mitry describes Chaplin's films as instances of "pure cinema" in that they are not simply "the expression of an idea existing in itself independently of the medium which translates it, serving merely as a support for something it has not actually created itself."[27] His films are instead self-defining, their actions occurring directly before us and recorded on the medium of film; Chaplin's images, in other words, happen in front of us, unfolding in space rather than in the sum of quick jumps between frames, creating "their own signification and emotion for and from themselves."[28] In one take that runs nearly a minute, for instance, Ogden prepares for his bath in real time, undressing and conversing with his valet without any urgency to cut or change the position of the camera. In another take just prior to the wedding that runs nearly as long, Chaplin fills the frame with ceaseless comings and goings and holds the camera as the captain enters the cabin and talks to Ogden, Hudson enters the cabin and talks to the captain, and finally Natascha enters the cabin and talks to them all. The long take is here not a visual flourish but a pervasive visual ideology—a way to organize and show to us the long, slow reality of this luxurious world at sea.

Yet it is hardly a static world. Chaplin does not quite break his stated prohibition against "the tedium of a traveling smear across the screen to see an actor move from one place to another," but his long takes are so mobile and intricately arranged that it is sometimes difficult to remember or even notice the absence of cutting.[29] Without dividing the space or foreclosing against a pervasive simultaneity, Chaplin weaves his camera through the mise-en-scène and renders the world alive and active, negotiating before our eyes between the demands of unbroken space and those of narrative direction and focus. Chaplin does not ultimately mask or naturalize the way in which his camera reveals the story to us; we can see and follow where it means to draw our attention, and we are constantly aware of what is being left outside the frame as the camera turns or tracks. It is an elegant and sometimes striking means of navigation, but it is also, just as important, a means that is remarkably open about its own concisions and omissions, making its narratorial choices in front of us rather than concealing them. In its transparency, Chaplin's cinematography here is a kind of apotheosis to his deep impulse in the silent and transitional films to discredit the illusion of narrative certainty and inevitability and to foreground the ways in which stories are crafted through exclusion.

It is also, on another level, a kind of visual compensation for the deeply deceptive world of the film itself. After struggling for so long to achieve some level of intellectual and emotional surety in his dialogue films, Chaplin has returned at last to the unstable and unreliable world that so defined his silent efforts and his early work with sound. As if by way of announcement, Chaplin's first major plot point in the film turns on a classic but unexpected instance of his famous object transformations, this time "Relationship/Relationship," to use one of Kamin's transformation categories.[30] Only a few minutes into the film, as he tries to decide what to do for a good time in Hong Kong, Ogden learns that an associate of his father who works in the city would like to see him and show him the town. He is, by Ogden's description, a "venerable old gentleman," and Harvey persuades his friend to feign the flu when the man arrives so that they can escape spending the day visiting the city's boring parks and museums. When the elderly gentleman appears, it seems to be even worse than Harvey imagines: he announces that he has three other friends waiting in the lounge whom he would like to introduce to Ogden. Ogden agrees against Harvey's silent protests, but he informs his father's friend that he is unfortunately too ill to go out to see the city's cultural landmarks. But that is not exactly what the old man had in mind. His three "friends" turn out to be three Russian prostitutes, and the "venerable old gentleman" is essentially acting as a pimp. It is perhaps as clear a statement as Chaplin could make on what we should expect in the film to come: anything can be subject to revision or transformation and nothing should be taken as certain.

Indeed, Chaplin goes further in *A Countess from Hong Kong* to blur the lines between content and composition than in any other film of his career, and the score is not left out of this exercise. Chaplin deliberately and consistently undercuts our narrative expectations through his collapsing of the distinction between diegetic and non-diegetic music. Early in the story, when the prostitutes first appear, Chaplin scores the scene with an up-tempo melody that is indicative of the sudden and exciting turn in events. Just as it is confirmed that the prostitutes will stay, the music cuts out at what seems like an appropriate point in the scene. But then one of the prostitutes protests: "No, no, don't turn it off. The music complements the champagne." Hudson, who was just seen reaching for some kind of knob, has turned the music off—it was coming from a radio in the suite all along. He turns it back on and a slower melody begins, again entirely appropriate to the mood of the scene. It is disconcerting enough the first time, but the gag happens several more times in the film. In one instance, as Ogden and Natascha prepare for bed, the scene seems to be underscored with romantic music, but it turns out to be the radio again—Ogden unexpectedly reaches over to adjust the radio volume in the middle of the scene and the volume of the diegetic music adjusts as well; it adjusts again as Natascha plays with the knob until Ogden tells her to leave it alone. Much later in the film, Chaplin begins a scene on the ship's deck with a jazzy song that fades away. The pretentious socialite from the ballroom scene happens to be carrying a small radio; she examines it as if it is broken and then hits it until the song comes back at full volume, startling the people around her. She was the source of the music, and it didn't fade out in the scene—her radio simply stopped working.

On one level, the persistently uncertain place of music in the film is simply a kind of metanarrative joke, a game of hide and seek with the audience. But it also has a much more unsettling role. The constant return to the joke leaves the viewer with no choice but to question the emotional register of the film at all times: it is never clear until a scene has completely ended whether the music underscoring it, which often does significant emotional work, is to be trusted. It may be that going to sleep in separate beds on their first night together has romantic undertones for Ogden and Natascha; or it may be that Ogden just likes to leave the radio on. Later, it may be that Chaplin for one of the few times in his career has chosen to use a popular song to underscore a scene and call out some particular emotional resonance that only it can capture. Or it may be that the song is simply being played on a radio by a fool and he associates such music with such people. To unsettle the capacity for the film's soundtrack to function properly within the film as Chaplin does is to deeply unsettle the idea that it might prove narratively or emotionally relevant or function as any kind of guide at all to what we see before us. In treating the soundtrack in this way, Chaplin essentially forfeits the right of the film to interpret itself to us as we watch it: anything it tells us might only be a tease, or anything it tells us might simply be wrong. We are left to confront on our own a world where nothing is as it first seems.

REMEMBERING THE TRAMP, REDISCOVERING DARKNESS

In terms of its composition, then, *A Countess from Hong Kong* is one of Chaplin's darkest films in years, a far cry from simply the "shipboard bedroom farce with much slamming of doors and peek-a-boo slapstick hijinks" of Kamin's description.[31] This is not the flagrantly macabre mode of *Monsieur Verdoux* or the self-pitying tragic register of *Limelight*. It is something far more subtle and sinister and more deeply antisocial: it displays a pervasive instability and unyielding lack of faith in certainty of any type, essentially a carryover from the profound cynicism that permeated Chaplin's silent-era work and that reached its peak in dark fables like *The Kid*. It goes even further than this, though, beyond the unsteady world that Chaplin constructs of constant object transformations and unreliable emotional and narrational cues. For all the glitz and glamour of the film's shipboard world, there is also a darkness embedded in the very visual register of *Countess* through a production design that is more in line with Chaplin's silent-era work than anything he had made since the 1920s. From *City Lights* onward, with a few moments of exception in *Modern Times*, Chaplin's films had started to take on more and more the visual quali-

ties of fairy tales, set in worlds that did not necessarily look like the fully en-
closed studio sets that they were but that did not look like anything grounded
in the dirt and grime of the real world either, no matter what kind of squalor
they purported to depict. But the sparkling dream kingdom of the ocean liner
in *Countess* is bookended by jarring reminders of the destitute and desperate
spaces of the world that used to be Chaplin's filmic home.

The film opens in a brothel, where tourists and American sailors can pay to
"dance with a countess for half a dollar"—the brothel specializes in refugees
from the former Russian aristocracy, and presumably they'll do a good deal
more than dance for a little extra cash. There is nothing particularly prurient
about the opening scenes, but they are as gloomy and hopeless as anything
Chaplin had ever put on film. The girls at best look despondent and at worst
emotionally dead; the johns look lonely and desperate, some of them pitifully
so and some of them chillingly so. As they spin across the dance floor in awkward circles, they become a paradoxical crowd made up of completely isolated
people—as though the whole dance hall from *The Gold Rush* were filled only
with versions of the Tramp. This is the world that Natascha comes from, and
it is the world to which she returns, briefly, at the film's end. Despite all the
reluctant kindness that Ogden has shown her, despite all his intimations that
he will help her and take care of her, Natascha does not trust him—she does
not trust anyone—and she risks her life to dive off the ocean liner when they
reach port in Hawaii. There is a vague plan in place to meet up with Harvey
again, but only if she survives the jump. She does, and she finds her way to
a luxury hotel on the island to rejoin her new wealthy quasi friends. But to
get there, she takes one of the strangest modes of transportation that Chaplin would put on film. Freezing and soaking wet, she hitchhikes alone in a
dirty alleyway. The only ride she can find is on the flatbed of a tractor-trailer
carrying a huge, filthy piece of construction equipment. The jarring image of
Sophia Loren sopping wet on the back of a construction transport—and the
complete naturalness with which she accepts this ride, grateful for any help at
all—is a brief but shocking reminder of how much her world is not the glam-
orous world of the ship. This world of dirt and discomfort and small favors that
hardly seem like favors at all is the world that she knows best.

And it is also the world that Chaplin knows best. Chaplin is back in the
universe of stark contrasts between rich and poor that had animated so much
of his best work, from *The Kid* to *A Woman of Paris* to *City Lights*. He even
opens the film with a purposefully offensive joke on these contrasts. Looking
through binoculars at the huddled masses of Hong Kong from the luxurious
ocean liner, Harvey jokes about their plight. "That's what I dislike about the
poor—they have no taste. They indulge in squalor. They pick the worst neigh-

borhoods to live in, eat the worst kind of food, and dress atrociously." The joke makes Ogden, the great advocate of brotherhood and world peace, begin to laugh a little; Harvey says it's "the first time I've seen you smile since I've been on this trip." Whatever else he is, Ogden is a very rich man who can appreciate a joke or two about people who have nothing. And whatever else she may be, Natascha is one of those souls on shore who "indulge in squalor." Chaplin has again populated his filmic world with the characters that have always been most familiar to him—not the political operators of *The Great Dictator* or the middle-class businessmen of *Monsieur Verdoux* or even the artists and comedians of *Limelight* or the media moguls of *A King in New York*. He is back to something much more elemental: people desperate from poverty and, ultimately, people desperate from wealth.

Chaplin pulls no punches. Natascha is not a prostitute with a heart of gold, and she is not a fallen woman searching for redemption. She is a prostitute whose former boyfriend was a violent gangster, who admits she is used to going hungry and sometimes sleeping on the street, who shows no particular kindness or sweetness anywhere in the film, and who has no interest in redemption of any sort other than the most material kind. She wants to escape Hong Kong and get to America, and she doesn't seem to care whom she has to compromise or disregard in order to do so, either at the beginning of the film or at the end. In one of her first scenes she blackmails Ogden with the threat of a sex scandal if he reports her, and she ends the film by risking her life jumping off the boat even though she knows Ogden would not want her to do it. She is, not surprisingly, a version of Goddard's Gamine, driven to the same degree by her material needs and her survival instinct but with any sentimental qualities worn away by hard and sad years. She has none of the Gamine's regard for domestic niceties and none of her happy pluck; she is too far gone for that. And in this sense, she is the perfect mate for Ogden, who is just as desperate emotionally as Natascha is materially. He is the son of the wealthiest oil man in the world. Money is nothing to him, and he uses it even more casually than the Millionaire in *City Lights*. He readily offers to buy Natascha a first-class cabin just to get rid of her; he has Harvey offer her $75,000 to try to get her to leave the ship. But for all his wealth, he seems to take no happiness in life. He is on the verge of divorce from a wife he never sees. He goes out for wild nights on the town but when he wakes up with telephone numbers scrawled across his shirt in lipstick, he just seems exhausted and disgusted at himself. He seems utterly trapped in his profession, reduced to giving passionless speeches to uninterested reporters in his hotel sitting room. Harvey tells him at one point that he is being considered as a possible secretary of state, but in fact he gets a glamourless ambassadorship to Saudi Arabia instead. Ogden comes to love

Natascha—or think, at least, that he loves her—not because of anything that she does or says or any particular way she treats him. He seems to come to love her because at least she is something different that he cannot predict. He cannot really fathom her desperation, just as she cannot really fathom his languor.

Natascha and Ogden are actually quite jarring as protagonists of a comedy, a point which seemed to translate directly into so many of the poor reviews that Brando in particular received. There seems to be no life to Brando's performance and no energy in his relationship with Natascha. Crowther declared his performance to be without any "real glimmers of comic talent or spirit," and Pauline Kael later said he had almost "never been worse or less interesting" in a film.[32] Writing in the *New Yorker*, Brendan Gill observed, "These days, Mr. Brando often gives the impression of being revolted by having to work in movies at all; in this picture his revulsion nearly succeeds in bringing a silly character to life by killing it."[33] But to expect some kind of dash or verve or even something approaching emotional honesty from this character seems to be missing the point, as Chaplin was at pains to repeat during interviews. "They picked on such puerile things to say," he observed of the film's critics. "'Brando is wooden'—but that's just the whole point!"[34] It's true that Brando is a terrible comedy lead, but he is actually quite perfect for the part. He delivers almost everything in a kind of deadpan mumble, as though he could hardly bring himself to find the liveliness needed for speech. Ogden is a diplomat, perfectly willing to smile and be basically polite, but in Brando's performance he seems almost as emotionally dead as the prostitutes in the opening dance hall, all of whom are also quite willing to smile lifelessly for the people whom they meet.

Ogden is not even alive enough to notice that Natascha seems to have little interest in him beyond his wealth. Chaplin does not judge her for this: her problems are real, and marrying Ogden is a real solution. But neither does he sentimentalize it. The film ends with what looks to be a triumphant reunion and a loving dance between Ogden and Natascha; Ogden has left his wife and he returns to the hotel ballroom where Natascha is sitting by herself. The final shots show the two of them twirling across the dance floor to lush, romantic music—though we might just as easily assume this is simply the music that the band is playing diegetically within the frame. Yet it is hardly an unequivocal triumph of love in Chaplin's construction. This scene of dancing has been preceded by three other dancing scenes in the film: one in the opening brothel, one where Ogden and Harvey are dancing with the Russian prostitutes, and one on the ocean liner where Natascha is recognized by one of her former johns. Each dance in the film has been tainted by prostitution—by something that might look from the outside like love but is nothing but an exchange of loneliness and money. There is no reason to believe that the ending dance is any different. In Chaplin's description, "It's a very sad story. This man who leaves his icicle of a wife for a girl who's a whore. I think the end, when they're dancing, is tragic."[35] It is certainly one of the darkest endings of Chaplin's career. Though it offers solutions to the immediate problems at hand, it offers nothing like a resolution.

Chaplin was endlessly frustrated by critics' stunned reactions to his last film, particularly in contrast to the way that he saw it himself. "The reviews of my pictures have always been mixed," he explained. "But what shocked me about the English reviews of the *Countess* was the fact that they were all unanimous. . . . It was such fun to do. I thought the whole world was going to go mad over it!"[36] But they were arguably looking at different films. Critics and scholars then and now seem, when they look at the film, to be looking for the Tramp. An unsigned review called "Time to Retire" in *Time* magazine was more telling than it perhaps meant to be in its central statement: "*Countess* is bad enough to make a new generation of moviegoers wonder what the Chaplin cult was all about."[37] But the "Chaplin cult" was always based on the figure of the Tramp—and with good reason. Between 1914 and 1940, Chaplin made only one film—*A Woman of Paris*—without the Tramp (or an obvious Tramp substitute like the Barber), and after that he spent his career making films that pointed backward to the heyday of his great creation. Yet, as Rohmer points out, *Countess* cannot be properly approached through this lens. This is not a film where one can "explain Chaplin by Charlie and his myth," as he says, and the Tramp is nowhere in the film in any kind of literal way.[38] Natascha is far too hard-nosed and self-interested to be his real heir; Ogden has none of his characteristics at all. For those who think of Chaplin primarily in terms of the Tramp, there is hardly anything on offer for them in the picture. It is simply a portrayal of a cold, strange, darkly cynical world filled with self-interested and in many ways emotionally dead individuals, calling itself a comedy.

But to Chaplin, this has always been his world, whether it includes the Tramp or not; this has always been the milieu around which he has crafted works that stand in contrast to classical modes of filmmaking and that seek a wider, steadier frame and a greater engagement with the world as it unfolds in all its simultaneous parts. And, for Chaplin, it has always been this harsh environment that undercuts its own story and its own direction, which asks us never to fully believe it and always to be aware of what it is leaving out. In other words, this is the filmic world in which the Tramp had always lived, though he was no longer in residence by 1967. But, in a way, his spirit was still present. As much as it departs from the shorts and features that centered only on the

Tramp, *A Countess from Hong Kong* also returns to the very beginning. The first Keystone short in which the Tramp character appeared, *Mabel's Strange Predicament,* was a bedroom farce set in a hotel. Mabel Normand had become trapped outside her room in her pajamas, and she constantly had to duck behind doors and into other rooms to hide from the people roaming the hallways. Her "strange predicament," in other words, was a version of Natascha's own tight spot in *Countess,* where she spends nearly half the film in Ogden's pajamas, hiding from anyone who might see her. (Chaplin might as easily have called the film *Natascha's Strange Predicament.*) And into the plain slapstick world of Mack Sennett's short walked a strange Tramp with a short mustache, utterly unsettling everything by operating according to his own universe of rules. Chaplin's world would begin in that short. *A Countess from Hong Kong,* which was every bit a part of that new world he had made, would mark a return.

The Chaplin Century

In his 1952 essay "Some Ideas on the Cinema," which functions as a kind of manifesto for the Neorealist movement, screenwriter Cesare Zavattini names those directors he considers to be most associated with the radical new approaches to filmmaking that he practiced and advocated: Roberto Rossellini, Vittorio De Sica, Luchino Visconti. And, at the end of the essay, he cites with reverence exactly one director outside of the movement: Charlie Chaplin. The esteem in which Chaplin was held by the Neorealists was extraordinary. Rossellini could compare him to only four other figures of veneration in his life—his father, Gandhi, Nehru, and Pope Paul VI.[1] For De Sica, he was simply a "monster" who had "discovered everything." After him, he said, "the cinema has become almost impossible."[2] Federico Fellini, who began his career among the Neorealists under Rossellini, would carry the reverence even further. For him, Chaplin was an inescapable mythological figure in both a public and private sense. "Chaplin is something like Santa Claus, like the mother," he told an interviewer for *Film Comment*.[3] He found Chaplin's influence "difficult to judge" because it was so originary and all-consuming.[4] In fact, as Wes Gehring has observed, the Neorealists were "doubly stirred" by Chaplin, as another of their major points of influence was René Clair, himself an admitted Chaplin acolyte. Clair, whose comedies are regularly compared to Chaplin's, saw himself as a kind of pupil of his American forerunner. When Clair's producers considered suing Chaplin over similarities between *Modern Times* and Clair's *Liberty for Us,* Clair persuaded them to drop the suit by reversing the direction of influence. "The whole of cinema has learned lessons from Chaplin," he contended.[5] Among French filmmakers of his generation, he was not alone in this opinion. His great contemporary Jean Renoir literally began making films on account of Chaplin, abandoning a career in the visual arts that followed in the footsteps of his luminary father, Pierre-Auguste, to pursue work in this fascinating new medium that Chaplin brought alive for him.[6] He would call Chaplin nothing less than "the master of masters, the film-maker of film-makers."[7] Jean Vigo was likewise a devoted Chaplin admirer who considered the filmmaker his "hero"; in *Zero for Conduct* (Franfilmdis/Argui-Film, 1933) alone he included visual quotations or allusions to *The Gold Rush, Easy Street, The Kid,* and *Shoulder Arms.*[8] Clair, Renoir, Vigo, Rossellini, De Sica—these were the influences from which the French New Wave was born. And with that new movement, the extraordinary expressions of esteem for Chaplin would only be compounded. Éric Rohmer credited him not just with the discovery of new cinematic techniques but with a new cinematic language, an "'allusive' mode of expression" that went beyond either "spoken language or mimicry."[9] For Jean-Luc Godard, Chaplin was far more than a cinematic innovator. He was foundational to the art and transcended commentary. "He is beyond praise because he is the greatest of all," he writes in his entry for *Cahiers du Cinéma's Dictionary of American Film-Makers.* "Today one says Chaplin as one says Da Vinci—or rather, Charlie, like Leonardo."[10] François Truffaut would echo Godard's reverence and take it even further. "Chaplin dominated and influenced fifty years of cinema," Truffaut declares in his essay "Who Is Charlie Chaplin?"[11] It was no small matter for a cinephile like Truffaut. As he famously told one interviewer, Chaplin meant more to him "than the idea of God."[12]

And yet, for many of these filmmakers, Chaplin was also a highly problematic figure—both an ancestor and an adversary. When Zavattini mentions him in "Some Ideas on the Cinema," the full citation is both praiseful and exclusionary. Chaplin is explicitly held apart from the Neorealists. "I am quite aware that it is possible to make wonderful films, like Charlie Chaplin's, and they are not neorealistic," he writes.[13] After all, the main thrust of Zavattini's manifesto is that "the true function of the cinema is not to tell fables."[14] In a similar vein, De Sica claimed, improbably, that the film director who "discovered everything" had influenced him "in no way." "I detest imitations," he declared when asked about Chaplin in one interview. "In fact, I sometimes don't go to see a certain film for fear I'll want to imitate it."[15] Fellini also came to question Chaplin (perhaps as one ultimately questions Santa Claus or even one's mother) and chided him for what he saw as "the emotional or ideological blackmail" in many of his films.[16] Rohmer criticized similar aspects of Chaplin's work. "How strange it is to proclaim Chaplin the most authentic genius of film!" he declared in contrast to fellow critics and directors Truffaut and Godard. "Beware of all winks to the audience, of the sly quest for complicity, of all calls, even discreet, for pity."[17] Truffaut maintained Chaplin's greatness, but at the same time he rendered the nature of his influence as a kind of problem. As much as Chaplin was "the most famous filmmaker in the world," Truffaut admitted that he was in some ways also "the most 'marginal' of the marginal."[18] Chaplin was ultimately more than a target of criticism or questioning for these filmmakers; the qualms he raised went further than the anxiety of influence. He was, deeply, a paradox: a figure who defined the medium but also in some sense misused it, a figure who "discovered everything" but supposedly influenced nothing. He was, in Godard's inimitable construction, perhaps the most important marginal figure ever to appear in any medium. As Godard writes in the *Dictionary of American Film-Makers*: "Charles Spencer Chaplin, while remaining marginal to the rest of cinema, ended up by filling this margin with more things (what other word can one use: ideas, gags, intelligence, honor, beauty, movement?) than all the other directors together have put into the whole book."[19]

What Godard does not mention (and does not need to mention) is that he himself and the filmmakers with whom he was most associated—his fellow directors of the French New Wave, his predecessors in Italian Neorealism, even to a certain extent antecedents like Clair or Vigo or Renoir—were in some sense also "marginal to the rest of cinema," and purposefully so. That is, they placed themselves self-consciously in distinction or in opposition to the hegemony of the classical style that dominated the American film industry in particular and the global film markets more generally throughout much of the twentieth century. Many of these directors—Truffaut and Godard especially—respected and even idolized classical American films. But those films were ultimately not the model for how they meant to construct their cinema. In Godard's words, the filmmakers of his epoch stood against unchallenged assumptions and doctrinal methods, the process of "elevating certain figures of style into a vision of the world, in investing some technical process or other with astrological pretensions it cannot possibly have."[20] They too wanted to fill the margins of film history with "intelligence, honor, beauty, movement," to show how the visual and stylistic possibilities left unexplored by the classical system were capable of sustaining entirely new approaches to filmic construction. And so they were met on this rebellious territory by Chaplin, who had long ago staked out a place on the edges of the dominant classical modes of filmmaking and began to fill it with his own unique compositions. But it was an uneasy alliance between Chaplin and the new counterclassical movements: as much as Chaplin was their greatest predecessor, he was also one of their greatest critics. Because Chaplin was, fundamentally, a skeptic. This was often quite literally true in the case of many postwar filmmakers. Chaplin was in fact friendly with a number of the leading new directors of the era—he was fast friends with Rossellini and knew De Sica professionally; Truffaut knew Chaplin through Rossellini. Yet he was not hesitant to be critical of his younger colleagues, no matter how much they worshipped him. He found much of the work of the Neorealists "beautiful" but also too "academic" in its concerns, while later works like Michelangelo Antonioni's *Blow-Up* (Bridge, 1966) were

simply "slow and boring."[21] His basic attitude toward any new artistic movement or trend was, in his own words, "cynical."[22] "I don't believe there is such a
thing as fashion," he explained to the London *Sunday Times* in 1967. "So much
has been done already. . . . We did all this stop action business in 1914: it was
very dull then and nobody paid much attention. . . . It's all right, but they put
it on in such a pretentious way now."[23] Chaplin was both a kind of conscience
and voice of history for the new filmmakers who found him inspirational. But
more than the issue of his personal judgments, Chaplin's filmmaking itself
seemed designed to scrutinize and question any mode or method that might
become too sure of itself; the skepticism embodied at its core would ultimately
serve to interrogate these new rebels and their own assumptions in much the
same way that he had once questioned that against which they were rebelling.
His figure would exist on the margin to their margins, as incredulous of the
new styles they propounded as he was of the ones that they rejected.

Hence the degree to which Zavattini both does and does not describe the
components of Chaplin's own cinematic style when he lays out the principles
of Neorealism. In describing Neorealism as a negative platform, Zavattini
offers substantial common ground with Chaplin's directorial methodology.
He describes Neorealism as the "elimination of technical-professional apparatus."[24] In this new filmic world, there will be no more classical orthodoxy:
"Handbooks, formulas, grammars, have no more application. . . . Neorealism
breaks all the rules, rejects all those canons which, in fact, exist only to codify
limitations."[25] On a narrative level, Neorealism "does not offer solutions" and
its endings are "particularly inconclusive."[26] On a visual level, the Neorealist
director will take a space or a scene and carefully "'remain' in it, because the
single scene itself can contain so many echoes and reverberations."[27] On the
level of direction, Neorealism will not predetermine or direct our experience
of each moment of the film through cinematography or editing. The Neorealists will "take things as they are" and allow them to "create their own special
significance" so that we see and understand "things we have never noticed
before."[28] What is Zavattini describing here but aspects of Chaplin's own technique: his refusal to comply with the dictates of classical construction; his
deeply ambivalent attitude toward narrative and his aversion to easy resolutions; his commitment to allowing action to unfold unbroken in the filmic
spaces before us, to "remain" in a space or a scene with a minimum of cutting;
his repudiation of the ways in which classical technique directs our attention
within a scene and predetermines the items of focus or significance; or his
disconcerting tendencies to force the items we think to be important into secondary positions within the scene. For all its differences from Chaplin's work,
Neorealism stands, in Zavattini's summary, in approximately the same posi-

tion vis-à-vis many of the classical paradigm's most central assumptions and dictates as does Chaplin himself.

Even on the broadest conceptual level, the Neorealists and Chaplin stand together in approximately the same relationship to the strange and imperfect process of trying to capture the world on film. In Zavattini's prescriptions, Neorealism must look at the world more broadly and more inclusively than classical technique will ever allow, consciously incorporating what a more traditional film might exclude, carefully focusing on what a more traditional film might ignore. Describing a potential film scenario involving the simple act of a woman buying a pair of shoes, he describes something close to the ever-expanding multiplicity of Chaplin's own approach. Zavattini's hypothetical film will show what the woman's son "is doing at the same moment"; it will inquire into the lives of its secondary characters—"the bargaining shopkeeper, who is he?"; it will present characters who seem to have no direct relation to the story—"the shopkeeper also has two sons, who eat and speak. . . . Here they are, in front of you."[29] A good Neorealist film, Zavattini writes, "opens to us a vast and complex world."[30] But Chaplin, in a way, had already shown us that world—in the minor characters suddenly thrust to the front of the frame or placed in close-up; in the moments where his protagonist disappears into the background of a shot as we focus on new personages; in the classic Chaplin sequences where three, four, or five different actions happen at once, multiple realities coexisting in the same shot as characters live their independent lives and perspectives adjacent to one another. In *A Woman of Paris,* Chaplin would rally these principles to a kind of extreme and create a version of the world of overlapping social and interpersonal realities to which Zavattini aspires.

But Chaplin's technique would not, in the end, be precisely the same as what Zavattini describes, as he would use these techniques only in flashes, in moments of subtle subversion to classical expectations just shocking enough to unsettle our assumptions about what it means to tell a story on film. Chaplin would be deeply skeptical of the visual and storytelling exigencies of classical style, but he would ultimately reinscribe elements of narrative construction and visual elision in a self-conscious and highly controlled manner rather than eliminate them altogether. Because Chaplin did not trust anything that might become a hard and fast rule. The opposition to such approaches was as dangerously limiting as the approaches themselves—the aesthetic paradox described by *The Great Dictator* writ large. Neorealism, in contrast, is based in Zavattini's description on a kind of absolute faith in everything that classical technique distrusts, de-mediating all that classical composition seeks to arrange and moderate. "However great a faith I might have in imagination," Zavattini writes, "I have a greater one in reality."[31] It is a position based in faith and a "love for reality" and, consequently, in a belief that it is possible "to capture the essence, the truth."[32] It is a rebellion that begins in distrust but that resolves to a new position of certainty. Thus, as much as it is a filmic approach that builds on the fissures in classical assumption that Chaplin helped to first expose, it is decidedly not the philosophy of the filmmaker who declared that he tries always to put across "the philosophic doubt I feel about things and people."[33]

Chaplin was, in this way, more radical than the radical descendants who worshipped him, more radical even than their other great Hollywood predecessor, Orson Welles. André Bazin places Welles above Chaplin as the origin point for the movements against classical technique that would define the postwar cinematic landscape, attributing to the director one of the first serious challenges to classical style made all the more impressive for being accomplished from within the broader classical paradigm. Welles's great insight, according to Bazin, was to recognize that "under the cover of the congenital realism of the screen a complete system of abstraction [had] been fraudulently introduced."[34] Welles understood that classical editing puts forth the misimpression that "limits have been set by breaking up the events according to a sort of anatomy natural to the action" when in fact it has "subordinated the wholeness of reality to the 'sense' of the action," imposing what Bazin calls "a forced breaking down where the logic of the shots controlled by the reporting of the action anesthetizes our freedom completely."[35] For Bazin, Welles's innovation was to reinscribe filmic space with the freedom of our own perceptual confrontations by using depth-of-field techniques that essentially force "the spectator to participate in the meaning of the film by distinguishing the implicit relations" and thereby help to bring "the spectator back to the real conditions of perception."[36] Welles, in this reading, brought the cinema back to a place of ambiguity that preceded classical certainty, opening filmic style to the possibility of alternate means of depicting and arranging the world that would be explored by the movements to come after him.[37] In Dudley Andrew's reading, Welles used the inherent visual ambiguity of depth of field—even while adhering in other manners to classical construction—to essentially dramatize "the ambiguity at the core of experience" and to visually "mark the starting point from which all of us try to construct provisionally the sense of our lives."[38]

Welles was, in a way, Chaplin's obverse. If Chaplin showed too little variation in his framing and shot construction, some early critics felt that Welles showed too much. If Chaplin was supposedly inept at his own medium, there were many who claimed that Welles was too adroit—too flashy and attention-seeking. Yet at their core, though Bazin did not ever explicitly recognize it, there is something profoundly similar in their approaches, a fact that Welles implicitly points to when he acknowledges Chaplin as an influence even as he claims that "there are not many filmmakers who have made much of an impression on me," only "a few isolated ones."[39] But if Bazin did not recognize the connection, Truffaut most certainly did. For Truffaut, Welles and Chaplin were nearly inseparable. As a boy, confined to a juvenile detention hall, he would ask his parents to send him only two things: his papers on Welles and his papers on Chaplin. As an adult, he would declare the filmmakers to be equally part of his pantheon and saw them both as partaking in what was at bottom a shared sense of cinematic space and composition, one that "emanates from the physical presence of the author-actor at the center of the screen."[40] But of the two, for Truffaut, Chaplin was the more incendiary. The ambiguity at the heart of Welles's depth of field is not quite the same as the fanatical insecurity that pervades Chaplin's work. If Welles made the world that cinema created brilliantly unsure, Chaplin made it actually untrustworthy. For Truffaut, the difference was reflected in the way that Welles and Chaplin dealt in their films with questions of identity, that which is always "the major theme of artistic creation."[41] In Chaplin's hands, questions of identity take on a kind of existentialist urgency unique to his work. He does not just ask, according to Truffaut, "Who am I?"[42] He asks, more fundamentally, "Do I exist?"[43] Chaplin, in other words, moves beyond a question steeped in ambiguity to one that openly confronts impossibility, that allows for a condition in which there is no possible answer or even one in which the answer negates the question itself. And as with any great cinematic issue for Truffaut, it was also a metafilmic question. Truffaut saw Chaplin questioning whether film itself might rightfully be said to exist, whether the idea of "film" as such might mean anything at all. In Rohmer's words, picking up on the same idea, Chaplin was so troubling in large part because he refused to accept in the end that "cinema is cinema" and tried to conspire "for it to turn against itself."[44] He was in this sense one of the most extremist filmmakers to ever pick up a camera, possessed in Truffaut's words of a unique "explosiveness."[45]

Chaplin was for these filmmakers a kind of monumental origin point that was also no origin point at all. He was both a patron saint to all those who would break from dominant classical modes of filmmaking and equally a point of critique to whatever new assumptions their point of breakage might create. He would always exist on the margins of "the rest of cinema," no matter what cinema that might be. Through his filmmaking, he opened doors to innumerable new avenues of cinematic construction that went beyond classical technique and then opened doors to new avenues on those avenues again. From this perspective, his cinematic legacy is far broader than most film histories allow. He is not just present in the moments of obvious homage to which his body of work gave rise, though these are certainly significant. There are the jokes taken from *City Lights* in Rossellini's *Rome, Open City* (Excelsa, 1945). There are the obvious thematic allusions between De Sica's *Umberto D*

(Rizzoli / De Sica / Amato, 1952) and *A Dog's Life* or between *Bicycle Thieves* (De Sica, 1948) and *The Kid*. There are the explicit parallels between Gelsomina and the Tramp in Fellini's *The Road* (Ponti–De Laurentiis Cinematografica, 1954), where even the title is evocative of Chaplin's famous imagery. There is the obvious homage to *The Circus* in *The Clowns* (RAI / Compagnia Leone Cinematografica, 1970), in which Fellini originally hoped that Chaplin would appear. There is Mel Brooks's appropriation of Chaplin's use of comic sound from *Modern Times* or aspects of his political and metafilmic satire from *The Great Dictator*. There is Woody Allen's lifelong admiration for Chaplin, his famous visual quotations from *City Lights* in *Manhattan* (United Artists, 1979). But there is also something more than what such films actually present, something that goes much deeper into how films outside the classical paradigm are made and the techniques they allow themselves to use. There are the long takes and unbroken spaces of the Neorealists, the way that they "remain" in a scene.[46] There are the ways that the filmmakers of the French New Wave would foreground and call out the formerly invisible elements of filmic style, drawing our attention to cuts and framing choices and camera movements. And there are the choices and approaches of later directors unconnected to any specific broader movement. There is the way that Robert Altman would deprivilege speech as a narrative device and allow for overlapping, unintelligible conversations of the kind that Chaplin predicted. There is the way that Stanley Kubrick would construct his narrative as much in the visual composition of the frame as in the editing of the story—and even, as with Chaplin, his obsessive reshoots until the composition was exactly right. There is the way that Wes Anderson would rehabilitate shot-as-scene construction and "frontality" in composition as viable artistic choices.[47] There is even the way that Paul Thomas Anderson would return in a film like *There Will Be Blood* (Paramount/Miramax, 2007) to movement within the static frame and sound (rather than speech) as the primary tools of narrative storytelling.

Most of these filmmakers surely give no thought to Chaplin; he is as forgotten as any deep ancestor will be. But the stylistic choices and avenues that these directors are able to explore were in many ways prepared by Chaplin's works and the critique of classical methodologies that they presented, even from the earliest days of classical consolidation. If, as Godard said, "one should mention Griffith in every discussion about the cinema," then Chaplin should perhaps be mentioned alongside.[48] Chaplin is the persistent critique to what the cinema became in Griffith's wake, the link back to what it was before and the bridge to what it might become anew. To borrow a phrase from Gilles Deleuze's *Cinema 2*, the filmic world that would emerge in the wake of classical cinema's paradigmatic decline was "always haunted . . . by a clown."[49]

Introduction

1. Sources for quotations are as follows: "I think I'm a better director ... " Richard Meryman, "Ageless Master's Anatomy of Comedy: Chaplin, An Interview," *Life*, March 10, 1967; "the only genius ... " Qtd. in Theodore Huff, *Charlie Chaplin* (New York: Henry Schuman, 1951), 8; "the single most important artist ... " Andrew Sarris, "Charles Spencer Chaplin," in *Cinema: A Critical Dictionary*, ed. Richard Roud (New York: Viking, 1980), 1:201; "among his age's first artists" Edmund Wilson, *The American Earthquake: A Documentary of the Twenties and Thirties* (New York: Macmillan, 1958), 73; "Chaplin's a great artist ... " Orson Welles and Peter Bogdanovich, *This Is Orson Welles* (1992; rev. ed., Cambridge, Mass.: Da Capo, 1998), 135; "a man of the cinema" Juan Cobos, Miguel Rubio, and J. A. Pruneda, "A Trip to Don Quixoteland: Conversations with Orson Welles," in *Orson Welles: Interviews*, ed. Mark W. Estrin (Jackson: University Press of Mississippi, 2002), 106; "a first-class picturemaker ... " Otis Ferguson, "Hallelujah, Bum Again," *New Republic*, February 19, 1936; "inadequate" and "every stylistic and technical change ... " Richard Schickel, "Hail Chaplin—The Early Chaplin," *New York Times*, April 2, 1972; "It is always difficult to separate ..." Qtd. in David Robinson, *Chaplin: The Mirror of Opinion* (London: Secker and Warburg, 1983), 167.

2. Dan Kamin, *The Comedy of Charlie Chaplin: Artistry in Motion* (Lanham, Md.: Scarecrow, 2008), 35.

3. Michael Roemer, "Chaplin: Charles and Charlie," in *The Silent Comedians*, ed. Richard Dyer MacCann (Lanham, Md.: Scarecrow, 1993), 142. Originally published in *Yale Review* 64, no. 2 (December 1974).

4. Kamin, 35.

5. Eric L. Flom, *Chaplin in the Sound Era: An Analysis of the Seven Talkies* (Jefferson, N.C.: McFarland, 1997), 260–61.

6. David A. Cook, *A History of Narrative Film* (New York: W. W. Norton, 1981), 203.

7. John Kimber, *The Art of Charlie Chaplin* (Sheffield, U.K.: Sheffield Academic Press, 2000), 13.

8. Charles Silver, *Charles Chaplin: An Appreciation* (New York: Museum of Modern Art, 1989), 75.

9. André Bazin, "Charlie Chaplin," in his *What Is Cinema?* ed. and trans. Hugh Gray (1967; Berkeley: University of California Press, 2005), 1:144.

10. Bazin, "The Myth of *Monsieur Verdoux*," in *What Is Cinema?* 2:118.

11. Ibid.

12. Andrew Sarris, *The American Cinema: Directors and Directions, 1929–1968* (Cambridge, Mass.: Da Capo, 1996), 41, 40.

13. Sarris, "Charles Spencer Chaplin," 201; Sarris, *"You Ain't Heard Nothin' Yet": The American Talking Film, History and Memory, 1927–1949* (Oxford: Oxford University Press, 1998), 151.

14. Kamin, 36.

15. Gilberto Perez, *The Material Ghost: Films and Their Medium* (Baltimore: Johns Hopkins University Press, 1998), 100.

16. Jeffrey Vance, *Chaplin: Genius of the Cinema* (New York: Harry N. Abrams, 2003), 56.

17. Ibid.

18. Ibid., 146.

19. Qtd. in Huff, 297.

20. Peter Bogdanovich, *Who the Hell's in It: Conversations with Hollywood's Legendary Actors* (New York: Ballantine, 2005), 353.

21. Ibid.

22. Gerald Mast, *The Comic Mind: Comedy and the Movies,* 2nd ed. (Chicago: University of Chicago Press, 1979), 65; 66; 66; 66; 67; 67.

23. Graham Petrie, "So Much and Yet So Little: A Survey of Books on Chaplin," in *The Silent Comedians,* ed. Richard Dyer MacCann (Lanham, Md.: Scarecrow, 1993), 117; 119; 115–16. Originally published in *Quarterly Review of Film Studies* (November 1977).

24. Ibid., 116; 123.

25. Ibid., 118.

26. Mast, 65.

27. David Bordwell, Janet Staiger, and Kristin Thompson, *The Classical Hollywood Cinema: Film Style and Mode of Production to 1960* (New York: Columbia University Press, 1985), xiii, xiv.

28. Kristin Thompson, "The Stability of the Classical Approach After 1917," in Bordwell, Staiger, and Thompson, 233.

29. Raymond Williams, *Marxism and Literature* (Oxford: Oxford University Press, 1977), 122.

30. Robert B. Ray, *A Certain Tendency of the Hollywood Cinema, 1930–1980* (Princeton: Princeton University Press, 1985), 33.

31. Bazin, "The Evolution of the Language of Cinema," in his *What Is Cinema?* 1:36.

32. Raoul Sobel and David Francis, *Chaplin: Genesis of a Clown* (London: Quartet Books, 1977), 218.

33. Charlie Keil, *Early American Cinema in Transition: Story, Style, and Filmmaking, 1907–1913* (Madison: University of Wisconsin Press, 2001), 12.

34. Schickel, "Hail Chaplin—The Early Chaplin."

35. Ibid.

36. David Bordwell, "The Bounds of Difference," in Bordwell, Staiger, and Thompson, 78.

37. Gilles Deleuze, *Cinema 2: The Time-Image,* trans. Hugh Tomlinson and Robert Galeta (1989; London: Continuum, 2005), xi.

38. Qtd. in Gilbert Seldes, *The Seven Lively Arts* (New York: Harper and Row, 1924), 361; emphasis in original.

39. Louis Delluc, *Charlie Chaplin,* trans. Hamish Miles (London: Bodley Head, 1922), 95.

40. Jean Mitry, *The Aesthetics and Psychology of the Cinema,* trans. Christopher King (Bloomington: Indiana University Press, 2000), 2–3.

41. Ibid., 357.

42. Deleuze himself can sometimes downplay the periodizing function of his theory, stating explicitly in the preface to the French edition of *Cinema 1* that "this study is not a history of the cinema." Rather, it is something more ahistorical—"a taxonomy, an attempt at the classification of images and signs." Deleuze's primary interest in *Cinema 1* and *Cinema 2* is a kind of cataloging and categorization of the conceptual framework on which he believes the cinema to operate. "The great directors of the cinema," he writes in the same preface, "may be compared . . . with thinkers. They think with movement-images and time-images instead of concepts" and the whole of both books might be considered an attempt "to isolate certain cinematographic concepts." Yet Deleuze also openly acknowledges the degree to which his taxonomy of filmic concepts broadly aligns to concepts of the classical and postclassical in film history, referring in the preface to the English edition to "the classical cinema of the movement-image" and the "modern cinema of the time-image." Deleuze takes Hitchcock as the fissure point between the two, a filmmaker who stands "at the juncture of the two cinemas, the classical that he perfects and the modern that he prepares." See Deleuze, *Cinema 1: The Movement-Image,* trans. Hugh Tomlinson and Barbara Habberjam (Minneapolis: University of Minnesota Press, 1986), xiv, ix, x.

43. Deleuze, *Cinema 1,* 22.

44. Ibid., 153, 171.

45. Éric Rohmer, *The Taste for Beauty,* trans. Carol Volk (Cambridge, U.K.: Cambridge University Press, 1989), 22–23.

46. Bazin, "The Virtues and Limitations of Montage," in his *What Is Cinema?* 1:50.

47. Ibid., 52.

48. J. Dudley Andrew, *The Major Film Theories: An Introduction* (Oxford: Oxford University Press, 1976), 166.

49. Carl Davis, qtd. in Vance, 348.

50. See Victor Saville, unpublished manuscript, 27. Victor Saville Collection, British Film Institute.

51. Vance, 56.

52. François Truffaut, *The Films in My Life,* trans. Leonard Mayhew (1978; Cambridge, Mass.: Da Capo, 1994), 61.

Chapter 1

1. Following David Robinson, most accounts take *Twenty Minutes of Love* as Chaplin's first turn behind the camera, though it is important to note the controversy around this film. In *My Autobiography,* written fifty years after he had left Keystone, Chaplin lists the later short *Caught in the Rain* (Keystone, 1914) as his first directorial effort, and studio records officially list a little-known figure named Joseph Maddern as

the director for *Twenty Minutes of Love*. However, in a letter to his half brother Sydney from later in 1914, discovered by Robinson in Chaplin's archives, Chaplin referred to *Twenty Minutes* as the first film that he could call "my own." He repeated a similar claim in an article in *Adelphi* from 1924. In all likelihood, Maddern had a mostly supervisory role on the film, essentially shepherding Chaplin into the beginning of his directorial career. Maddern was a relatively marginal figure at Keystone—a no-frills technician who worked there only briefly, mostly directing educational subjects rather than comedy shorts. Chaplin was a rising star, already one of the company's most popular performers after only a few months on the job and openly eager to begin directing his own work. In James L. Neibaur's account, the pairing was a pragmatic one orchestrated by Keystone founder and impresario Mack Sennett: "Not wanting the resulting film to be unreleasable due to the possibility of Chaplin's not fully understanding the filmmaking process, Sennett chose to assign a nominal director like Maddern, who would comfortably take orders and allow Chaplin as much creative input as he desired. . . . Maddern was a veritable traffic cop . . . chiefly there to make sure things moved along, on budget and on time, and a releasable film was ready when expected." In line with the information that has come to light about the film and about the likely production processes behind it, treating *Twenty Minutes of Love* as essentially Chaplin's own has become standard convention. See David Robinson, *Chaplin: His Life and Art* (New York: McGraw-Hill, 1985), 121; Charles Chaplin, "Does the Public Know What It Wants?" *Adelphi* 1, no. 8 (January 1924): 702; James L. Neibaur, *Early Charlie Chaplin: The Artist as Apprentice at Keystone Studios* (Lanham, Md.: Scarecrow Press, 2012), 63.

2. Technically, *Kid Auto Races at Venice,* released on February 7, 1914, was the first short released to the public in which the Tramp appeared. Chaplin first developed the role for a bit part in Henry Lehrman and Mack Sennett's short *Mabel's Strange Predicament,* which was filmed earlier than *Kid Auto Races* but released two days after it on February 9, 1914.

3. Ted Okuda and David Maska, *Charlie Chaplin at Keystone and Essanay: Dawn of the Tramp* (Lincoln, Neb.: iUniverse, 2005), 67.

4. The story of the confrontation with Sennett is sometimes attached to Chaplin's second directorial effort, *Caught in a Cabaret* (Keystone, 1914). However, in line with the primary status now given to *Twenty Minutes of Love,* most commentators connect the dispute to the impetus behind that film. See, for example, Joyce Milton, *Tramp: The Life of Charlie Chaplin* (New York: HarperCollins, 1996), 69; and Vance, 34.

5. Cook, 13; emphasis in original.

6. See André Gaudreault and Tom Gunning, "Le Cinéma des premier temps: Un défi a histoire du film?" in *Histoire du cinema: Nouvelles approches,* ed. J. Aumont, A. Gaudreault, and M. Marie (Paris: Publications de la Sorbonne, 1989), 49–63.

7. See Marshall Deutelbaum, "Structural Patterning in the Lumière Films," in *Film Before Griffith,* ed. John L. Fell (Berkeley: University of California Press, 1983), 299–310; and André Gaudreault, "Film, Narrative, Narration: The Cinema of the Lumière Brothers," in *Early Cinema: Space, Frame, Narrative,* ed. Thomas Elsaesser (London: British Film Institute, 1984), 68–75.

8. John Fell explores the connection between the development of the cartoon strip and the development of narrative film in depth in a chapter titled "Mr. Griffith, Meet Windsor McCay." See John L. Fell, *Film and the Narrative Tradition* (Norman: University of Oklahoma Press, 1974).

9. Charles Musser, *The Emergence of Cinema: The American Screen to 1907* (New York: Scribner's, 1990), 335.

10. See Thompson, "From Primitive to Classical," in Bordwell, Staiger, and Thompson; see also Robert C. Allen, "Contra the Chaser Theory," *Wide Angle* 3, no. 1 (1979): 4–11; Charles Musser, "Another Look at the 'Chaser Theory,'" *Studies in Visual Communication* 10, no. 4 (1984): 24–44; and Robert C. Allen, "Looking at 'Another Look at the "Chaser Theory,"'" *Studies in Visual Communication* 10, no. 4 (1984): 45–50.

11. André Gaudreault, "Temporality and Narrativity in Early Cinema, 1895–1908," in *Film Before Griffith,* ed. John L. Fell (Berkeley: University of California Press, 1983), 322.

12. *Billboard,* March 16, 1907, 32.

13. In Charlie Keil's words, "Knowledge of the industry's structure permits us to see how filmmakers operated within an atmosphere of sustained competition. In this context, companies attempted to attain a level of quality in order to promote name recognition, such as that established early on by the most dominant American manufacturers of the period, especially Biograph and Vitagraph." See Keil, 12.

14. Charles Musser, "The Nickelodeon Era Begins: Establishing the Framework for Hollywood's Mode of Representation," *Framework,* nos. 22/23 (Autumn 1983): 4.

15. See John L. Fell, *A History of Films* (New York: Holt, Rinehart and Winston, 1979); André Gaudreault, "Detours in Film Narrative: The Development of Cross-Cutting," *Cinema Journal* 19 (Fall 1979): 39–59; and Barry Salt, "Film Form, 1900–1906," *Sight and Sound* 47 (Summer 1978): 148–53.

16. Thompson, "From Primitive to Classical," 159.

17. Keil, 12, 11.

18. Tom Gunning, "I film Vitagraph e il cinema dell'integrazione narrativa," in *Vitagraph Co. of America: Il cinema prima di Hollywood,* ed. Paolo Cherchi Usai (Pordenone, Italy: Edizioni Studio Tesi, 1987), 231–32.

19. Keil, 12. In fact, Thompson argues that we should extend the "transitionary phase" itself from around 1909 through to 1916. (See Thompson, "Formulation," 159.) Keil, however, makes a compelling case that there is a fundamental distinction between the filmmaking work in the years immediately before 1913, when American cinema was marked by extensive experimentation with new techniques, and those immediately after 1913, which represent for him a process of consolidation of techniques rather than new experimentations.

20. Barry Salt, "The Early Development of Film Form," in *Film Before Griffith,* ed. John L. Fell (Berkeley: University of California Press, 1983), 284.

21. Ibid., 285.

22. Keil is particularly adamant about the important insight that trade press publications give us into the mentalities of the early film industry, as they commented on and judged filmmaking trends not for the general public but for an audience of studio heads, directors, actors, and scenarists. In his words: "The trade press played a signal role in aiding filmmakers to develop solutions to their problems. . . . If we understand trade press reaction in terms of feedback, it helps amplify our sense of how filmmakers continued to craft solutions to the problems posed by more complex narratives." See Keil, 29.

23. David S. Hulfish, "Art in Moving Pictures," *Nickelodeon,* May 1909.

24. "Too Near the Camera," *Moving Picture World,* March 25, 1911; "On Filming a Classic," *Nickelodeon,* January 7, 1911.

25. Epes Winthrop Sargent, "The Photoplaywright: Scenes and Leaders," *Moving Picture World,* August 10, 1912.

26. Tom Gunning, "Non-Continuity, Continuity, Discontinuity: A Theory of Genres in Early Films," *Iris* 2, no. 1 (1984): 105.

27. Precursors to the chase films of the transitionary period lie in Williamson's *Stop Thief!* and others of the early 1900s like Frank S. Mottershaw's *A Daring Daylight Burglary* (Sheffield, 1903) and Walter Haggar's *A Desperate Poaching Affray* (Haggar and Sons, 1903). By 1904 the genre had become, in Gunning's words, "one of the staples of international cinema." See Tom Gunning, *D. W. Griffith and the Origins of American Narrative Film: The Early Years at Biograph* (Chicago: University of Illinois Press, 1991), 67.

28. Gunning, *D. W. Griffith and the Origins of American Narrative Film,* 67.

29. Ibid.

30. Keil, 86.

31. Gunning, *D. W. Griffith and the Origins of American Narrative Film,* 68.

32. Ibid., 65.

33. This last point would become a typical Griffith trope and would frequently take on an overtly religious valence. Its clearest expression may come in the publicity material for *Corner in Wheat* (Biograph, 1909), a short which introduces a situation of injustice only to resolve that injustice through a fatal accident rather than the action of the characters themselves: "There is no vengeance possible here but the hand of God." See Eileen Bowser, ed., *Biograph Bulletins, 1908–1912* (New York: Farrar, Straus and Giroux, 1973), 150.

34. "Technique of the Photoplay," *Moving Picture World,* July 22, 1911. This is, of course, essentially Chaplin's solution in *Twenty Minutes of Love.*

35. David Bordwell, *On the History of Film Style* (Cambridge, Mass.: Harvard University Press, 1997), 198.

36. Ibid., 185.

37. Ibid.

38. Unsigned review of *Uncle's Birthday Gift, Nickelodeon* 5, no. 4 (January 28, 1911): 110.

39. For all of its obvious limitations, it was a notably popular device, particularly with Biograph and Vitagraph films. Examples include *Ben Hur* (Kalem, 1907), *Deaf-Mutes' Masquerade* (Biograph, 1907), *At the French Ball* (Biograph, 1907), *Man in the Box* (Biograph, 1908), *The Black Viper* (Biograph, 1908), *Oliver Twist* (Vitagraph, 1909), *Romance of the Umbrella* (Vitagraph, 1909), and *Hiawatha* (IMP, 1909).

40. Keil, 108.

41. Ibid., 105.

42. Ibid., 109.

43. Ibid., 107.

44. Sergei Eisenstein, "Dickens, Griffith, and the Film Today," in his *Film Form: Essays in Film Theory,* trans. and ed. Jay Leyda (Orlando: Harcourt, 1949), 200. We may surmise, of course, that Eisenstein's story is more apocryphal than historical, though it has entered into the lore of film history almost as fact.

45. Gunning, *D. W. Griffith and the Origins of American Narrative Film,* 42–43.

46. Eisenstein, *Film Form,* 200.

47. Keil offers a comparison of the average number of shots per thousand-foot reel between Griffith's Biograph shorts and those of other studios of the era. In 1913, the

year of *The Mothering Heart,* Griffith averaged 87.8 shots per reel, with 52 shots per reel being the average at other studios. Early years showed ever greater disparities, peaking in 1911 with a Griffith average of 71.4 versus a studio average of 24.1. See Keil, 173.

48. Tom Gunning, "Early American Film," in *The Oxford Guide to Film Studies,* ed. John Hill and Pamela Church Gibson (New York: Oxford University Press, 1998), 266.

49. Roger Ebert, "The Birth of a Nation," Rogerebert.com, *Chicago Sun-Times,* March 30, 2003, http://rogerebert.suntimes.com. Griffith's supposed atonement would begin early, for there was no shortage of controversy at the film's debut. Protests led by the National Association for the Advancement of Colored People met premieres of the film in many cities, with riots breaking out in Boston and Philadelphia. Griffith, improbably, pleaded ignorance of the depth of racism in the film, claiming in an intertitle that "This is an historical presentation of the Civil War and Reconstruction Period, and is not meant to reflect on any race or people of today." Yet Griffith clearly felt compelled to cleanse himself in some way of the film. His next effort, *Intolerance* (Wark, 1916), would be widely regarded as what Ebert calls "an attempt at an apology," and his 1919 film *Broken Blossoms* (United Artists), though deeply problematic in its own right, would depict in a positive light the first interracial love affair on film. Griffith even attempted at one point to create a version of *The Birth of a Nation* cutting out all the scenes of the Ku Klux Klan, all but eviscerating the narrative he originally meant to tell. Melvyn Stokes provides an excellent consideration of the history and legacy in *D. W. Griffith's "The Birth of a Nation": A History of "The Most Controversial Motion Picture of All Time"* (New York: Oxford University Press, 2007). See *The Birth of a Nation,* directed by D. W. Griffith (1915; New York: Kino International, 2002), DVD; Ebert, "The Birth of a Nation." All subsequent quotations from *The Birth of a Nation* are from this release of the film.

50. Salt, in comparing *The Birth of a Nation* to the technical experiments in earlier non-Griffith shorts of the era, is explicit on this point: "Generally, compared with the films we have been discussing, D. W. Griffith's *Birth of a Nation* is technically retarded, though of course other qualities outside our concern at the moment compensate as far as its absolute aesthetic value is in question. In the two hours of this film's duration there is not one use of a subjective shot or more generally of the angle-reverse angle combination, even in scenes crying out for these devices such as Flora Cameron's pursuit by the negro and leap from the cliff. Always the camera moves straight in from the established 'audience' side for closer shots. And there are not very many closer shots compared to the usage in the films previously mentioned. Cuts on action are almost completely absent as well, and of course all this still stems from Griffith's technique of using varied improvisation on each take. These features would tend to produce a very slow moving film but for the well-known feature of Griffith's style, the cross-cutting between parallel actions. This produces a series of very strong cuts between shots which propel the film forward and compensates for the relatively static nature of the individual shots due to the distance of the actors from the camera and hence the small amount of movement within the frame." See Salt, "The Early Development of Film Form," 295.

51. *Intolerance,* directed by D. W. Griffith (1916; New York: Kino International, 2002), DVD. All subsequent quotations from *Intolerance* are from this release of the film.

52. This kind of move in Griffith's visual style has traditionally been regarded as a manifestation of his shift away from a theatrically motivated visuality and conception of space, as seen in many other shorts of the transitional period and before. But

Noël Burch offers a powerful revision of this idea, figuring Griffith's abstraction from theatrical space as a compensation for the silent cinema's muting of theatrical dialogue and the opportunities for characterization and thematization it affords: "It is not until the system of narrative editing, with its close-ups, matching devices, etc., was fully developed that it became possible to recover the theatre's power of characterization, personalization, etc. Paradoxically it is for the development of this system that Griffith is celebrated as the man who brought cinema out of the theatrical stage!" See Noël Burch, *To the Distant Observer: Form and Meaning in the Japanese Cinema,* rev. and ed. Annette Michelson (Berkeley: University of California Press, 1979), 76.

53. Lillian Gish recounted of the film, "Its depiction of German brutality bordered on the absurd. Whenever a German came near me, he beat me or kicked me." Lillian Gish, with Ann Pinchot, *The Movies, Mr. Griffith, and Me* (Upper Saddle River, N.J.: Prentice-Hall, 1969), 201.

54. Indeed, Joyce E. Jesionowski argues that questions of proximity are a core component of Griffith's general methodology of building suspense: "The question of 'where' is a major dramatic issue in Griffith's films (how close is the villain? how near is the hero?) and one that finds expression specifically in terms of composition, shot order, and the direction of activity through the world of the film. The audience may not know the exact location in terms of city streets, but has a very clear sense of where in the film characters are located with respect to each other." See Joyce E. Jesionowski, *Thinking in Pictures: Dramatic Structure in D. W. Griffith's Biograph Films* (Berkeley: University of California Press, 1987), 179.

55. Gunning, *D. W. Griffith and the Origins of American Narrative Film,* 26.

56. Ibid., 292.

57. Ray, 32.

58. Ibid., 32–33.

59. Jesionowski, 184.

60. Ibid., 2, 5.

61. Stanley Cavell, *The World Viewed: Reflections on the Ontology of Film,* rev. ed. (1971; Cambridge, Mass.: Harvard University Press, 1979), 25; emphasis in original.

62. Ibid., 101–2.

63. James Agee, *Agee on Film* (New York: Putnam, 1983), 1:311.

64. Jean-Luc Godard, *Godard on Godard,* trans. Tom Milne (New York: Viking, 1972), 135.

65. Harry Carr, "Chaplin Explains Chaplin," *Motion Picture Magazine* 30 (November 1925): 88.

Chapter 2

1. Richard Abel, "Guarding the Borders in Early Cinema: The Shifting Ground of French-American Relations," in *Celebrating 1895: The Centenary of Cinema,* ed. John Fullerton (Bloomington: Indiana University Press, 1998), 46.

2. Barry Salt, "D. W. Griffith Shapes Slapstick," in *Slapstick Comedy,* ed. Tom Paulus and Rob King (New York: Routledge, 2010), 37.

3. Don Fairservice, *Film Editing: History, Theory, and Practice* (Manchester, U.K.: Manchester University Press, 2001), 57.

4. Richard Abel, *The Ciné Goes to Town: French Cinema, 1896–1914* (Berkeley: University of California Press, 1998), 221.

5. Fairservice, 57.

6. Peter Krämer, "Vitagraph, Slapstick and Early Cinema," *Screen* 29, no. 2 (1988): 100.

7. Tom Paulus and Rob King, "Restoring Slapstick to the Historiography of American Film," in *Slapstick Comedy,* ed. Tom Paulus and Rob King (New York: Routledge, 2010), 6–7.

8. David Bordwell, *Narration in the Fiction Film* (Madison: University of Wisconsin Press, 1985), 280, 61.

9. Kristin Thompson, "The Concept of Cinematic Excess," *Cine-Tracts* 1 (Summer 1977): 55–56; David Bordwell and Kristin Thompson, *Film Art: An Introduction* (New York: Knopf, 1986), 142–46.

10. Henry Jenkins, *What Made Pistachio Nuts? Early Sound Comedy and the Vaudeville Aesthetic* (New York: Columbia University Press, 1992), 97.

11. It would, for one, inspire the Russian novelist Andrei Bely to muse on the new power of the cinema that "man is a cloud of smoke. He catches a cold, he sneezes and bursts; . . . the cinematograph has crossed the borders of reality. More than the preachings of scholars and wise men, this has demonstrated to everyone what reality is: it is a lady suffering from a cold who sneezes and explodes." Qtd. in Yuri Tsivian, *Early Russian Cinema and Its Cultural Reception* (London: Routledge, 1994), 151.

12. Keil, 86.

13. Gunning, *D. W. Griffith and the Origins of American Narrative Film,* 67.

14. For variations on this argument across the decades see Salt ("he was a man lacking a real comic touch"), Walter Kerr ("he hated slapstick and all of its relatives"), and Mast ("Sennett claimed that Griffith cared very little about comedy, and the artistic carelessness of many of the Griffith Biograph comedies supports the claim"). See Salt, "D. W. Griffith Shapes Slapstick," 37; Walter Kerr, *The Silent Clowns* (New York: Knopf, 1975), 58; Mast, 45.

15. Kerr, *Silent Clowns,* 58, 59–60.

16. Salt, "D. W. Griffith Shapes Slapstick," 37–38. Salt somewhat overstates the case for Griffith's unrecognized comedic innovations. Though Griffith's contributions to film comedy figure marginally if at all in most major studies of his work, certain film historians—and particularly those of slapstick comedy—have been more adamant in acknowledging and understanding his influence. Beyond Kerr, Gunning makes a case that a work like Griffith's *The Curtain Pole* "seems to predict the future of American film comedy." Moreover, one of the tenets of Paulus and King's essay "Restoring Slapstick to the Historiography of American Film," their introduction to the collection in which Salt's essay appears, is that studies in slapstick must take greater account of "the history of cinematic style and technique," particularly an examination of "how D. W. Griffith's innovations in dramatic filmmaking provided a framework within which filmmakers like Mack Sennett elaborated new formal directions for American comic cinema." See Gunning, *D. W. Griffith and the Origins of American Narrative Film,* 132; Paulus and King, 10.

17. Mack Sennett, with Cameron Shipp, *King of Comedy* (1954; Charlotte, N.C.: Baker and Taylor / Textstream, 2000), 151.

18. Salt, "D. W. Griffith Shapes Slapstick," 38.

19. Ibid., 41.

20. Donald Crafton, "Pie and Chase: Gag, Spectacle and Narrative in Slapstick Comedy," in *Classical Hollywood Comedy,* ed. Kristine Brunovska Karnick and Henry Jenkins (New York: Routledge, 1995), 107.

21. Tom Gunning, "Crazy Machines in the Garden of Forking Paths: Mischief Gags and the Origins of American Film Comedy," in *Classical Hollywood Comedy,* ed. Kristine Brunovska Karnick and Henry Jenkins (New York: Routledge,1995), 89.

22. Noël Carroll, "Notes on the Sight Gag," in *Comedy/Cinema/Theory,* ed. Andrew Horton (Berkeley: University of California Press, 1991), 26–27. For a general overview of theories of humor and particularly the place of humor in the history of philosophy, see Peter L. Berger, *Redeeming Laughter: The Comic Dimension of Human Experience* (Berlin: Walter de Gruyter, 1997). Lisa Trahair connects this history directly to the study of slapstick in *The Comedy of Philosophy: Sense and Nonsense in Early Cinematic Slapstick* (Albany: State University of New York Press, 2007).

23. Carroll, 26.

24. Crafton, "Pie and Chase," 107. Though Crafton's essay holds a certain pride of place in slapstick studies, others have made a similar case. Eileen Bowser positions slapstick as generically distinct from other forms on the basis of the gag in *The Transformation of Cinema* (Berkeley: University of California Press, 1994), also based on a paper she delivered at the MoMA Slapstick Symposium. Though Tom Gunning has published a response to certain points in Crafton's essay, he has also spoken to the unique nature of the gag in the history of film comedy in "Crazy Machines in the Garden of Forking Paths: Mischief Gags and the Origins of American Film Comedy," collected with Crafton's essay and Gunning's response to it in *Classical Hollywood Comedy.* Henry Jenkins also presents a similar argument in his history of the gag in *What Made Pistachio Nuts?*

25. Crafton, "Pie and Chase," 116, 117.

26. Ibid., 111.

27. Mast, 38.

28. See Paul Woodruff, *The Necessity of Theatre: The Art of Watching and Being Watched* (Oxford: Oxford University Press, 2008).

29. In Sergei Eisenstein's words: "The art of cinematography is not in selecting a fanciful framing, or in taking something from a surprising camera-angle. The art is in every fragment of a film being an organic part of an organically conceived whole. With such organically thought-out and photographed parts of one large significant and general conception, these must be segments of some whole." See Sergei Eisenstein, "A Course in Treatment," in his *Film Form,* 92.

30. See Tom Gunning, " 'Now You See It, Now You Don't': The Temporality of the Cinema of Attractions," *Velvet Light Trap* 32 (Fall 1993): 3–12.

31. Mack Sennett, "The Psychology of Film Comedy," in *The Silent Comedians,* ed. Richard Dyer MacCann (Lanham, Md.: Scarecrow Press, 1993), 52.

32. Carroll, 26.

33. Alan Dale, *Comedy Is a Man in Trouble: Slapstick in American Movies* (Minneapolis: University of Minnesota Press, 2000), 3.

34. Ibid., 4, 3.

35. Alex Clayton, *The Body in Hollywood Slapstick* (Jefferson, N.C.: McFarland, 2007), 13.

36. James Agee, "Comedy's Greatest Era," *Life,* September 3, 1949.

37. It is, in this way, a not-too-distant cousin of certain other semi-anomalous narrative forms like the musical, as Crafton and Gunning both observe. There, the spectacle of the dancing body and even the singing body take on an interest and significance that can be extracted from their larger narrative context, although where

slapstick finds indignity and degradation in the body the musical arguably finds in it dignity and splendor. One might also include here later genres like the martial arts film, where the spectacle of bodies in artful combat takes on a significance above and beyond its narrative moment. Robert Knopf even makes a case in *The Theatre and Cinema of Buster Keaton* (Princeton: Princeton University Press, 1999) for the modern martial arts film, particularly the work of Jackie Chan, as a direct derivative of Keaton's work.

38. George Wead, *Buster Keaton and the Dynamics of Visual Wit* (New York: Arno, 1976), 307.

39. Henri Bergson, "Laughter," in *Comedy,* ed. Wylie Sypher, trans. Fred Rothwell (Baltimore: Johns Hopkins University Press, 1991), 79.

40. Ibid., 92.

41. Ibid., 78.

42. Walter Benjamin, *Selected Writings,* ed. Marcus Bullock and Michael W. Jennings, 4 vols. (Cambridge, Mass.: Belknap Press of Harvard University Press, 1996–2003), 3:94.

43. Michael North, *Machine-Age Comedy* (Oxford: Oxford University Press, 2009), 3.

44. Ibid., 5.

45. Rob King, "Uproarious Inventions: The Keystone Film Company, Modernity, and the Art of the Motor," in *Slapstick Comedy,* ed. Tom Paulus and Rob King (New York: Routledge, 2010), 115.

46. Eileen Bowser, "Mack Sennett vs. Henry Ford," in *Slapstick Comedy,* ed. Tom Paulus and Rob King (New York: Routledge, 2010), 107.

47. Sennett, "The Psychology of Film Comedy," 51.

48. Kerr, *Silent Clowns,* 70.

49. Gunning, *D. W. Griffith and the Origins of American Narrative Film,* 42, 204.

50. Simon Joyce, "Genre Parody and Comedic Burlesque: Keystone's Meta-Cinematic Satires," in *Slapstick Comedy,* ed. Tom Paulus and Rob King (New York: Routledge, 2010), 54.

51. Agee, "Comedy's Greatest Era."

52. Mast, 57.

53. Kerr, *Silent Clowns,* 270.

54. Mast, 165; Richard Dyer MacCann, "Lloyd and Langdon," in *The Silent Comedians,* ed. Richard Dyer MacCann (Lanham, Md.: Scarecrow Press, 1993), 194.

55. Qtd. in Mast, 169.

56. "Brought into Focus," *New York Times,* April 17, 1921.

57. Rob King, *The Fun Factory: The Keystone Film Company and the Emergence of Mass Culture* (Berkeley: University of California Press, 2009), 132.

58. Ibid., 249.

59. Sennett, *King of Comedy,* 29.

60. James R. Quirk, "Mabel Normand," *Photoplay,* August 1915, 41.

61. "Short Comedies Wanted," *Photoplay,* June 1915, 131.

62. Thompson, "From Primitive to Classical," 161.

63. Jenkins, 97.

64. Some of the textbooks in question include Bordwell and Thompson's *Film Art,* 9th edition (McGraw-Hill, 2009), Louis Giannetti's *Understanding Movies,* 12th edition (Allyn and Bacon, 2010), and David A. Cook's *History of Narrative Film,* 4th edition (W. W. Norton, 2003). Such straightforward designations of *The General* are highly

problematic, as will be discussed in chapter 3, but they are not unreasonable. *The General*, like all of Keaton's work, is actively in dialogue with classical technique, even if it is not always a perfect example of classical style.

65. Bryony Dixon, "The Good Thieves: On the Origins of Situation Comedy in the British Music Hall," in *Slapstick Comedy*, ed. Tom Paulus and Rob King (New York: Routledge, 2010), 22–23.

66. Ibid., 22.

67. Knopf, 82.

68. Lupino Lane, *How to Become a Comedian* (London: F. Muller, 1945).

69. David Madden, *Harlequin's Stick, Charlie's Cane: A Comparative Study of Commedia dell'arte and Silent Slapstick Comedy* (Madison: University of Wisconsin Press / Popular Press, 1975), 72.

70. Dixon, 23.

71. Knopf, 82.

72. Ibid.; Perez, 101.

Chapter 3

1. Harry C. Carr, "Charlie Chaplin's Story, Part I," *Photoplay*, July 1915.

2. Harry C. Carr, "Charlie Chaplin's Story, Part II," *Photoplay*, August 1915.

3. Harry C. Carr, "Charlie Chaplin's Story, Part IV," *Photoplay*, October 1915.

4. Agee, "Comedy's Greatest Era."

5. Frank Krutnik, "A Spanner in the Works? Genre, Narrative and the Hollywood Comedian," in *Classical Hollywood Comedy*, ed. Kristine Brunovska Karnick and Henry Jenkins (New York: Routledge, 1995), 17.

6. Ibid.

7. Ibid.

8. Marc Wanamaker, *Beverly Hills: 1930–2005* (Charleston, S.C.: Arcadia, 2006), 76.

9. Lloyd's greatest accomplishment before entering the world of film was some eighteen roles that he played between 1912 and 1913 in productions at the San Diego School of Expression, where he also taught acting.

10. Although Lloyd's rise to stardom came well after Chaplin's, Lloyd was actually the first of the great silent clowns to appear on screen: even before his adventures at Keystone, he was cast as an extra—a Yaqui Indian—in a short titled *The Old Monk's Tale* (Edison, 1913).

11. Harold Lloyd, with Wesley Winans Stout, *An American Comedy* (Mineola, N.Y.: Dover, 1971), 127, 128.

12. Qtd. in Kerr, *The Silent Clowns*, 108.

13. Qtd. in Kevin Brownlow, *The Parade's Gone By . . .* (Berkeley: University of California Press, 1968), 460.

14. Ibid.

15. Lloyd, 107.

16. Dale, 69.

17. Lloyd, 59.

18. See Kerr, *Silent Clowns*, 206. For direction of his works, Lloyd relied initially on Roach and then on the directing pairs of Fred Newmeyer / Sam Taylor and Ted Wilde / J. A. Howe.

19. Dale, 66–67. What is surprising, Dale notes, is "that there's only one feature in which Harold has to overcome the objections of the girl's father," evidence perhaps of

the degree to which the romantic plot of Lloyd's films is just a cover for a story of self-improvement. See Dale, 66.

20. Kerr, *Silent Clowns,* 196.

21. See Crafton, "Pie and Chase."

22. The "human fly" was a rarefied but not unheard-of profession in the era. Bill Strother, who plays "The Pal" in *Safety Last,* was in fact not an actor but a professional "human fly."

23. Mast, 160n.

24. Mast, 9; emphasis in original.

25. *Safety Last,* directed by Fred Newmeyer and Sam Taylor (1923; New York: New Line Home Entertainment, 2005), DVD.

26. In fact, Lloyd and his crew tried to film the football sequence first when shooting the film but found that they couldn't make it work until after they had completed the earlier scenes, so they would know how the sequence would connect to the rest of the story. The football game, filmed largely during breaks in an actual University of California Berkeley–Stanford game at Pasadena Stadium, would end up being the last sequence that they shot before wrapping production. See Lloyd, 127.

27. Crafton, "Pie and Chase," 116, 117.

28. See, for example, David Bordwell, *The Way Hollywood Tells It: Story and Style in Modern Movies* (Berkeley: University of California Press, 2006); Kristin Thompson, *Breaking the Glass Armor: Neoformalist Film Analysis* (Princeton: Princeton University Press, 1988); Donald McCaffrey, *4 Great Comedians: Chaplin, Lloyd, Keaton, Langdon* (London: Zwemmer, 1968); and Daniel Moews, *Buster Keaton: The Silent Features Close Up* (Berkeley: University of California Press, 1977).

29. Mast, 131.

30. Kerr, *Silent Clowns,* 118.

31. Buster Keaton, with Charles Samuels, *My Wonderful World of Slapstick* (New York: Da Capo, 1960), 93.

32. Ibid.

33. Kerr, *Silent Clowns,* 127.

34. Knopf, 6.

35. Kerr, *Silent Clowns,* 127.

36. Steve Massa, "Rediscovering Roscoe: The Careers of 'Fatty' Arbuckle," program notes, Museum of Modern Art (April 20–May 15, 2006).

37. Keaton, 12.

38. Keaton's father would, at various points, try to avert the prohibitions of the society by claiming that Buster was not his son but a talented midget performer or, as Buster continued to grow, conspiring with vaudeville producers to add years to the boy's age. For a detailed look at Keaton's young vaudeville career and the family dynamics it entailed see Knopf, *The Theatre and Cinema of Buster Keaton.*

39. Keaton, 13.

40. Qtd. in Dale, 78.

41. Moews, 2.

42. Ibid., 14.

43. Luis Buñuel, "Buster Keaton's *College,*" in *The Shadow and Its Shadow: Surrealist Writings on the Cinema,* 3rd ed., ed. and trans. Paul Hammond (San Francisco: City Lights, 2000), 62.

44. Keaton, 207.

Chapter 4

1. Robert Nichols, "Future of the Cinema: Mr. Charles Chaplin," *Times* (London), September 3, 1925.

2. Ibid.

3. Ibid.

4. Gunning, *D. W. Griffith and the Origins of American Narrative Film,* 25.

5. David Bordwell, *Narration in the Fiction Film,* 164.

6. Cavell, 104.

7. One of the most comprehensive accounts of this ascendancy can be found in Charles J. Maland, *Chaplin and American Culture: The Evolution of a Star Image* (Princeton: Princeton University Press, 1991).

8. Unsigned review of *A Woman of Paris,* directed by Charles Chaplin, *Photoplay,* December 1923; and Barr, qtd. in Richard Roud, *A Passion for Films: Henri Langlois and the Cinémathèque Française* (New York: Viking, 1983), 33.

9. Harcourt Farmer, "Is the Charlie Chaplin Vogue Passing?" *Theatre Magazine,* October 1919.

10. George Jean Nathan, *Passing Judgments* (New York: Knopf, 1934), 210.

11. David Bordwell, *On the History of Film Style* (Cambridge, Mass.: Harvard University Press, 1997), 9.

12. Ibid., 34.

13. Ibid., 33.

14. Sergei Eisenstein, "The Cinematographic Principle and the Ideogram," in his *Film Form,* 28.

15. Mitry, 2.

16. Charles Chaplin, *My Autobiography* (New York: Simon and Schuster, 1964), 255.

17. Rudolf Arnheim, *Film as Art* (1933; rpt. Los Angeles: University of California Press, 1979), 151.

18. Béla Balázs, *Theory of the Film: Character and Growth of a New Art,* trans. Edith Bone (1952; rpt. New York: Dover, 1970), 26; emphasis in original.

19. Wes D. Gehring, *Charlie Chaplin: A Bio-Bibliography* (Westport, Conn.: Greenwood Press, 1983), 82.

20. Chaplin, *My Autobiography,* 255.

21. See Kenneth S. Lynn, *Charlie Chaplin and His Times* (New York: Simon and Schuster, 1997), 100.

22. Chaplin imitation was both a mass cultural phenomenon and a lucrative subindustry in the 1910s and 1920s, part and parcel of Chaplin's overwhelming rise to fame. Charles J. Maland offers an account of the Chaplin imitation phenomenon in *Chaplin and American Culture: The Evolution of a Star Image,* as does Jennifer M. Bean in "The Art of Imitation: The Originality of Charlie Chaplin and Other Moving-Image Myths," in *Slapstick Comedy,* ed. Tom Paulus and Rob King (New York: Routledge, 2010), 236–61.

23. Louis Delluc, "Max Linder's and Elsie Codd's Views on the Working Method," trans. Hamish Miles, in *Focus on Chaplin,* ed. Donald W. McCaffrey (Englewood Cliffs, N.J.: Prentice-Hall, 1971), 58.

24. Thompson, "From Primitive to Classical," 159.

25. As a side note to issues of style, it is remarkable the degree to which the universe of references in Chaplin's films is tied to the cinema of the preclassical era. His 1916 Essanay short *Burlesque on Carmen,* for instance, contains a classic front-and-back of

the gate sequence, a visual quote from very early attempts to navigate the use of multiple spaces on camera from films like *Ben Hur* in 1907 and *The Last Cartridge* in 1908. *Police* (Essanay, 1916) essentially replicates, in slapstick form, the burglary and rescue motif of Griffith's Biograph short *The Lonely Villa* from 1909, which Sennett himself parodied directly in *Help! Help!* in 1912 while he too was still at Biograph. Similarly, a classic Mutual short like *The Vagabond* (1916) seems both to quote from and provide an alternate continuation for the story line of Griffith's influential 1908 chase film *The Adventures of Dollie,* wherein a young girl is abducted from her wealthy family by a band of traveling gypsies; Edna Purviance might as well be playing the fully grown version of Dollie when the Tramp rescues her and returns her to her wealthy family through a series of chase sequences of his own. Even a short as late as *A Dog's Life* (First National, 1918) ends with what appears to be a direct visual quotation from Griffith's 1909 *Corner in Wheat,* when the Tramp suddenly becomes a farmer working alone in his well-tilled fields with costume and shot composition to match Griffith's iconic image of the agrarian laborer alone.

26. Thompson, "The Stability of the Classical Approach After 1917," 231.

27. Chaplin, *My Autobiography,* 254.

28. Ibid.

29. Ibid.

30. Gunning, *D. W. Griffith and the Origins of American Narrative Film,* 43.

31. Carr, "Charlie Chaplin's Story, Part IV."

32. Carr, "Chaplin Explains Chaplin."

33. Gunning, *D. W. Griffith and the Origins of American Narrative Film,* 40.

34. Bordwell, *On the History of Film Style,* 198, 158. As Bordwell notes, practices of staging in depth continued to be used with some regularity in Europe even after the consolidation of classical techniques in the United States, and on both continents elements of the technique could still be seen in select moments within more traditional classical constructions. "Historically," he writes, "they often functioned as flexible, nonexclusive options. Many directors synthesized the schemas available from continuity editing and from depth staging." See Bordwell, *On the History of Film Style,* 199.

35. Griffith himself would occasionally try to master narrative storytelling within individual shots of large crowds, as in the epic celebrations and battles in the Babylon portions of *Intolerance,* but the individual shots are remarkably hard to follow from a storytelling perspective beyond the most basic narrative communications: a celebration is occurring, people are fighting. Kerr is effusive on this point: "*Intolerance,* still called a masterwork by some though it seems to me a complete failure on its own terms, would be psychologically unintelligible if it were not for verbal signposts slapped in our faces every minute or oftener explaining just what is in the minds of certain ancient priests of Babylon, of a mountain girl who loves Belshazzar, of a Rhapsode who loves the mountain girl. We never do understand the intent of the conniving priests from anything they do on the screen; in fact, we scarcely recognize them from scene to scene. Here psychology has not been filmed, it has been interpolated." See Kerr, *Silent Clowns,* 46.

36. Nichols, "Future of the Cinema."

37. Chaplin, *My Autobiography,* 151.

38. In this manner, directors could maintain the shot-as-scene construction that was the standard mode of filmmaking at the time, but they could use individual rooms or exterior spaces to connote a change or development in the story—the rooms them-

selves essentially doing the work of the classical camera by subdividing the story into individual pieces. For more on the use of individuated spaces as a tool for narrative clarity in early cinema, see chapter 1.

39. *The Floorwalker,* directed by Charles Chaplin, on *The Chaplin Mutual Comedies* (1916; Los Angeles: Image Entertainment, 2006), DVD.

40. The comment, undocumented but often repeated, comes from an anecdote director Peter Bogdanovich tells during an interview with Orson Welles, transcribed in *This Is Orson Welles.* Bogdanovich recounts a performance in which "the director came up to Barrymore and said, 'There isn't any doubt about it, Jack, you're still the greatest actor in the world.' Barrymore gave out one of those famous snorts. 'Don't give me that,' he said. 'There are only two great actors—Charles Chaplin and Orson Welles.'" See Welles and Bogdanovich, 35.

41. Kamin, 22.

42. Sennett, *King of Comedy,* 179.

43. Clayton, 27; emphasis in original.

44. Cavell, 37.

45. Bogdanovich, 353; emphasis in original.

46. Carr, "Chaplin Explains Chaplin," 33.

47. Tim Smith, "Watching You Watch *There Will Be Blood,*" *Observations on Film Art* (blog), February 14, 2011, http://www.davidbordwell.net.

48. Ibid.

49. Ibid.

50. Chaplin, *My Autobiography,* 255.

51. Sergei Eisenstein, "Word and Image," in *The Film Sense,* ed. and trans. Jay Leyda (Boston: Houghton Mifflin Harcourt, 1947), 28.

52. Ibid., 23.

53. Ibid., 24.

54. Ibid.

55. Ibid.

56. There is, at the same time, a more sinister motivating force behind Eisenstein's revision to his theory of montage, based in the Soviet government's growing disapproval of the formalism of the 1920s as elitist and counterrevolutionary. Bringing Chaplin into the fold of montage theory was a way to claim less formalist bona fides for the theory, and it did not hurt that the social messaging of Chaplin's films was generally well received in Russia.

57. References in this chapter are to the silent-era version of *The Gold Rush,* released in 1925. Chaplin reissued the film in 1942 with several significant changes, including, most prominently, the addition of a narrative track. While most definitive copies of the silent version were lost in the years after the reissue, filmmakers David Gill and Kevin Brownlow released a painstaking restoration in 1993 based on available prints and continuities. Readings of the 1925 film are based on this restoration, from the 2012 Criterion Collection release. Differences between the 1925 and 1942 versions of the film are discussed in more detail in chapter 8.

58. Qtd. in John McCabe, *Charlie Chaplin* (New York: Doubleday, 1978), 28.

59. According to one knowledgeable observer, fellow tumbler Dick Van Dyke, Laurel and Chaplin were perhaps the two greatest physical comedians ever to make films, though Van Dyke felt Laurel ultimately to be the superior craftsman: "Chaplin is great,

a genius, but with Chaplin I can always see the technique showing. Lord knows it's great technique, and I admire it very much—but with Stan the technique never shows. Never. And that to me is proof that he is a better craftsman than Chaplin." Qtd. in Al Kilgore and John McCabe, *Laurel and Hardy* (New York: Ballantine, 1976), 11.

60. Qtd. in McCabe, 29.

61. Delluc, "Max Linder's and Elsie Codd's Views on the Working Method," 61.

62. Ibid.

63. See Kamin, 97.

64. Delluc, "Max Linder's and Elsie Codd's Views on the Working Method," 55.

Chapter 5

1. Brian Taves, "Charlie Dearest," *Film Comment* (March–April 1988): 64.

2. Ibid., 63.

3. Ibid.

4. Ibid.

5. Ibid., 69.

6. Jack Spears, *Hollywood: The Golden Era* (New York: Castle Books, 1971), 247.

7. Deleuze, *Cinema 1,* 153.

8. Bazin, "The Virtues and Limitations of Montage," 50.

9. Ibid.

10. Bazin, "Charlie Chaplin," 147.

11. Deleuze, *Cinema 1,* 153.

12. Ibid.

13. Ibid., 169–70.

14. Bazin, "The Evolution of the Language of Cinema," 36.

15. Though it is separate from issues of technical construction and visual style as such, it is in large part for scenes like this that Lea Jacobs describes *A Woman of Paris* as a key point in the "decline of sentiment" in American cinema after the First World War, arguing that the film augured a shift toward the "cynical amorality and nonemphatic presentation" of the later silent era comedies particularly and a move away from film-making styles that were "excessively pathetic" or "too intent on achieving big dramatic effects" more broadly. See Lea Jacobs, *The Decline of Sentiment: American Film in the 1920s* (Berkeley: University of California Press, 2008).

16. References in this chapter are to the 1925 version of *The Gold Rush,* which was changed in several significant ways in Chaplin's 1942 reissue of the film. The differences between the two versions of the film are discussed in more detail in chapter 8. See also chapter 4, n. 57.

17. Carr, "Chaplin Explains Chaplin."

18. Bazin, "The Virtues and Limitations of Montage," 49n.

19. Ibid.

20. Ibid., 50n.

21. Balázs, 63.

22. *The Gold Rush,* directed by Charles Chaplin, restored by David Gill and Kevin Brownlow (1925; New York: The Criterion Collection, 2012), DVD. All subsequent quotations from *The Gold Rush* in this chapter are from this restoration of the film.

23. Chaplin, *My Autobiography,* 151.

24. Bazin, "The Virtues and Limitations of Montage," 49n.

25. In fact, the tramp in *A Woman of Paris* bears a remarkable visual similarity to another tramp figure who will appear in the cigar-stealing sequence nearly a decade later in *City Lights*.

26. Ray, 33.

27. Deleuze, *Cinema 1*, 170.

28. *The Vagabond*, directed by Charles Chaplin, on *The Chaplin Mutual Comedies* (1916; Los Angeles: Image Entertainment, 2006), DVD.

29. Kerr, *Silent Clowns*, 88.

30. Kamin, 175.

31. Tellingly, Chaplin would remove the kiss (and the photographer's comment) from his revised version of *The Gold Rush* for its 1942 reissue, even though the film otherwise greatly simplifies the relationship between Georgia and the Tramp. In the 1942 version, the note that Chaplin receives is indeed intended for him, indicating that Georgia is open to a reconciliation and that she has some degree of real affection for him. The exclusion of the kiss is something of a mystery for most commentators, though arguably it is far too tentative in the way that it is staged to allow for the emotional climax the new version required. Chaplin instead cuts off the ending sequence at the moment when Chaplin and Georgia are heading up to the first-class deck. The changes between the 1925 and the 1942 versions of the film are discussed in more detail in chapter 8.

32. Bazin, "Charlie Chaplin," 144.

33. Ibid.

34. Ibid.

35. Ibid.

36. Kerr, *Silent Clowns*, 84.

37. Ibid., 85.

38. Ibid., 82.

39. Kamin is explicit on this point: "Chaplin's rapid advancement as a filmmaker and the development of his character is accurately tracked in many books about him. What is not often noted, however, is that his gestural vocabulary is virtually complete from his earliest Keystone films; many of the most endearing comic moments and sequences from his later comic masterpieces are seen in virtually identical form in the Keystones." See Kamin, 24.

40. Kerr, *Silent Clowns*, 340; emphasis in original.

41. Dale, 38, 36.

42. Qtd. in Dale, 37.

43. Chaplin, *My Autobiography*, 144.

44. Kerr, *Silent Clowns*, 91, 92.

45. Kamin has provided a detailed accounting of this kind of transformational gag humor across Chaplin's films, from which a number of the preceding examples were drawn. For a more complete account of the role that these transformations play in Chaplin's comedy, see Kamin, 56–72.

46. Bazin, "Charlie Chaplin," 145.

47. Qtd. in Sobel and Francis, 179.

48. One of the great ironies and tensions within Chaplin's filmmaking, of course, is the degree to which this radically open position is achieved through a meticulous and

painstaking control of visual elements in the frame, including most of all the physical bodies of his other actors. Chaplin's filmmaking can be thought of in this sense as enacting a dialectic between the free and the controlled, played out in the tension between its diegetic content and its process of production.

49. Nichols, "Future of the Cinema."

50. Ibid.

51. Lynn, 71.

52. Benjamin de Casseres, "The Hamlet-Like Nature of Charlie Chaplin," *New York Times Book Review and Magazine,* December 12, 1920. It should be noted that Chaplin's recollections of his early life were sometimes notoriously unreliable, and he often embellished moments or transposed facts for greater narrative effect. Whether or not the incident with the apple occurred exactly as Chaplin describes it here is impossible to discern, though the story undoubtedly expressed for him an emotional truth about his childhood experience.

53. De Casseres, 5.

54. Deleuze, *Cinema 2,* xi.

55. Deleuze, *Cinema 1,* 205.

Chapter 6

1. Charles Chaplin, interviewed by Peter Bogdanovich, February 8, 1973. Qtd. in Charles J. Maland, *City Lights* (New York: Macmillan, 2007), 11.

2. Alexander Woollcott, *While Rome Burns* (New York: Grosset and Dunlap, 1936), 236.

3. Agee, "Comedy's Greatest Era."

4. Kerr, *Silent Clowns,* 345.

5. Arthur Knight, "One Man's Movie," *Saturday Review,* May 6, 1972.

6. Alexander Walker, *The Shattered Silents: How the Talkies Came to Stay* (New York: William Morrow, 1980), vii. Donald Crafton has since gone a long way toward refining and complicating the picture of breakneck transformation that Walker presents, arguing for "the transition to sound as partly rational and partly confused." It was a remarkably rapid transition, but, in his words, "if a revolution is a sudden event which throws over the past regime and substitutes a new oppositional rule, then the conversion to sound was certainly no revolution. The talkies were not instantaneous, although once sound film was in place, it was accepted very quickly." See Donald Crafton, *The Talkies: American Cinema's Transition to Sound, 1926–1931* (Berkeley: University of California Press, 1999), 5, 267.

7. Gunning, *D. W. Griffith and the Origins of American Narrative Film,* 40.

8. Bordwell, "The Introduction of Sound," in Bordwell, Staiger, and Thompson, *The Classical Hollywood Cinema,* 306.

9. Ray, 33.

10. Hence the strange logic of Mary Pickford's famous comment on the coming of sound: "Isn't all art development a process of simplification . . . a search for a universal idea, a universal medium? It would have been more logical if silent pictures had grown out of the talkie instead of the other way round." Silent and sound pictures were ultimately of a kind compositionally, so much so that the former seemed almost like a simplification of the latter. See Anne O'Hare McCormick, "Searching for the Mind of

Hollywood: An Inquiry into the Influences Molding the Vast Flow of Motion Pictures," *New York Times Magazine,* December 13, 1931.

11. Jean Epstein, "Slow-Motion Sound," trans. Robert Lamberton, in *Film Sound: Theory and Practice,* ed. Elisabeth Weis and John Belton (New York: Columbia University Press, 1985), 143.

12. Mary Ann Doane, "Ideology and the Practice of Sound Editing and Mixing," in *Film Sound: Theory and Practice,* ed. Elisabeth Weis and John Belton (New York: Columbia University Press, 1985), 57.

13. Nathan, 214.

14. This manner of having specific musical instruments or the general music of the scene closely follow the action on screen would become known as "mickey-mousing," for the frequency with which it is used in comic animation.

15. *City Lights,* directed by Charles Chaplin (1931; Burbank: Warner Home Video and MK2, 2004), DVD. All subsequent quotations from *City Lights* are from this release of the film.

16. Epstein, 143.

17. Kamin, 126; emphasis in original.

18. L'Estrange Fawcett, *Films: Facts and Forecasts* (London: Geoffrey Bles, 1930), 153.

19. Ibid.

20. Huff, 241, 240.

21. Bazin, "The Evolution of the Language of Cinema," 36.

22. Qtd. in Chaplin, *My Autobiography,* 192.

23. Mast, 106.

24. Huff, 238.

25. Gunning, *D. W. Griffith and the Origins of American Narrative Film,* 40, 25.

26. Kerr, *Silent Clowns,* 247–49.

27. Chaplin, *My Autobiography,* 151.

28. In fact, Chaplin had originally considered opening the film with a scene that would mark the Tramp's embarrassment at his own being and his desire to escape himself even more acutely. In a discarded scenario, the film would open with Chaplin as an aristocrat, dressed in formal military garb and dripping in medals. Just as this noble prince is about to kiss his princess, Chaplin would reveal it all to be a dream: the more familiar Tramp is sleeping in a doorway and the kiss from the princess is actually a lick from a stray dog. The scenario never moved beyond some test footage, but it helps to confirm the degree to which the girl affords the Tramp a chance to secretly act the part of the valorous prince that he imagines himself to be, the degree to which she allows him to secretly transcend the material realities of his condition. See Flom, 63.

29. Jonathan Rosenbaum, *Goodbye Cinema, Hello Cinephilia: Film Culture in Transition* (Chicago: University of Chicago Press, 2010), 89.

30. Ibid.

31. Qtd. in Thomas M. Pryor, "How Mr. Chaplin Makes a Movie," *New York Times Magazine,* February 17, 1952; emphasis in original.

32. Kerr, *Silent Clowns,* 88.

33. Slavoj Žižek, *Enjoy Your Symptom! Jacques Lacan in Hollywood and Out,* 2nd ed. (East Sussex, U.K.: Psychology Press, 2001), 5.

34. Ibid., 7.

35. Nichols, "Future of the Cinema."

Chapter 7

1. Charlie Chaplin, "Pantomime and Comedy," *New York Times*, January 25, 1931. How seriously we were ever meant to take such a statement is a matter of some debate. It is perhaps unlikely that Chaplin ever truly believed that *City Lights* would "change [the] trend of [the] film world," as one of his press releases put it, and Eric Flom chalks up the entire set of Chaplin's public statements about the enduring qualities of pantomime to part of his "promotion" for the film. The only person Chaplin seems to have truly convinced with these sentiments was Winston Churchill, who visited Chaplin during the filming of *City Lights* and who penned an essay in 1935 supporting Chaplin's brave stance against the tide of the talkies. For Churchill, there was a kind of colonial mission behind Chaplin's stance—though we have no reason to believe Chaplin himself agreed with this assessment. "The English-speaking nations have here a great opportunity—and a great responsibility. The primitive mind thinks more easily in pictures than in words. The thing seen means more than the thing heard. The films which are shown amid the stillness of the African tropical night or under the skies of Asia may determine, in the long run, the fate of empires and of civilizations." Of course, if Churchill thought that Chaplin's indigent Tramp was an effective or appropriate standard-bearer for the great advantages of "empires and of civilizations," he was perhaps not watching Chaplin's films very closely. See *City Lights* press release, qtd. in Maland, *Chaplin and American Culture*, 115; Flom, 77; Winston Churchill, "Everybody's Language," *Collier's*, October 26, 1935.

2. "Charles Chaplin: Film Comedian's Welcome," *Times* (London), February 20, 1931.

3. Chaplin, *My Autobiography*, 387.

4. Charles Chaplin Jr., with N. and M. Rau, *My Father, Charlie Chaplin* (New York: Random House, 1960), 119.

5. Siegfried Kracauer, *Theory of Film: The Redemption of Physical Reality* (1960; Princeton: Princeton University Press, 1997), 104.

6. *Modern Times*, directed by Charles Chaplin (1936; Burbank: Warner Home Video and MK2, 2003), DVD. All subsequent quotations from *Modern Times* are from this release of the film.

7. Timothy Brock, "Modern Times," last modified 2004, http://www.timothybrock .com/articles_modern_times.htm.

8. Chaplin, *My Autobiography*, 366.

9. Kracauer, 104.

10. Crafton, "Pie and Chase," 110, 109.

11. Kamin, 149.

12. Indeed, Chaplin would take steps to better ensure the unresolvability of the tension between these layers of meaning. In his 1954 reissue of the film, he would cut out the final verse of the song (creating an awkward jump cut between the new conclusion of the song and the immediate next scene in the antechamber), making sure that the tale of prostitution that he pantomimes cuts out at the moment that the ring is transferred and never resolves with the woman trying to pawn the ring. Arguably, the ending verse slightly overdetermines the nature of the song: the woman finds out that the ring is a fake, making the whole song essentially build to a punch line of sex sold for nothing. Ending the song in this way works in some part to resolve the tension between the jaunty music and the sordid tale, turning the whole thing into a kind of

extended dirty joke. By taking out the final verse, Chaplin helps ensure that neither the music nor the content ever comes to unification or resolution.

13. Kamin, 153, n. 25.

14. The film's classification on the Internet-based Progressive Silent Film List (PSFL) is indicative of its strange relationship to both silent and sound film. PSFL is one of the largest and most comprehensive available databases of silent-era films. It readily includes *City Lights,* but it excludes *Modern Times* with the following explanation: "we firmly judge *Modern Times* to be a mute sound film." See "The Top 100 Silent Era Films," http://www.silentera.com/info/top100.html.

15. Chaplin, *My Autobiography,* 387.

16. Kerr, *Silent Clowns,* 166.

17. Ferguson, "Hallelujah, Bum Again."

18. Kerr, *Silent Clowns,* 355.

19. Ferguson, "Hallelujah, Bum Again."

20. Qtd. in Kamin, 145.

21. Ibid., 146.

22. Chaplin seems even to confirm the strange sense of ordering and sequencing in the film in a subtle misconfiguration of Eisensteinian technique in the film's opening. Chaplin starts the film with an homage to Eisenstein's theory of montage (indicative perhaps of his supposed turn to "modern times"), showing us an image of sheep crowding together and cutting to an image of workers crowding from the subway on their way to work. Yet the most exact parallel for this image of sheep is not the one that follows it but one that occurs almost halfway through the film. The image of sheep shows us a single black sheep making its way through the crowd of white sheep, but no parallel is to be found in the image of workers leaving the subway station. Where the parallel to that image appears is in the Tramp's effort to break through the crowd of workers clamoring to get into the reopened factory much later in the story, the Tramp's trademark black outfit clearly distinguishing him as he makes his way through the packed collection of workers huddled together like so many sheep from that opening image. Even the film's ability to follow the basic prescriptions of montage theory—to simply order its own images correctly—seems to have ceased to function properly.

23. By way of a narrative codex: the Tramp begins by working in a factory, he is sent to a hospital, the Gamine escapes being sent to an orphanage, the Tramp goes to jail, the Tramp receives food in jail, the Tramp makes himself a comfortable home in jail, the Gamine steals food at the bakery, the Tramp steals food at the restaurant, the Tramp and the Gamine pretend to have a comfortable home in the suburbs, the Tramp and the Gamine steal food in the department store, the Tramp and the Gamine make themselves a home in the department store, the Tramp goes back to jail, the Tramp and the Gamine make themselves a home in the hovel, the Tramp goes back to work in the factory, the Tramp and the Gamine find work in a restaurant.

24. *The Great Dictator,* directed by Charles Chaplin (1940; Burbank: Warner Home Video and MK2, 2003), DVD. All subsequent quotations from *The Great Dictator* are from this release of the film.

25. As noted earlier, Frank Krutnik is explicit on this later point, describing the verbal comedies of the 1930s as a form that aligned more easily with classical prescriptions than did slapstick film. It was, in his words, an arena in which "the twin demands of representation and presentation are articulated and contained within a stable and predictable formal mode." See Krutnik, 17.

26. It is well covered in the critical literature how Chaplin did not fully understand the depth of the horror of the Nazi state when he made *The Great Dictator*. By his own admission, "Had I known the actual horrors of the German concentration camps, I could not have made *The Great Dictator;* I could not have made fun of the homicidal insanity of the Nazis." But it should not be overlooked how brutal even his parodic version of Nazi Germany actually is in the film. The characters speak openly of the state-sanctioned torture and murder of fellow citizens, the disappearance of dissidents to prison camps, and the persecution and ghettoization of the Jews. Chaplin's imagined version of Nazi Germany does not begin to approach mass industrial genocide, but neither is it particularly whitewashed. It ultimately looks like a brutal apartheid-style regime bent on controlling its population through terror. See Chaplin, *My Autobiography*, 392.

27. Mast, 117.

28. Walter Kerr, "The Lineage of *Limelight*," in *Focus on Chaplin*, ed. Donald W. McCaffrey (Englewood Cliffs, N.J.: Prentice-Hall, 1971), 147; originally published in *Theatre Arts* 36 (November 1952). The tide against the speech is in fact so strong that Sanjeev Verma felt it necessary to offer an entire essay in its defense, arguing that Chaplin "became unfunny to instill hope in people fearful of the megalomania of the Führer" and asking "what could be wrong with that?" See Sanjeev Verma, "Tramp as Dictator," in *Chaplin: The Dictator and the Tramp*, ed. Frank Scheide and Hooman Mehran (London: British Film Institute, 2004), 15.

29. Ella Winter, "But It's Sad, Says Chaplin, It's Me," *Observer*, September 15, 1957.

30. George Wallach, "Charlie Chaplin's *Monsieur Verdoux* Press Conference," in *Charlie Chaplin Interviews*, ed. Kevin J. Hayes (Jackson: University Press of Mississippi, 2005), 106. Originally printed in *Film Comment* 5 (Winter 1969).

Chapter 8

1. De Casseres, "The Hamlet-Like Nature of Charlie Chaplin."

2. Thomas Burke, *City of Encounters: A London Divertissement* (London: Little, Brown, 1932), 143.

3. Ibid., 142.

4. Charles Chaplin, "A Comedian Sees the World," *Woman's Home Companion* 60 (December 1933): 23.

5. Ibid., 17.

6. Ibid., 17, 102.

7. Robinson, *Chaplin: His Life and Art*, 455.

8. Nichols, "Future of the Cinema."

9. Ted Le Berton, "Absolutely, Mr. Chaplin! Positively, Mr. Freud!: Psychoanalysis Comes to the Movies," *Motion Picture Classic*, August 17, 1923.

10. Nichols, "Future of the Cinema."

11. Chaplin, *My Autobiography*, 417.

12. Qtd. in James Bacon, *Hollywood Is a Four Letter Town* (Washington, D.C.: Regnery, 1976), 29.

13. Kracauer, 108.

14. Kerr, "The Lineage of *Limelight*," 146, 145.

15. Ibid., 146, 148.

16. Ibid., 147.

17. Allardyce Nicoll, *The World of Harlequin* (London: Cambridge University Press, 1963), 18.

18. Kerr, "The Lineage of *Limelight,*" 146.

19. Kracauer, 108.

20. Bazin, "The Grandeur of *Limelight,*" in his *What Is Cinema?* 2:132.

21. This was in some sense even literally true. Charlie Chaplin Jr. would later recount that his father had a penchant for narrating his own films in much the manner that he did with the reissue of *The Gold Rush* when he screened them for his children privately at home. See Charles Chaplin Jr., 92–93.

22. Vance, 166; see Agee, 1:23.

23. *The Gold Rush,* directed by Charles Chaplin (1942; New York: Criterion Collection, 2012), DVD. All subsequent quotations from *The Gold Rush* in this chapter are from this release of the film.

24. Kamin, 174.

25. Ibid., 17.

26. Kerr, "The Lineage of *Limelight,*" 144; emphasis in original.

27. Bordwell, *Narration in the Fiction Film,* 245.

28. Mitry, 357.

29. Timothy J. Lyons, "Interview with Roland H. Totheroh," *Film Culture* (Spring 1972), 230–85: 285.

30. Ibid.

31. *Monsieur Verdoux,* directed by Charles Chaplin (1947; Burbank: Warner Home Video and MK2, 2004), DVD. All subsequent quotations from *Monsieur Verdoux* are from this release of the film.

32. Arthur Schopenhauer, *Philosophical Writings,* ed. and trans. Wolfgang Schirmacher (New York: Continuum, 2005), 46.

33. *Limelight,* directed by Charles Chaplin (1952; Burbank: Warner Home Video and MK2, 2003), DVD. All subsequent quotations from *Limelight* are from this release of the film.

34. Qtd. in Lynn, 349.

35. Karl Marx and Frederick Engels, *The Communist Manifesto,* trans. Samuel Moore (1848; London: Verso, 1998), 38, 39.

36. *A King in New York,* directed by Charles Chaplin (1957; Burbank: Warner Home Video and MK2, 2004), DVD. All subsequent quotations from *A King in New York* are from this release of the film.

37. For more on types of transformations in Chaplin's films, see the discussion of Dan Kamin's catalog of Chaplin transformations in chapter 5.

38. Kenneth Burke, *Terms for Order,* ed. Stanley Edgar Hyman (Bloomington: Indiana University Press, 1964), 84; emphasis in original.

39. Bazin, "The Myth of *Monsieur Verdoux,*" 112–13; emphasis in original.

40. Rosenbaum, 88.

41. The degree of noble martyrdom to be inferred from the moment can perhaps be best assessed in contrast to an earlier version of the scene. In interviews with Peter Bogdanovich, Orson Welles claimed to have written an early draft of a full screenplay for *Verdoux.* (Chaplin counterclaimed that Welles only gave him the idea for the film, for which he was duly paid and even given credit on the film's title card.) In Welles's description of the original concept, Verdoux was a teetotaler who had never tasted any alcohol before. Given a drink of rum before his execution, he is suddenly called to rethink how he has spent his life. Welles describes him "thinking, you know, 'What I've

missed! I killed all these women, had this wonderful life, but I *could* have been doing *that.'* And goes off to the guillotine." In Welles's treatment of the rum scene, Verdoux seems to have traces of the kind of magnetic, amoral, and self-indulgent narcissism of so many of Welles's great villains—he seems a kind of Harry Lime in training—but he is hardly the semi-sainted figure of Chaplin's conclusion. See Welles and Bogdanovich, 136.

42. Parker Tyler, "Movie Letter: Charlie Verdoux," *Kenyon Review* 9, no. 3 (Summer 1947): 459.

43. Kenneth Tynan, "Looking Back in Anger," *Observer,* September 1957 (clipping, Chaplin file, 1950–59, MoMA).

44. Though Chaplin lived in fear of testifying before the House Un-American Activities Committee like many of his Hollywood peers, he never did.

45. Tynan, "Looking Back in Anger."

46. Bazin, "The Myth of *Monsieur Verdoux*," 105.

47. Mast, 122.

48. Sarris, *"You Ain't Heard Nothin' Yet,"* 151.

49. Bazin, "The Myth of *Monsieur Verdoux*," 109; emphasis in original.

50. Ibid., 105–6; emphasis in original.

51. See Parker Tyler, *Chaplin, Last of the Clowns* (New York: Vanguard Press, 1948).

52. Kracauer, 106, 108.

53. "The Last Silent Film," *Greely Daily Tribune,* March 14, 1936. Qtd. in William M. Drew, *The Last Silent Picture Show: Silent Films on American Screens in the 1930s* (Lanham, Md.: Scarecrow Press, 2010), 108.

Chapter 9

1. Brendan Gill, "The Current Cinema," *New Yorker,* March 25, 1967; Paul D. Zimmerman, "Chasing the Dream," *Newsweek,* April 3, 1967; Alexander Walker, *Evening Standard,* qtd. in Robinson, *Chaplin: The Mirror of Opinion,* 167.

2. Bosley Crowther, " 'A Countess from Hong Kong': New Movie by Chaplin Opens at the Sutton, Miss Loren and Brando in an Antique Farce," *New York Times,* March 17, 1967.

3. Mast, 258.

4. Kamin, 207.

5. Jay Leyda, ed., *Voices of Film Experience: 1894 to the Present* (New York: Macmillan, 1977), 46; David Downing, *Marlon Brando* (New York: Stein and Day, 1984), 120.

6. Lawrence Grobel, *Conversations with Brando* (New York: Hyperion, 1991), 75.

7. Flom, 274.

8. Kamin, 207.

9. Francis Wyndham, "Chaplin on the Critics, the Beatles, the Mood of London," *Sunday Times* (London), March 26, 1967.

10. Meryman, "Ageless Master's Anatomy of Comedy."

11. Wyndham, "Chaplin on the Critics, the Beatles, the Mood of London."

12. Carr, "Chaplin Explains Chaplin."

13. Mast, 122.

14. Andrew Sarris, *Confessions of a Cultist: On the Cinema, 1955–1969* (New York: Simon and Schuster, 1970), 295.

15. Wyndham, "Chaplin on the Critics, the Beatles, the Mood of London."

16. Ibid.

17. They were not entirely alone. The director and screenwriter Tim Hunter, best known for such films as *Over the Edge* (Orion, 1979) and *River's Edge* (Hemdale/ Island, 1986), was an undergraduate at Harvard when the film came out. In his review in the *Harvard Crimson* he declares, "*A Countess From Hong Kong* is a fascinating film, in my own opinion his best." See Tim Hunter, "A Countess from Hong Kong," *Harvard Crimson*, April 25, 1967, http://www.thecrimson.com/article/1967/4/25/a-countess-from-hong-kong-palong/.

18. Kamin, 207.

19. It is unclear why Chaplin abandoned the film when he did, though the reason may have had something to do with Goddard herself, who was sometimes quite willing to butt heads with her husband and mentor and whose career was already starting to take off on its own. By 1939, Goddard was in serious running for the part of Scarlett O'Hara in *Gone with the Wind*, which gave her significant cachet in Hollywood. During the filming of *The Great Dictator*, she even had her agent try to negotiate her billing status with her own husband. Offering Goddard a career platform like *Countess* may simply, in the end, not have seemed like a good strategy for Chaplin either professionally or personally.

20. *A Countess from Hong Kong*, directed by Charles Chaplin (1967; Universal City, Calif.: Universal Studios Home Entertainment, 2005), DVD. All subsequent quotations from *A Countess from Hong Kong* are from this release of the film.

21. *The Great Dictator*, directed by Charles Chaplin (1940; Burbank: Warner Home Video and MK2, 2003), DVD. All subsequent quotations from *The Great Dictator* are from this release of the film.

22. Brownlow, 505. Even in interviews, Chaplin could still hardly remember the lines from his film, not even the gist. In one description of a scene, he says, "I've got a scene in this picture—*The* [*sic*] *Countess*. Marlon Brando is very sulky, and he just sits. His wife, Tippi Hedren, comes on, very beautiful, saying, 'Your Excellency, so-and-so and so-and-so.' She kids him a little about this bra she finds in his drawer. He doesn't say a word. I don't care who the writer is, nothing is more eloquent than his silence." See Meryman, "Ageless Master's Anatomy of Comedy."

23. Brownlow, 507.

24. Gehring, 163.

25. Kerr, "The Lineage of *Limelight*," 147.

26. Éric Rohmer, "La Comtesse de Hong Kong," in André Bazin and Éric Rohmer, *Charlie Chaplin* (Paris: Les Éditions du Cerf, 1972), 106; translation mine.

27. Mitry, 357.

28. Ibid.

29. Chaplin, *My Autobiography*, 254.

30. Kamin, 68.

31. Ibid., 207.

32. Crowther, "'A Countess from Hong Kong'"; Pauline Kael, "The Small Winner," *New Yorker*, March 8, 1969, qtd. in Stefan Kanfer, *Somebody: The Reckless Life and Remarkable Career of Marlon Brando* (New York: Vintage, 2009), 224.

33. Gill, "The Current Cinema."

34. Wyndham, "Chaplin on the Critics, the Beatles, the Mood of London."

35. Ibid.

36. Ibid.

37. "Time to Retire," *Time,* March 31, 1967.

38. Rohmer, "La comtesse," 106; translation mine.

Epilogue

1. See Tag Gallagher, *The Adventures of Roberto Rossellini: His Life and Films* (Cambridge, Mass.: Da Capo, 1998), 669.

2. Qtd. in Roy Armes, *Patterns of Realism: A Study of Italian Neo-Realist Cinema* (New York: A. S. Barnes, 1971), 144.

3. Irving R. Levine, "'I Was Born for the Cinema': A Conversation with Federico Fellini," in *Federico Fellini: Interviews,* ed. Bert Cardullo (Jackson: University Press of Mississippi, 2006), 58. Originally published in *Film Comment* (Fall 1966).

4. Ibid.

5. Qtd. in Larry Langman, *Destination Hollywood: The Influence of Europeans on American Filmmaking* (Jefferson, N.C.: McFarland, 2000), 39.

6. See Mast, 232.

7. Jean Renoir, *My Life and My Films,* trans. Norman Denny (New York: Atheneum, 1974), 205.

8. Marina Warner, "*L'Atalante,*" in *British Film Institute Film Classics,* vol. 1, ed. Rob White and Edward Buscombe (London: British Film Institute, 2003), 293.

9. Rohmer, *The Taste for Beauty,* 22.

10. Godard, 202.

11. Truffaut, 62.

12. Sylviane Gold, "Truffaut's Small Charges," *New York Post,* October 1, 1976.

13. Cesare Zavattini, "Some Ideas on the Cinema," in *Vittorio De Sica: Contemporary Perspectives,* ed. Stephen Snyder and Howard Curle (Toronto: University of Toronto Press, 2000), 61. Originally published in *Sight and Sound* 23, no. 2 (October–December 1953).

14. Ibid., 53.

15. Bert Cardullo, *Vittorio De Sica: Director, Actor, Screenwriter* (Jefferson, N.C.: McFarland, 2002), 181.

16. Anna Muzzarelli, "Fellini in Conversation," in *Federico Fellini: Interviews,* ed. Bert Cardullo (Jackson: University Press of Mississippi, 2006), 58. Originally published in *Sight and Sound* 3, no. 4 (April 1993).

17. Rohmer, *The Taste for Beauty,* 42.

18. Truffaut, 60, 62.

19. Godard, 202.

20. Ibid., 30.

21. Gallagher, 251; Vittorio De Sica, "Money, the Public and *Umberto D,*" in *Vittorio De Sica: Contemporary Perspectives,* ed. Stephen Snyder and Howard Curle (Toronto: University of Toronto Press, 2000), 25 (originally published in *Films and Filming* 2, no. 4 [January 1956]); Wyndham, "Chaplin on the Critics, the Beatles, the Mood of London."

22. Wyndham, "Chaplin on the Critics, the Beatles, the Mood of London."

23. Ibid.

24. Zavattini, 58.

25. Ibid.

26. Ibid., 56.

27. Ibid., 52.

28. Ibid., 53, 54.

29. Ibid., 57.

30. Zavattini, 58.

31. Ibid., 61.

32. Ibid., 55, 61.

33. Nichols, "Future of the Cinema."

34. André Bazin and Jean Cocteau, *Orson Welles* (Paris: Editions du Chavanne, 1950), 57. Translation by Dudley Andrew in *André Bazin* (1978; New York: Columbia University Press, 1990).

35. Ibid., 57, 58.

36. André Bazin, *Orson Welles: A Critical View,* trans. Jonathan Rosenbaum (New York: Harper and Row, 1978), 80.

37. It is important to note that the originality that Bazin ascribes to Welles's use of deep space is not universally agreed upon. In contrast to Bazin, David Bordwell claims that Welles represented only one manifestation of a negotiation between analytical editing and composition in the frame that had long been part of the development of classical style. "As a decoupage-based style came to dominate American films," he writes, "depth staging was mobilized for particular functions within that." Bordwell's rereading in fact helps to further confirm that Chaplin and Welles were engaging in similar negotiations between an ambiguous and decentered form of composition in the frame and a degree of adherence to classical dictates in the overall construction of narrative, though we might say they were coming at this negotiation from opposite sides. See Bordwell, *On the History of Film Style,* 201.

38. Dudley Andrew, *André Bazin* (1978; New York: Columbia University Press, 1990), 130, 129.

39. André Bazin, Charles Bitsch, and Jean Domarchi, "Interview with Orson Welles (II)," trans. Alisa Hartz, in *Orson Welles: Interviews,* ed. Mark W. Estrin (Jackson: University Press of Mississippi, 2002), 76. Originally published in *Cahiers du Cinéma,* September 1958.

40. Truffaut, 283.

41. Ibid., 62.

42. Ibid.

43. Ibid.

44. Rohmer, *The Taste for Beauty,* 42.

45. Truffaut, 61.

46. Even the use of amateur actors common to Neorealism has a kind of origin in Chaplin's openness to working with untrained performers (Virginia Cherrill being the most famous example), though in Chaplin's case this was about being able to shape their performance rather than an attempt to capture authenticity.

47. Mark Browning, *Wes Anderson: Why His Movies Matter* (Santa Barbara, Calif.: Praeger, 2011), 143.

48. Godard, 135.

49. Deleuze, *Cinema 2,* 196.

Abel, Richard. *The Ciné Goes to Town: French Cinema, 1896–1914.* Berkeley: University of California Press, 1998.

———. "Guarding the Borders in Early Cinema: The Shifting Ground of French-American Relations." In *Celebrating 1895: The Centenary of Cinema,* edited by John Fullerton, 45–54. Bloomington: Indiana University Press, 1998.

Agee, James. *Agee on Film.* Vol. 1. New York: Putnam, 1983.

———. "Comedy's Greatest Era," *Life,* September 3, 1949.

Allen, Robert C. "Contra the Chaser Theory." *Wide Angle* 3, no. 1 (1979): 4–11.

———. "Looking at 'Another Look at the "Chaser Theory,"'" *Studies in Visual Communication* 10, no. 4 (1984): 45–50.

Andrew, Dudley. *André Bazin.* 1978. New York: Columbia University Press, 1990.

———. *The Major Film Theories: An Introduction.* Oxford: Oxford University Press, 1976.

Armes, Roy. *Patterns of Realism: A Study of Italian Neo-Realist Cinema.* New York: A. S. Barnes, 1971.

Arnheim, Rudolf. *Film as Art.* 1933. Los Angeles: University of California Press, 1979.

Bacon, James. *Hollywood Is a Four Letter Town.* Washington, D.C.: Regnery, 1976.

Balázs, Béla. *Theory of the Film: Character and Growth of a New Art.* Translated by Edith Bone. New York: Dover, 1970.

Bazin, André. "Charlie Chaplin." In his *What Is Cinema?* 1:144–53.

———. "The Evolution of the Language of Cinema." In his *What Is Cinema?* 1:23–40.

———. "The Grandeur of *Limelight.*" In his *What Is Cinema?* 2:128–39.

———. "The Myth of *Monsieur Verdoux.*" In his *What Is Cinema?* 2: 102–23.

———. *Orson Welles: A Critical View.* Translated by Jonathan Rosenbaum. New York: Harper and Row, 1978.

———. "The Virtues and Limitations of Montage." In his *What Is Cinema?* 1:41–52.

———. *What Is Cinema?* 2 vols., edited and translated by Hugh Gray. Berkeley: University of California Press, 2005.

Bazin, André, Charles Bitsch, and Jean Domarchi. "Interview with Orson Welles (II)." Translated by Alisa Hartz. In *Orson Welles: Interviews,* edited by Mark W. Estrin, 48–76. Jackson: University Press of Mississippi, 2002. Originally published in *Cahiers du Cinéma,* September 1958.

Bazin, André, and Jean Cocteau, *Orson Welles*. Paris: Editions du Chavanne, 1950.

Bazin, André, and Éric Rohmer. *Charlie Chaplin*. Paris: Les Éditions du Cerf, 1972.

Bean, Jennifer M. "The Art of Imitation: The Originality of Charlie Chaplin and Other Moving-Image Myths." In *Slapstick Comedy*, edited by Tom Paulus and Rob King, 236–61. New York: Routledge, 2010.

Benjamin, Walter. *Selected Writings*. 4 vols., edited by Marcus Bullock and Michael W. Jennings. Cambridge, Mass.: Belknap Press of Harvard University Press, 1996–2003.

Berger, Peter L. *Redeeming Laughter: The Comic Dimension of Human Experience*. Berlin: De Gruyter, 1997.

Bergson, Henri. "Laughter." In *Comedy*, edited by Wylie Sypher, 61–192. Translated by Fred Rothwell. Baltimore: Johns Hopkins University Press, 1991.

Bogdanovich, Peter. *Who the Hell's in It: Conversations with Hollywood's Legendary Actors*. New York: Ballantine, 2005.

Bordwell, David. "The Bounds of Difference." In Bordwell, Staiger, and Thompson, *The Classical Hollywood Cinema*, 70–84.

———. "The Introduction of Sound." In Bordwell, Staiger, and Thompson, *The Classical Hollywood Cinema*, 298–308.

———. *Narration in the Fiction Film*. Madison: University of Wisconsin Press, 1985.

———. *On the History of Film Style*. Cambridge, Mass.: Harvard University Press, 1997.

———. *The Way Hollywood Tells It: Story and Style in Modern Movies*. Berkeley: University of California Press, 2006.

Bordwell, David, Janet Staiger, and Kristin Thompson. *The Classical Hollywood Cinema: Film Style and Mode of Production to 1960*. New York: Columbia University Press, 1985.

Bordwell, David, and Kristin Thompson. *Film Art: An Introduction*. New York: Knopf, 1986.

Bowser, Eileen, ed. *Biograph Bulletins, 1908–1912*. New York: Farrar, Straus and Giroux, 1973.

———. "Mack Sennett vs. Henry Ford." In *Slapstick Comedy*, edited by Tom Paulus and Rob King, 107–13. New York: Routledge, 2010.

———. *The Transformation of Cinema*. Berkeley: University of California Press, 1994.

Browning, Mark. *Wes Anderson: Why His Movies Matter*. Santa Barbara, Calif.: Praeger, 2011.

Brownlow, Kevin. *The Parade's Gone By . . .* Berkeley: University of California Press, 1968.

Buñuel, Luis. "Buster Keaton's College." In *The Shadow and Its Shadow: Surrealist Writings on the Cinema*. 3rd ed., translated and edited by Paul Hammond. San Francisco: City Lights, 2000.

Burch, Noël. *To the Distant Observer: Form and Meaning in the Japanese Cinema*. Revised and edited by Annette Michelson. Berkeley: University of California Press, 1979.

Burke, Kenneth. *Terms for Order*. Edited by Stanley Edgar Hyman. Bloomington: Indiana University Press, 1964.

Burke, Thomas. *City of Encounters: A London Divertissement*. London: Little, Brown, 1932.

Cardullo, Bert, ed. *Fellini: Interviews*. Jackson: University Press of Mississippi, 2006.

———. *Vittorio De Sica: Director, Actor, Screenwriter*. Jefferson, N.C.: McFarland, 2002.

Carr, Harry. "Chaplin Explains Chaplin." *Motion Picture Magazine* 30 (November 1925).

———. "Charlie Chaplin's Story." 4 parts. *Photoplay,* July–October 1915.

Carroll, Noël. "Notes on the Sight Gag." In *Comedy/Cinema/Theory,* edited by Andrew Horton, 25–42. Berkeley: University of California Press, 1991.

Cavell, Stanley. *The World Viewed: Reflections on the Ontology of Film.* Rev. ed. Cambridge, Mass.: Harvard University Press, 1979.

Chaplin, Charles. "A Comedian Sees the World." *Woman's Home Companion* 60 (December 1933).

———. "Does the Public Know What It Wants?" *Adelphi* 1, no. 8 (January 1924).

———. *My Autobiography.* New York: Simon and Schuster, 1964.

———. "Pantomime and Comedy." *New York Times,* January 25, 1931.

Chaplin, Charles, Jr., with N. and M. Rau. *My Father, Charlie Chaplin.* New York: Random House, 1960.

Churchill, Winston. "Everybody's Language." *Collier's* 96 (October 26, 1935).

Clayton, Alex. *The Body in Hollywood Slapstick.* Jefferson, N.C.: McFarland, 2007.

Cobos, Juan, Miguel Rubio, and J. A. Pruneda. "A Trip to Don Quixoteland: Conversations with Orson Welles." In *Orson Welles: Interviews,* edited by Mark W. Estrin, 96–125. Jackson: University Press of Mississippi, 2002.

Cook, David A. *A History of Narrative Film.* New York: W. W. Norton, 1981.

Crafton, Donald. "Pie and Chase: Gag, Spectacle and Narrative in Slapstick Comedy." In *Classical Hollywood Comedy,* edited by Kristine Brunovska Karnick and Henry Jenkins, 106–19. New York: Routledge, 1995.

———. *The Talkies: American Cinema's Transition to Sound, 1926–1931.* Berkeley: University of California Press, 1999.

Crowther, Bosley. "'A Countess from Hong Kong': New Movie by Chaplin Opens at the Sutton, Miss Loren and Brando in an Antique Farce." *New York Times,* March 17, 1967.

Dale, Alan. *Comedy Is a Man in Trouble: Slapstick in American Movies.* Minneapolis: University of Minnesota Press, 2000.

De Casseres, Benjamin. "The Hamlet-Like Nature of Charlie Chaplin." *New York Times Book Review and Magazine,* December 12, 1920.

Deleuze, Gilles. *Cinema 1: The Movement-Image.* Translated by Hugh Tomlinson and Barbara Habberjam. Minneapolis: University of Minnesota Press, 1986.

———. *Cinema 2: The Time-Image.* Translated by Hugh Tomlinson and Robert Galeta. London: Continuum, 2005.

Delluc, Louis. *Charlie Chaplin.* Translated by Hamish Miles. London: Bodley Head, 1922.

———. "Max Linder's and Elsie Codd's Views on the Working Method." Translated by Hamish Miles. In *Focus on Chaplin,* edited by Donald W. McCaffrey, 55–62. Englewood Cliffs, N.J.: Prentice-Hall, 1971.

De Sica, Vittorio. "Money, the Public and *Umberto D.*" In *Vittorio De Sica: Contemporary Perspectives,* edited by Stephen Snyder and Howard Curle, 25–6. Toronto: University of Toronto Press, 2000. Originally published in *Films and Filming* 2, no. 4 (January 1956).

Deutelbaum, Marshall. "Structural Patterning in the Lumière Films." In *Film Before Griffith,* edited by John L. Fell, 299–310. Berkeley: University of California Press, 1983.

Dixon, Bryony. "The Good Thieves: On the Origins of Situation Comedy in the British Music Hall." In *Slapstick Comedy,* edited by Tom Paulus and Rob King, 21–36. New York: Routledge, 2010.

Doane, Mary Ann. "Ideology and the Practice of Sound Editing and Mixing." In *Film Sound: Theory and Practice,* edited by Elisabeth Weis and John Belton, 54–62. New York: Columbia University Press, 1985.

Downing, David. *Marlon Brando.* New York: Stein and Day, 1984.

Drew, William M. *The Last Silent Picture Show: Silent Films on American Screens in the 1930s.* Lanham, Md.: Scarecrow Press, 2010.

Ebert, Roger. "The Birth of a Nation." Rogerebert.com. *Chicago Sun-Times,* March 30, 2003. http://rogerebert.suntimes.com.

Eisenstein, Sergei. *Film Form: Essays in Film Theory.* Translated and edited by Jay Leyda. Orlando: Harcourt, 1949.

———. "Word and Image." In *The Film Sense,* translated and edited by Jay Leyda, 3–68. Boston: Houghton Mifflin Harcourt, 1947.

Epstein, Jean. "Slow-Motion Sound." Translated by Robert Lamberton. In *Film Sound: Theory and Practice,* edited by Elisabeth Weis and John Belton, 143–44. New York: Columbia University Press, 1985.

Estrin, Mark W., ed. *Orson Welles: Interviews.* Jackson: University Press of Mississippi, 2002.

Fairservice, Don. *Film Editing: History, Theory, and Practice.* Manchester, U.K.: Manchester University Press, 2001.

Farmer, Harcourt. "Is the Charlie Chaplin Vogue Passing?" *Theatre Magazine,* October 1919.

Fawcett, L'Estrange. *Films: Facts and Forecasts.* London: Geoffrey Bles, 1930.

Fell, John L. *Film and the Narrative Tradition.* Norman: University of Oklahoma Press, 1974.

———, ed. *Film Before Griffith.* Berkeley: University of California Press, 1983.

———. *A History of Films.* New York: Holt, Rinehart and Winston, 1979.

Ferguson, Otis. "Hallelujah, Bum Again." *New Republic,* February 19, 1936.

Flom, Eric L. *Chaplin in the Sound Era: An Analysis of the Seven Talkies.* Jefferson, N.C.: McFarland, 1997.

Gallagher, Tag. *The Adventures of Roberto Rossellini: His Life and Films.* Cambridge, Mass.: Da Capo, 1998.

Gaudreault, André. "Detours in Film Narrative: The Development of Cross-Cutting." *Cinema Journal* 19 (Fall 1979): 39–59.

———. "Film, Narrative, Narration: The Cinema of the Lumière Brothers." In *Early Cinema: Space, Frame, Narrative,* edited by Thomas Elsaesser, 68–75. London: British Film Institute, 1984.

———. "Temporality and Narrativity in Early Cinema, 1895–1908." In *Film Before Griffith,* edited by John L. Fell, 311–29. Berkeley: University of California Press, 1983.

Gaudreault, André, and Tom Gunning. "Le Cinéma des premier temps: Un défi a histoire du film?" In *Histoire du cinema: Nouvelles approches,* edited by J. Aumont, A. Gaudreault, and M. Marie, 49–63. Paris: Publications de la Sorbonne, 1989.

Gehring, Wes D. *Charlie Chaplin: A Bio-Bibliography.* Westport, Conn.: Greenwood Press, 1983.

Giannetti, Louis. *Understanding Movies.* 12th ed. Boston: Allyn and Bacon, 2010.

Gill, Brendan. "The Current Cinema." *New Yorker,* March 25, 1967.

Gish, Lillian, with Ann Pinchot. *The Movies, Mr. Griffith, and Me.* Upper Saddle River, N.J.: Prentice-Hall, 1969.

Godard, Jean-Luc. *Godard on Godard.* Translated by Tom Milne. New York: Viking, 1972.

Gold, Sylviane. "Truffaut's Small Charges." *New York Post,* October 1, 1976.

Grobel, Lawrence. *Conversations with Brando.* New York: Hyperion, 1991.

Gunning, Tom. "Crazy Machines in the Garden of Forking Paths: Mischief Gags and the Origins of American Film Comedy." In *Classical Hollywood Comedy,* edited by Kristine Brunovska Karnick and Henry Jenkins, 87–104. New York: Routledge, 1995.

———. *D. W. Griffith and the Origins of American Narrative Film: The Early Years at Biograph.* Chicago: University of Illinois Press, 1991.

———. "Early American Film." In *The Oxford Guide to Film Studies,* edited by John Hill and Pamela Church Gibson, 255–71. New York: Oxford University Press, 1998.

———. "I film Vitagraph e il cinema dell'integrazione narrativa." In *Vitagraph Co. of America: Il cinema prima di Hollywood,* edited by Paolo Cherchi Usai, 225–39. Pordenone, Italy: Edizioni Studio Tesi, 1987.

———. "Non-Continuity, Continuity, Discontinuity: A Theory of Genres in Early Films." *Iris* 2, no. 1 (1984): 101–12.

———. "'Now You See It, Now You Don't': The Temporality of the Cinema of Attractions." *Velvet Light Trap* 32 (Fall 1993): 3–12.

Hayes, Kevin J., ed. *Chaplin Interviews.* Jackson: University Press of Mississippi, 2005.

Huff, Theodore. *Charlie Chaplin.* New York: Henry Schuman, 1951.

Hulfish, David S. "Art in Moving Pictures." *Nickelodeon,* May 1909.

Hunter, Tim. "A Countess from Hong Kong." *Harvard Crimson,* April 25, 1967. http://www.thecrimson.com/article/1967/4/25/a-countess-from-hong-kong-palong/.

Jacobs, Lea. *The Decline of Sentiment: American Film in the 1920s.* Berkeley: University of California Press, 2008.

Jenkins, Henry. *What Made Pistachio Nuts? Early Sound Comedy and the Vaudeville Aesthetic.* New York: Columbia University Press, 1992.

Jesionowski, Joyce E. *Thinking in Pictures: Dramatic Structure in D. W. Griffith's Biograph Films.* Berkeley: University of California Press, 1987.

Joyce, Simon. "Genre Parody and Comedic Burlesque: Keystone's Meta-Cinematic Satires." In *Slapstick Comedy,* edited by Tom Paulus and Rob King, 49–66. New York: Routledge, 2010.

Kamin, Dan. *The Comedy of Charlie Chaplin: Artistry in Motion.* Lanham, Md.: Scarecrow Press, 2008.

Kanfer, Stefan. *Somebody: The Reckless Life and Remarkable Career of Marlon Brando.* New York: Vintage Books, 2009.

Karnick, Kristine Brunovska, and Henry Jenkins, eds. *Classical Hollywood Comedy.* New York: Routledge, 1995.

Keaton, Buster, with Charles Samuels. *My Wonderful World of Slapstick.* New York: Da Capo, 1960.

Keil, Charlie. *Early American Cinema in Transition: Story, Style, and Filmmaking, 1907–1913.* Madison: University of Wisconsin Press, 2001.

Kerr, Walter. "The Lineage of Limelight." In *Focus on Chaplin,* edited by Donald W. Mc-
Caffrey, 143–48. Englewood Cliffs, N.J.: Prentice-Hall, 1971. Originally published
in *Theatre Arts* 36 (November 1952).
———. *The Silent Clowns.* New York: Knopf, 1975.
Kilgore, Al, and John McCabe. *Laurel and Hardy.* New York: Ballantine Books, 1976.
Kimber, John. *The Art of Charlie Chaplin.* Sheffield, U.K.: Sheffield Academic Press,
2000.
King, Rob. *The Fun Factory: The Keystone Film Company and the Emergence of Mass
Culture.* Berkeley: University of California Press, 2009.
———. "Uproarious Inventions: The Keystone Film Company, Modernity, and the Art
of the Motor." In *Slapstick Comedy,* edited by Tom Paulus and Rob King, 114–36.
New York: Routledge, 2010.
Knight, Arthur. "One Man's Movie." *Saturday Review,* May 6, 1972.
Knopf, Robert. *The Theatre and Cinema of Buster Keaton.* Princeton: Princeton Uni-
versity Press, 1999.
Kracauer, Siegfried. *Theory of Film: The Redemption of Physical Reality.* Princeton:
Princeton University Press, 1997.
Krämer, Peter. "Vitagraph, Slapstick and Early Cinema." *Screen* 29, no. 2 (1988): 98–104.
Krutnik, Frank. "A Spanner in the Works? Genre, Narrative and the Hollywood Come-
dian." In *Classical Hollywood Comedy,* edited by Kristine Brunovska Karnick and
Henry Jenkins, 17–38. New York: Routledge, 1995.
Lane, Lupino. *How to Become a Comedian.* London: F. Muller, 1945.
Langman, Larry. *Destination Hollywood: The Influence of Europeans on American Film-
making.* Jefferson, N.C.: McFarland, 2000.
Le Berton, Ted. "Absolutely, Mr. Chaplin! Positively, Mr. Freud!: Psychoanalysis Comes
to the Movies." *Motion Picture Classic,* August 17, 1923.
Levine, Irving R. "'I Was Born for the Cinema': A Conversation with Federico Fellini."
In *Federico Fellini: Interviews,* edited by Bert Cardullo, 54–67. Jackson: University
Press of Mississippi, 2006. Originally published in *Film Comment* (Fall 1966).
Leyda, Jay, ed. *Voices of Film Experience: 1894 to the Present.* New York: Macmillan,
1977.
Lloyd, Harold, with Wesley Winans Stout. *An American Comedy.* Mineola, N.Y.: Dover,
1971.
Lynn, Kenneth S. *Charlie Chaplin and His Times.* New York: Simon and Schuster, 1997.
Lyons, Timothy J. "Interview with Roland H. Totheroh." *Film Culture* (Spring 1972):
230–85.
MacCann, Richard Dyer. "Lloyd and Langdon." In *The Silent Comedians,* edited by
Richard Dyer MacCann, 192–204. Metuchen, N.J.: Scarecrow Press, 1993.
Madden, David. *Harlequin's Stick, Charlie's Cane: A Comparative Study of Commedia
dell'arte and Silent Slapstick Comedy.* Madison: University of Wisconsin Press/
Popular Press, 1975.
Maland, Charles J. *Chaplin and American Culture: The Evolution of a Star Image.* Prince-
ton: Princeton University Press, 1991.
———. *City Lights.* New York: Macmillan, 2007.
Marx, Karl, and Frederick Engels. *The Communist Manifesto.* Translated by Samuel
Moore. 1848; London: Verso, 1998.

Massa, Steve. "Rediscovering Roscoe: The Careers of 'Fatty' Arbuckle." Program notes. Museum of Modern Art, April 20–May 15, 2006.

Mast, Gerald. *The Comic Mind: Comedy and the Movies.* 2nd ed., Chicago: University of Chicago Press, 1979.

Mayer, David. *Stagestruck Filmmaker: D. W. Griffith and the American Theatre.* Iowa City: University of Iowa Press, 2009.

McCabe, John. *Charlie Chaplin.* New York: Doubleday, 1978.

McCaffrey, Donald. *4 Great Comedians: Chaplin, Lloyd, Keaton, Langdon.* London: Zwemmer, 1968.

McCormick, Anne O'Hare. "Searching for the Mind of Hollywood: An Inquiry into the Influences Molding the Vast Flow of Motion Pictures." *New York Times Magazine,* December 13, 1931.

Meryman, Richard. "Ageless Master's Anatomy of Comedy: Chaplin, An Interview." *Life,* March 10, 1967.

Milton, Joyce. *Tramp: The Life of Charlie Chaplin.* New York: HarperCollins, 1996.

Mitry, Jean. *The Aesthetics and Psychology of the Cinema.* Translated by Christopher King. Bloomington: Indiana University Press, 2000.

Moews, Daniel. *Buster Keaton: The Silent Features Close Up.* Berkeley: University of California Press, 1977.

Musser, Charles. "Another Look at the 'Chaser Theory,'" *Studies in Visual Communication* 10, no. 4 (1984): 24–44.

———. *The Emergence of Cinema: The American Screen to 1907.* New York: Scribner's, 1990.

———. "The Nickelodeon Era Begins: Establishing the Framework for Hollywood's Mode of Representation." *Framework,* nos. 22/23 (Autumn 1983): 4–11.

Muzzarelli, Anna. "Fellini in Conversation." In *Federico Fellini: Interviews,* edited by Bert Cardullo, 173–79. Jackson: University Press of Mississippi, 2006. Originally published in *Sight and Sound* 3, no. 4 (April 1993).

Nathan, George Jean. *Passing Judgments.* New York: Knopf, 1934.

Neibaur, James L. *Chaplin at Essanay: A Film Artist in Transition, 1915–1916.* Jefferson, N.C.: McFarland, 2008.

———. *Early Charlie Chaplin: The Artist as Apprentice at Keystone Studios.* Lanham, Md.: Scarecrow Press, 2012.

Nichols, Robert. "Future of the Cinema: Mr. Charles Chaplin." *Times* (London), September 3, 1925.

Nicoll, Allardyce. *The World of Harlequin.* London: Cambridge University Press, 1963.

North, Michael. *Machine-Age Comedy.* Oxford: Oxford University Press, 2009.

Okuda, Ted, and David Maska. *Charlie Chaplin at Keystone and Essanay: Dawn of the Tramp.* Lincoln, Neb.: iUniverse, 2005.

"On Filming a Classic." *Nickelodeon,* January 7, 1911.

Paulus, Tom, and Rob King. "Restoring Slapstick to the Historiography of American Film." In *Slapstick Comedy,* ed. Tom Paulus and Rob King, 1–18. New York: Routledge, 2010.

———, eds. *Slapstick Comedy.* New York: Routledge, 2010.

Perez, Gilberto. *The Material Ghost: Films and Their Medium.* Baltimore: Johns Hopkins University Press, 1998.

Petrie, Graham. "So Much and Yet So Little: A Survey of Books on Chaplin." In *The Silent Comedians*, ed. Richard Dyer MacCann, 114–29. Metuchen, N.J.: Scarecrow Press, 1993. Originally published in *Quarterly Review of Film Studies* (November 1977).

Pryor, Thomas M. "How Mr. Chaplin Makes a Movie." *New York Times Magazine*, February 17, 1952.

Quirk, James R. "Mabel Normand." *Photoplay*, August 1915.

Ray, Robert B. *A Certain Tendency of the Hollywood Cinema, 1930–1980*. Princeton: Princeton University Press, 1985.

Renoir, Jean. *My Life and My Films*. Translated by Norman Denny. New York: Atheneum, 1974.

Robinson, David. *Chaplin: His Life and Art*. New York: McGraw-Hill, 1985.

———. *Chaplin: The Mirror of Opinion*. London: Secker and Warburg, 1983.

Roemer, Michael. "Chaplin: Charles and Charlie." In *The Silent Comedians*, edited by Richard Dyer MacCann, 130–45. Metuchen, N.J.: Scarecrow Press, 1993. Originally published in *Yale Review* 64, no. 2 (December 1974).

Rohmer, Éric. "La Comtesse de Hong Kong." In André Bazin and Éric Rohmer, *Charlie Chaplin*, 106–22. Paris: Les Éditions du Cerf, 1972.

———. *The Taste for Beauty*. Translated by Carol Volk. Cambridge, U.K.: Cambridge University Press, 1989.

Rosenbaum, Jonathan. *Goodbye Cinema, Hello Cinephilia: Film Culture in Transition*. Chicago: University of Chicago Press, 2010.

Roud, Richard. *A Passion for Films: Henri Langlois and the Cinémathèque Française*. New York: Viking, 1983.

Salt, Barry. "D. W. Griffith Shapes Slapstick." In *Slapstick Comedy*, edited by Tom Paulus and Rob King, 37–48. New York: Routledge, 2010.

———. "The Early Development of Film Form." In *Film Before Griffith*, edited by John L. Fell, 284–98. Berkeley: University of California Press, 1983.

———. "Film Form, 1900–1906." *Sight and Sound* 47 (Summer 1978): 148–53.

Sargent, Epes Winthrop. "The Photoplaywright: Scenes and Leaders." *Moving Picture World*, August 10, 1912.

Sarris, Andrew. *The American Cinema: Directors and Directions, 1929–1968*. Cambridge, Mass.: Da Capo, 1996.

———. "Charles Spencer Chaplin." In *Cinema: A Critical Dictionary*, edited by Richard Roud, 1:201–11. New York: Viking, 1980.

———. *Confessions of a Cultist: On the Cinema, 1955–1969*. New York: Simon and Schuster, 1970.

———. *"You Ain't Heard Nothin' Yet": The American Talking Film, History and Memory, 1927–1949*. Oxford: Oxford University Press, 1998.

Schickel, Richard, "Hail Chaplin—The Early Chaplin." *New York Times*, April 2, 1972.

Schopenhauer, Arthur. *Philosophical Writings*. Translated and edited by Wolfgang Schirmacher. New York: Continuum, 2005.

Seldes, Gilbert. *The Seven Lively Arts*. New York: Harper and Row, 1924.

Sennett, Mack. "The Psychology of Film Comedy." In *The Silent Comedians*, edited by Richard Dyer MacCann, 50–53. Metuchen, N.J.: Scarecrow Press, 1993.

———, with Cameron Shipp. *King of Comedy*. 1954; Charlotte, N.C.: Baker and Taylor / Textstream, 2000.

"Short Comedies Wanted." *Photoplay,* June 1915.

Silver, Charles. *Charles Chaplin: An Appreciation.* New York: Museum of Modern Art, 1989.

Smith, Tim. "Watching You Watch *There Will Be Blood.*" *Observations on Film Art* (blog), February 14, 2011. http://www.davidbordwell.net.

Sobel, Raoul, and David Francis. *Chaplin: Genesis of a Clown.* New York: Quartet Books, 1977.

Spears, Jack. *Hollywood: The Golden Era.* New York: Castle Books, 1971.

Stokes, Melvyn. *D. W. Griffith's "The Birth of a Nation": A History of "The Most Controversial Motion Picture of All Time."* New York: Oxford University Press, 2007.

Taves, Brian. "Charlie Dearest." *Film Comment* (March–April 1988): 63–9.

"Technique of the Photoplay." *Moving Picture World,* July 22, 1911.

Thompson, Kristin. *Breaking the Glass Armor: Neoformalist Film Analysis.* Princeton: Princeton University Press, 1988.

———. "The Concept of Cinematic Excess." *Cine-Tracts* 1 (Summer 1977): 54–65.

———. "From Primitive to Classical." In Bordwell, Staiger, and Thompson, *The Classical Hollywood Cinema,* 157–73.

———. "The Stability of the Classical Approach After 1917." In Bordwell, Staiger, and Thompson, *The Classical Hollywood Cinema,* 231–40.

"Too Near the Camera." *Moving Picture World,* March 25, 1911.

Trahair, Lisa. *The Comedy of Philosophy: Sense and Nonsense in Early Cinematic Slapstick.* Albany: State University of New York Press, 2007.

Truffaut, François . *The Films in My Life.* Translated by Leonard Mayhew. Cambridge, Mass.: Da Capo, 1994.

Tsivian, Yuri. *Early Russian Cinema and Its Cultural Reception.* London: Routledge, 1994.

Tyler, Parker. *Chaplin, Last of the Clowns.* New York: Vanguard Press, 1948.

———. "Movie Letter: Charlie Verdoux." *Kenyon Review* 9, no. 3 (Summer 1947): 457–64.

Tynan, Kenneth. "Looking Back in Anger." *Observer,* September 1957 (clipping, Chaplin file, 1950–59, MoMA).

Vance, Jeffrey. *Chaplin: Genius of the Cinema.* New York: Harry N. Abrams, 2003.

Verma, Sanjeev. "Tramp as Dictator." In *Chaplin: The Dictator and the Tramp,* edited by Frank Scheide and Hooman Mehran, 13–16. London: British Film Institute, 2004.

Walker, Alexander. *The Shattered Silents: How the Talkies Came to Stay.* New York: William Morrow, 1980.

Wallach, George. "Charlie Chaplin's *Monsieur Verdoux* Press Conference." In *Charlie Chaplin Interviews,* edited by Kevin J. Hayes, 103–18. Jackson: University Press of Mississippi, 2005. Originally printed in *Film Comment* 5 (Winter 1969).

Wanamaker, Marc. *Beverly Hills: 1930–2005.* Charleston, S.C.: Arcadia, 2006.

Warner, Marina. "*L'Atalante.*" In *British Film Institute Film Classics,* vol. 1, edited by Rob White and Edward Buscombe, 272–96. London: British Film Institute, 2003.

Wead, George. *Buster Keaton and the Dynamics of Visual Wit.* New York: Arno, 1976.

Welles, Orson, and Peter Bogdanovich. *This Is Orson Welles.* 1992. Rev. ed., Cambridge, Mass.: Da Capo, 1998.

Williams, Raymond. *Marxism and Literature.* Oxford: Oxford University Press, 1977.

Wilson, Edmund. *The American Earthquake: A Documentary of the Twenties and Thirties.* New York: Macmillan, 1958.

Winter, Ella. "But It's Sad, Says Chaplin, It's Me." *Observer,* September 15, 1957.

Woodruff, Paul. *The Necessity of Theatre: The Art of Watching and Being Watched.* Oxford: Oxford University Press, 2008.

Woollcott, Alexander. *While Rome Burns.* New York: Grosset and Dunlap, 1936.

Wyndham, Francis. "Chaplin on the Critics, the Beatles, the Mood of London." *Sunday Times* (London), March 26, 1967.

Zavattini, Cesare. "Some Ideas on the Cinema." In *Vittorio De Sica: Contemporary Perspectives,* edited by Stephen Snyder and Howard Curle, 50–61. Toronto: University of Toronto Press, 2000.

Zimmerman, Paul D. "Chasing the Dream." *Newsweek,* April 3, 1967.

Žižek, Slavoj. *Enjoy Your Symptom! Jacques Lacan in Hollywood and Out.* 2nd ed. East Sussex, U.K.: Psychology Press, 2001.